QUICKBOOKS
2005
QuickSteps

CINDY FOX

McGraw-Hill/Osborne

New York Chicago San Francisco
Lisbon London Madrid Mexico City
Milan New Delhi San Juan
Seoul Singapore Sydney Toronto

McGraw-Hill/Osborne
2100 Powell Street, 10th Floor
Emeryville, California 94608
U.S.A.

To arrange bulk purchase discounts for sales promotions, premiums, or fund-raisers, please contact McGraw-Hill/Osborne at the above address. For information on translations or book distributors outside the U.S.A., please see the International Contact Information page inside the back cover of this book.

Intuit®, QuickBooks®, Quicken®, and TurboTax® are registered trademarks of Intuit, Inc. in the United States and other countries.

Microsoft® and Windows® are registered trademarks of Microsoft Corporation in the United States and other countries.

This book was composed with Adobe® InDesign®.

Information has been obtained by McGraw-Hill/Osborne from sources believed to be reliable. However, because of the possibility of human or mechanical error by our sources, McGraw-Hill/Osborne, or others, McGraw-Hill/Osborne does not guarantee the accuracy, adequacy, or completeness of any information and is not responsible for any errors or omissions or the results obtained from use of such information.

QUICKBOOKS® 2005 QUICKSTEPS

1234567890 WCK WCK 0198765

ISBN 0-07-225951-5

VICE PRESIDENT, GROUP PUBLISHER / Philip Ruppel

VICE PRESIDENT, PUBLISHER / Jeffrey Krames

ACQUISITIONS EDITOR / Megg Morin

ACQUISITIONS COORDINATOR / Agatha Kim

SERIES CREATORS & EDITORS / Marty and Carole Matthews

TECHNICAL EDITOR / Ed Van Patten

COPY EDITOR / Lisa McCoy

PROOFREADERS / Harriet O'Neal, Kellen Diamanti

INDEXER / Valerie Perry

LAYOUT ARTIST / Bailey Cunningham

ILLUSTRATORS / Kathleen Edwards, Pattie Lee, Bruce Hopkins

SERIES DESIGN / Bailey Cunningham

COVER DESIGN / Pattie Lee

Contents at a Glance

Chapter 1   **Stepping into QuickBooks 2005**............................ 1
Start QuickBooks, open a company file, use the menu and icon bars and the Navigators, customize the desktop and icon bar, get help

Chapter 2   **Creating a Company File** 25
Use an existing file or migrate to QuickBooks, complete the New Company Wizard, determine opening balances, set up multiple users

Chapter 3   **Working with Lists**.. 49
Use and print lists; understand accounts; use menu buttons; add, delete, and edit accounts; use Customer:Job list, enter service items

Chapter 4   **Set Up and Use Your Bank Accounts** 73
Create a new account, activate and use online banking, write checks, make deposits, manage business credit cards and reconcile accounts

Chapter 5   **Entering and Paying Bills**.................................... 95
Use the Vendor List, setup and print 1099s, enter and pay bills, memorize transactions and manage memorized transactions

Chapter 6   **Selling Products and Services**........................... 119
Edit customers, set up sales tax, create estimates, invoices, sales receipts and statements, process payments, and issue credit memos

Chapter 7   **Managing Inventory Items** 143
Create inventory items, assembly items, and groups; use purchase orders and sales orders; receive items; ship items; adjust inventory

Chapter 8   **Customizing and Maintaining QuickBooks** 161
Automate your backup, customize preferences, view reminders, use the Find feature, write letters, customize forms

Chapter 9   **Paying Employees and Taxes and Tracking Time** .. 181
Set up payroll, review employee information, create and print paychecks, enter weekly timesheets, review and pay taxes

Chapter 10   **Creating Reports** 203
Use the Report Navigator; set report preferences; customize and memorize reports; print, e-mail, and export reports

Index... 225

To my boys,

Mark, Lane, and Richie. Thank you for making my life complete.

Acknowledgments

I never realized how many people it takes to make a book! Thank you to all my editors. **Megg Morin** ruled the ship, **Marty** kept tabs, **Ed** made notes, **Lisa** kept my English straight, **Bailey** laid out the look, and **Harriet** proofed all of us. There are a whole lot of other people whom I didn't work directly with, but who are just as important in the existence of this book. The Credits page in the front is filled with real people full of real talent! Thank you, all!

Thank you most to my family, who tolerated me. Mark, Lane, and Richie, I love you boys!

About the Author

Cindy Fox (www.cindyfox.com) has been working with computers in some form—hardware, software, networking, programming, management, writing, and teaching—since 1986. Cindy owns Butterfly Consulting, LLC, which provides database and Web design, hosting, programming, training, and writing services to a diverse client base. A certified college instructor, she has taught SCUBA and philosophy, in addition to a variety of computer courses. She also writes and teaches online courses for companies such as HP and CNET, with up to 25,000 students in each class. In addition, she is always learning, most currently through the eyes of her five-year-old son, as they perform science experiments; play; and attend symphonies, art museums, and plays as part of his unschooling curriculum. Cindy lives with her husband Mark, sons Richie and Lane, and their three cats in Mesa, AZ.

Contents

Acknowledgments..iv

Introduction x

Chapter 1 Stepping into QuickBooks 2005 1

Learn about the QuickBooks Family...2
Start QuickBooks 4
   Use the Start Menu to Open QuickBooks...4
   Open a Sample Company File..5
   Updating Older Company Files to Work with QuickBooks 2005..................7
   Registering QuickBooks 2005..8
Tour the QuickBooks Window 8
   Explore the Menu Bar..9
   Use the Icon Bar...10
   Use the Open Window List..11
   Opening Other Company Files (.qbw)..12
   Learn Accounting Flow from Navigators...12
Customize QuickBooks...12
   Use the View Menu to Customize Your Desktop.....................................13
   Edit the Icon Bar...15
   Delete, Edit, and Rearrange Icons...16
Find Help within QuickBooks 19
   Ask a Help Question..19
   Use the How Do I? Drop-Down Menu 20
   Use the Help Menu 20
   Use Keyboard Shortcuts..21
Exit QuickBooks...22
   Close the Company File 22
   Close QuickBooks..22

Chapter 2 Creating a Company File 25

Use a Company File.. 25
   Use an Existing File...26
   Migrate to QuickBooks..26
Create a New Company File..27
   Gather Information and Choose a Start Date...27
   Gathering Data for a New Company File 28
   Complete the General Section 28
   Using Accrual- vs. Cash-Based Accounting 36
   Complete the Income & Expense Section 36
   Receiving Payments..39
   Edit Income Details...39
   Determine Opening Balances..41
   Creating Liability Accounts...44
   Review What's Next 45
   Set Up Multiple Users 46

3   Chapter 3   **Working with Lists** 49

Understand Lists 50
    Use Lists 50
    Examine List Similarities 53

Understand Accounts 54
    Understand Balance Sheet Accounts 55
    Understand Income and Expense Accounts 57
    Understanding Cost of Goods Sold Accounts 58

Review and Edit Your Chart of Accounts 58
    Use Menu Buttons for Actions and Reports 58
    Move and Sort Accounts and Subaccounts 59
    Customize Columns 61
    Add Accounts and Subaccounts 62
    Delete Accounts and Subaccounts 63
    Editing an Account 64
    Make an Account Inactive 64
    Rename and Merge Accounts 65
    Print Lists of Accounts 65

Use Name Lists to Manage Information 67
    Use the Customer:Job List to Track Balances and Jobs ... 67
    Naming Customers 70

Track Service, Inventory, and Taxes Using the Item List ... 70
    Enter Service Items 70
    Enter Non-Inventory Items 72

4   Chapter 4   **Set Up and Use Your Bank Accounts** 73

Use the Banking Navigator 73
    Choosing a Bank 75

Set Up Bank Accounts 75
    Create a New Account 75
    Activate Online Banking 76
    Order Checks and Forms 78

Manage Your Accounts on a Daily Basis 79
    Write Checks 79
    Edit, Void, or Delete Checks 81
    Make Deposits 82
    Sending and Receiving Online Transactions 84
    View and Edit Bank Account Registers 86
    Transferring Funds between Accounts 87
    Manage Business Credit Cards 87
    Set Up a Credit Card Account 87
    Enter Credit Card Transactions 88
    Receive and Enter Online Business Credit Card Transactions ... 90

Manage Your Accounts on a Monthly Basis 91
    Reconcile Credit Card Accounts 91
    Reconcile Bank Accounts 93

Chapter 5 **Entering and Paying Bills** 95

Manage Vendors..95
  Use the Vendor Navigator 96
  Use the Vendor List...97
  Add a Vendor...98
  Merge, Delete, or Make Vendors Inactive.......................103
  Set Up and Print 1099s..104
  Add Customized Fields to Your Name Lists....................108
  Use the Vendor Detail Center 109
Pay Bills...109
  Writing Checks 110
  Enter and Pay Bills 110
Use Cost of Goods Sold Accounts.......................................113
  Create Items with Purchase Information.........................113
  Use Items on a Bill...115
Memorize Transactions 116
  Memorize Reminder Transactions.....................................116
  Memorize Automatic Transactions....................................117
  Manage Memorized Transactions......................................117

Chapter 6 **Selling Products and Services** 119

Manage Customers and Jobs... 120
  Use the Customer Navigator..120
  Edit Customers in the Customer:Job List 121
  Use the Customer Detail Center 124
Track Sales in QuickBooks... 125
  Set Up Sales Tax Items..125
  Changing Tax Preferences..129
  Create Invoices 129
  Edit Invoices..132
  Charge for Cost of Goods...133
  Adding an Invoice to Memorized Transactions 134
  Send Statements to Customers..134
  Enter Sales Receipts 136
  Create Estimates 137
  Accepting Credit Cards from Customers 138
Receive Payments... 139
  Process Cash Payments and Checks.................................139
  Process Credit Card Payments 140
  Make Deposits 141
  Issue Credit Memos 142

7

Chapter 7 **Managing Inventory Items** 143

Create and Purchase Inventory Items 144

Activate Inventory in Preferences...144

Create Inventory Items...145

Create and Build Inventory Assembly Items.................................146

Create Inventory Groups..150

Understanding Inventory Item Types...151

Use Purchase Orders...151

Receive Items..154

Ship Items...155

Use the Shipping Manager 157

Monitor and Maintain Inventory Items....................................... 159

Take Inventory...159

Manually Adjust Inventory 160

8

Chapter 8 **Customizing and Maintaining QuickBooks**......... 161

Maintain and Access Your Data.. 162

Automate Your Backup 162

Restore Your Data...164

Verify Your Data 165

Work with an Accountant's Copy 165

Storing Your Backups...166

Network Your QuickBooks File 168

Edit Your QuickBooks Preferences 168

Customize Company Preferences...169

Customize My Preferences 170

Use the Find Feature 170

View Reminders 172

Communicate with Customers 173

Write Collection Letters to Customers 173

Create Mailing Labels..176

Customize Forms 177

9

Chapter 9 **Paying Employees and Taxes and Tracking Time**... 181

Set Up Payroll Options 182

Activate Payroll in Preferences 182

Set Up Payroll...183

Choosing a Payroll Service...184

Set Up Company Information 185

Enter Default Payroll Settings 187

Enter and Review Employee Information.......................................189

Run and Maintain Payroll 192
    Create Paychecks...192
    Print Paychecks 193
    Edit or Void Paychecks...194
Track Time 196
    Turn on Time Tracking 196
    ⊕ Entering a Single Activity 197
    Enter Weekly Timesheets 197
Paying Taxes 199
    Review and Pay Payroll Taxes...199
    Review and Pay Sales Taxes 201

Chapter 10 **Creating Reports** 203

Create Company and Financial Reports 204
    Use the Report Navigator 204
    Use the Report Menu..206
Navigate and Modify Reports 208
    Set Report Preferences 209
    Use the Button Bar 211
    Customize Reports..213
    Memorize Reports...217
    Use Memorized Reports..217
    Organize Memorized Reports...218
    ⊕ Printing to a File 220
Print, E-Mail, and Export Reports 220
    Print Reports 221
    ⊕ E-Mailing Reports in PDF Format 222
    Export Reports..222

Index..225

Introduction

QuickSteps books are recipe books for computer users. They answer the question "How do I...?" by providing quick sets of steps to accomplish the most common tasks in a particular operating system or application.

The sets of steps are the central focus of the book. QuickSteps sidebars show how to quickly perform many small functions or tasks that support primary functions. Notes, Tips, and Cautions augment the steps, presented in a separate column so as not to interrupt the flow of the steps. Introductions are minimal rather than narrative, and numerous illustrations and figures, many with callouts, support the steps.

QuickSteps books are organized by function and the tasks needed to perform that function. Each function is a chapter. Each task, or "How To," contains the steps needed for accomplishing the function with the relevant Notes, Tips, Cautions, and screenshots. You can easily find the tasks you need through:

- The Table of Contents, which lists the functional areas (chapters) and tasks in the order they are presented

- A How To list of tasks on the opening page of each chapter

- The index, which provides an alphabetical list of the terms that are used to describe the functions and tasks

- Color-coded tabs for each chapter or functional area with an index to the tabs in the Contents at a Glance (just before the Table of Contents)

Conventions Used in this Book

QuickBooks 2005 QuickSteps uses several conventions designed to make the book easier for you to follow. Among these are

- A in the table of contents and in the How To list in each chapter references a QuickSteps sidebar in a chapter and a references a QuickFacts sidebar.

- **Bold type** is used for words or objects on the screen that you are to do something with—for example, "click the **Start** menu, and then click **My Computer**."

- *Italic type* is used for a word or phrase that is being defined or otherwise deserves special emphasis.

- <u>Underlined type</u> is used for text that you are to type from the keyboard.

- SMALL CAPITAL LETTERS are used for keys on the keyboard such as **ENTER** and **SHIFT**.

- When you are expected to enter a command, you are told to press the key(s). If you are to enter text or numbers, you are told to type them.

How to...

- *Use the Start Menu to Open QuickBooks*
- *Open a Sample Company File*
- *Updating Older Company Files to Work with QuickBooks 2005*
- *Registering QuickBooks*
- *Explore the Menu Bar*
- *Use the Icon Bar*
- *Use the Open Windows List*
- *Opening Other Company Files (.qbw)*
- *Learn Accounting Flow from Navigators*
- *Use the View Menu to Customize Your Desktop*
- *Edit the Icon Bar*
- *Delete, Edit, and Rearrange Icons*
- *Ask a Help Question*
- *Use the How Do I? Drop-Down Menu*
- *Use the Help Menu*
- *Use Keyboard Shortcuts*
- *Close the Company File*
- *Close QuickBooks*

Chapter 1

Stepping into QuickBooks 2005

QuickBooks is a powerful yet easy accounting program that keeps the finances of your business in shape and at your fingertips. This book uses QuickBooks Premier 2005, but much of it will apply to different versions and editions of QuickBooks. This chapter explains how to open QuickBooks and your company file (if you have one) or the sample file included with QuickBooks. You'll use this sample file to learn how to move around the program, get help, and close QuickBooks. Creating a new QuickBooks file will be covered in Chapter 2.

NOTE

The term "version" refers to the release of QuickBooks, such as 2005, and "edition" refers to the level of features within the program, such as QuickBooks Basic.

TIP

While this book will show you *how* to do things, to determine *what* to do, consult your accountant. Your accountant (who hopefully knows QuickBooks) can help you with local laws and industry-specific advice. He or she can also help you set up new processes or evaluate your options.

Learn about the QuickBooks Family

QuickBooks is a family of programs that includes three basic editions: QuickBooks Basic, QuickBooks Pro, and QuickBooks Premier, as well as a variety of business-specific editions. The core of these QuickBooks programs is the same. Where appropriate, Tips and Notes will be used to point out special features of some products, but this book is here to help you get started, understand important features, run your business, and give you step-by-step directions on features most businesses need to use, such as creating invoices and sales receipts, making deposits, paying bills, running reports, and managing inventory.

Table 1-1 compares the three most popular QuickBooks editions. A complete list of all features is available online at www.intuit.com or on the back of any QuickBooks package.

QuickBooks Pro is the best overall solution for most businesses since it includes payroll, job costing, and multiuser capabilities. QuickBooks Premier is also popular and comes in business-specific editions, which include specialized reports for specific industries, such as construction, manufacturing, and retail. If you are using a version older than 2005 or are interested in a specific industry version, you can request a free trial of any of these programs at www.intuit.com.

Three other editions of QuickBooks are also available: QuickBooks Enterprise Solutions, QuickBooks Pro 6.0 for Mac, and QuickBooks Online Edition. You'll find that many chapters will apply to these editions as well, but your computer screen will not always look like the pictures in this book.

TABLE 1-1: COMPARISON OF THE THREE MOST POPULAR QUICKBOOKS EDITIONS

FEATURE	QUICKBOOKS BASIC	QUICKBOOKS PRO	QUICKBOOKS PREMIER
Price	$99.95 - $199.95	$199.95 - $749.95	$379.95 - $1,499.95
Purchase Options	Single User	Single User/Five-User Pack	Single User/Five-User Pack
Number of simultaneous users	N/A	Up to five	Up to five
Ability to print packing slips and labels		X	X
Ability to e-mail and save forms and reports as PDFs		X	X
Compatible with Microsoft Office and 250 other applications		X	X
Form customization and designs		X	X
Extended detail area on forms and statements		X	X
Price-level customization for customer types (up to 100 price levels)		X	X
Individual item price levels			X
Job-costing reports		X	X
Estimate capability		X	X
Time-tracking capability		X	X
Budget creation capability		X	X
Project cash flow capability		X	X
Ability to track vehicle mileage		X	X
Ability to manage loans		X	X
Ability to track fixed assets		X	X
Remote data access			X
Employee organizer for tracking detailed information			X
Business plan creator			X
Forecast creation			X
Expert analysis			X
Other advanced accounting features			X
Ability to create inventory assemblies (for manufacturers of finished goods)			X
Ability to create purchase orders from sales orders			X

Start QuickBooks

QuickBooks stores all your financial data in a single file called a *company file*. You may have multiple company files if you have multiple companies or locations.

In this chapter you will open a sample file and examine the layout of the QuickBooks program. If you have a company file of your own, you may use that for this chapter; however, your screens will not look exactly the same.

Use the Start Menu to Open QuickBooks

A normal installation of QuickBooks includes a listing on the Start menu and a shortcut on the desktop. You may double-click the shortcut on the desktop to open QuickBooks or use the Start menu. To open QuickBooks using the Start menu:

1. Start your computer, if it is not running, and log on to Windows if necessary.

2. Click **Start**. The Start menu opens.

3. Click **All Programs**, click **QuickBooks**, and then click **QuickBooks 2005**.

If this is the first time you've used QuickBooks, you will see a license agreement, which, once you click **Yes** in response to, will never show up again. QuickBooks now opens with the last company file used, or, if no company file is open, you will see the screen in Figure 1-1. From here, you can view a tutorial video about QuickBooks, explore QuickBooks by opening one of the two sample files included, create a new company file, or open an existing company file.

If you have a QuickBooks file from another computer or from a coworker, you can choose the option to open or restore an existing data file. If QuickBooks was installed for you and a company file has been set up, QuickBooks will open that file by default (you may be prompted for a password). If you are opening your own company file, QuickBooks will open to whatever screen was last saved.

NOTE

The QuickBooks company file always ends in a .qbw extension. QuickBooks backup files always end with a .qbw extension. Backups will be covered in Chapter 2.

NOTE

QuickBooks can have many levels of passwords. If you are working with an existing file, check with the owner to see what level of access you have.

Open a Sample Company File

QuickBooks comes with two sample (.qbw) files for you to explore and practice with before setting up your own files. One is a service-based company (Landscape Larry), and one is a product-based company (Rock Castle Construction). To open a sample company file:

1. Click the **Explore QuickBooks** button. A drop-down menu is displayed, giving you the option to open the sample product-based business or sample service-based business.

2. Click **Product Based Company.** One of two dialog boxes appear, either notifying you that you are opening a sample file or prompting you to update this file to a newer version. If you are prompted to update, this is a one-time process. See the QuickSteps "Updating Older Company Files to Work with QuickBooks 2005" for more information.

QuickBooks Information

i This is the QuickBooks sample file. Use it as an example or for practice while learning QuickBooks.

While using this file QuickBooks will set today's date to December 15, 2007.

Do not use this file as your company file.

[OK]

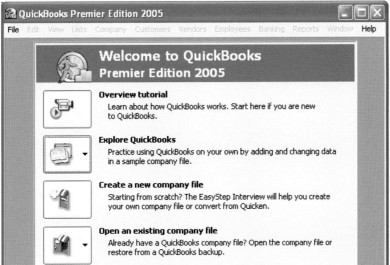

Figure 1-1: The QuickBooks 2005 Welcome screen presents you with four items from which to choose.

2

3

4

5

6

7

8

9

10

If the registration screen is displayed, you will have to register QuickBooks within seven uses. See the QuickSteps "Registering QuickBooks" for more information on the registration process.

3. Click **OK** to acknowledge that this is a practice file. You will see either the registration screen or the QuickBooks Welcome screen with the QuickBooks Learning Center displayed, as shown in Figure 1-2. The QuickBooks Learning Center is available at any time on the Help menu.

4. Click **Begin Using QuickBooks**.

Open Window List gives quick access to Navigators and currently open windows

Icon bar provides quick access to forms, lists, and register objects

The QuickBooks Learning Center provides tutorial videos

Close button

Title bar

Menu bar

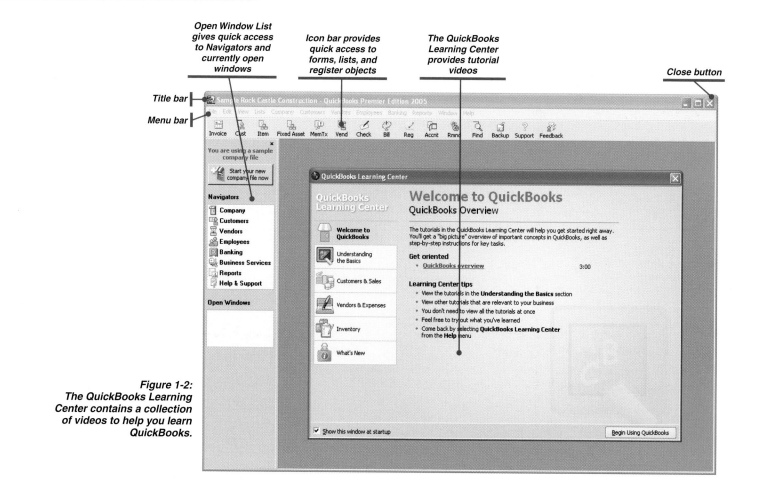

Figure 1-2:
The QuickBooks Learning Center contains a collection of videos to help you learn QuickBooks.

QUICKSTEPS

UPDATING OLDER COMPANY FILES TO WORK WITH QUICKBOOKS 2005

If you have an older QuickBooks file, you can easily update it to work with the latest version of QuickBooks. The only reason you would *not* want to upgrade is if you need to share the file with someone who has an older version of QuickBooks. QuickBooks is *not* backwards-compatible, so while any file can be upgraded, once you make entries in the current version, you cannot open that version with an older copy of QuickBooks. To update an older company file:

1. Open the company file you want to update.

2. If QuickBooks asks you to update your file to a newer version, type yes in the white box, and click **OK**.

3. Click **OK** to back up the file. The Quick-Books Backup dialog box appears (see Figure 1-3). Review the file name and location, and change these items if necessary.

4. Click **OK**. A dialog box appears regarding backing up files on a local drive and confirming that you want to back up your data to your hard drive.

5. Click **Yes**. A dialog box appears, notifying you that if multiple users are using this file, they cannot access it until they update their QuickBooks program once the update is complete. You are asked if you want to continue with the update process.

6. Click **Yes**. The backup and file update process takes place in less than two minutes for most files.

Update File to New Version

Your data file needs to be updated to work with this version of QuickBooks.

Depending on the version of QuickBooks you were previously using, QuickBooks might rebuild your file to verify the integrity of your data. This is a multi-step process that can take more than 30 minutes depending on the size of your file.

Once your data file is updated to this new version, it will not work with your previous version of QuickBooks. Before we begin updating your data file, QuickBooks will assist you in making a backup of your current data file.

You can always use this backup data file with your previous version of QuickBooks, but any data entered in this new version of QuickBooks will have to be re-entered in that case.

Type 'YES' if you want to update your data file.   YES

[OK]   [Cancel]

NOTE

You can update your file to a newer version unless you need to share data with people who must use older versions of QuickBooks.

QuickBooks Backup   Ask a help question [Ask]   ▽ How Do I?   ☒

Current Company:

You are about to make a backup of your QuickBooks company file. Use Restore to retrieve your backup.

Filename: sample_product-based business.qbw

Location: D:\Program Files\Intuit\QuickBooks 2005\

Back Up Current Company:

Select a backup option. If backing up to a 3.5-inch disk or other removable storage, put the disk in the drive before clicking OK.

⦿ Disk: Filename: sample_product-based business.QBB

Location: D:\Program Files\Intuit\QuickBooks...   [Browse]

○ Online: Protect your company files now. Automatically back them up with QuickBooks Online Backup.   [Tell Me More]

Back Up Options:

Selecting either option will increase time.

☐ Verify data integrity   [Set Defaults...]

☐ Format each floppy disk during backup

[OK]   [Cancel]   [Help]

Figure 1-3: Back up files to your hard disk when upgrading, but normally use floppies, CDs, or other removable media and store them offsite to prevent data loss.

QUICKSTEPS

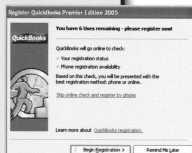

REGISTERING QUICKBOOKS

You are required to register QuickBooks in order to use the product. A reminder window opens each time you start QuickBooks up to seven uses. After that, you will not be able to proceed past the registration screen without registering. To register QuickBooks:

1. Click **Begin Registration**. A screen appears with a series of registration questions. Providing this information is optional.

2. Click **Next**. A dialog box appears notifying you that QuickBooks needs to start your web browser, which may be useful to see each time if you need to connect to a dialup line. Click the **Do Not Display In Future** check box if you don't want to see this message again.

3. Click **OK** and wait for your computer to connect to the Internet. If you cannot connect to the Internet, you will be notified to call a toll-free number to register your product. If your computer connects successfully, you will see a registration page. Enter information in any field that has an asterisk.

4. Click **Next**. The Thank You page is displayed.

5. Click **Next**. A page appears with advertisements for other Intuit products.

6. Click **Finish Registration** and click **Yes** in response to the dialog box that appears, notifying you that the web page you are viewing is trying to close this window. Your registration is now complete.

Tour the QuickBooks Window

When you first start QuickBooks, no windows are open (see Figure 1-2). The title bar displays the name of the currently open company file and the program—in this case, Sample Rock Castle Construction - QuickBooks Premier Edition 2005. Below the title bar are the menu bar and icon bar.

The *menu bar* contains menus familiar to most Windows users, such as File, Edit, View, Window, and Help, and menus specific to QuickBooks, such as Lists, Company, Customers, Vendors, Employees, Banking, and Reports.

The *icon bar* (usually called a toolbar in other programs) contains shortcuts to frequently used objects, such as forms, lists, registers, and reports. As you move your cursor over the icon bar, you will see yellow ToolTips for each button. This icon bar can be completely customized to streamline your business according to your company's needs. For example, Chart of Account is abbreviated "Accnt," but when you move your mouse over it, you see the whole name.

You can use any of the following methods to accomplish a task in QuickBooks:

- Click the corresponding button on the icon bar.
- Click the corresponding menu and select the desired option.
- Click the corresponding icon on the Navigator.
- Use a keyboard shortcut to quickly open a window.

On the left side of the screen, the Open Window List is visible. QuickBooks has many different windows that can be open at any given time, and most items throughout QuickBooks can be customized.

Explore the Menu Bar

Most Windows programs use similar menu headings. For example, most programs have File, Edit, and Help menus. If you are new to QuickBooks, focus on those aspects that are similar to Windows programs, such as how to open and close a program and get help, and then focus on what you need to know for your business, such as daily data entry and report generation. Don't worry or get overwhelmed by features you don't yet know. You can add skills as you need them.

Click **File** and move your cursor along the menu bar to view each menu. An arrow indicates that a submenu is available. Move your cursor over that menu topic to see the next menu level, as shown in Figure 1-4.

Some items are listed on more than one menu. For example, both the Company and Banking menus contain an item called Chart of Accounts, because it is related to multiple areas. To the right of Chart of Accounts is **CTRL+A** (hold down **CTRL** while pressing **A**). This is the keyboard shortcut that opens this window.

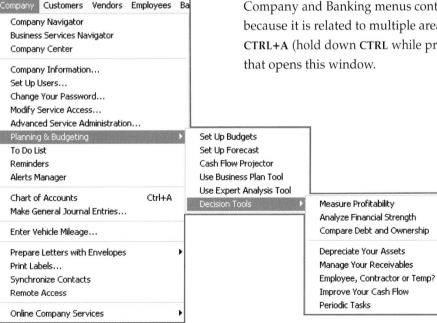

Figure 1-4: The arrows indicate that a submenu is available for a menu item.

TIP

You can easily add and remove icons to customize the icon bar for your business needs.

Use the Icon Bar

One reason QuickBooks is easy to use is because of the consistent interface of forms, lists, and registers. Once you learn to navigate in one of these types of objects, you'll be able to transfer your skills to similar objects:

- Examples of forms: Checks, Deposits, and Receive Payments
- Examples of lists: Chart of Accounts, Customer:Job List, and Reminders List
- Examples of registers: Checking Account, Accounts Receivable, and Accounts Payable

To open any of these objects, simply click the one you want on the icon bar, such as the Chart of Accounts, shown in Figure 1-5, or click the corresponding menu and click the desired option.

The Chart of Accounts contains your bank accounts, credit cards, fixed assets, other liabilities, accounts receivable, accounts payable, income, and expenses. It will be covered in detail in Chapter 3.

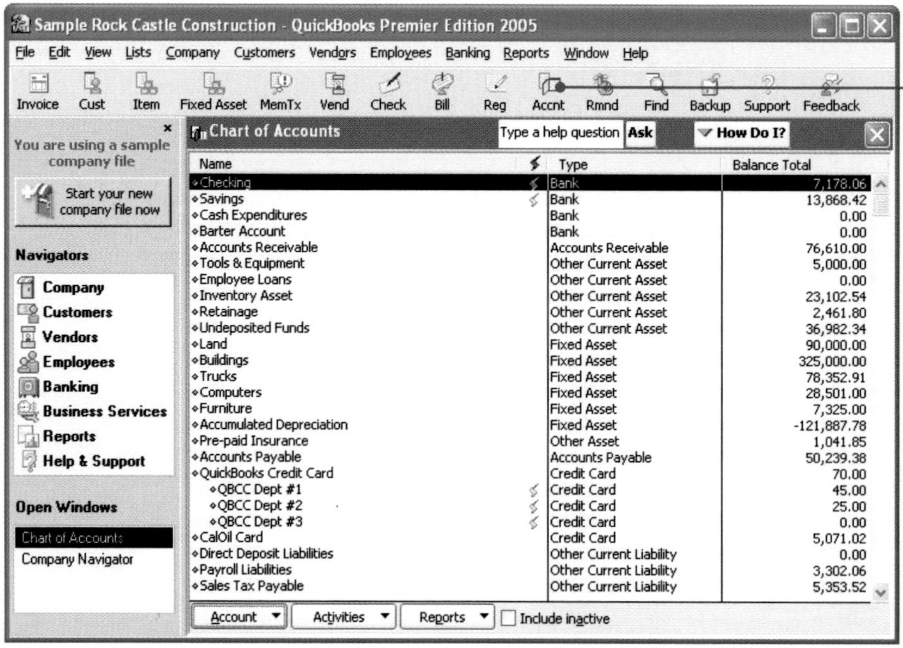

Figure 1-5: Chart of Accounts shows a list of all balance sheet, income, and expense accounts.

Use the Open Window List

The Open Window List displays the names of all the windows you have open in QuickBooks. For example, if you open Chart of Accounts, you will see it listed in the Open Window List (see Figure 1-5).

When multiple windows are open, you can switch from one window to another by clicking the window name in the Open Window List. You can also click the Window menu and choose the desired window from the list, as shown in Figure 1-6. A check mark next to a window name indicates that this is the currently active window. You may close any of these windows by clicking the X in the upper-right corner of the window.

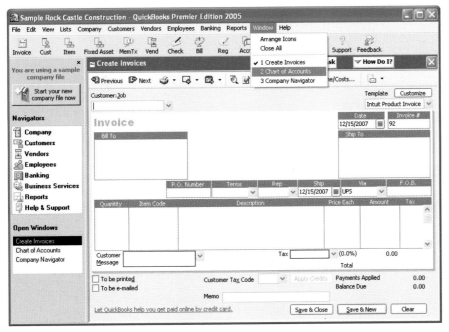

Figure 1-6: Select the Chart of Accounts window to work in it.

QUICKSTEPS

OPENING OTHER COMPANY FILES (.qbw)

You can open a different company file at any time. You may have multiple companies or simply want to practice something in the sample file before trying it in your real file. When you open a new company file, the current company file automatically closes. Two methods exist by which you can open a company file.

USE A DIALOG BOX TO OPEN A COMPANY FILE

1. Click the **File** menu and click **Open Company**. The current company file will close and the Open A Company dialog box will appear.

2. Click the **Look In** list down arrow, or click any of the buttons on the left (for example, **My Recent Documents**), and browse to the company file you want.

3. When you have located the file you wish to open, click the file to select it, and then click the **Open** button. Alternatively, you can double-click the file to open it, or your file may be set to open on one click.

USE OPEN PREVIOUS COMPANY TO OPEN A COMPANY FILE

Click the **File** menu, click **Open Previous Company**, and click the file you want to open. The currently open company file closes and the new file opens.

To set the number of previously open company files displayed in the list, click the **File** menu, click **Open Previous Company**, and click **Set Number Of Previous Companies**. Enter a number from 1 to 20.

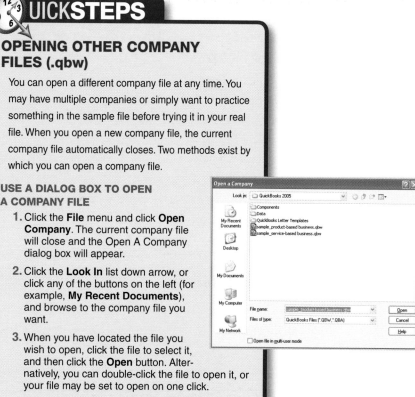

Learn Accounting Flow from Navigators

Navigators are windows with clickable images that explain the normal business flow for each section of QuickBooks. Each image is a link to the actual object. If you are new to accounting, using Navigators is a good way to understand how each section of QuickBooks works. They will slow you down in the long run, however, and are really more of a reference as to what a particular section of QuickBooks includes than a daily work tool.

The Navigators list is above the Open Window List and lists all the Navigators available in QuickBooks. For example, click **Company** on the Navigators list to open the Company Navigator, as seen in Figure 1-7.

Navigators are available for every major area of QuickBooks: Company, Customers, Vendors, Employees, Banking, Business Services, Reports, and Help & Support. Click each of the Navigators in the Navigators list to see the resources available to you.

Customize QuickBooks

Many ways exist whereby you can customize QuickBooks to meet your needs. You can customize the desktop, icon bar, and shortcut list; turn features on and off; and edit invoices, statements, and estimates. This chapter will cover customizing the desktop and icon bar.

NOTE

If you are in a multiuser environment, be sure to select the Open File In Multi-User Mode check box in the Open A Company dialog box.

CAUTION

If you are sharing a file on a network, map your network drive for the most stable environment. See Chapter 8 for more information.

NOTE

If you can't find your file, click **Cancel**, and your screen will return to the No Company Open screen.

Use the View Menu to Customize Your Desktop

The View menu contains a number of options to customize your QuickBooks company file, including a number of toggle items. A *toggle item* is an object that can be clicked once to turn it on. Clicking the item again turns it off. A check mark or dot next to a toggle item indicates that it is turned on.

TOGGLE THE OPEN WINDOW LIST ON AND OFF

Click the **View** menu and then click **Open Window List** to toggle the Open Window List off. Repeat this step to turn it back on.

TOGGLE THE ICON BAR ON AND OFF

Click the **View** menu and then click **Icon Bar** to toggle the icon bar off. Repeat this step to turn it back on.

Figure 1-7: The Company Navigator shows a summary of your business and common company-related actions you can perform.

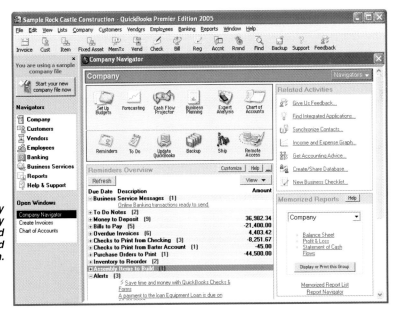

NOTE

Each time you open a window, it will open to the same size you set it to.

TURN THE SHORTCUT LIST ON AND OFF

The Shortcut list operates in a similar fashion as the icon bar. Click the **View** menu and then click **Shortcut List** to toggle the Shortcut list on. Repeat this step to turn it off.

VIEW ONE WINDOW OR MULTIPLE WINDOWS

By default, QuickBooks displays only one window at a time. The View One Window setting won't let you resize or move windows. If you would like to see multiple windows at the same time, you can toggle between the one-window view and the multiple-window view. For example, Figure 1-8 shows the screen with both the Item List window and the Customer:Job List window displayed.

1. Click the **View** menu and then click **Multiple Windows** to be able to tile, move, and resize windows on the screen.
2. Click the **Customer** icon to open the Customer list.
3. Click the **Item** icon to open the Item list.
4. Click the **View** menu and then click **One Window** to see only the active window filling the screen.
5. Click **View** and then click **Multiple Windows** to see a layout like that shown in Figure 1-8.

Figure 1-8: You can display multiple windows at a time in QuickBooks.

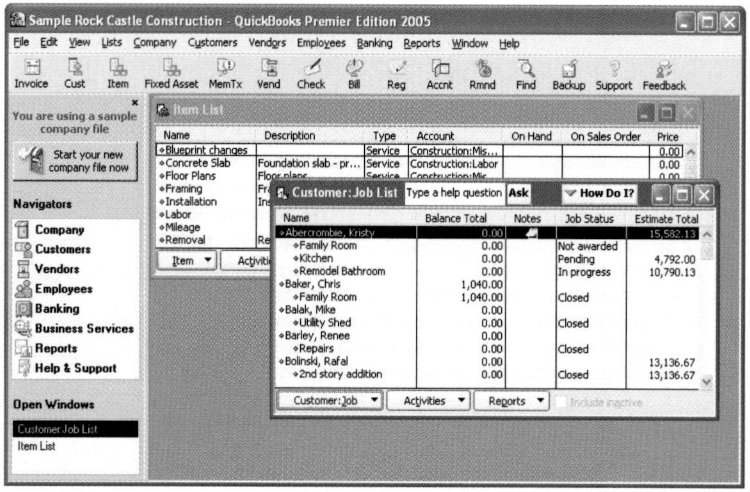

Windows in QuickBooks can be maximized, minimized, or closed using the standard Windows symbols in the upper-right corner. Resize a window by moving your mouse pointer to the edge of a window until the mouse pointer changes to a double-headed arrow and then clicking and dragging (press and hold the mouse button while moving the mouse). Move a window by clicking and dragging the title bar.

USE THE WINDOW MENU

With multiple-windows view, you will have additional choices on the Window menu.

Click the **Window** menu and click **Cascade**, **Tile Vertically**, or **Tile Horizontally**.

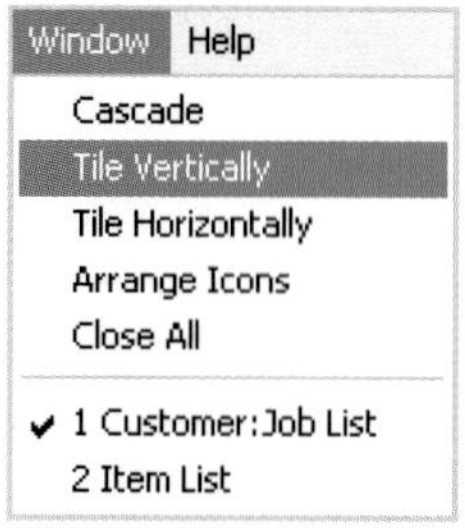

TABLE 1-2: TYPICAL ACCOUNTING-RELATED TASKS

DAILY/WEEKLY TASKS:

- Create estimates
- Order products (purchase orders)
- Receive inventory
- Create invoices
- Receive payments (cash, check, or credit card)
- Make deposits
- Enter bills
- Pay bills
- Write checks
- Enter credit card charges (made by the business)
- Run payroll

MONTHLY/QUARTERLY TASKS:

- Reconciliation
- Pay taxes (sales, employee, and so on)
- Review reports and compare against the budget

ANNUAL TASKS:

- Review year
- Manually adjust inventory

Edit the Icon Bar

The icon bar contains commonly used buttons, but you can add, delete, move, and rename buttons to customize the icon bar to meet your company's specific needs.

DETERMINE YOUR COMPANY'S WORK FLOW

Before you edit the icon bar, determine the needs of your company. By organizing your icon bar in the order in which tasks are done, you'll make your daily QuickBooks work flow go more smoothly and have an easier time remembering how to access the less frequent tasks. Table 1-2 shows some suggestions for tasks that companies typically do and the order in which they do them.

PLANNING YOUR ICON BAR

Identify the tasks your company performs on a regular basis, and group the relevant icons on the icon bar according to function and in order of typical use. Figure 1-9 shows a typical consulting business's company flow.

The icons in Figure 1-9 are arranged for a specific company flow from left to right. Use your own priorities on your icon bar.

ADD AN ICON TO THE ICON BAR

1. On the menu bar, click the **Customers** menu and click **Receive Payments**. The Receive Payments window opens.

2. Click the **View** menu and click **Add "Receive Payments" To Icon Bar**. The Add Window To Icon Bar dialog box appears.

3. Scroll through the list on the left, and click the image you want to represent the new icon.

4. Edit the **Label** and **Description** fields. The label is what you see on the icon bar. The description is what pops up in a ToolTip when you hover over the icon.

5. Click **OK** when finished. The new icon is added to the right end of the icon bar.

6. Close the Receive Payments window.

Delete, Edit, and Rearrange Icons

After you have used QuickBooks for a while and become familiar with it, you may find that you need to delete, edit, or rearrange icons to better reflect the tasks you perform.

TIP

When you customize reports to meet your needs, you can add them to your icon bar for easy daily creation.

DELETE AN ICON

To delete an icon from the icon bar (in this case, the Register icon):

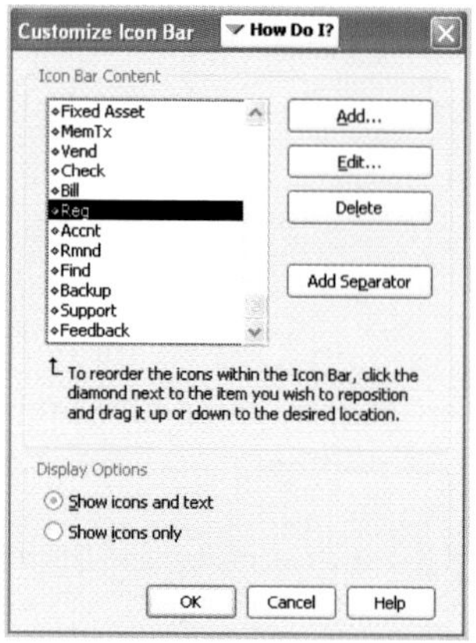

1. Click the **View** menu and click **Customize Icon Bar**. The Customize Icon Bar dialog box appears.

2. In the Icon Bar Content pane on the left, click **Reg**.

3. Click the **Delete** button on the right. The Register icon is immediately deleted.

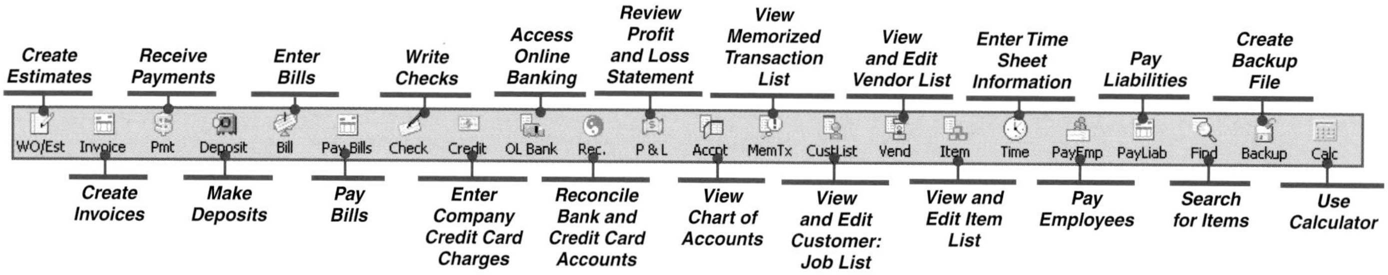

Figure 1-9: Icons may be arranged for specific company flow.

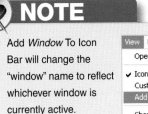

NOTE

Add *Window* To Icon Bar will change the "window" name to reflect whichever window is currently active.

View Lists Company Customers Vendors

Open Window List

✔ Icon Bar
Customize Icon Bar...

Add "Receive Payments" to Icon Bar...

Shortcut List
Customize Shortcut List...
Add Window to Shortcut List...

One Window
● Multiple Windows

Customize Desktop...

TIP

In the Customize Icon Bar window, click the **Show Icons And Text** check box or the **Show Icons Only** check box, and you will immediately see the change.

TIP

Consider adding budget, cash flow, and other tools to your icon bar to help in daily business management.

EDIT AN ICON

To edit an icon (in this case, the Support icon):

1. Click the **View** menu and click **Customize Icon Bar**. The Customize Icon Bar dialog box appears.
2. In the Icon Bar Content pane on the left, click **Support**.
3. Click the **Edit** button on the right. The Edit Icon Bar Item dialog box appears.
4. Scroll through the list on the left, and click the new image you want to represent the icon.
5. Click in the **Label** field.
6. Delete the word "Support," and type Help.
7. Edit the Description field, if desired.
8. Click **OK** when finished. The edited icon is displayed on the icon bar.

REARRANGE THE ORDER OF ICONS

To rearrange the order in which icons appear on the icon bar:

1. Click the **View** menu and click **Customize** Icon Bar. The Customize Icon Bar dialog box appears.
2. Click the diamond to the left of the icon you want to move, and drag up or down to the new location for the icon. A dashed line and arrow indicate where the icon will be placed.
3. Release the mouse button, and the icon is now present in its new place.
4. Click **OK** when finished.

TIP

Not all items are listed in the Add Icon Bar Item list, which is why you can also add icons using the procedure described in the "Add an Icon to the Icon Bar" section.

ADD A SEPARATOR BETWEEN ICON BUTTONS

To group your icons into meaningful sections, you can add separators between any two icons.

1. Click the **View** menu and click **Customize Icon Bar**. The Customize Icon Bar dialog box appears.

2. In the Icon Bar Content pane on the left, click the icon above where you would like to add a space.

3. Click the **Add Separator** button. A space (and a line) is created below (to the right of) the selected icon.

ADD AN ICON TO THE ICON BAR

In a previous section, you learned how to add a window to the icon bar. You can also add icons to the icon bar beyond the standard icons already included in the Customize Icon Bar window. To add an icon to the icon bar:

1. Click the **View** menu and click **Customize Icon Bar**. The Customize Icon Bar dialog box appears.

2. In the Icon Bar Content pane on the left, click the icon above (and to the left of) where you would like the new icon to be added.

3. Click the **Add** button. The Add Icon Bar Item dialog box appears.

4. Scroll through the list on the left, and click the task for which you want to make an icon. QuickBooks will recommend an icon, label, and description. If you don't want to use QuickBooks's recommendation, select a different icon and edit the Label and Description fields.

5. Click **OK** when finished. The new icon is added to the icon bar.

CAUTION

Many help topics will take you online for the latest information. If you have a dial-up connection, you may need to connect before accessing some help topics.

Find Help within QuickBooks

Help is available in three places within QuickBooks:

- Type a question in the Help field, and click the Ask button.
- Use the How Do I? drop-down menu to find the relevant topic.
- Use the Help menu located on the menu bar.

Ask a Help Question

The following procedure demonstrates how to get help using the Write Checks-Checking window as an example. Figure 1-10 shows the different options available to you when seeking answers to your questions.

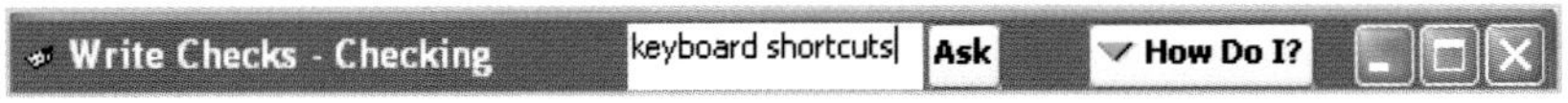
Write Checks - Checking
keyboard shortcuts
Ask
How Do I?

1. With QuickBooks open, click the **Check** icon on the icon bar.
2. Click in the **Type A Help Question** text box, and type keyboard shortcuts.
3. Click the **Ask** button. A QuickBooks Help window opens, displaying the help topics that relate to your question, as shown in Figure 1-10.
4. Click the **QuickBooks Keyboard Shortcuts** topic, and detailed information is displayed in the pane on the right.
5. Review the help information and close the window when you are finished.

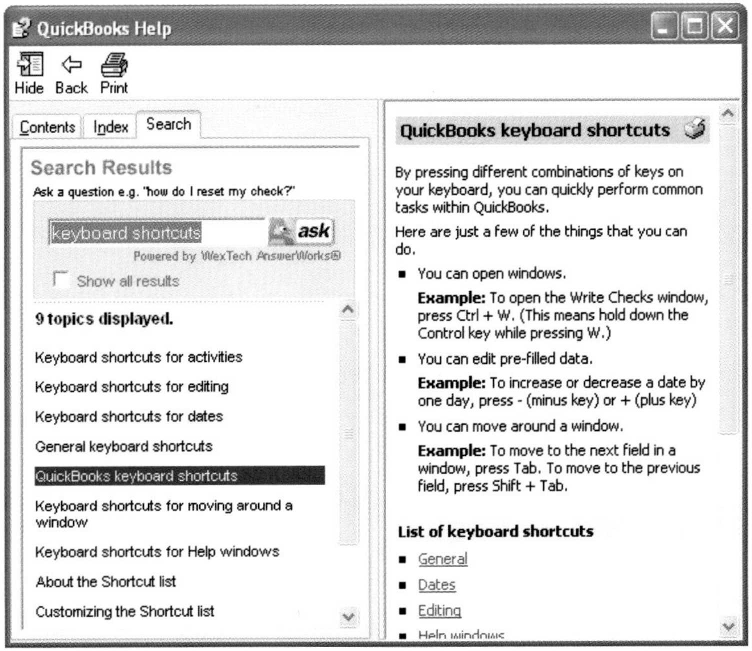
QuickBooks Help
Hide
Back
Print
Contents
Index
Search
Search Results
Ask a question e.g. "how do I reset my check?"
keyboard shortcuts
ask
Powered by WexTech AnswerWorks®
Show all results
9 topics displayed.
Keyboard shortcuts for activities
Keyboard shortcuts for editing
Keyboard shortcuts for dates
General keyboard shortcuts
QuickBooks keyboard shortcuts
Keyboard shortcuts for moving around a window
Keyboard shortcuts for Help windows
About the Shortcut list
Customizing the Shortcut list
QuickBooks keyboard shortcuts
By pressing different combinations of keys on your keyboard, you can quickly perform common tasks within QuickBooks.
Here are just a few of the things that you can do.
You can open windows.
Example: To open the Write Checks window, press Ctrl + W. (This means hold down the Control key while pressing W.)
You can edit pre-filled data.
Example: To increase or decrease a date by one day, press - (minus key) or + (plus key)
You can move around a window.
Example: To move to the next field in a window, press Tab. To move to the previous field, press Shift + Tab.
List of keyboard shortcuts
General
Dates
Editing

Figure 1-10: QuickBooks Help can quickly provide you with answers to your questions.

Use the How Do I? Drop-Down Menu

The How Do I? drop-down menu contains helpful information pertaining only to the currently active window. Continuing to use the Write Checks-Checking window as an example:

1. Click the **How Do I?** down arrow, click **Print Checks**, and click **Print One Check**. A window similar to the QuickBooks Help window shown in Figure 1-10 opens, displaying instructions on how to print a single check.

2. Review the help information and close the window when finished.

Use the Help Menu

The Help menu, which is located on the menu bar, provides you with a variety of ways to access additional help in using QuickBooks:

- Click the **Help** menu and click **QuickBooks Help** to access the general help files. These are the same files accessed when using the Type A Help Question text box and the How Do I? drop-down menu.

- Click the **Help** menu and click **QuickBooks Learning Center** to access a collection of tutorial videos, such as Welcome to QuickBooks, Understanding the Basics, Customers and Sales, and What's New.

- Click the **Help** menu and click **Help & Support** to go directly to the search function. This is an online function, so you must be connected to the Internet.

- Click the **Help** menu and click **Help On This Window** for context-sensitive help.

- Click the **Help** menu and click **QuickBooks Pro 2005** for information pertaining to your QuickBooks installation, such as the install key code and registration number. You will need this information if you ever have to reinstall QuickBooks.

TABLE 1-3:
DATA-ENTRY KEYBOARD SHORTCUTS

KEYBOARD SHORTCUT	ACTION PERFORMED
TAB	Move through fields in a form
SHIFT+TAB	Move backwards through fields in a form
CTRL+INS	Insert a new line (for example, in an invoice)
CTRL+DEL	Delete the current line

TABLE 1-4:
GENERAL KEYBOARD SHORTCUTS

KEYBOARD SHORTCUT	ACTION PERFORMED
ALT+F4	Exit QuickBooks
F1	Open a Help window
F2	Show QuickBooks software product information
CTRL+I	Open a Create Invoice form
CTRL+W	Open a Write Checks form
CTRL+D	Delete the current transaction (invoice, check, and so on)
CTRL+F	Open a Find window
CTRL+A	Open the Chart of Accounts list
CTRL+J	Open the Customer:Job List
CTRL+M	Memorize the current transaction or report
CTRL+P	Open a Print window
CTRL+T	Open the Memorized Transactions list

Use Keyboard Shortcuts

Since QuickBooks is an accounting program, it involves a lot of data entry via the keyboard. *Keyboard shortcuts*—combinations of keystrokes that can be used to perform tasks that would otherwise require the use of the mouse—will save you time in the long run. Some shortcuts are easy and intuitive, while others require regular use before being committed to memory. Table 1-3 lists the most common data-entry keyboard shortcuts used in QuickBooks. Table 1-4 lists the most common keyboard shortcuts used to perform general commands in QuickBooks. Table 1-5 lists the most common keyboard shortcuts used when working with lists in QuickBooks.

You can also use keyboard shortcuts to access menus. Just as with most Windows programs, the menu items in QuickBooks give an easy clue as to their keyboard shortcuts. Press **ALT** and look for the underlined letter in each menu item name. While holding **ALT**, press the key corresponding to that letter, and you can open any menu you want. Table 1-6 lists the most common keyboard shortcuts used in QuickBooks to access menus.

QuickBooks also gives you the ability to use shortcuts when entering dates, which can be useful when entering lists of past transactions. Table 1-7 lists the most common keyboard shortcuts used in QuickBooks for entering dates.

Sample Rock Castle Construction - QuickBooks Premier Edition 2005
File Edit View Lists Company Customers Vendors Employees Banking Reports Window Help

TABLE 1-5:
KEYBOARD SHORTCUTS FOR LISTS

KEYBOARD SHORTCUT	ACTION PERFORMED
CTRL+N	Open an Enter New Item window
CTRL+E	Edit a list item
CTRL+D	Delete the current item
CTRL+Q	View a QuickReport of a current item

TABLE 1-6: KEYBOARD SHORTCUTS FOR MENUS

KEYBOARD SHORTCUT	CORRESPONDING MENU
ALT+F	File
ALT+E	Edit
ALT+V	View
ALT+L	Lists
ALT+C	Company
ALT+U	Customers
ALT+O	Vendors
ALT+B	Banking
ALT+R	Reports
ALT+W	Windows
ALT+H	Help

CAUTION

When you press **CTRL+DEL** to delete the current line, you will not see a dialog box confirming this action, nor can you undo this action. If you accidentally press **CTRL+DEL**, you will need to retype whatever you deleted.

Exit QuickBooks

It's a good idea to exit QuickBooks every night to protect your company file from corruption should a power failure occur and to prevent others from viewing or changing your data.

Close the Company File

When you close QuickBooks, the company file closes automatically. The next time you open QuickBooks, the same company file will open. For most users, this is convenient and preferred. If you have multiple companies, however, you may not want a company file to open by default. In this case, close the company file before exiting QuickBooks.

Click the **File** menu and click **Close Company**. The No Company Open screen will be displayed. You can then open a different file or exit QuickBooks.

Close QuickBooks

To close, or exit, QuickBooks, click the **Close** button (the X in the upper-right corner) in the QuickBooks window, or click the **File** menu and click **Exit**. QuickBooks saves all of your transactions as you make them, so you don't need to worry about saving information before you exit. If you have an incomplete transaction, you will see a dialog box notifying you of such and prompting you to record the transaction. If you click **Yes**, QuickBooks will save the current transaction and close. If you click **No**, QuickBooks will not save the transaction but will close. If you click **Cancel**, QuickBooks will not close and will display the transaction in question.

File	Edit	View	Lists	Company	Custor

New Company...
Open Company...
Open Previous Company ▶
EasyStep Interview
Close Company
Switch to Multi-user Mode

Back Up...
Restore...
Import ▶
Export ▶
Archive & Condense Data...
Utilities ▶
Timer ▶
Accountant's Review ▶

Print Check...   Ctrl+P
Save as PDF...
Print Forms ▶
Printer Setup...
Send Forms...
Shipping ▶

Update QuickBooks...
Exit   Alt+F4

CAUTION

Always confirm your entries have the correct date. QuickBooks will use today's date when you first open your file, but if you change your date to enter old transactions, that date becomes the new default until the file is closed or until the date is changed, even if you switch to other windows.

TABLE 1-7: KEYBOARD SHORTCUTS FOR DATE FIELDS

KEYBOARD SHORTCUT	DATE ENTERED
T	Today's date.
+	The next day's date. The date will continue to increase by one day each time this key is pressed.
-	The previous day's date. The date will continue to decrease by one day each time this key is pressed.
W	The date of the first day of the week. This will be Sunday's date unless you have changed your preferences. The date will change to that of the previous Sunday each time this key is pressed. See Chapter 8 for more information on changing your preferences.
K	The date of the last day of the week. This will be Saturday's date unless you have changed your preferences. The date will change to that of the previous Saturday each time this key is pressed. See Chapter 8 for more information on changing your preferences.
M	The date of the first day of the current month. The date will change to that of the first day of the previous month each time this key is pressed.
H	The date of the last day of the current month. The date will change to that of the last day of the next month each time this key is pressed.
Y	The date of the first day of the current year. The date will change to that of the first day of the previous year each time this key is pressed.
R	The date of the last day of the current year. The date will change to that of the last day of the next year each time this key is pressed.

How to...

- *Use an Existing File*

- *Migrate to QuickBooks*

- *Gather Information and Choose a Start Date*

- *Gathering Data for a New Company File*

- *Complete the General Section*

- *Using Accrual- vs. Cash-Based Accounting*

- *Complete the Income and Expenses Section*

- *Receiving Payments*

- *Edit Income Details*

- *Determine Opening Balances*

- *Creating Liability Accounts*

- *Review What's Next*

- *Set Up Multiple Users*

Chapter 2

Creating a Company File

If you already have a company file set up, this chapter will help you review and fine-tune it further. If you are new to QuickBooks, this chapter will show you how to use the EasyStep Interview to set up your company and follow up with manual adjustments. Later chapters will cover how to customize additional settings.

Use a Company File

You have three options regarding company files in QuickBooks:

- You can use an existing file, if one exists, including a file from an older version of QuickBooks.

- You can migrate to QuickBooks from another accounting system and use that company file.

- You can create a new company file.

Use an Existing File

If your company is already using QuickBooks, open the existing company file as shown in Chapter 1. If the existing company file was created using the same version of QuickBooks, it will open.

If the company file you are attempting to open was created using an earlier version of QuickBooks, the program will automatically update your file to the current version but will ask you to make a backup and confirm that all users have the same QuickBooks version. See Chapter 1 for update instructions.

Migrate to QuickBooks

When migrating to QuickBooks from another accounting system, you will need to manually enter the information from the old system. You may follow the steps in the next section to do this, but make sure you have gathered the following information from your old system first:

- Balance sheet
- Customer list with balances owed
- Vendor list with balances owed
- Employee list with all payroll information
- Most current tax returns, including:
  - Federal
  - State
  - Payroll
- Current inventory list with costs and quantities

How much information you enter into QuickBooks is up to you. If your old system is less than a year old, you should enter all information in QuickBooks so that your entire business history is available for reports. If you've used an alternative accounting system for 15 or more years, find a logical point in time from which all data will be entered in the new QuickBooks system. You can refer to the old system if historical data is needed prior to that point.

TIP

If there are multiple users of QuickBooks in your company, you may see a dialog box warning you that the file you want to open is already open on another system. If this happens, you need to ask that person to click the File menu and click Switch To Multi-User so that you can also open the file.

CAUTION

Make sure that all QuickBooks users in your company have the latest version installed before you update a company file.

CAUTION

If you are converting to QuickBooks from another accounting system, make sure to choose your start date carefully and match your balance sheets between systems. You may want to have an accountant or bookkeeper help you with the transfer and/or reconciliation of accounts.

Create a New Company File

The rest of this book will use the sample company Butterfly Books and Bytes to demonstrate procedures. Concerns for other businesses will be pointed out using Tips and Notes.

Butterfly Books and Bytes is a retail shop selling computer-related books, coffee, and snacks. Inventory will need to be maintained, and ISBN numbers will be used to identify the books; coffee, coffee supplies, and snack items will be identified by descriptions or vendor IDs.

Four employees run the shop, and the owner has one business checking account. The shop was started with $50,000: $20,000 from a capital investment and $30,000 from a private loan.

Gather Information and Choose a Start Date

It's important to choose an appropriate start date when setting up a new company file. If you are starting a new company with no current accounting system in place, use the first day of your fiscal year as the date you start your business. If you have no reason to choose a different date, use the calendar year (January 1–December 31) as your fiscal year. It will make your tax returns and other paperwork easier to do.

If you are migrating to QuickBooks from another system, choose an easy-to-remember date, such as the beginning of a quarter: January 1, April 1, July 1, or December 1. Once you've set up your new file, you can run identical reports from each system to make sure everything is set up correctly.

Butterfly Books and Bytes opened its doors on April 1, 2005, but business transactions started before that, so the QuickBooks start date will be January 1, 2005, so that the business's financial reporting dates will line up with the traditional calendar year. The farther back your start date is, the more historical information you will have to enter; however, this will give you more accurate reporting and control in the long run.

NOTE

The start date you pick for QuickBooks does not have to be the start of your fiscal year or calendar year. If your company has been in business for a while, you already have year-end and year-start dates, which are not easy to change. So, unless you are near those dates, pick another start date for QuickBooks.

NOTE

The start date is key to all balances in the EasyStep Interview. For example, if you have a checking account with $4,000 in it but it was opened after the start date, then in the EasyStep Interview, the opening balance would be zero. You will add transactions later.

GATHERING DATA FOR A NEW COMPANY FILE

Before creating a new company file, gather as much of the following information as you can. If you are missing some information, you can add it later, but your transition to QuickBooks will be smoother with accurate information entered as soon as possible:

- Company name, address, phone number, fax number, and e-mail and web addresses

- Company EIN (employer identification number), fiscal year, tax structure/income tax form, and type of business

- Number of QuickBooks users and their names

- Employee names (see Chapter 9 for information on setting up payroll)

- All bank statements for account numbers, types, entries, and balances back to your start date

- Balance sheet from current accounting system (if existing)

- List of customer names and balances owed as of the company start date (this will be zero if your start date is also the actual start date of your company)

- List of vendor names and balances due as of the company start date (this will be zero if your start date is also the actual start date of your company)

- List of credit cards, lines of credit, loans, notes, and other debts and amounts owed as of the company start date (this will be zero if your start date is also the actual start date of your company)

- List of assets and their value as of the company start date

- All transactions made since your start date

- Sales tax number, rate, and agencies' names (state, county, city)

- List of items you sell, including services, inventory, and non-inventory items

- Whether your company will report on a cash or accrual basis

Complete the General Section

The EasyStep Interview process begins with the General section. In this section, you will enter your company information, choose your preferences, and enter your start date. This section *must* be completed before any other section. To begin the EasyStep Interview process:

1. Open QuickBooks.

2. Click the **File** menu and click **New Company**. If a company file is currently open, QuickBooks closes it and the EasyStep Interview starts. If no company file is open, click the **Create A New Company** button, as seen in Figure 2-1. The EasyStep Interview starts, as shown in Figure 2-2. In the lower-left area of the screen are the Previous and Next buttons. Click the **Leave** button in the lower-right area to exit the EasyStep Interview and return to it later.

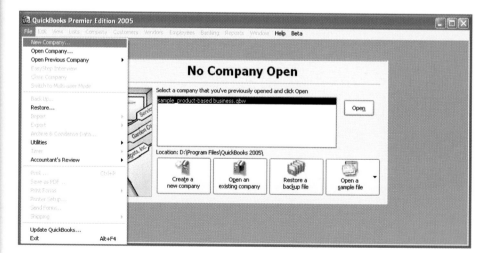

Figure 2-1: You can start a new company using the File menu or the Create A New Company button.

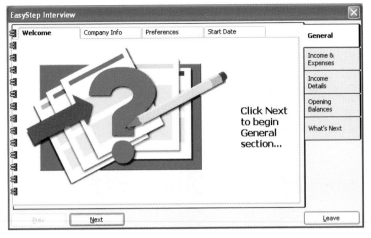

Figure 2-2: The EasyStep Interview simplifies the process of creating a new company file.

The EasyStep Interview consists of five sections, listed on the right side of the screen:

- General
- Income & Expenses
- Income Details
- Opening Balances
- What's Next

The General Section contains four tabs, listed across the top of the screen:

- Welcome
- Company Info
- Preferences
- Start Date

THE WELCOME TAB

The Welcome tab is the starting place for the General section.

1. Click **Next** to begin the General section of the EasyStep Interview. A message displays information on how you can obtain certified help in using QuickBooks. Click the blue link to open a web site to find a professional advisor if you feel the need for additional help.

> **Do you need assistance in setting up QuickBooks?**
>
> The EasyStep Interview provides step-by-step instructions for setting up your company. If you need further assistance, contact a Certified QuickBooks ProAdvisor to answer your questions or to have an advisor properly set up QuickBooks for your type of business.
>
> Click Find a Certified QuickBooks ProAdvisor or enter www.quickbooks.com/qbsetup into your browser to connect to the Internet and choose from our network of advisors.
>
> ⌁ Find a Certified QuickBooks ProAdvisor
>
> Click Next to continue the interview.

> Are you converting your data from Quicken to QuickBooks?
>
> ⚠ If your Company data file is in Quicken format and you wish to convert it to QuickBooks, click the Convert Quicken Data button to continue.
>
> [Convert Quicken Data...]
>
> Are you setting up a new company in QuickBooks?
>
> Click Next to continue with the EasyStep interview.

2. Click **Next** to continue. If you are migrating from Quicken to QuickBooks, click the **Convert Quicken Data** button. A dialog box appears, from which you can browse to the location of your Quicken data file. You will exit this EasyStep Interview, and another window will open. Click the **View Help** button in the Important Documentation window, and follow all directions. Your Quicken data will still be accessible after converting to QuickBooks.

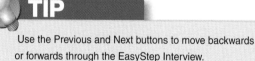

TIP

If you have set up a company file but want to return to the EasyStep Interview, you can click the **File** menu and click **EasyStep Interview** at any time.

TIP

Use the Previous and Next buttons to move backwards or forwards through the EasyStep Interview.

3. If you are not migrating from Quicken, then click **Next** to continue. You are given a choice: you can skip the rest of the EasyStep Interview and use a minimum amount of company information to create a file and then manually enter all information, or you can continue with the EasyStep Interview. It's recommended that you continue through the EasyStep Interview steps.

Setting up a new QuickBooks company

We've designed this interview to help you set up your NEW QuickBooks company.

We'll walk you through choosing and setting up various QuickBooks features.

If you don't want to use this interview and prefer to add minimal information to get started, click this button:

Skip Interview

Click Next to continue the interview.

4. Click **Next** to continue. You will see pointers on how to use the EasyStep Interview.

Navigating around the interview

While you're working in the interview, use the following buttons to move around:
- Click Next to move to the next screen.
- Click Prev to move to the previous screen.
- Click Leave to leave the interview and return to the regular QuickBooks program. You may return later by choosing "EasyStep Interview" from the File menu.

Important

Be sure to complete the General section of the interview first!

5. Click **Next**. You will see an explanation of the EasyStep Interview layout.

Sections and topics

The interview is divided into major sections listed on the right side of the window. Each major section is divided into topics shown on the tabs at the top of the window.

When all the sections are checked off, you've completed the interview and will be off to a great start with QuickBooks!

6. Click **Next** again. A message appears, notifying you that you can go back and change your answers during the EasyStep Interview process.

7. Click **Next**. You've completed the Welcome tab of the General section and will now see a check mark next to the Welcome tab.

Your company name

Enter your company name as you would like it to appear on invoices, statements, and reports. This is your "Doing Business As..." name:

Company Name

Butterfly Books and Bytes

Enter your company name as you need to have it on legal documents:

Legal name

Butterfly Consulting LLC

Other company information

Enter the federal tax ID number that you use on your federal income tax returns: (employer identification number or social security number)

20-1234567

Enter the first month of your income tax year:

January

Enter the first month in your fiscal year:

January

THE COMPANY INFORMATION TAB

The Company Information tab is the second tab in the General section and where you provide general information pertaining to your company.

1. Click **Next**. You'll see an overview of the Company Info section.

2. Click **Next** again. Type your company name (DBA) and your legal name (if different). The company name will show up on invoices, reports, and other correspondence you create using QuickBooks.

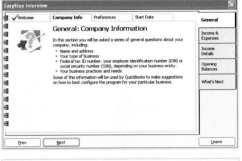

3. Click **Next** to continue. Enter your company contact information. You may leave blank anything you don't know or that doesn't apply to you, such as a web site address.

Your company information

Enter your company's full address here including street address, city, state, and zip code.

Address: 27 East Main Street

City: Mesa State: AZ Zip: 85201

Country: U.S.

Phone #: 480-507-4952

FAX #: 480-507-4953

Email: info@butterflybooks.org

Web Site: www.butterflybooks.org

4. Click **Next** again. Enter the company's EIN or your social security number (SSN) and the first month of your income tax year and fiscal year. Leave the default month (January) unless you have reason to change it. You may leave the EIN or SSN fields blank if you do not have this information yet. You can obtain an EIN from the IRS (www.irs.gov) and will need it if you will be running payroll.

5. Click **Next** to continue. Select the income tax form your company will be using. If you don't have this information yet, you can reenter the EasyStep Interview later and provide it.

Your company income tax form

What income tax form does your company use?

Form 1120S (S Corporation)

- Form 1120 (Corporation)
- ✓ Form 1120S (S Corporation)
- Form 1065 (Partnership)
- Form 990 (Exempt Organization)
- Form 990-PF (Ret of Priv Foun...
- Form 990-T (Bus Tx Ret)
- Form 1040 (Sole Proprietor)
- <Other/None>

...ation to automatically assign your accounts to
...it easier and quicker at tax time, by creating tax
...g up your data for your accountant or for
...Tax or ProSeries products.

TIP

You can't change your company type, but you can create and delete accounts within the Chart of Accounts QuickBooks creates based on this selection.

TIP

If you have an established business with a Chart of Accounts, you will be able to create your own set of accounts at this point.

CAUTION

Be sure you know where your company file will be stored on your computer and what its name is. All of your financial data is stored in this file. Write down the location and name you choose, and keep it in a safe place.

6. Click **Next**. Select your type of business. Don't worry if your exact company type is not present. Choose whatever is closest to it. The choice you make here will determine your initial list of income and expense accounts shown in the Chart of Accounts; however, these can all be edited, deleted, and added, as you will see in Chapter 3.

Select your type of business

Select your business type from the scrollable list.

⚠ Choose your company type carefully. You can not change your company type later.

Industry
Nonprofit Organization
Property Management
Real Estate Brokerage
Restaurant
Retail: General
Service Business

7. Click **Next** again. Green arrows indicate specific tips regarding the type of business you have chosen.

8. Click **Next**. A warning message is displayed regarding the creation of a company file name.

9. Click **Next** to continue. The Filename For New Company window opens. The default location to store your new file is C:\Program Files\Intuit\QuickBooks 2005, but consider storing it in the My Documents folder so that it will be backed up on a regular basis with all of your other files. The default name reflects your company name, such as "Butterfly Books and Bytes.qbw." You can keep this name or change it.

Filename for New Company

Save in: QuickBooks 2005

📁 Components
📁 Data
📁 QuickBooks Letter Templates
sample_product-based business.qbw
sample_service-based business.qbw

My Recent Documents
Desktop
My Documents
My Computer
My Network

File name: Butterfly Books and Bytes.QBW

Save as type: QuickBooks Files (*.QBW,*.QBA)

Save
Cancel
Help

CAUTION

User names and passwords must be typed exactly, as these fields are case-sensitive.

CAUTION

Once you enter the Administrator's Name password, if you forget it, you won't be able to get into your file, so make sure to correctly note it and securely store it.

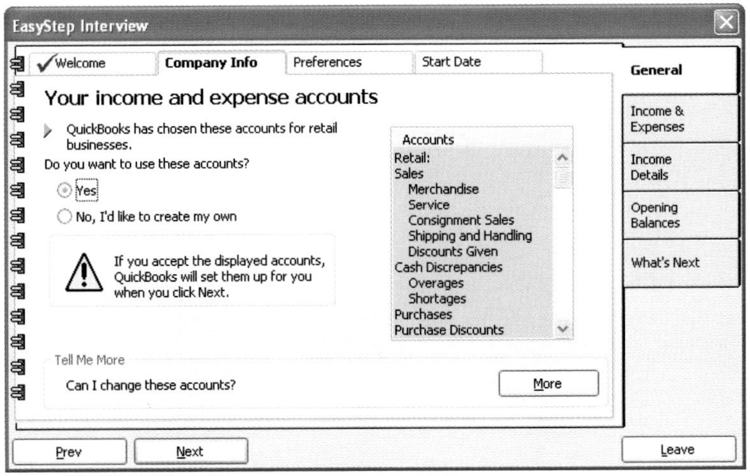

10. Click **Save**. The company file is created. You will now see your company name at the top of the window and a suggested Chart of Accounts (see Figure 2-3). The accounts were set up based on the company type you chose. (See Chapter 3 for more information on working with the Chart of Accounts.) Leave the **Yes** option selected.

11. Click **Next**. Enter the number of additional people who will need to access your QuickBooks file. You can add access levels later. If you are the only one using the file, leave the number at zero. In this example, since there are four employees and the owner, we will type 4.

Accessing your company

How many people (besides yourself) will have access to your QuickBooks company?

12. Click **Next** again. A dialog box appears with fields for you to enter the administrator's name and password. If you run a small, single-person business (sole proprietorship), you can leave the password field blank; however, anyone can open your financial records. You can change the default name in the Adminstrator's Name field, but make it something you can remember, as it will need to be entered *exactly* as you have typed it here, including the use of spaces and upper- and lowercase characters. Write this information down and put it in a secure place where other employees do not have access. You'll enter other employee passwords at the end of the EasyStep Interview.

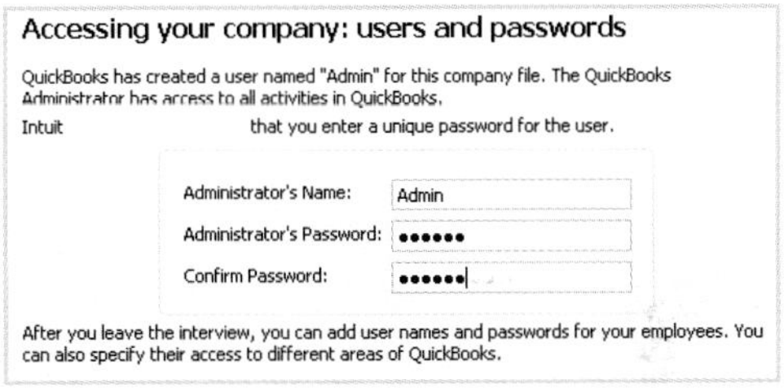

Accessing your company: users and passwords

QuickBooks has created a user named "Admin" for this company file. The QuickBooks Administrator has access to all activities in QuickBooks.

Intuit   that you enter a unique password for the user.

Administrator's Name: Admin

Administrator's Password: ••••••

Confirm Password: ••••••

After you leave the interview, you can add user names and passwords for your employees. You can also specify their access to different areas of QuickBooks.

EasyStep Interview

✓Welcome   **Company Info**   Preferences   Start Date

Your income and expense accounts

▷ QuickBooks has chosen these accounts for retail businesses.

Do you want to use these accounts?

⊙ Yes

○ No, I'd like to create my own

⚠ If you accept the displayed accounts, QuickBooks will set them up for you when you click Next.

Tell Me More

Can I change these accounts?   More

Prev   Next   Leave

Accounts
Retail:
Sales
  Merchandise
  Service
  Consignment Sales
  Shipping and Handling
  Discounts Given
Cash Discrepancies
  Overages
  Shortages
Purchases
Purchase Discounts

General

Income & Expenses

Income Details

Opening Balances

What's Next

13. Click **Next**. You have now completed the Company Info tab of the General section.

Figure 2-3: When your new company file is created, a list of income and expense accounts is created as well.

TIP

If you make a mistake at any point, simply click the **Back** button to return to the previous screen.

Your invoice format

QuickBooks has several invoice formats to fit different types of businesses. Select the format you prefer to use:

- ⊙ Product
- ○ Professional
- ○ Service
- ○ Custom

You can change this format at any time.

Invoice

DATE INVOICE #

BILL TO: SHIP TO:

P.O. # TERMS REP SHIP VIA F.O.B. PROJECT

QUANT. CODE DESCR. PRICE AMOUNT

TOTAL

THE PREFERENCES TAB

The Preferences tab is the third step in the General section and where you determine how information will be presented, stored, and so on.

1. Click **Next**. Read the Preferences overview. You may change any or all of these selections later.

2. Click **Next** to continue. Even if you collect taxes, leave the default option **No** selected at this point. You will set up your tax information later (see Chapter 9).

3. Click **Next** again. Select the type of invoice you prefer. Click each type to see a preview of how it will look. You may use several types of invoices within your business as well as set up custom invoices. Invoices are covered in more detail in Chapter 6.

4. Click **Next**. Click **Yes** if you will use sales orders. Sales orders are only available in the Premium version of QuickBooks and are used for back orders or for services not yet completed; these are later converted into invoices once sales are complete. Butterfly Books and Bytes will use sales orders. This feature, like most QuickBooks choices, can be changed later.

5. Click **Next** again. Click **Yes** if you have employees; click **No** if you don't. Setting up payroll will be covered in Chapter 9.

6. Click **Next** to continue. Click **Yes** if you will use QuickBooks to prepare or track estimates, proposals, bids, or quotes. If you create estimates using a custom form, you may choose not to use QuickBooks' Estimates feature (in which case, click **No**). If you want to do progress invoicing based on estimates, however, you must use the Estimates feature to automate the process. The Estimates feature can be turned on or off later as well.

7. Click **Next**. If you are using the Estimates feature, click **Yes** if you want to use progress invoicing, which basically means creating an estimate for a total amount and then billing for portions of that estimate as the work is completed or according to a prearranged time frame. If you have chosen not to use the Estimates feature, this page will not appear.

8. Click **Next** again. Decide whether you would like to track time spent on projects. If you are a consultant, time tracking is useful in your billing. If you have employees, time tracking is useful when entering payroll data. In this example, Butterfly Books and Bytes will use time tracking for research services and for weekly payroll.

9. Click **Next**. Decide whether to use classes. Classes add a third layer of accuracy to your data, but can be confusing. For example, if you want to track an expense by department, location, or other non-customer, non-item–related topic, you will benefit from classes. If you are unsure, click **No**. You can go back later and click Yes if you decide you need to use classes.

10. Click **Next** again. Select the method you want to use to manage your bills and payments. The first option is to enter the checks directly. This method presumes that you receive bills and wait on paying them until you are ready to write all checks. The second option (Enter The Bills First And Then Enter The Payments Later) assumes you will enter the bills upon receipt, along with the date due, and then go back and create checks using the Pay Bills feature when you are ready. The first option (Enter The Checks Directly) is easier and usually preferred by small companies. The second option is more accurate and often preferred in larger companies or in situations where one person enters the bills and another person pays them. Butterfly Books and Bytes will use the second method in order to have a true accrual system.

Two ways to handle bills and payments

Choose one of the two following ways to track your bills and payments.

- ○ Enter the checks directly.
- ⊙ Enter the bills first and then enter the payments later.

The first option is simple since it only involves one step.

The second option is a two-step process. QuickBooks reminds you when your bills are due, so that you can pay at the last possible moment or in time to get early payment discounts.

11. Click **Next**. The Reminders list summarizes your pending tasks in QuickBooks. It includes overdue invoices, checks to print, e-mails to send, online transactions to send, bills to pay, and various other reminders. Select one of these items to do now. You may change it later. Butterfly Books and Bytes will have the Reminders list show at start up.

12. Click **Next** again. Choose between accrual- or cash-based reporting. The choice you make will not affect how transactions are recorded, only how they are reported. Most accountants prefer the accrual method, which shows your liabilities and assets as of the date a debt was incurred. See the QuickFacts "Using Accrual- vs. Cash-Based Accounting" for more information. Butterfly Books and Bytes will use accrual-based accounting.

13. Click **Next**. You've completed the Preferences tab of the General section.

Accrual- or cash-based reporting

Do you prefer to view reports on an accrual or cash basis?

- ○ Cash-based reports
- ⊙ Accrual-based reports

For cash-based reports, income is reported when you receive the payment on an invoice, and an expense is reported when you pay a bill.

For accrual-based reports, income is reported as soon as you write an invoice, and an expense is reported as soon as you receive a bill.

▷ If you haven't already done so, consider using accrual-based reporting, since it may give you a more accurate picture of your business than cash-based reporting.

USING ACCRUAL- VS. CASH-BASED ACCOUNTING

The difference between accrual-based accounting and cash-based accounting is best demonstrated by way of example. In this example, the current date is June 25. On this day, you charge $20 worth of supplies on your business credit card and make a sale to a customer over the phone worth $50, billed to the customer's account. On July 15 you pay the credit card bill, and on July 1 you receive the money from your customer.

ACCRUAL-BASED ACCOUNTING METHOD

Under the *accrual-based* accounting method, on June 25, your business has a net income of $30 (the $50 sale—your profit—minus the $20 you spent in supplies—your expense). Your balance sheet reflects these transactions as having taken place in June.

CASH-BASED ACCOUNTING METHOD

Under the *cash-based* accounting method, transactions are reflected as occurring when money actually changes hands. In this example, your balance sheet shows July 15 as the date the $20 expense was incurred and July 1 as the day the income was incurred—the day the client's check arrives in the mail. Thus, these two transactions look like they happened in July, rather than June.

The accrual-based method provides a more accurate day-to-day picture of your finances; however, you don't want to pay taxes on income you haven't received yet. No matter which method you choose, you can change the reporting at any time in QuickBooks. All transactions will still be entered on the date they actually occurred; only the reports are affected by this choice.

THE START DATE TAB

The Start Date tab is the final tab in the General section. After completing the information needed on the Preferences tab:

1. Click **Next**. Enter your company's start date. Butterfly Books and Bytes will use January 1, 2005. It is highly recommended that you use the beginning of a year.

2. Click **Next** to continue. You've completed the General section.

> **Select a start date for your company's books**
>
> QuickBooks uses a start date as the point at which you begin entering your business transactions. You must enter all transactions between your start date and today to ensure complete accounting records for your business.
>
> ○ I **want** to start entering detailed transactions as of : **01/01/2004**
> Many QuickBooks users base their accounting records on their fiscal year so they can see detailed transactions for the entire year.
>
> ◉ I **want** to **s**tart entering detailed transactions as of : 01/01/2005 🗒
> Select a specific date to start entering your transactions. For example, you could choose today, the first of the month, etc.

Complete the Income & Expenses Section

In this section, you will review the Chart of Accounts that QuickBooks created for you based on your choice of business type. Butterfly Books and Bytes is a retail store, so if you chose a different type of business, your screen will look different from the images in Figures 2-4 and 2-5.

CREATE INCOME ACCOUNTS

Income accounts are the categories by which you choose to track your income. Butterfly Books and Bytes will be tracking book sales and food sales. Using these two income accounts will give a quick view on the profit and loss statement of the income these two areas are producing.

To see the details of book sales or food sales, various sales reports may be used to provide individual item-level detail.

Upon completing the General section:

1. Click **Next** to proceed automatically to the Income & Expenses section.

2. Click **Next** again. An overview of income accounts is displayed.

If you need to leave the EasyStep Interview at this time, you can return by opening QuickBooks, clicking the **File** menu, and clicking **EasyStep Interview**. You will return to the point at which you left the EasyStep Interview.

TIP

If you're ever unsure what choices to make when using the EasyStep Interview, it's best to accept the default choices QuickBooks presents to you. You can always go back and change most of this information later if needed.

3. Click **Next**. A list of income accounts that QuickBooks has created based on your chosen company type is displayed, as shown in Figure 2-4. Although it is possible to have only one income account, simply called Sales, most companies want to break down their sales (and expenses) into the various types so they can quickly see what is most profitable and what is most costly in their business.

4. Click **No** in response to the question, "Do you want to add an income account now?"

5. Click **Next** to continue. You have completed the income account portion of the Income & Expenses section.

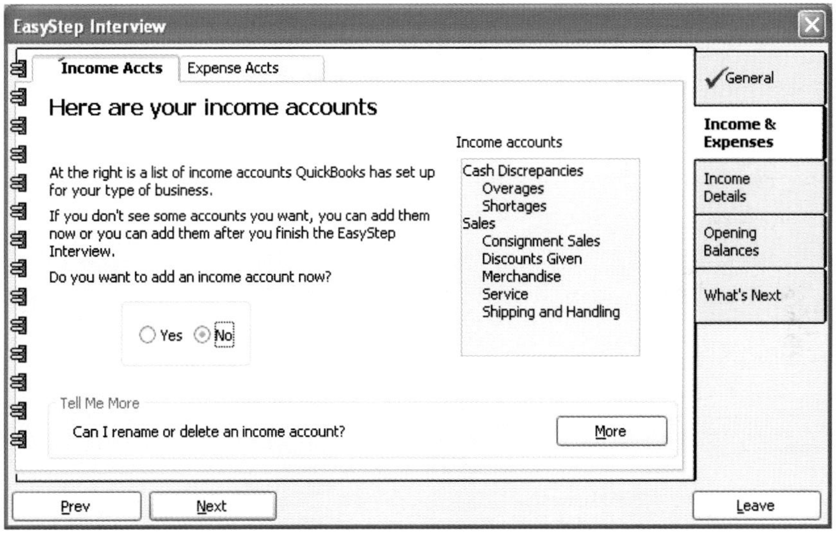

EasyStep Interview

| **Income Accts** | Expense Accts |

Here are your income accounts

At the right is a list of income accounts QuickBooks has set up for your type of business.

If you don't see some accounts you want, you can add them now or you can add them after you finish the EasyStep Interview.

Do you want to add an income account now?

○ Yes ⦿ No

Tell Me More

Can I rename or delete an income account? [More]

Income accounts

Cash Discrepancies
 Overages
 Shortages
Sales
 Consignment Sales
 Discounts Given
 Merchandise
 Service
 Shipping and Handling

✓ General

Income & Expenses

Income Details

Opening Balances

What's Next

[Prev] [Next] [Leave]

Figure 2-4: Income accounts can be easily renamed, added, and deleted.

TIP

You can create subaccounts under expense accounts for more detailed information, such as Gas, Insurance, and Repairs under Automobile Expense.

CREATE EXPENSE ACCOUNTS

Expense accounts track expenses related to your business overhead, for example, rent, utilities, computer supplies, paper, and so on. These are items you need to pay for whether or not a customer walks in your door. People often get these confused with cost of goods. *Cost of goods* are direct costs that you wouldn't have if you didn't sell any products or services, for example, books, coffee, cups, bags, and so on. Some business—for example, service-related businesses—may have little to no cost of goods. After creating your income accounts:

1. Click **Next**.
2. Click **More Details** if you want to read more about expense accounts (you'll see three screens to read).

   –Or–

   Click **No Thank You** if you don't want to read this information.
3. Continue to click **Next** until you see the screen displayed in Figure 2-5. This is a list of expense accounts that QuickBooks has created based on your chosen company type.
4. Click **No** in response to the question, "Do you want to add an expense account now?"
5. Click **Next** to continue. You have completed the expense account portion of the Income & Expenses section.

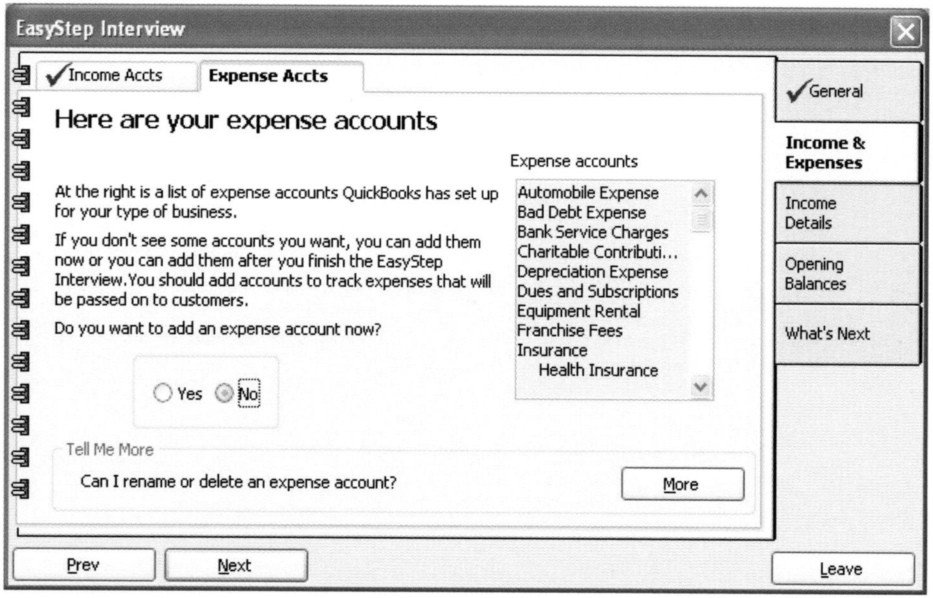
EasyStep Interview
Income Accts
Expense Accts
Here are your expense accounts
At the right is a list of expense accounts QuickBooks has set up for your type of business.
If you don't see some accounts you want, you can add them now or you can add them after you finish the EasyStep Interview. You should add accounts to track expenses that will be passed on to customers.
Do you want to add an expense account now?
Yes
No
Expense accounts
Automobile Expense
Bad Debt Expense
Bank Service Charges
Charitable Contributi...
Depreciation Expense
Dues and Subscriptions
Equipment Rental
Franchise Fees
Insurance
Health Insurance
Tell Me More
Can I rename or delete an expense account?
More
General
Income & Expenses
Income Details
Opening Balances
What's Next
Prev
Next
Leave

Figure 2-5: You can add subaccounts, such as Health Insurance, for more insight into the details of your business.

Edit Income Details

The Income Details section is the third section in the EasyStep Interview and pertains to your invoicing and statement needs. If you sell items only at your store location and receive payments right away upon the completion of a sale, you may choose to use sales receipts rather than invoices. If you sell some items via phone orders, for example, and receive payment later, you should use invoices as well as receipts. After completing the Income & Expenses section:

1. Click **Next**.

2. Click **Next** again. An overview of the Income Details section is displayed.

3. Click **Next**. Decide if you need to track what clients owe you. If you are paid immediately upon the completion of a sale, click **No**. If you make some transactions based on customer credit, click **Sometimes**.

   Receipt of payment

   Do you receive full payment at the time (or before) you provide a service or sell a product?

   ○ Always   ⦿ Sometimes   ○ Never

   If you answer "Always", the interview assumes you do NOT need to track how much money customers or clients owe you because they pay you immediately.

   If you answer "Sometimes" or "Never", the interview assumes you DO need to track how much money customers or clients owe you. That is, you need to track accounts receivable.

4. Click **Next**. Sometimes is chosen for the purposes of our example, but will work in most situations. The Statement Charges page is displayed.

   Statement Charges

   Some businesses issue regular monthly statements which list all of the customer's activity for a month and carry balances forward.

   Will you be using statement charges? If you are unsure, answer "No". You can always change your mind later.

   ○ Yes   ⦿ No

   ▷ Most retailers do not send monthly statements.
   Limitations: QuickBooks statements do not calculate percentages. Therefore, you cannot add sales tax or percentage discounts, however, you can add flat-rate discounts.

5. Click **No** and click **Next**. No is chosen for the purposes of our example. You may choose whichever is applicable for your business.

ITEMS

Items are extremely important in understanding QuickBooks. Basically, everything you sell is an item, regardless of whether it is a service or a product. Research, coffee, and books are all items, but they can be different item types, including Service, Non-Inventory, Other Charges, and Inventory. Chapter 3 will cover item types in more detail. To complete the Items topic of the Income Details section:

1. Click **Next**.

2. Click **Next** again. The next page asks if you have any service items to sell (this would include consulting, research, painting, and so on). If you are a consulting company, you may want to create several types of service items. Our example company will create a Research item in Chapter 3 so that you may see how to work with the Item list and create items.

3. Click **No** and then click **Next** to continue. QuickBooks asks if you have any non-inventory items to sell. If you already use a custom program to track your inventory, you might want to use QuickBooks to track your non-inventory items. Some people prefer to use non-inventory items for a simpler system, such as a business in which pencils are bought by the case but sold individually, since counting might not be a concern.

4. Click **No** and then click **Next**. QuickBooks asks if you have any other charges you would like to set up. This includes fees for shipping and handling, delivery, travel, and so on.

5. Click **No** and then click **Next**. You've completed the Items topic.

INVENTORY

Inventory consists of items you purchase to hold for resale, such as in a retail store. If you are primarily a service company and use parts for repair, you might want to talk with your accountant to determine if you are better off holding inventory or purchasing items as you need them. Inventory will be covered in more detail in Chapter 7. To complete the Inventory topic after finishing the Items section:

1. Click **Next**.

2. Click **Next** again. You may set up inventory or skip that for now.

3. Click **Skip Inventory Setup** and click **Next** to continue.

NOTE

Non-inventory items include items that are purchased specifically for a customer (as is often the case with consulting companies), items you make (for manufacturers), and any other item that you don't wish to track as inventory (such as seeds you grow into plants).

Determine Opening Balances

The Opening Balances section is the fourth phase in the EasyStep Interview. It is important that you match your entries in this section with the start date you chose because each entry here is referring to that date in time.

In this section you will enter customer and vendor information as well as their current balances (if you are moving from another system) as of the date you chose to start this company file. You will then enter the opening balances in all of your other asset and liability accounts, such as bank accounts, credit cards, lines of credit, and loans. You will have better reporting and tracking if you enter a zero balance for customers (and vendors) and then enter each outstanding invoice (or bill) with the balance and date; however, this may not be practical if you have a large number of customers (or vendors) with outstanding balances.

Upon completing the Income Details section of the EasyStep Interview:

1. Click **Next**. An overview of the Opening Balances section is displayed.

2. Click **Next** again. Make sure you have the following items on hand:

   - Bank statements back to your starting date
   - The value of any assets, liabilities, and credit cards as of your starting date
   - Customer names and balances as of your starting date
   - Vendor names and balances as of your starting date

3. Click **Next** to continue. An overview explaining customers is displayed.

4. Click **Next** again. If you are starting a new company or plan to enter all transactions back to your start date, you do not need to enter any customer information here. You can add customer information at any time using the Customer:Job List, which will be covered in Chapter 3.

5. Click **No** and then click **Next** to continue. If you selected the Enter The Checks Directly option earlier, you will skip to the Accounts section. If you selected the Enter The Bills First And Then Enter The Payments Later option earlier, you will provide your vendor information next.

Enter customers

Do you have any customers who owed you money on your start date to add?

○ Yes ⦿ No

TIP

Don't enter customer balances when you enter customers. Enter outstanding invoices with their correct number for accurate tracking.

TIP

Go ahead and set up your accounts here if you are creating your own company account. Enter zero as the starting balance if you did not open the account before your start date or if you plan to enter the related transactions later.

CAUTION

Credit cards as referred to here are ones you use for expenses, not credit cards you accept from your customers as a merchant.

VENDORS

Vendors are the people from whom you buy goods and services. Subcontractors are also considered vendors, and you will learn how to set up IRS Form 1099 for those vendors in Chapter 5. To enter vendor information:

1. Click **Next**. Enter vendor information and their balances as of the start date you chose and not today's date.

2. If you don't have any vendor information to enter at this time, click **No**.

3. Click **Next**.

ACCOUNTS

Within your Chart of Accounts are two categories: Balance Sheet Accounts and Income and Expense Accounts.

Income and Expense Accounts track the flow of your income and expenses, but the actual money will be added or subtracted from your bank account or posted to Accounts Payable (money you owe people) or Accounts Receivable (money people owe you).

Balance Sheet Accounts track the actual value of your business at any given point in time. Thus, the two most important reports you will later generate will be the Profit and Loss report, based on Income and Expense Accounts, and the Balance Sheet report, based on the Balance Sheet Accounts. To set up your accounts after providing your vendor information:

1. Click **Next**. An overview explaining accounts is displayed.

2. Click **Next** again. If you use a business credit card, you may set up an account for that at this time. If you have a debit card with a credit card logo, that will not be set up here as it is considered part of your checking account.

Credit card accounts

Would you like to set up a credit card account? Note that you should NOT set up an account for a personal credit card which you sometimes use for business.

○ Yes ⦿ No

You must set up one QuickBooks credit card account for each credit card account you have.

Adding lines of credit

Do you have any lines of credit?

○ Yes ● No

3. Click **No** and click **Next** to continue. If you have any lines of credit, you may enter that information. QuickBooks treats lines of credit like credit cards.

4. Click **No** and click **Next**. If you have any loans or notes payable, you may enter that information. Our sample company began with a $30,000 loan, so it will be entered here.

Loans and Notes Payable

Would you like to set up an account to track a loan or note payable? Loans and notes payable are tracked in "liability" accounts.

○ Yes ● No

You must set up a separate QuickBooks liability account for each loan account you have.

Loans and notes are the two most common examples of liability accounts. QuickBooks sets up some kinds of liability accounts for you automatically if you charge sales tax, use payroll, or use accounts payable.

If you have other kinds of liabilities you would like to track with QuickBooks, enter them now as well.

5. Click **No** (see the QuickSteps "Creating Liability Accounts" if you want to click Yes), and click **Next** to continue.

CAUTION

In the case of a liability account, you will be asked if it is short- or long-term (anything longer than a year is considered long-term). The answer you provide will only make a difference in where this account is listed in related reports.

CREATE A BANK ACCOUNT

Bank accounts include money market, savings, and checking accounts. You will have at least one bank account. You can modify your banking account information at any time. After setting up your other account information (see the previous section):

1. Ensure that **Yes** is selected, and click **Next** to continue.

2. Type the name of the account, for example, Checking, and click **Next**.

Adding a bank account

Name

Checking

Enter the name of your bank account, (for example "checking", "savings", "State National Bank", etc). For petty cash accounts, you can use "Petty Cash" or "Cash Drawer".

3. If you want, provide the following information on the Bank Account Setup page (doing so is optional):

- Statement ending date (if different from your start date)

- Statement ending balance (if this is not a new account; if you opened it after your start date, leave the amount as 0)

- Bank account number

- Check reorder number (if you want QuickBooks to remind you when it's time to reorder checks)

Bank account setup

Statement Ending Date

01/01/2005

Enter the date of the last bank statement you received whose ending date was ON OR BEFORE 01/01/2005 (the date you chose as the starting date for transaction entry).

Statement Ending Balance

30,000.00

Enter the ending balance from the statement

Bank Account Number

03-123456

Enter bank account number.

Check Reorder Number

450

Remind me to order checks when I print this check number

CREATING LIABILITY ACCOUNTS

The process whereby you add accounts is similar throughout the EasyStep Interview. In this section, the specific task is creating a liability account, but you can apply this process to bank or asset accounts as well. A liability account includes any type of account to which you owe money, such as a credit card, line of credit, loan, or note payable. If you want to add a liability account during the EasyStep Interview:

1. Click **Yes** in response to the question, "Would you like to set up an account to track a loan or note payable?" and click **Next**. The Adding A Loan (Liability) Account page is displayed. Fill in the Name and Unpaid Balance fields. Make sure that the unpaid balance is the amount as of your start date and not today's date. Choose whether this is a long-term loan.

Adding a loan (liability) account

Name
| Startup Loan - Personal | Enter the name of your loan. |

Unpaid Balance on 01/01/2005
| 30,000.00 | Enter the balance of the loan (NOT the original amount of the loan) as of your start date. If you obtained this loan after your start date, enter 0 for the balance of the loan. After you finish the EasyStep interview, use QuickBooks to enter a loan deposit for the date on which you received the loan. |

| ☑ Long Term Liability | Click here if this loan will not be paid off in a year. See Tell Me More below for further explanation. |

2. Click **Next** and wait while QuickBooks creates the account. You will see it added to the Loan Accounts list, located to the right.

3. Click **No** if you don't want to create any more liability accounts, and click **Next**.

Adding another loan

You have just added a liability account. To the right is your current list of loan accounts.

Would you like to add a liability account for another loan or note payable?

○ Yes ⊙ No

Loan Accounts
Payroll Liabilities
Sales Tax Payable
Startup Loan - Personal

4. Click **Next**. Your bank accounts are created and displayed in the Bank Accounts list.

5. Click **No** in response to the question, "Would you like to add another bank account?" and click **Next**. You are asked if you will print checks and deposit slips from QuickBooks.

Adding another bank account

You have just added a bank account. To the right is your current list of bank accounts.

Would you like to add another bank account?

○ Yes ⊙ No

Bank Accounts
Checking

Remember, QuickBooks classifies all checking, savings, and money market accounts as bank accounts. We also recommend that you set up your petty cash accounts as bank accounts.

6. Click **No** (or click **Yes** if you wish to learn how to print checks and deposit slips on your printer). If you click Yes, help on printing checks and deposit slips will pop up when you use QuickBooks at a later time. Click **Next** to continue.

ASSETS

Asset accounts include loans payable to you, furniture, property, and so on. If you have purchased these items since the start of your business, don't enter them here; enter them as a transaction against one of your accounts. If you have assets you are transferring to the business, you may want to enter them here. This could include a computer, telephone equipment, a vehicle, or tools. Consult your accountant for determination of value.

1. After providing information on your bank accounts and clicking **Next**, read the overview explaining assets.

2. Click **Next**. You will have the opportunity to enter any assets you may have.

3. Click **No** in response to the question, "Would you like to set up an asset account?" (or click **Yes** if you know their value as of your start date). You can enter this information at a later time.

Asset accounts

Would you like to set up an asset account?

○ Yes ⊙ No

4. Click **Next**.

EQUITY ACCOUNTS

Equity accounts track the difference between what you owe and what you own. You can review and edit this account, and may wish to consult with your accountant as to the accuracy of these accounts once your business is set up and data is entered. QuickBooks automatically generates an Opening Balance Equity account or an Owner's Equity account based on the initial opening balances you entered. To review your equity account:

1. After providing information on your assets and clicking **Next**, review the accounts QuickBooks has set up for you in the Equity Accounts list. You may edit these in the Chart of Accounts if needed.

2. Click **Next** again. You have completed the Opening Balances section of the EasyStep Interview.

Review What's Next

The What's Next section is the final step in the EasyStep Interview. It tells you what your options are once you've successfully created a new company file. Upon completing the Opening Balances section:

1. Click **Next** and read the recommendations as to what you should do next.

2. Continue clicking **Next** to read through the following topics:

- Backing up your data (See Chapter 1)

- Entering historical transactions (See Chapters 5 and 6)

- Setting up users and passwords (See "Set Up Multiple Users and Passwords" later in this chapter)

- Customizing forms (See Chapter 6)

- Setting up 1099 tracking (See Chapter 5)

- Signing up for payroll services (See Chapter 8)

- Ordering checks and forms, such as deposit slips, tax forms, or shipping labels (See Chapter 4)

NOTE

If pop-up windows appear while you are working with your company file reminding you of certain tasks, you may click OK and do them later.

TIP

Create regular backups. The busier your business, the more frequently you should back up your data.

3. Click the **Leave** button when you have read through all of the topics. You have finished the EasyStep Interview, and your new company file is open and ready for you to work in, as shown in Figure 2-6.

4. Click the **Begin Using QuickBooks** button at the lower-right corner of the screen to close the QuickBooks Learning Center and examine your company file.

Set Up Multiple Users

If you are the sole employee of your business, you don't need to worry about multiple users. If you have employees and only one copy of QuickBooks on one computer, it is possible to allow everyone to take turns opening QuickBooks and only have a single user set up, but you should create a separate user account for each person who will use your accounting files in order to ensure other users do not go into (or change) areas where they do not have authority. Set up individual user accounts, and restrict access to areas and privileges so that some people can only enter data while others can make changes to data.

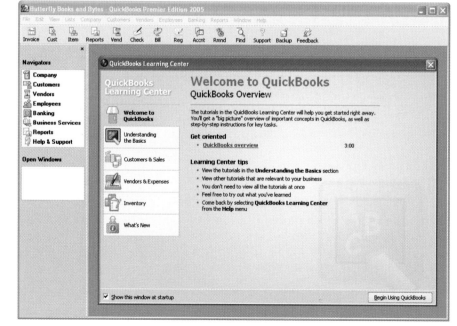

If you have multiple computer locations that need to use QuickBooks, such as a front register and a back office, then you will not only need separate user accounts, but you will also need a separate copy of QuickBooks for each computer. Keep in mind that even though each user will have a copy of QuickBooks on his or her computer, they will all share the same company file.

Figure 2-6: When you complete the EasyStep Interview, you can then begin working in your new company file.

CAUTION

You *cannot* merge separate QuickBooks files. It is imperative that all users share a single file or you will be missing data. That file can be accessed by multiple computers at the same time, but each user must have the same version of QuickBooks installed.

To set up user accounts:

1. Click the **Company** menu and click **Set Up Users**. The User List appears displaying the Admin User. If you didn't set up an Admin User in the EasyStep Interview, you will be asked to create one before seeing the User List.

2. Click the **Add User** button. The Set Up User Password And Access screen is displayed.

3. Type a user name, such as Register, and a password that you will easily remember. Use descriptive names rather than employees's personal names to ease employee turnover transitions. Keep in mind that both the User Name and Password fields are case-sensitive and must be typed *exactly* as they are entered here.

Access for user: Register

What do you want this user to have access to?

◉ Selected areas of QuickBooks
(You will make the selections in the screens that follow)

○ All areas of QuickBooks

4. Click **Next**. Select the level of access you want this user to have. For the purposes of our example, we will give this user a selective level of access.

5. Click **Selected Areas Of QuickBooks**, and click **Next**. In each of the following nine areas, choose the level of access you want this user to have, clicking **Next** after each selection:

- Sales and Accounts Receivable (Create And Print Transactions has been selected for this account because the Register will be creating invoices and cash sales and printing them for customers). The Register user will not have any other access.

○ No Access
○ Full Access
◉ Selective Access
  ○ Create transactions only
  ◉ Create and print transactions
  ○ Create transactions and create reports

NOTE

A closing date is the date you chose—usually the end of the previous year—at which point transactions prior to the closing date are locked. This protects sensitive tax information from being changed by accident.

- Purchases and Accounts Payable (you may want to give a manager account this type of access but not someone who just runs the register unless he or she must order items as well)

- Checking and Credit Cards

- Time Tracking

- Payroll and Employees

- Sensitive Accounting Activities

- Sensitive Financial Reporting

- Changing or Deleting Transactions

- Access for User (review the summary of access for this user; click the **Previous** button to go back and change any of your previous choices, or click **Finish** if you are satisfied with the levels of access you have created for this user)

6. The user account is created and displayed in the User List window. Click **Close** to exit the User List window.

From the User List window you can perform the following actions:

- Click **Add User** to continue to add users.

- Click **Edit User** to return to previous screens and change access levels for this user.

- Click **Delete User** to remove this user from the User List.

- Click **View User** to see the summary of the user's access levels.

How to...

- *Use Lists*
- *Examine List Similarities*
- *Understand Balance Sheet Accounts*
- *Understand Income and Expense Accounts*
- *Understanding Cost of Goods Sold Accounts*
- *Use Menu Buttons for Actions and Reports*
- *Move and Sort Accounts and Subaccounts*
- *Customize Columns*
- *Add Accounts and Subaccounts*
- *Delete Accounts and Subaccounts*
- *Editing an Account*
- *Make an Account Inactive*
- *Rename and Merge Accounts*
- *Print Lists of Accounts*
- *Use the Customer: Job List to Track Balances and Jobs*
- *Naming Customers*
- *Enter Service Items*
- *Enter Non-Inventory Items*

Chapter 3

Working with Lists

One of the major advantages in learning QuickBooks is the consistency found throughout the forms, lists, registers, and reports. Once you learn how to work with one type of object, you'll find your skills easily transfer to other objects of the same type. Lists are at the heart of QuickBooks in helping you easily manage your business. In this chapter, you'll explore the various types of lists, including the Chart of Accounts, and learn to edit, add, and delete items in the Chart of Accounts list. Other lists use the same steps, although in each list different entry forms are displayed. Registers will be covered in the next chapter, and forms will be covered in more detail in their related chapters.

Understand Lists

You can access most lists by clicking the Lists menu, as shown in Figure 3-1. Some lists also appear on a second related menu, and a few are found only on a menu other than the Lists menu. The list items you see are dependent, to a degree, on the choices you made when setting up your company file, so you may not see all of the same items pictured in this chapter. Click and explore what is listed on your menus.

Use Lists

When you determine the lists you use most often, you can add them to your icon bar for quick access, as you learned in Chapter 1. Until then, or at any time, you can access lists through the menus in the following sections.

THE LISTS MENU

The Lists menu contains almost all of the lists included in QuickBooks. Table 3-1 describes each of the choices on the Lists menu, and Table 3-2 describes the choices available in the submenu called Customer & Vendor Profile Lists (which can be accessed from the Lists menu).

Lists	Company	Customers	Vendors	Empl
Chart of Accounts			Ctrl+A	
Item List				
Fixed Asset Item List				
Price Level List				
Sales Tax Code List				
Payroll Item List				
Customer:Job List			Ctrl+J	
Vendor List				
Employee List				
Other Names List				
Customer & Vendor Profile Lists ▶				Sales Rep List
Templates				Customer Type List
				Vendor Type List
Memorized Transaction List			Ctrl+T	Job Type List
				Terms List
				Customer Message List
				Payment Method List
				Ship Via List
				Vehicle List

Figure 3-1: The Lists menu provides a quick way to access most lists.

THE COMPANY MENU

The Company menu includes two special company lists that are not available on the Lists menu:

To Do List	
Reminders	
Alerts Manager	
Chart of Accounts	Ctrl+A

- **To Do List** contains notes that you enter and that appear on dates you set.
- **Reminders** tracks online banking transactions that need to be completed, To Do notes, deposits that need to be made, bills to pay, overdue invoices, checks, invoices, purchase orders, and receipts to be printed, as well as inventory to reorder, assembly items to build (in Premier), and other business alerts.

TABLE 3-1: LISTS ACCESSIBLE FROM THE LISTS MENU

LIST NAME	DESCRIPTION
Chart of Accounts	Lists balance sheet and income and expense accounts. (Also on the Company and Banking menus.)
Item list	Tracks items and services you sell on a detailed level. Each item is linked to one or more accounts in the Chart of Accounts, but by using the Items list, you can view more detailed reports for use in job costing. (Also on the Customers and Vendors menus.)
Fixed Asset Item list	Tracks furniture, vehicles, equipment, and other assets used over a long term (more than a year), and provides a means to manage depreciation.
Price Level list	Provides flexibility in designating prices, discounts, or surcharges for specific customers and items.
Sales Tax Code list	Lists different types of taxes that you might need to track. (Also on the Vendors Sales Tax menu.)
Payroll Item list	Includes items that may appear on a paycheck, including salaries, hourly wages, additions (such as bonuses and reimbursement), and deductions (such as taxes, direct deposits, and insurance). (Also on the Employee menu.)
Customer: Job List	Tracks information for your customers and the individual jobs (or projects) you set up for them, as well as their current balances, notes, and job status. (Also on the Customer menu.)
Vendor list	Tracks information for your vendors (including 1099s), as well as their current balances and notes. (Also on the Vendor menu.)
Employee list	Tracks information for your employees, including their tax status and any custom fields you care to add, such as licensing, spouse, or birthday, as well as their social security number and notes. (Also on the Employee menu.)
Other Names list	Tracks information for anyone who doesn't fit into one of the previous lists. This is a limited category, but the advantage is the ability to later move an entry in this list into any of the other three, so someone just hired may be entered as an "other" name if you are unsure whether he or she will have a 1099 (vendor) or employee status. (Also on the Banking menu.)
Templates list	Lists all form templates in one location to easily manage the look of invoices, credit memos, sales receipts, purchase orders, statements, estimates, and sales orders. Editing templates will be covered in Chapter 6.
Memorized Transactions list	Tracks recurring transactions. Once a transaction is entered, you can configure it so that it is automatically entered on a regular basis or so that QuickBooks reminds you to manually enter the transaction.

TABLE 3-2: LISTS ACCESSIBLE FROM THE CUSTOMER & VENDOR PROFILE LISTS

LIST NAME	DESCRIPTION
Sales Rep list	Keeps a reference of salespeople's names, type, and initials for use on invoices and other sales forms. You can use this list to identify names on the Vendors, Employees, or Other Names lists to indicate who is responsible for a sale.
Type lists	Allows you to categorize your customers, vendors, and jobs by industry, location, source, or any other way your business is structured and includes: Customer Type list, Vendor Type list, and Job Type list.
Terms list	Allows you to determine payment schedules for clients, including discounts and deadlines used in billing. Standard terms are included, but you can add others.
Customer Message list	Allows custom messages to be added to the bottom of invoices and estimates. These can also be easily added on the fly.
Payment Method list	The Payment Method list includes commonly used payment methods, such as cash, check, and credit cards, but you can easily add new methods, such as store credit or PayPal.
Ship Via list	Contains a simple list of shipping methods, such as FedEx, USPS, and UPS. You can add custom items, such as pick up or delivery, either in this list or the first time you need it, using the Quick Add feature.
Vehicle list	Tracks all company vehicle mileage for tax, billing, and depreciation purposes.

Throughout QuickBooks, if you enter a name, item, or message that is not already on a list, you will see a dialog box prompting you to add, set up, or cancel this item. If you believe you made a mistake, click **Cancel**; otherwise, click **Quick Add** to add the name or item to the list, or click **Set Up** to open a detailed entry form.

Consider naming your users according to their function rather than by name to easily identify the level of access.

THE VENDOR MENU

The Vendor menu includes one list that is not on the Lists menu, which is useful for those businesses that use purchase orders. The Purchase Orders list shows outstanding purchase orders by default, but you can also view all purchase orders and receive items and run reports.

> Vendor List
> Item List
> Purchase Orders List

THE REPORTS MENU

The Reports menu includes one additional list, the Memorized Reports list, which tracks customized reports, allowing you to run groups of reports and manage memorized (custom) reports.

> Reports   Window   Help
> Report Navigator
> Memorized Reports   ▶   Memorized Report List

OTHER LISTS

Two more important lists in QuickBooks not on the Lists menu include:

- **User List** (click the **Company** menu and click **Set Up Users**) allows you to assign passwords and rights to multiple users in QuickBooks Pro and QuickBooks Premier. Once you have entered the first user, the User List is displayed, from which you can add, delete, and edit users (see Chapter 2 for more information).

- **Item Types** (Click the **Lists** menu and click **Item List**; then click the **Item** menu, and click **New**) lists types of items you can create, such as service, inventory part, inventory assembly, non-inventory part, other charge, subtotal, group, discount, payment, sales tax item, and sales tax group. These item types cannot be edited (see Chapter 9 for more information).

Examine List Similarities

Although this chapter focuses primarily on the Chart of Accounts, if you substitute the word "item," almost everything that will be covered in this chapter using the Chart of Accounts as an example applies to every other list within QuickBooks as well. The Customer:Job List and Item list are slightly different and are discussed separately at the end of this chapter.

LIST TYPES

The three major groups of lists in QuickBooks are:

- **Main lists** are the lists that are critical to QuickBooks, such as Chart of Accounts, Item list, and Memorized Transaction.

- **Name lists** include the Customer:Job List and the Vendor, Employee, and Other lists.

- **Sublists** include drop-down lists on forms, such as Payment Method list or Sales Rep list. These lists typically have no detail level other than their name, unlike the other lists, which include detailed fields for each item.

LIST CAPACITY

The lists in QuickBooks can hold a large number of entries. For example, Item list and Memorized Transaction list can hold 14,500 entries. The four name lists (Customer:Job, Vendor, Employee, and Other) share a common source of data and can also hold a total of 14,500 names. Price Levels is a special list that links other lists and can hold up to 100 entries. The sublists Class, Terms, Payment Method, Customer Type, Vendor Type, Job Type, and Customer Message can hold up to 10,000 entries each.

Understand Accounts

The most important list of all is your Chart of Accounts. It lists your balance sheet accounts, such as bank and loan accounts, and your income and expense accounts, such as sales and rent.

1. Open QuickBooks and your last used file will open—either your new company file or the sample file. Use whichever you prefer.

2. Click the **Company** menu.

3. Click **Chart Of Accounts**.

You will see a list of accounts for your company or a more comprehensive list of accounts in the sample company file, as shown in Figure 3-2.

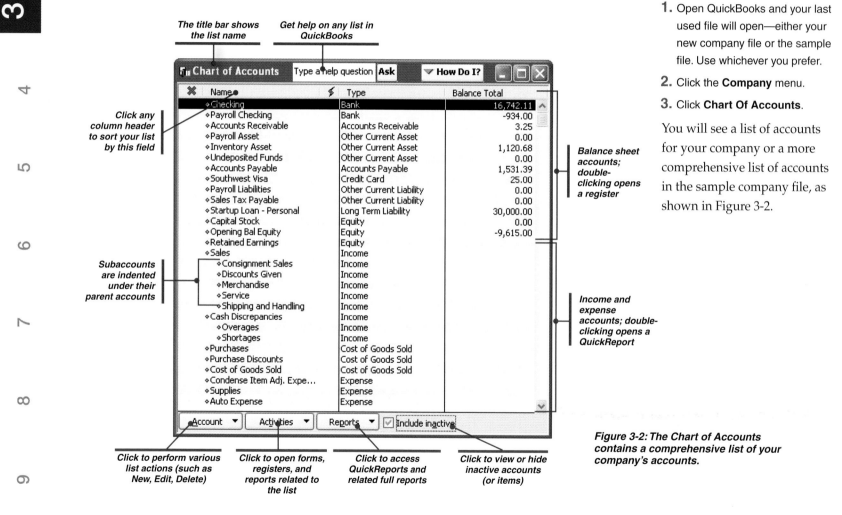

The title bar shows the list name

Get help on any list in QuickBooks

Click any column header to sort your list by this field

Subaccounts are indented under their parent accounts

Balance sheet accounts; double-clicking opens a register

Income and expense accounts; double-clicking opens a QuickReport

Click to perform various list actions (such as New, Edit, Delete)

Click to open forms, registers, and reports related to the list

Click to access QuickReports and related full reports

Click to view or hide inactive accounts (or items)

Figure 3-2: The Chart of Accounts contains a comprehensive list of your company's accounts.

The four basic types of accounts in QuickBooks are:

- Balance sheet accounts
- Income and expense accounts
- Cost of Goods Sold accounts
- Other income and expense accounts

Understand Balance Sheet Accounts

Balance sheet accounts list what your company owns and what it owes. The Balance Sheet report is created using the reports function of QuickBooks. It shows your company's current position in terms of your assets, liabilities, and equity (the difference between assets and liabilities), an example of which is shown in Figure 3-3. Equity, also called net worth, tells you how much the business is actually worth. All areas should combine to equal zero in a balance sheet.

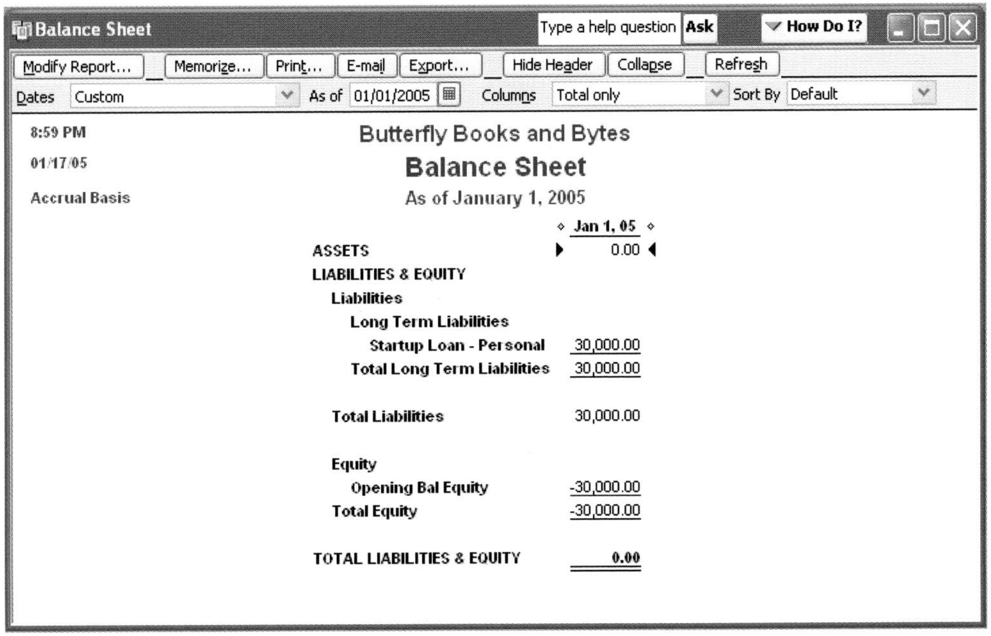

Three types of accounts are present on a balance sheet:

- Assets
- Liabilities
- Equity

These accounts each have a register. If you refer back to the Chart of Accounts in Figure 3-2, you will see the current balance for all of the balance sheet accounts.

Figure 3-3: The Balance Sheet report provides you with a picture of your company's health at any given point in time.

| Balance Sheet | | | Type a help question | Ask | How Do I? |

| Modify Report... | Memorize... | Print... | E-mail | Export... | Hide Header | Collapse | Refresh |
| Dates | Custom | As of | 01/01/2005 | Columns | Total only | Sort By | Default |

8:59 PM
01/17/05
Accrual Basis

Butterfly Books and Bytes
Balance Sheet
As of January 1, 2005

	Jan 1, 05
ASSETS	▶ 0.00 ◀
LIABILITIES & EQUITY	
Liabilities	
Long Term Liabilities	
Startup Loan - Personal	30,000.00
Total Long Term Liabilities	30,000.00
Total Liabilities	30,000.00
Equity	
Opening Bal Equity	-30,000.00
Total Equity	-30,000.00
TOTAL LIABILITIES & EQUITY	0.00

ASSETS

Assets include:

- Bank accounts, such as checking and savings accounts
- Accounts receivable (A/R), which are the current outstanding balances of your clients
- Fixed assets, such as furniture, buildings, and cars
- Other assets, such as investments and loans made to others
- Other current assets, such as advances made to employees

LIABILITIES

Liability accounts track what your business owes and include:

- Accounts payable (A/P), which are often unpaid bills from vendors
- Credit cards, which reflect balances owed on company credit cards and not the credit cards customers use (these are a part of A/R)
- Other current liabilities, such as sales tax and payroll tax to be paid to the government
- Long-term liabilities, such as loans and mortgages

EQUITY

Equity accounts show a company's net worth and reflect the differences between assets and liabilities. Equity changes in two ways:

- Money invested in or removed from the company (usually in the form of owner investment or draws)
- Profits and losses in the business

Equity accounts can include:

- Opening balance
- Retained earnings
- Owner's equity
- Owner's draws
- Capital investment
- Capital stock

Understand Income and Expense Accounts

Income and expense accounts do not have a register where you can enter information, as do balance sheet accounts; however, most transactions you enter in QuickBooks require an income or expense account to be specified. This allows you to run reports, such as the profit and loss (P & L) statement, shown in Figure 3-4, which shows where your money is coming from and where it is going. An even more accurate way to track this information (and which is required for job costing) is to use items. This method will be introduced in this chapter and covered in more detail in Chapters 6, 7, and 10.

INCOME ACCOUNTS

Income accounts can be lumped into one category, such as sales, or set up as separate accounts or subaccounts, such as book sales, coffee sales, and other sales, depending on the level of detail desired by the owner. Three to five categories of income accounts is usually sufficient since reports run using items can give more detailed sales information.

EXPENSE ACCOUNTS

While income accounts tend to be few, expense accounts can be numerous. The level of detail in subaccounts might include a utilities account with subaccounts of water, electric, and phone. Exactly how they are arranged depends on the level of information needed by the company owner or investors.

When you begin using QuickBooks, it is actually better to have too many accounts as opposed to too few; it's easier to merge accounts than it is to go through a list of combined transactions and accurately move transactions into new accounts.

OTHER INCOME AND EXPENSE ACCOUNTS

Other income and expense accounts are used for any income or expense not generated by your primary business. Businesses use them for such things as interest or losses on investments, as these are things that affect you but that are not generated by your primary business.

Rock Castle Construction
Profit & Loss
December 15, 2007

	◇ Dec 15, 07 ◇
Ordinary Income/Expense	
Income	
Construction	
Labor	5,694.00
Materials	18,008.30
Miscellaneous	1,260.00
Subcontractors	8,016.38
Total Construction	32,978.68
Total Income	32,978.68
Cost of Goods Sold	
Cost of Goods Sold ▶	2,656.15 ◀
Total COGS	2,656.15
Gross Profit	30,322.53
Expense	
Insurance	
Disability Insurance	50.00
Liability Insurance	350.00
Work Comp	275.00
Total Insurance	675.00
Job Expenses	
Subcontractors	670.00
Total Job Expenses	670.00
Utilities	
Gas and Electric	122.68
Total Utilities	122.68
Total Expense	1,467.68
Net Ordinary Income	28,854.85
Net Income	28,854.85

Figure 3-4: A profit and loss statement shows you the source and outflow of your company's money.

UNDERSTANDING COST OF GOODS SOLD ACCOUNTS

Cost of Goods Sold accounts are similar to expense accounts but hold a different place on the profit and loss report, as seen in Figure 3-4. They are subtracted from the total income to give a gross profit. Expenses are then subtracted to give a net profit or loss for the time period of the report.

The difference between Cost of Goods Sold and expense accounts can be easily determined by asking yourself if you would need to pay for something whether or not a sale had occurred. For example, your telephone bill, electric bill, and rent are considered expenses and need to be paid whether or not you've made any sales. Cost of Goods, however, are items you purchase for resale, for example, books, coffee, and snacks. Items used as an ancillary to the main products, such as milk and sugar, can be considered a supply item, which may be considered an expense.

Review and Edit Your Chart of Accounts

In looking at the Chart of Accounts in Figure 3-2, you will see certain features that are common to most lists in QuickBooks, including the How Do I? and Type a Help Question areas at the top and the Account, Activities, and Reports menu buttons at the bottom.

Use Menu Buttons for Actions and Reports

At the bottom of every list are one to three menu buttons:

- List Name
- Activities
- Reports

Every standard list has a list name menu button on the left, which allows you to perform common activities, such as create a new account, edit an account, or delete an account.

The name of this menu button generally reflects the name of the list. For example:

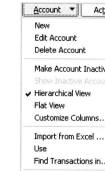

- Account menu button on the Chart of Accounts list
- Item menu button on the Fixed Asset Items and Items lists
- Employee menu button on the Employee list
- Shipping Method menu button on the Ship Via list
- Vendor Type menu button on the Vendor Type list
- Payment Method menu button on the Payment Method list

Some lists have an Activities menu button in the middle, allowing you to quickly access related activities, such as Receive Payments in the Customer:Job List and Process Payroll in the Employee list. These choices are the same as the choices on the related menu.

Activities ▼	Reports ▼	Includ
Write Checks		
Make Deposits		
Enter Credit Card Charges		
Transfer Funds		
Make General Journal Entries		
Reconcile		
Use Register		Ctrl+R

Most lists also have a Reports menu button on the right listing commonly used reports for the area to which the list relates. This is a quick way to access reports that are also on the Reports menu. The exception is the QuickReport, which gives you a list of transactions for the currently selected account.

Reports ▼	Include inactive			
QuickReport: Checking Ctrl+Q				
Income Tax Preparation				
Account Listing				
Reports on All Accounts ▶	Profit & Loss ▶	Standard		
	Balance Sheet ▶	YTD Comparison		
	Cash Flow ▶	Prev Year Comparison		
	Budget ▶	Itemized		
	Payroll ▶			
	Other ▶			
	Graphs ▶			

Move and Sort Accounts and Subaccounts

The Chart of Accounts is normally sorted first by account type and then alphabetically. Other lists are normally sorted just alphabetically. You can change the list's sort order or move any account within its account type. Although some companies use account numbers in the Chart of Accounts, in which case the accounts are sorted numerically, we will use the default sort order in our examples. The advantage of using the default sort order is that it's an easy-to-remember system and account names will automatically appear, as you will see later. Some people recommend using account numbers in order to have more consistency in data entry, but merging and renaming accounts is an easy task if you make a mistake.

MOVE ACCOUNTS WITHIN LISTS

To move accounts within lists:

1. Move your cursor to rest over one of the small diamonds next to any list item, for example, to the left of Cash Discrepancies. The cursor changes to a four-headed arrow.

◇Retained Earnings	Equity
◇Sales	Income
◇Consignment Sales	Income
◇Discounts Given	Income
◇Merchandise	Income
◇Service	Income
◇Shipping and Handling	Income
◇Cash Discrepancies	Income
◇Overages	Income
◇Shortages	Income
◇Purchase Discounts	Cost of Goods Sold

2. Drag the account up or down the list.

3. When you are at the desired location, release your mouse button.

You can only move an account within the group to which it belongs. If you move an account too far above or below the group it was part of, you will get an error message when you release it, and it will remain where it was.

SORT LISTS

You can sort a list according to a given column heading by clicking it. For example, clicking the Name column heading sorts your list alphabetically by name (as indicated by the up arrow next to the column name). Click the Name column heading again to sort the list in reverse-alphabetical order (as indicated by the down arrow next to the column name).

Chart of Accounts   Typ

◈ Name ▲	⚡ Type
◇Automobile Expense	Expense
◇Bad Debt Expense	Expense
◇Bank Service Charges	Expense
◇Capital Stock	Equity
◇Cash Discrepancies	Income
◇Overages	Income
◇Shortages	Income
◇Charitable Contributions	Expense
◇Checking	Bank
◇Depreciation Expense	Expense

RETURN TO THE DEFAULT ORDER

When you have the list sorted in a non-standard way, that is non-alphabetically, you will see a diamond to the left of the Name heading. Click the diamond to return the list to the normal sort order.

If you want to return your list to its default order, in order of account type and then alphabetical:

1. Click the **Account** button.

2. Click **Re-Sort List**.

3. Click **OK** when asked if you are sure.

Customize Columns

The column headings at the top of any list can be customized to better meet your needs.

1. Click the **Account** button.

2. Click **Customize Columns**.
   A window opens with the available column headings on the left and the currently active column headings on the right.

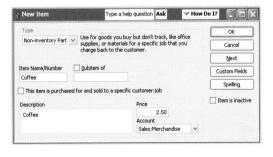

3. Double-click **Description** (or any item) in the left column to move it to the right (or click the item and click **Add**).

4. Click **Description** (or any item) on the right, and click the **Move Up** or **Move Down** button to move it left or right across the top of the column headings.

5. Click **OK** when you are finished. Click **Cancel** if you decide not to make these changes.

TIP

You can return to the default column headings by clicking the **Default** button at any time.

Add Accounts and Subaccounts

You will probably add new accounts as your business grows and changes, such as adding a new product line, incurring a new expense, opening a new bank account or credit card, purchasing a new piece of equipment, or any other business change. You can also create subaccounts, for example, if you wanted to refine your Auto Expenses category to track spending on gas, insurance, and repairs.

To create a new account:

1. Click the **Account** button.

2. Click **New**. The New Account window opens.

3. Click the **Type** down arrow, and click **Expense**.

4. Click in the **Name** field, and type Auto Expense. You can fill in the Description or Note fields also if you want, but it is not necessary.

5. Click **OK**. The Auto Expense account is created.

ADD SUBACCOUNT

To create a subaccount for this account:

1. Click the **Account** button.

2. Click **New**. The New Account window will open.

3. Click the **Type** down arrow.

4. Click **Expense**.

5. Click in the **Name** field.

6. Type <u>Gas</u>.

7. Click the **Subaccount Of** check box, click the down arrow, and click **Auto Expense**.

8. Click **OK**.

9. Repeat steps 1–8 to add the Insurance and Repairs subaccounts (see the Tip).

TIP

If you are entering multiple accounts, click **Next** instead of **OK** in step 8.

Delete Accounts and Subaccounts

You can delete an account at any time with the exception of the Payroll Liabilities and Payroll Expenses accounts. However, if you have entered transactions into an account, you cannot delete it unless you first delete or change the transactions within the account. In that case, you can choose to make the account inactive or merge it with another account. You must also delete or move any subaccounts before you delete a parent account.

To delete an account:

1. Click the name of the account you want to delete (for example, **Franchise Fees**).

2. Click the **Account** button and then click **Delete**. If you have subaccounts, items, or transactions within this account, you will receive a notice that the account cannot be deleted; otherwise, the Delete Account dialog box appears.

3. Click **OK**.

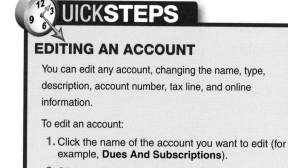

EDITING AN ACCOUNT

You can edit any account, changing the name, type, description, account number, tax line, and online information.

To edit an account:

1. Click the name of the account you want to edit (for example, **Dues And Subscriptions**).

2. Click the **Account** button and click **Edit**.

    –Or–

    Right-click the account name and click **Edit**.

3. Type the new account name or make any other desired changes, and click **OK**.

Make an Account Inactive

In some cases, you may no longer need to use an account, but QuickBooks will not allow you to delete it because it has transactions in it. As your business grows and changes, you will not want to see old items in the list and on your reports. To allow for this situation, you have the capability of making that account inactive.

1. Click the name of the account you want to make inactive (for example, **Equipment Rental**).

2. Click the **Account** button and then click **Make Account Inactive**. If you have sub-items or transactions in this account, QuickBooks will automatically make those accounts inactive as well.

To review your inactive accounts, click the **Include Inactive** check box at the bottom of the List window, and you will see all your list items, with an X next to the inactive accounts, as shown in Figure 3-5.

Figure 3-5: View or hide your inactive accounts by selecting or clearing the Include Inactive check box.

Rename and Merge Accounts

A common mistake users make in QuickBooks is misnaming or creating duplicate accounts. Fortunately, QuickBooks makes it easy to correct these mistakes. You can rename an account or, if you have duplicate accounts with different names, such as Auto Expense and Automobile Expense, you can merge the accounts by renaming one account to the other account.

To rename or merge an account:

1. Click the name of the account you want to rename (for example, **Automobile Expense**).

2. Click the **Account** button and click **Edit**.

   –Or–

   Right-click the account name and click **Edit**.

3. Make your desired changes and click **OK**. If the account name is not currently in use, your changes will take effect immediately. If it is, a confirmation dialog box appears.

4. Click **Yes** if you want to merge these two accounts.

Merge

This name is already being used. Would you like to merge them?

Yes   No

Print Lists of Accounts

The Reports menu is the best means by which you can print a list of your accounts or items. In addition to simple lists, you can print phone and contact lists for customers, employees, vendors, and others.

1. Click the **Reports** menu and then click **List** to see a list of available reports you can print.

2. Click **Account Listing** to see a report on your accounts, an example of which is shown in Figure 3-6.

3. Click the **Print** button at the top of the screen to send the report to your printer.

4. Click the **Close** button (the X) in the upper-right corner of the report window to close it.

Reports   Window   Help

Report Navigator
Memorized Reports   ▸
Process Multiple Reports

Company & Financial   ▸
Customers & Receivables ▸
Sales   ▸
Jobs, Time & Mileage   ▸
Vendors & Payables   ▸
Employees & Payroll   ▸
Banking   ▸
Accountant & Taxes   ▸
Budgets & Forecasts   ▸
List   ▸

Custom Summary Report
Custom Transaction Detail Report

QuickReport   Ctrl+Q
Transaction History
Transaction Journal

Account Listing
Item Price List
Item Listing
Payroll Item Listing
Fixed Asset Listing

Customer Phone List
Customer Contact List
Vendor Phone List
Vendor Contact List
Employee Contact List
Other Names Phone List
Other Names Contact List

Terms Listing
To Do Notes
Memorized Transaction Listing

The advantage of printing from the Reports menu is added detail and the ability to customize the lists and save reports. However, not all lists can be printed from the Reports menu. You can print any list by clicking the **File** menu and clicking **Print List** or by clicking the **Account** menu and clicking **Print**. This will give just a basic report, listing the account name and account type.

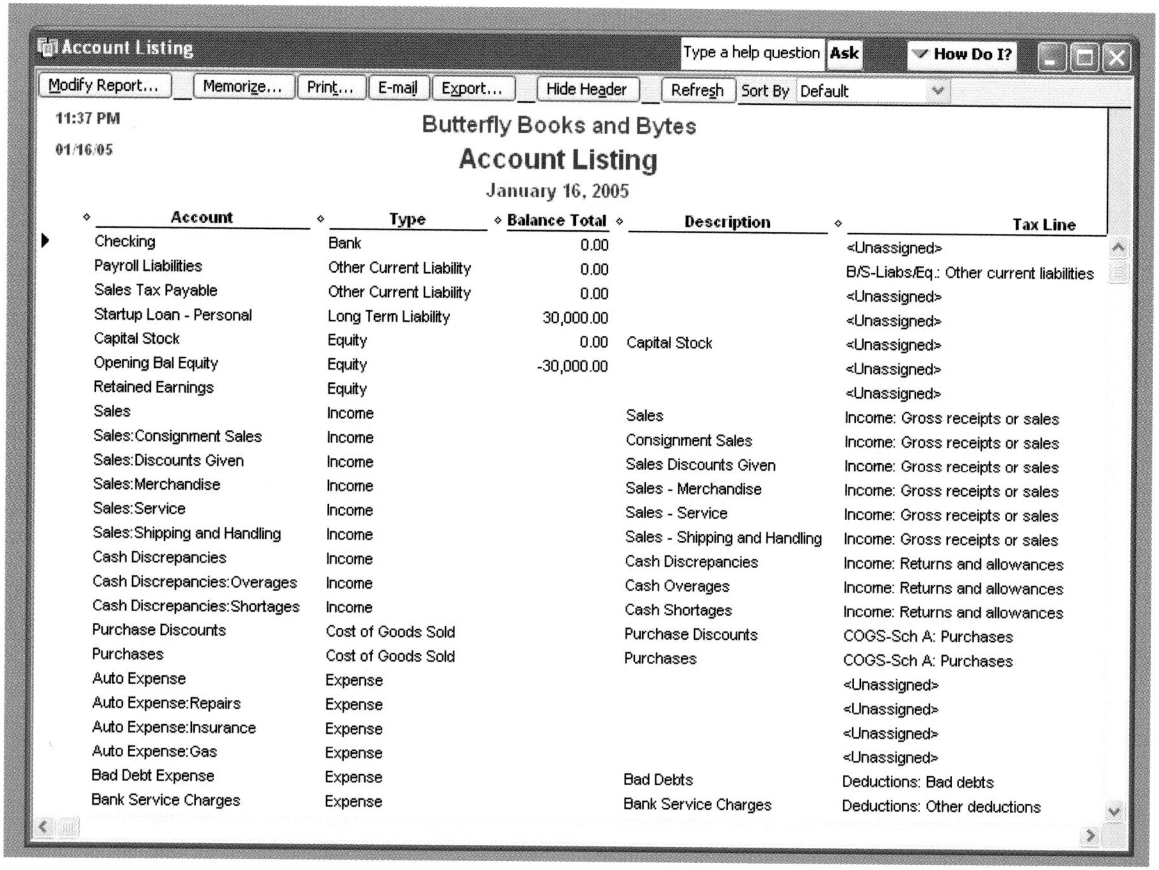

11:37 PM
01/16/05

Butterfly Books and Bytes
Account Listing
January 16, 2005

Account	Type	Balance Total	Description	Tax Line
Checking	Bank	0.00		<Unassigned>
Payroll Liabilities	Other Current Liability	0.00		B/S-Liabs/Eq.: Other current liabilities
Sales Tax Payable	Other Current Liability	0.00		<Unassigned>
Startup Loan - Personal	Long Term Liability	30,000.00		<Unassigned>
Capital Stock	Equity	0.00	Capital Stock	<Unassigned>
Opening Bal Equity	Equity	-30,000.00		<Unassigned>
Retained Earnings	Equity			<Unassigned>
Sales	Income		Sales	Income: Gross receipts or sales
Sales:Consignment Sales	Income		Consignment Sales	Income: Gross receipts or sales
Sales:Discounts Given	Income		Sales Discounts Given	Income: Gross receipts or sales
Sales:Merchandise	Income		Sales - Merchandise	Income: Gross receipts or sales
Sales:Service	Income		Sales - Service	Income: Gross receipts or sales
Sales:Shipping and Handling	Income		Sales - Shipping and Handling	Income: Gross receipts or sales
Cash Discrepancies	Income		Cash Discrepancies	Income: Returns and allowances
Cash Discrepancies:Overages	Income		Cash Overages	Income: Returns and allowances
Cash Discrepancies:Shortages	Income		Cash Shortages	Income: Returns and allowances
Purchase Discounts	Cost of Goods Sold		Purchase Discounts	COGS-Sch A: Purchases
Purchases	Cost of Goods Sold		Purchases	COGS-Sch A: Purchases
Auto Expense	Expense			<Unassigned>
Auto Expense:Repairs	Expense			<Unassigned>
Auto Expense:Insurance	Expense			<Unassigned>
Auto Expense:Gas	Expense			<Unassigned>
Bad Debt Expense	Expense		Bad Debts	Deductions: Bad debts
Bank Service Charges	Expense		Bank Service Charges	Deductions: Other deductions

Figure 3-6: The Account Listing report provides an overview of your accounts, including type, balance, and description.

NOTE

Just as you customized column headings in the Chart of Accounts, you can follow those same steps to customize headings in the Customer:Job List. You have 47 fields to choose from, from address fields to project-related information, to create a list that gives you the information you need.

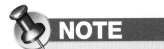

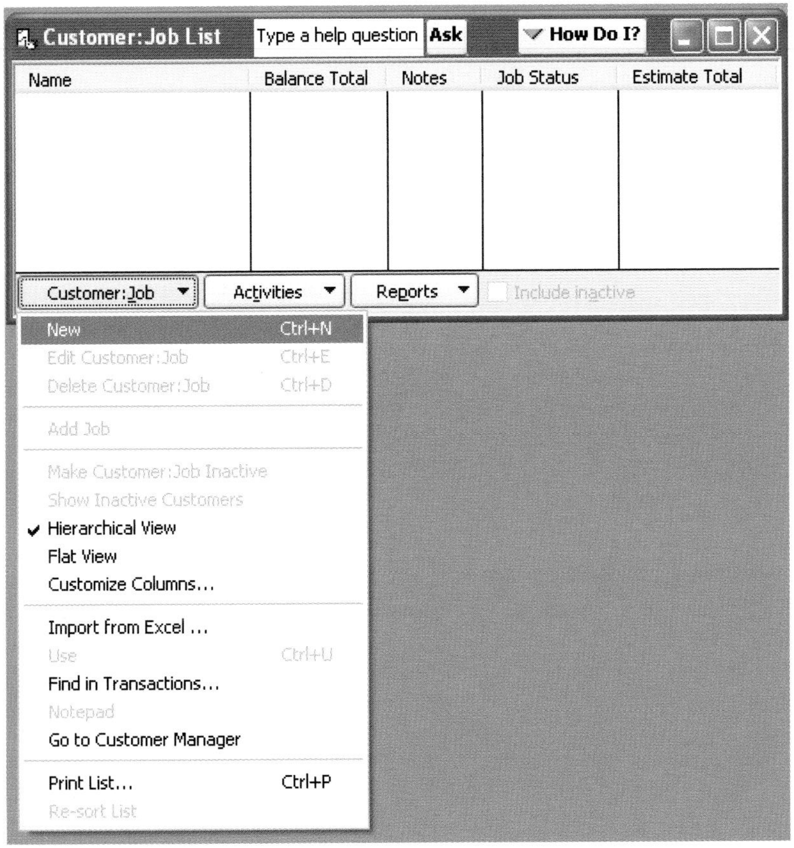

Figure 3-7: The Customer: Job List shows three buttons similar to the Chart of Accounts list.

Use Name Lists to Manage Information

QuickBooks contains four name lists, all of which are related to each other, so you must use unique names throughout the lists. If you try to add a name that already exists, you will receive a warning message.

Use the Customer:Job List to Track Balances and Jobs

When you create a new company file, no customers or jobs are initially present, as seen in Figure 3-7. For most businesses, their customers are obvious; but for a nonprofit organization, members or donors may be their "customers." A *job* is a customer subcategory, allowing you to track different departments, projects, or other categories of a business pertaining to a specific customer. This is particularly useful for contractors who may want to do job costing based on a specific job but have repeat customers with different jobs. As with accounts and entries on other lists, you can make jobs inactive.

You can add customers and jobs from the Customer:Job menu button (located at the bottom), or as you need them (see Chapter 9).

It's always a good idea to have a generic customer name, such as Cash, if you have a retail store. A 50-cent sale from someone who is not likely to return to the store is not worth setting up an account for. Also, some people refuse or resist giving any contact information, so plan on asking but using a generic account if your customer prefers to not give you any information.

ADD A CUSTOMER TO THE CUSTOMER:JOB LIST

1. Click the **Lists** menu and then click **Customer:Job List**. The Customer: Job List window opens.

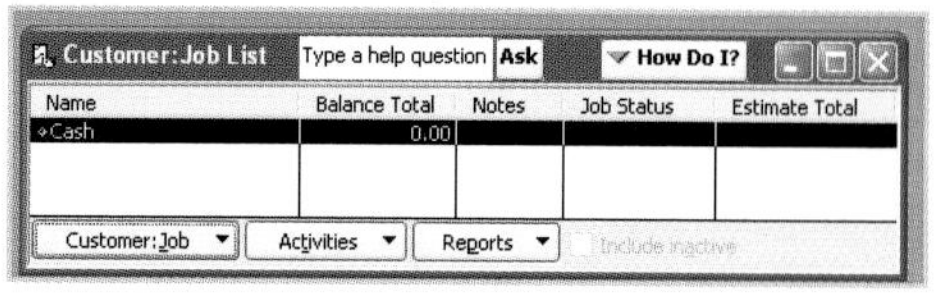

2. Click the **Customer:Job** menu button and click **New**. A New Customer form is displayed, as shown in Figure 3-8.

3. Type the customer name (for example, <u>Cash</u>), and click **OK**. The customer name is the minimum amount of information you need to provide. You will now see your new customer in your Customer:Job List.

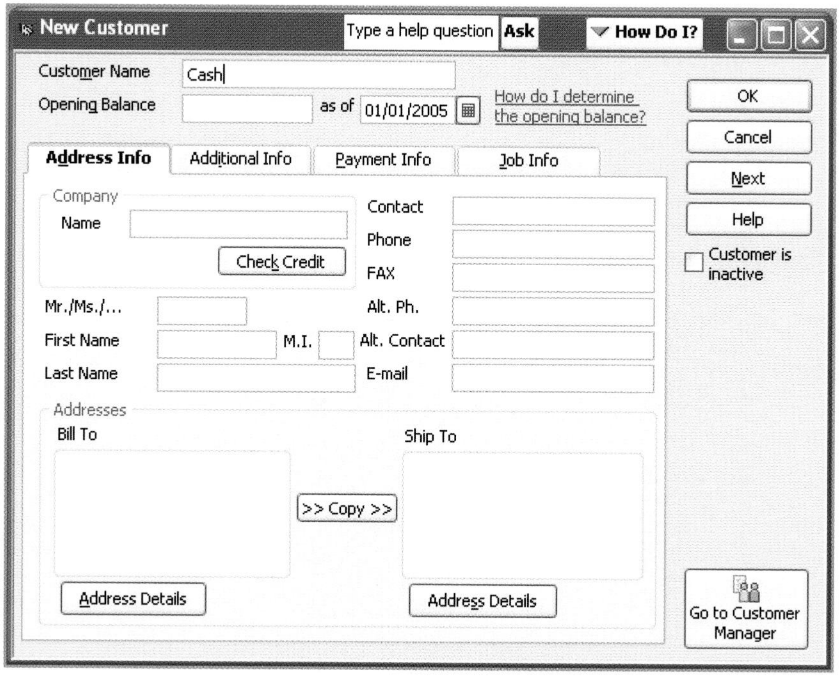

Figure 3-8: The New Customer form gives you the ability to record a great deal of information about your customers.

ADD A JOB TO THE CUSTOMER:JOB LIST

The process whereby you add a job is similar to that for adding a customer.

1. In the Customer:Job List, click **Cash**.

2. Click the **Customer:Job** menu button, and click **Add Job**. A New Job form is displayed, as shown in Figure 3-9.

3. Type the job name (for example, <u>Show</u>), and click **OK**. The job name is the minimum amount of information you need to provide. You will now see your new job under your customer in your Customer: Job List.

4. Repeat steps 1–3 to add a job called In Store.

Figure 3-9: Jobs provide a means whereby you can record customer category information.

Track Service, Inventory, and Taxes Using the Item List

An important feature of QuickBooks is the way it uses items to track anything you buy and sell. While your Chart of Accounts is the most important list and provides a large overview, your Item list is the next most important list and provides the details of how your business runs. Inventory will be covered in Chapter 7, but regardless of whether you track inventory or not, you need to use items in order to use invoices or sales receipts. The only time someone would not use items is if a custom computer program is in use that tracks all that information. Even then, those companies often enter a daily invoice with sales listed by item based on their daily receipts. When you set up a new item, choose the item type from the Item drop-down list.

Service
✓ Service
Non-inventory Part
Other Charge
Subtotal
Group
Discount
Payment

Enter Service Items

If your company primarily provides services, you will want to create a number of service items to represent what you do. For example, a computer company might have service items for consulting, training, development, and maintenance; and a construction company will likely have a different service item for each trade. Butterfly Books has only one service item, Research. To set up a service item:

1. Click the **Lists** menu and then click **Item List**. If you have a new company, your Item list will be empty.

2. Click the **List** menu button, and click **New**. The New Item window opens with the Item Type drop-down list displaying **Service** as the default selection, as shown in Figure 3-10.

3. Press the **TAB** key to accept this default selection and move to the next field.

4. Type Research in the Item Name field. Your customers won't see this name. It is for your use only.

5. Click in the **Description** field, and type Research Services. Customers will see this name on invoices and sales receipts.

6. Press the **TAB** key to move to the next field, and type 50 for the hourly rate.

7. Press the **TAB** key to move to the next field, and type S. The Chart of Accounts Income list is displayed. Notice the subaccount called Service.

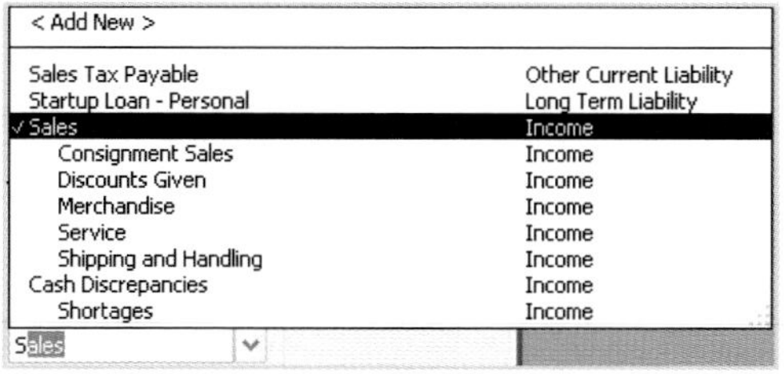

< Add New >	
Sales Tax Payable	Other Current Liability
Startup Loan - Personal	Long Term Liability
✓ Sales	Income
Consignment Sales	Income
Discounts Given	Income
Merchandise	Income
Service	Income
Shipping and Handling	Income
Cash Discrepancies	Income
Shortages	Income

8. Click the **Service** account.

9. Click **OK** to save the new item (or click **Next** if you will be setting up a number of items).

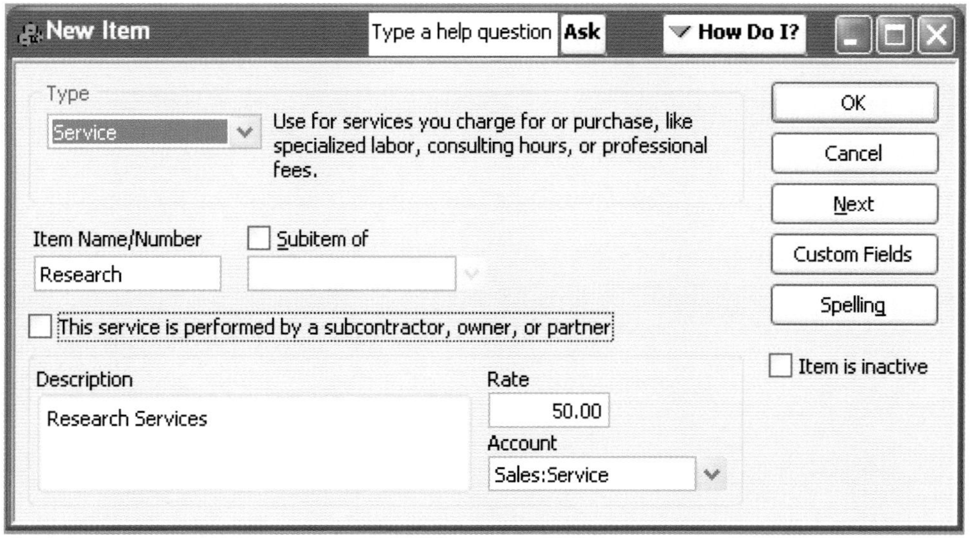

Figure 3-10: Items can have sub-items just as the other lists do.

NOTE

You can integrate QuickBooks with a POS (Point of Sale) system to better handle retail situations, using a register for high-volume sales, or enter information directly into a computer equipped with QuickBooks.

Enter Non-Inventory Items

Non-inventory items are things you sell that you do not track. In the case of Butterfly Books and Bytes, this will include coffee, as a cup of coffee is not by itself an inventory item. Coffee beans and other items used to make coffee can be treated as supply expenses or cost of goods.

1. Click the **Lists** menu and then click **Item List**. If you have a new company, your Item list will be empty.
2. Click the **List** menu button, and click **New**. The New Item window opens, as shown in Figure 3-11.
3. Click the **Item Type** down arrow, and click **Non-Inventory Part**.
4. Press the **TAB** key to move to the next field.
5. Type <u>Coffee</u> in the Item Name field.
6. Click in the **Description** field, and type <u>Coffee</u>.
7. Press the **TAB** key to move to the next field, and type <u>2.50</u> for the price.
8. Press the **TAB** key to move to the next field, and type <u>M</u>. The Chart of Accounts Income list is displayed. Notice the subaccount called Merchandise.
9. Click the **Merchandise** account.
10. Click **OK** to save the new item (or click **Next** if you will be setting up a number of items).

The more non-inventory items you enter, the better you can track your sales. However, you don't want to overburden your employees and frustrate your customers if the complexity slows down your line.

Figure 3-11: Non-inventory parts can also include vendor information (click the This Item Is Purchased And Sold To A Specific Customer:Job check box).

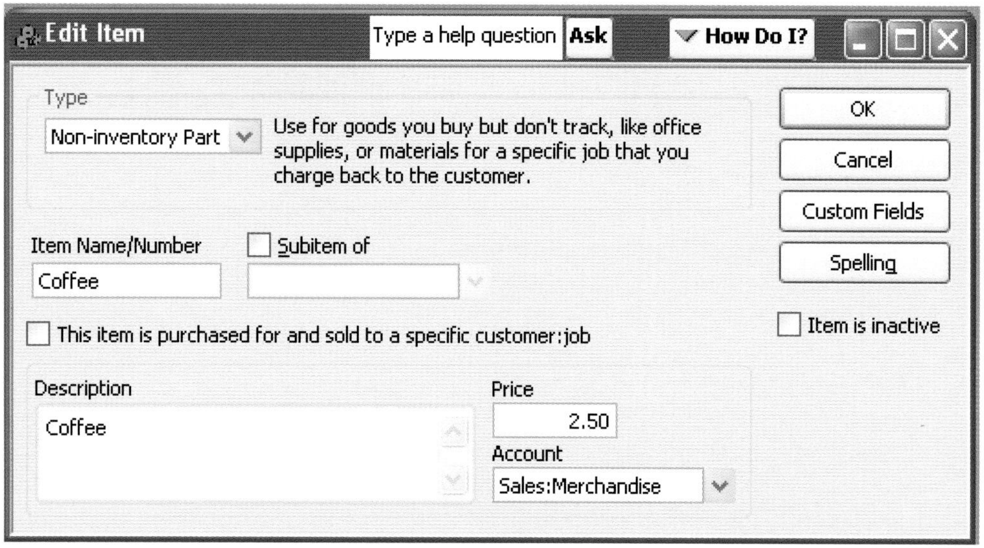

How to...

- ✏ *Choosing a Bank*
- • *Create a New Account*
- • *Activate Online Banking*
- • *Order Checks and Forms*
- • *Write Checks*
- • *Edit, Void, or Delete Checks*
- • *Make Deposits*
- ⚙ *Sending and Receiving Online Transactions*
- • *View and Edit Bank Account Registers*
- ⚙ *Transferring Funds between Accounts*
- • *Manage Business Credit Cards*
- • *Set Up a Credit Card Account*
- • *Enter Credit Card Transactions*
- • *Receive and Enter Online Business Credit Card Transactions*
- • *Reconcile Credit Card Accounts*
- • *Reconcile Bank Accounts*

Chapter 4

Set Up and Use Your Bank Accounts

Maintaining a good cash flow, knowing where you stand on a daily basis, and reviewing and revising your collections and bill payment methods are all integral to your business's success. The Banking Navigator, along with a variety of other banking functions in QuickBooks, automates the way you deal with many of these finance-related tasks.

Use the Banking Navigator

The Banking Navigator (seen in Figure 4-1) gives you a big-picture view of your business's finances and quick access to common banking functions, such as:

- Writing checks
- Making deposits
- Online banking
- Transferring funds
- Credit card charges
- Reconciling accounts

You can access the Banking Navigator by one of two ways:

- Click the **Banking** menu and then click **Banking Navigator**.
- From the Navigator list on the left side of the screen, click **Banking**.

You may use the Banking Navigator, the Banking menu, or the icon bar to access any banking-related function in QuickBooks.

Flowcharts include clickable icons to help you quickly get to where you need to go

The Related Activities list provides a quick link to common banking actions

The Memorized Reports list provides customized reports specific to your banking needs

Banking Solutions are add-on services that you can use to augment your banking

The Accounts list contains all your current banking accounts

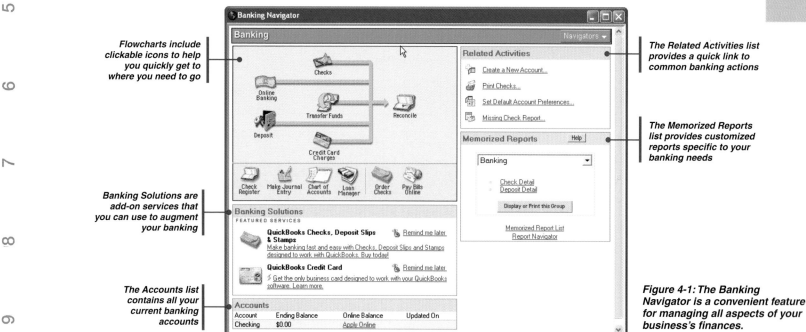

Figure 4-1: The Banking Navigator is a convenient feature for managing all aspects of your business's finances.

CHOOSING A BANK

You may already have a bank, but your bank may not support the features that are important to you in your business; for example, online banking is a convenient feature that you'll want in a bank that serves your business. When comparing banks, use the following checklist as a guide to determine what features are important to you, and see if they are supported by the bank you choose:

- Online banking through QuickBooks.
- Online viewing of checks.
- Debit card.
- Sweep accounts (moves money in excess of preset limits from a checking to a savings account automatically).
- Employee direct deposit (some banks offer this as a free benefit).
- No minimum balance (or compare minimums).
- No monthly fees (or compare fees). Don't forget to compare check fees, deposit fees, overage fees, stop payment fees, telephone transfer fees, and any other fees that might apply to your business.

NOTE

All of the examples in this chapter reflect the default settings in QuickBooks Preferences. If your file does not exactly match the examples, refer to Chapter 8 for details on setting your preferences.

Set Up Bank Accounts

If you set up a new company file in Chapter 2, you have already set up a checking account. Many businesses use two checking accounts: one for deposits and bill payments, and one strictly for payroll. Some businesses may also use a money market or savings account if they hold large amounts of cash, such as in the construction business, so that they may receive interest on that cash.

Create a New Account

If you want to create a new account in QuickBooks, it is a simple process.

1. Click the **Banking** menu and then click **Chart Of Accounts**.

2. Click the **Account** menu button, and then click **New**. The New Account window opens.

3. Type the account name in the Name field (for example, Payroll Checking).

4.

Account ▼	Activities ▼	
New	Ctrl+N	
Edit Account	Ctrl+E	
Delete Account	Ctrl+D	
Make Account Inactive		
Hide Inactive Accounts		
✓ Hierarchical View		
Flat View		
Customize Columns...		
Import from Excel ...		
Use	Ctrl+U	
Find Transactions in...		
Print List...	Ctrl+P	
Re-sort List		

Click **OK**. The account is created and will appear in the Accounts list.

TIP

Online access can be used for more than just bank accounts. Many credit card companies also allow you to download transactions, thus saving you time when doing data entry.

Activate Online Banking

Online banking is convenient and safe. It pays for itself in time and cost savings since you no longer have to print, stamp, and mail payments to vendors. Many banks support online banking. If you are not sure if your current bank does, the simplest way to find out is to try to set up an account online and see if your bank is listed.

To set up an online banking account, you first need your bank to set up the account for online banking, and then you need to activate that account within QuickBooks for use with online banking.

Figure 4-2: The first step in setting up an online banking account in QuickBooks is to find your bank from the list.

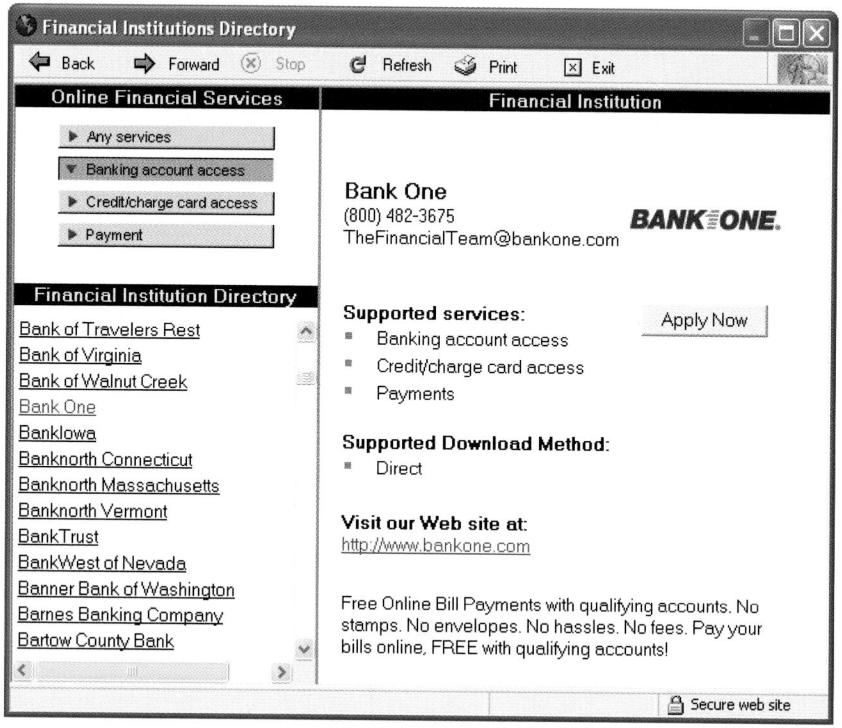

REVIEW AND APPLY TO BANK FOR ONLINE BANKING

1. Click the **Banking** menu, click **Set Up Online Financial Services**, and then click **Online List Of Available Financial Institutions**. The Financial Institutions Directory window opens, as shown in Figure 4-2.
2. Click one of the four buttons in the upper-left area of the screen to indicate the type of account you want to access, and then click your bank from the list located underneath (you may have to scroll down to find your bank). The middle of the page displays a summary of what that bank offers in the way of online banking. Look for the word "Direct" under Supported Download Method, which indicates that your bank can link up directly with QuickBooks.
3. Click the **Apply Now** button to find out exactly how to activate online banking. You may be able to directly apply online, or you may need to call or go into your local branch.
4. Once you have chosen a bank, click the **Close** button (the X in the upper-right corner) to close the window. QuickBooks will note which institution you selected and update your list of banks.

ENABLE QUICKBOOKS BANK ACCOUNT FOR USE WITH ONLINE BANKING

Once you have received confirmation from your bank that online banking is activated:

1. Click the **Banking** menu, click **Set Up Online Financial Services**, and then click **Set Up Account For Online Access**.

2. Click **Yes** if you see a dialog box notifying you that QuickBooks needs to close all open windows. The Online Banking Setup Interview Wizard starts.

3. Click **Next**. QuickBooks ask you what type of account you want to set up for online access.

4. Click **Bank Account Or QuickBooks Bill Pay Service**, and click **Next**.

5. Click **I Have Already Completed An Application With My Institution**, and click **Next**.

6. Click **Next** after reading about waiting for your financial institution to set up your accounts.

7. Click **Next** after reading about confirming your account information.

8. Click your bank from the drop-down list, and click **Next**. If your bank is not on the list, click **Leave** and repeat the steps in the previous section "Review and Apply to Bank for Online Banking."

9. Click **Yes. I've Received My Confirmation Letter From** *Your Bank*. Click **Next**.

10. Type your routing number in the Routing Number field, and type your customer ID in the Customer ID field. These numbers should be in the letter you received from your bank. Click **Next**.

11. Click the account name from the drop-down list. Click **Next**.

12. Click the account type from the list, and type your account number in the Account Number field. Click the **Online Account Access** and **Online Payment** options. (Do not click the Online Payment option if your bank doesn't offer this service.) Click **Next**.

13. Review your information, confirm that **No** is selected (unless you want to configure additional accounts), and click **Next**.

14. Click **OK** in response to the dialog box that appears, asking you to acknowledge that these services are provided by your banking institution and not by Intuit.

15. Click **No** in response to the dialog box that appears, asking if you want to set up accounts at another institution, and click **Next**.

16. Read the congratulations message and click **Leave**. You can verify that your account is active by looking at your Chart of Accounts. Notice the blue lightning bolt next to the checking account, which denotes that it is now an active online account.

NOTE

Your QuickBooks online banking account uses a different password from your QuickBooks user account, so keep this password private to prevent unauthorized persons from sending electronic checks.

TIP

Unless you need to handwrite a large number of checks away from the office, you can use QuickBooks-compatible checks rather than standard checks.

Figure 4-3: You can order QuickBooks-compatible deposit slips and many other forms.

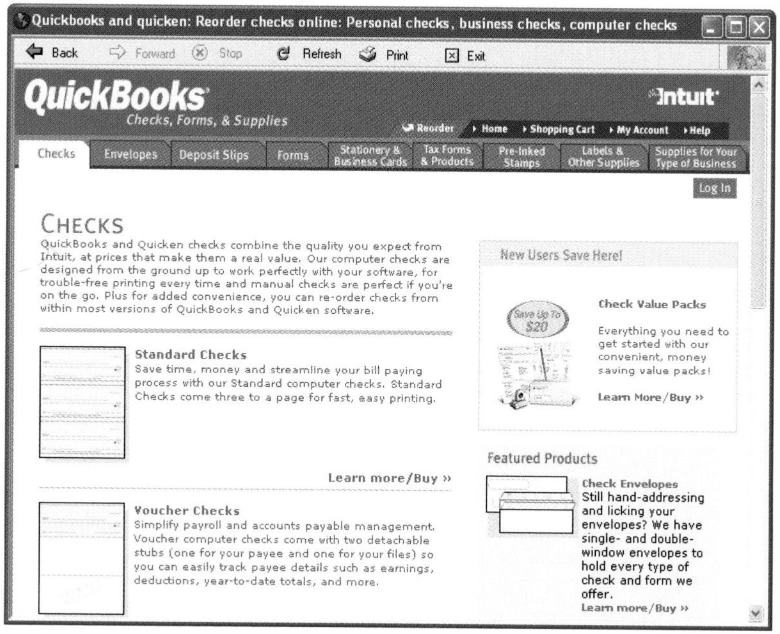

Order Checks and Forms

Many forms are required when running a business, but when you use QuickBooks, you need only a few. Banks still require special forms for checks and deposit slips, and the IRS still requires the use of certain forms, but for the rest of your business activities, you can print custom forms on plain paper using QuickBooks.

You have three choices for creating checks with QuickBooks:

- Use the Online Bill Payment method, which does not require you to purchase any forms.
- Print checks on bank-approved, QuickBooks-style checks.
- Handwrite checks on any checks, and then enter the information in QuickBooks.

Deposit slips can also be printed or handwritten. If you currently have standard checks, you can continue to use those and also enter the check in QuickBooks; however, if you process a large number of checks each month, consider online banking or getting checks that will fit in your printer.

To order checks:

1. Click the **Banking** menu, click **Order Checks & Envelopes**, and click **Order Checks**. The Order Supplies window opens.
2. Click **Ordering From Intuit For The First Time**.
3. Click **Order Now**. The ordering options are displayed, as shown in Figure 4-3.
4. Click **Standard Checks**. You may prefer to use the Voucher checks (seen in Figure 4-4) for payroll or vendor payment. The order page will appear.
5. Scroll down, click the **Printer Type** down arrow, and click your printer type.
6. If you chose a dot matrix printer, click **Single** or **Duplicate** (meaning carbon copy). This option is not available for laser or inkjet printers.

Don't press the **ESC** key or the window will close and your choices will be lost.

Many companies offer QuickBooks-compatible checks. If you want to purchase checks from another company or from your bank, verify their compatibility first.

7. Click the **Quantity/Price** down arrow, and click your preferred quantity.

8. Click **Continue**. The Product Style page appears, and you will now have the opportunity to select the style, color, personalization, logo, font, and print color and to enter routing and account numbers.

9. Click your desired color and click **Next**.

10. Type your company name and address as you want it to appear on your checks. Click one signature line or two, and type any additional text you would like above the signature line. Click **Next**.

11. If you choose to add a logo for an additional charge, do so and then click **Next**.

12. If you choose to add colors and fonts for an additional charge, do so and then click **Next**.

13. Type your routing number, account number, and starting check number. Click **Reverse Numbering** if you place checks in your printer face-down. Click **Next**. A sample of how your check will appear is seen in Figure 4-4.

14. Click the **Approval** check box at the bottom of the screen (you may have to scroll down), and click **Add To Cart**. You will need to register to use this site further.

Figure 4-4: Be sure to verify your routing number and account number, as well as your name, address, and other data.

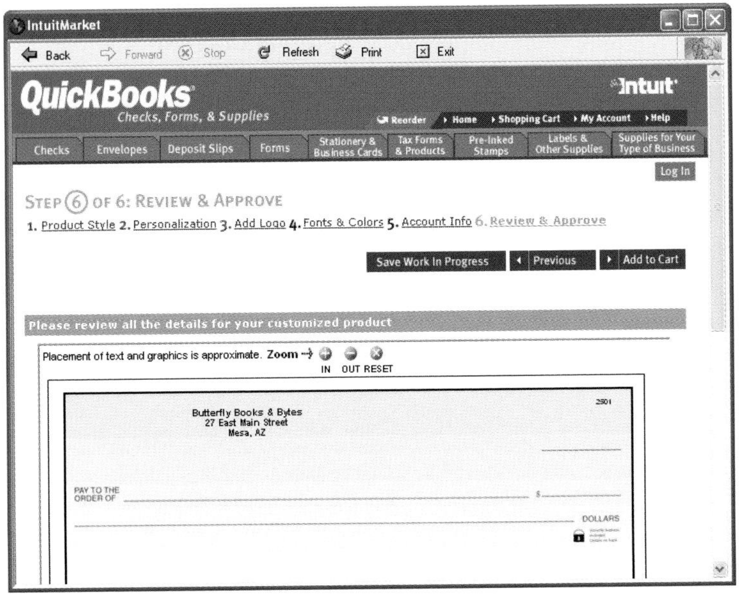

Manage Your Accounts on a Daily Basis

The following sections show how to accomplish daily tasks such as making deposits, transferring funds, and reviewing transactions.

Write Checks

QuickBooks makes it easy to write checks. Whether you are handwriting checks and then entering the information into QuickBooks for bookkeeping, entering checks to be printed on check forms, or entering checks to be sent online, the process is basically the same.

NOTE

QuickStatements are a great way to find out if a check has cleared or a transaction has occurred, but they don't take the place of your monthly paper statement. It's always good to do a periodic review of transactions during reconciliation.

CAUTION

Do not use the Write Checks feature to create paychecks. (See Chapter 9 for more information on payroll.)

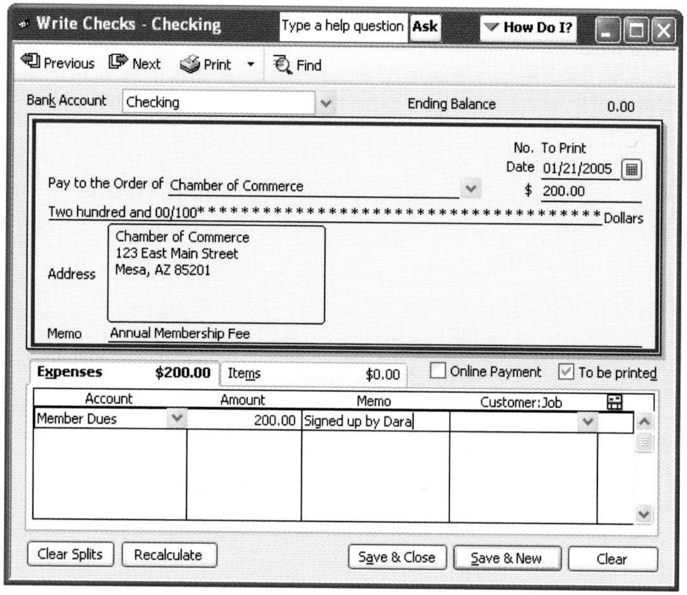

Figure 4-5: The Write Checks feature in QuickBooks makes writing checks a breeze.

1. Click the **Banking** menu and click **Write Checks** (or click the **Check** icon on the icon bar). The Write Checks window opens, as shown in Figure 4-5. Confirm that you are in the correct bank account from which to write a check.
2. Press the **TAB** key to move to the Date field. Click the **calendar** icon to select the date from a drop-down calendar, or type the date in the field.
3. Press the **TAB** key again to move to the Pay To The Order Of line.
4. Type the payee's name, for example, Chamber of Commerce.
5. Press the **TAB** key again to move to the Amount line. If the payee's name is not in the Name list, the Name Not Found dialog box appears.

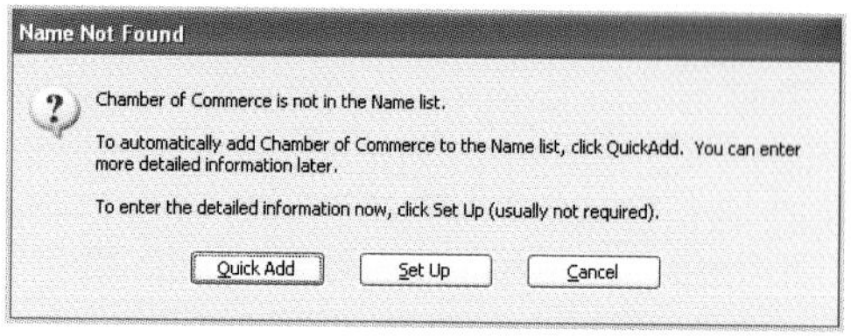

6. Click the **Quick Add** button. The Select Name Type dialog box appears. The Vendor option is chosen by default since you are writing a check.
7. Click **OK**. The payee (in this case, Chamber of Commerce) is added to the Vendor Name list.

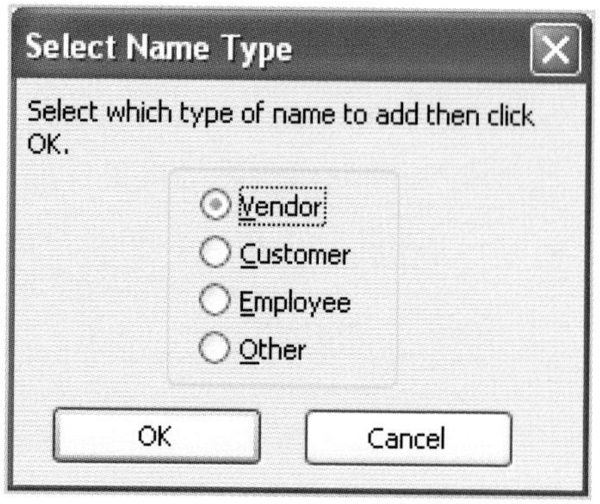

8. Click in the Amount line, and type 200.
9. Press the **TAB** key again. QuickBooks automatically fills in the Dollars field with the correct wording based on the Amount field.
10. Press the **TAB** key to move to the Address area, where the payee's name has already been filled in by QuickBooks.
11. Press the **ENTER** key to move to the next line, and type the payee's address.
12. Press the **TAB** key to move to the Memo field.
13. Type a relevant memo, for example, Annual Membership Fee.

Name Information Changed

You have changed the Address for Chamber of Commerce. Would you like to have this new
information appear next time?

Yes   No   Cancel

14. Click the **To Be Printed** check box if you will be printing this check (the words "To
Print" will appear in the No. line). Click the **Online Payment** check box if you have
online banking enabled. If you are handwriting a check, make sure both these check
boxes are clear, and type the check number in the No. field (located above the date).

15. Click in the drop-down list under Account (in the bottom portion of the screen), and
type <u>Member Dues</u>. (You may find that just typing <u>Me</u> causes Member Dues to automatically appear in this field.)

16. Press the **TAB** key twice to move to the Memo column. What you type here is designed
to serve as a memo for you and will not be printed on the check sent to the payee.

17. Click the **Save & Close** button. If the address for the payee doesn't match the one
QuickBooks has on file, a dialog box will appear, asking you to confirm the new address.
Click **Yes** if you want to use this address when writing future checks to this payee.

Edit, Void, or Delete Checks

If you make a mistake when writing a check, you can edit, void, or delete the
check. Once a check has been sent, however, you should not change the check
itself, just the items in the bottom portion of the Write Checks window.

1. Click the **Banking** menu and then click **Write Check**.

2. Click **Previous** to see the last check you wrote.

3. Click the **Edit** menu. You will see a list of options to use on
this check.

4. Click **Void Check**. The check amount is changed to $0, and
the Memo line on the check reads VOID. The void action is not
yet carried out at this point. If you click **Delete Check**, however, a dialog box appears, confirming the action. If you click
Yes, QuickBooks immediately carries out this action.

5. Click the **Save & Close** button. A dialog box appears, asking if
you want to save your changes.

6. Click **Yes** to save the changes.

Edit	View	Lists	Company	Custome
Undo Typing			Ctrl+Z	
Revert				
Cut			Ctrl+X	
Copy			Ctrl+C	
Paste			Ctrl+V	
New Check			Ctrl+N	
Delete Check			Ctrl+D	
Memorize Check			Ctrl+M	
Void Check				
Copy Check			Ctrl+O	
Go To Transfer			Ctrl+G	
Transaction History...			Ctrl+H	
Show List			Ctrl+L	
Use Register			Ctrl+R	
Notepad				
Change Account Color...				
Use Calculator				
Find Checks...			Ctrl+F	
Preferences...				

> **TIP**
>
> The Edit menu changes throughout QuickBooks, depending on what area you are in. Click it to see what options you have throughout your QuickBooks user session.

> **TIP**
>
> See Chapter 8 to learn how to find transactions quickly.

> **TIP**
>
> If you have already sent the check to the recipient, don't change anything on the face of the check in the Write Checks window. Change only the information below the check, such as accounts, items, memo, or classes.

> **TIP**
>
> If you use another system for tracking sales but use QuickBooks for tracking expenses, enter a single daily sales receipt so that you can more readily identify income areas. See Chapter 6 for more information.

Make Deposits

Often, beginning QuickBooks users enter their checks, but not their deposits. As a result, their bank accounts look like negative holes. To keep accurate records, you need to track your deposits in QuickBooks as well as your checks. QuickBooks has three ways by which you can enter deposit information:

- Sales Receipt form
- Receive Payments window
- Make Deposits window

Use the first two methods for more accurate reporting. Chapter 6 will cover the sales receipts and receive payments methods.

THE MAKE DEPOSITS WINDOW

1. Click the **Banking** menu and click **Make Deposits**. The Make Deposits window opens, as shown in Figure 4-6. If the default account in the Deposit To drop-down list is not the one you want to use, click the down arrow and select the correct account.

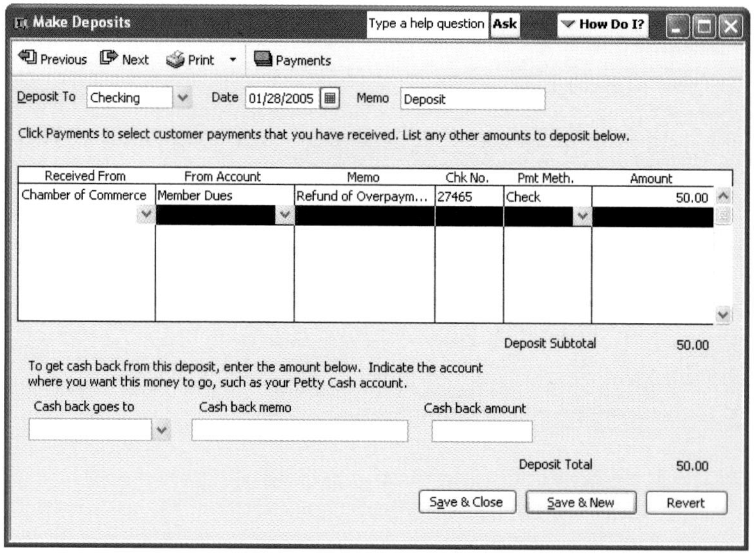

Figure 4-6: QuickBooks gives you the ability to easily record and track your deposits using the Make Deposits window.

2. Press the **TAB** key to move to the Date field. Click the **calendar** icon to select the date from a drop-down calendar, or type the date in the field.

3. Press the **TAB** key to move to the Memo field. The word "Deposit" is there by default. You can highlight this and type something different if you want.

4. Press the **TAB** key to move to the Received From column. Click the down arrow and select the relevant name. If you type the first few letters of the name in that field, the correct name will automatically appear in the drop-down list. For example, typing Ch causes "Chamber of Commerce" to automatically appear.

5. Press the **TAB** key to move to the From Account column. Click the down arrow and select the relevant account. If you type the first few letters of the name in that field, the correct account will automatically appear in the drop-down list. For example, typing Me causes "Member Dues" to automatically appear.

6. Press the **TAB** key to move to the Memo column, and type a memo pertaining to the deposit, for example, Refund of Overpayment.

7. Press the **TAB** key to move to the Check Number column, and type the check number, for example, 27465.

8. Press the **TAB** key to move to the Payment Method column. Click the down arrow and select the relevant payment method. If you type the first few letters of the payment method, the correct name will automatically appear in the drop-down list. For example, typing Ch causes "Check" to automatically appear.

9. Press the **TAB** key to move to the Amount column, and type the check amount, for example, 50.

10. Press the **TAB** key again. The cursor moves to the beginning of the next line and updates the Deposit Subtotal and Deposit Total amounts. If you have more entries to add to this deposit, repeat steps 4–10. You could continue entering checks and cash that will be part of that deposit.

11. If you are finished entering this deposit, click the **Save & Close** button.

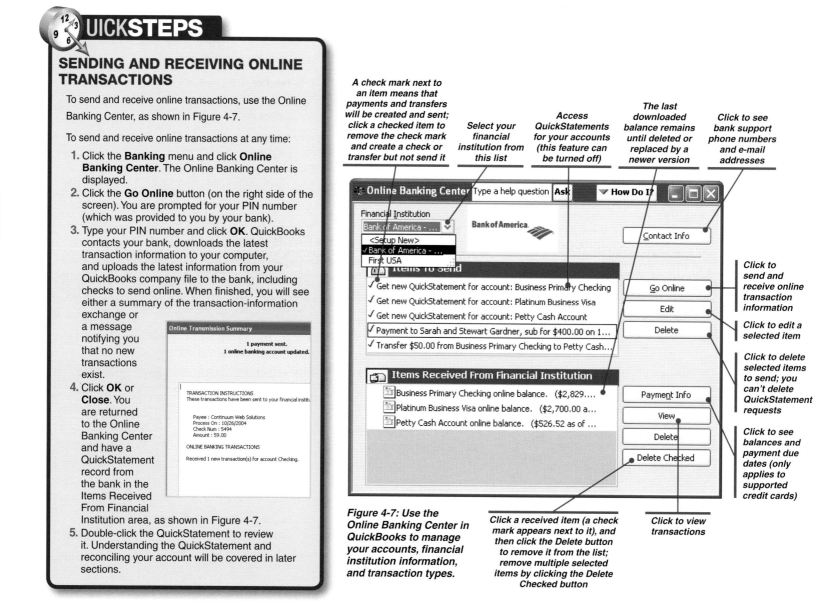

QUICKSTEPS

SENDING AND RECEIVING ONLINE TRANSACTIONS

To send and receive online transactions, use the Online Banking Center, as shown in Figure 4-7.

To send and receive online transactions at any time:

1. Click the **Banking** menu and click **Online Banking Center**. The Online Banking Center is displayed.

2. Click the **Go Online** button (on the right side of the screen). You are prompted for your PIN number (which was provided to you by your bank).

3. Type your PIN number and click **OK**. QuickBooks contacts your bank, downloads the latest transaction information to your computer, and uploads the latest information from your QuickBooks company file to the bank, including checks to send online. When finished, you will see either a summary of the transaction-information exchange or a message notifying you that no new transactions exist.

4. Click **OK** or **Close**. You are returned to the Online Banking Center and have a QuickStatement record from the bank in the Items Received From Financial Institution area, as shown in Figure 4-7.

5. Double-click the QuickStatement to review it. Understanding the QuickStatement and reconciling your account will be covered in later sections.

A check mark next to an item means that payments and transfers will be created and sent; click a checked item to remove the check mark and create a check or transfer but not send it

Select your financial institution from this list

Access QuickStatements for your accounts (this feature can be turned off)

The last downloaded balance remains until deleted or replaced by a newer version

Click to see bank support phone numbers and e-mail addresses

Click to send and receive online transaction information

Click to edit a selected item

Click to delete selected items to send; you can't delete QuickStatement requests

Click to see balances and payment due dates (only applies to supported credit cards)

Figure 4-7: Use the Online Banking Center in QuickBooks to manage your accounts, financial institution information, and transaction types.

Click a received item (a check mark appears next to it), and then click the Delete button to remove it from the list; remove multiple selected items by clicking the Delete Checked button

Click to view transactions

TIP

If you want a deposit summary or to see how the deposit slip will print before using a preprinted deposit slip, print your deposit on a blank sheet of paper as a test.

PRINT A DEPOSIT SLIP

To print a deposit slip for use with your actual bank deposit:

1. Click the **Banking** menu and click **Make Deposits**. The Make Deposits window opens. If the default account in the Deposit To drop-down list is not the one you want to use, click the down arrow and select the correct account.

2. Click the **Previous** button to return to the last deposit you made. If you have preprinted deposit slips for your printer, you can follow these steps to print this deposit. If not, you will need to handwrite a deposit slip. Make sure the amounts match the QuickBooks entry.

3. Load your preprinted deposit slip into your printer.

4. Click the **Print** button. The Print Deposit dialog box appears.

5. Click **Deposit Slip And Deposit Summary** if you have QuickBooks-compatible deposit slips. Otherwise, click **Deposit Summary Only** and use this to prepare a handwritten deposit slip or for reporting purposes and record keeping. Click **OK**. The Print Deposit Slips window opens, as shown in Figure 4-8.

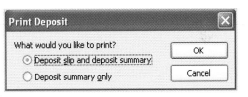

6. Make sure you have your deposit slip in the printer the correct way (you may want to test it with a blank sheet first), and then click the **Print** button.

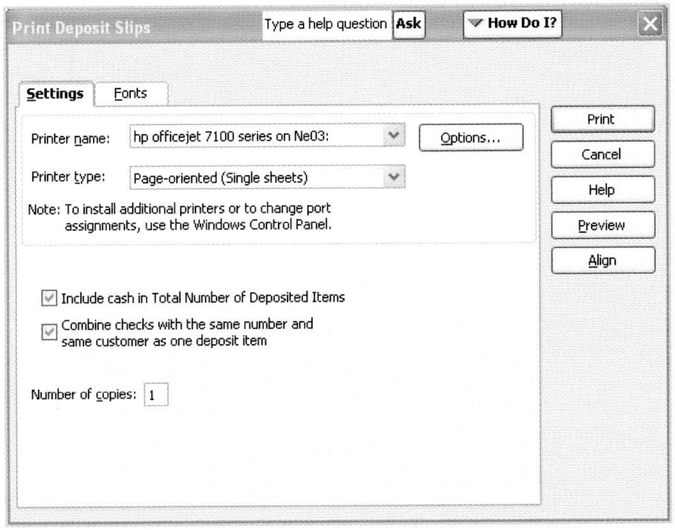

Figure 4-8: The Print Deposit Slips window enables you to include cash in your deposits and combine multiple deposits from the same customer.

View and Edit Bank Account Registers

QuickBooks is driven by forms, such as those found in the Write Checks, Make Deposits, and Transfer Funds windows, but all transactions are kept in a register, which you can view and edit. The easiest way to view your register is through the Chart of Accounts.

1. Click the **Company** menu and click **Chart Of Accounts**.

2. Double-click the **Checking** account. The check register is displayed, as shown in Figure 4-9. You can edit directly in this register, or click a transaction and click the **Edit Transaction** button to open the form the transaction refers to (Make Deposit, Write Checks, Transfer Funds, and so on). Follow the steps in previous sections, such as "Edit, Void, and Delete Checks," for specific information on editing a given transaction.

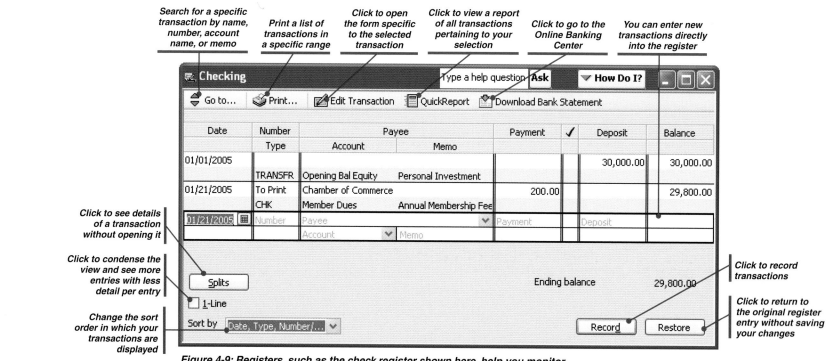

Search for a specific transaction by name, number, account name, or memo

Print a list of transactions in a specific range

Click to open the form specific to the selected transaction

Click to view a report of all transactions pertaining to your selection

Click to go to the Online Banking Center

You can enter new transactions directly into the register

Click to see details of a transaction without opening it

Click to condense the view and see more entries with less detail per entry

Change the sort order in which your transactions are displayed

Click to record transactions

Click to return to the original register entry without saving your changes

Figure 4-9: Registers, such as the check register shown here, help you monitor your transactions and, as a result, your company's financial health.

If you use multiple accounts, you can transfer funds online or manually and enter these transactions into QuickBooks to keep your balances accurate. The Transfer Funds feature is used mostly for transferring monies from bank account to bank account, but this example will use it to show the infusion of funds from the owner.

1. Click the **Banking** menu and click **Transfer Funds**. The Transfer Funds Between Accounts window opens.
2. Click in the **Date** field, and type the date. Alternatively, you can click the **calendar** icon to select the date from a drop-down list.
3. Press the **TAB** key to move to the Transfer Funds From field. Click the down arrow and select the relevant account. Notice that all your bank accounts and asset, liability, and equity accounts are listed.
4. Press the **TAB** key to move to the Transfer Funds To field. Click the down arrow and select the relevant account (for example, **Checking**). Alternatively, you can type the first few letters of the account name (for example, Ch) and the correct name may automatically appear in the drop-down list.
5. Press the **TAB** key twice to move to the Transfer Amount line. If the account you are transferring money from and the account you are transferring money to are both online, click the **Online Funds Transfer** check box.
6. Type the transfer amount (for example, 20,000).
7. Press the **TAB** key to move to the Memo field, and type a note reminding you of the reason for the transfer, for example, Cash Deposit from Owner.
8. Click the **Save & Close** button.

Manage Business Credit Cards

This section refers to credit cards you use to buy things for your business as opposed to merchant accounts—credit cards you accept as payment from your clients. If you use a business credit card, it's important to keep it separate from your personal credit card account. In rare cases, for example, if your business uses a credit card only occasionally, it may be more convenient to put your business expenses on a personal credit card and reimburse yourself with a check from your business account. This procedure is not advised, however, and you should check with your accountant as to the best course of action to take.

Set Up a Credit Card Account

To set up a credit card account:

1. Click the **Company** menu and click **Chart of Accounts**.
2. Click the **Account** menu and click **New**. The New Account window opens, as shown in Figure 4-10.

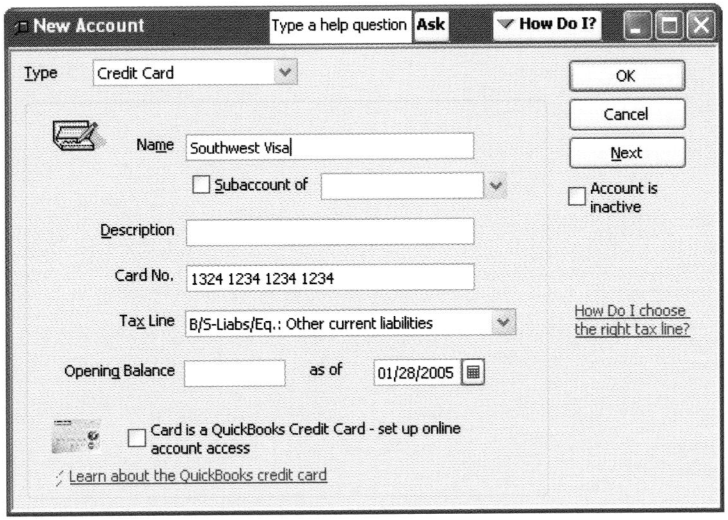

Figure 4-10: When setting up a new credit card account, click the How Do I Choose The Right Tax Line? link for more information.

TIP

You can create credit card subaccounts if you have multiple cards (for employees) issued on one account.

NOTE

You can create multiple credit card accounts, one for each card you use for your business, such as Visa, Discover, MasterCard.

CAUTION

Most of the time you will be entering charges. Be careful when entering a credit, because the next time you enter a transaction, QuickBooks will default to the last type of entry, which may have been a credit entry. Click the **Credit** and **Charge** options, and notice how the color changes in the Enter Credit Card Charges window.

3. Click the **Type** down arrow, and click **Credit Card**.

4. Click in the **Name** field, and type your credit card name, for example, Southwest Visa. This is the only required field in this form

5. Click in the **Card No.** field, and type your account number. This field is optional, as are the rest in this form.

6. Click **OK**.

Enter Credit Card Transactions

Entering credit card transactions in QuickBooks is similar to entering checks. You enter the vendor, date, and amount at the top of the form, and then fill in the account and memo information at the bottom of the form.

1. Click the **Banking** menu, click **Record Credit Card Charges**, and click **Enter Credit Card Charges**. The Enter Credit Card Charges window opens, as shown in Figure 4-11.

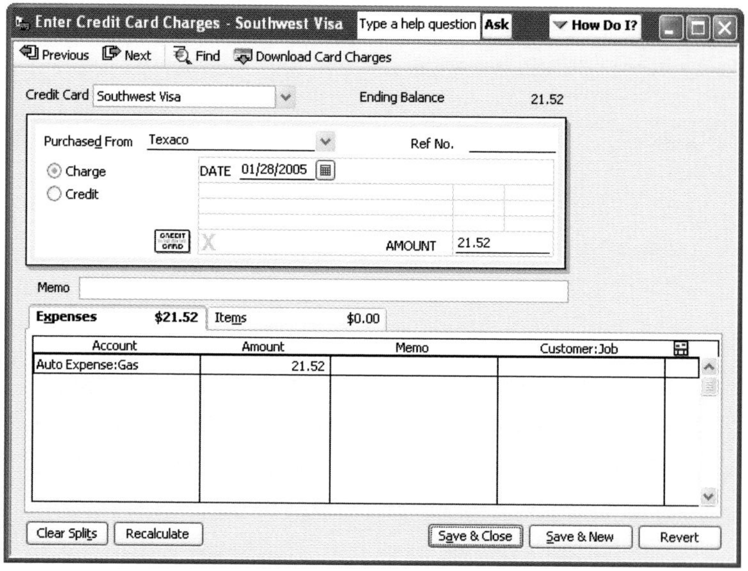

Figure 4-11: When entering credit card transactions, click the Credit option if you are entering a refund or credit to the account.

2. If the default account in the Credit Card drop-down list is not the one you want to use, click the down arrow and select the correct account.

3. Press the **TAB** key to move to the Purchased From field, and type the vendor name, for example, <u>Texaco</u>. If you have used this vendor before, typing the first few letters of the name will cause the correct name to appear in the field automatically; otherwise, QuickBooks will prompt you to add this name.

4. Click in the **Date** field, and type the date. Alternatively, you can click the **calendar** icon to select the date from a drop-down list.

5. Press the **TAB** key to move to the Amount field. Type the amount of the charge, for example, <u>21.52</u>.

6. Press the **TAB** key twice to move to the Account column at the bottom.

7. Type the account name, for example, <u>Auto Expense</u>. If this is an account you have used before, typing <u>A</u> may cause this name to automatically appear in the field. If not, click the Quick Add button to add it.

8. Type a colon (:) to accept the Auto Expense category and enter a subcategory.

9. Type <u>G</u> and "Gas" appears.

10. Press the **TAB** key to move to the Amount column. The amount—21.52—should come up automatically.

11. Press the **TAB** key to move to the Memo column. If you need a reminder as to why this charge was incurred, type it here.

12. Press the **TAB** key to move to the Customer:Job column. This column is used to track expenses that are reimbursable from clients or to track for whom you bought supplies.

13. Press the **TAB** key to move to the last column. This column is used to identify whether this charge is billable to the client. Press **SPACEBAR** to insert a check mark in this column, thereby identifying the charge as a billable one.

14. When finished, click **Save & Close**.

NOTE

When you type G, "Gas" appears because you have few data-item accounts listed. Experiment with your names. Change them if typing the same few letters is liable to bring up different accounts. For example, typing the letters GA might cause both "Gas" and "Garbage" to appear, so you might change "Garbage" to "Trash."

Figure 4-12: Compare your downloaded transactions to your register in order to reconcile an account.

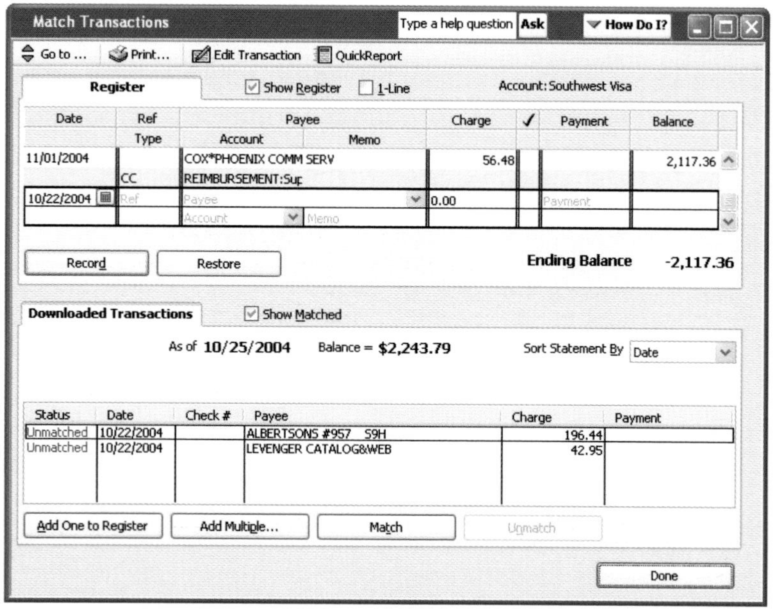

Receive and Enter Online Business Credit Card Transactions

Receiving online credit card transactions is just like receiving online banking transactions, except you use a different account.

1. Click the **Banking** menu and click **Online Banking Center**. The Online Banking Center is displayed.

2. If the default account in the Financial Institution drop-down list is not the one you want to use, click the down arrow and select the correct account.

3. Click **Go Online**. You are prompted for your PIN.

4. Type your PIN (or password), and click **OK**. QuickBooks connects to your bank and downloads any new transactions. When finished, a summary is displayed.

5. Click **Close** after reviewing the new transactions (click **OK** if you are notified that there are no new transactions). You are returned to the Online Banking Center, and the new downloaded transactions are listed in the Items Received From Financial Institution area in the bottom portion of the screen.

VIEW AND ENTER TRANSACTIONS

Once your transactions are downloaded, you can view them and match them to entries already in your credit card register or add them to your register, either one at a time or all at once (this is a new feature in QuickBooks 2005).

1. Double-click the relevant QuickStatement in the bottom portion of the Online Banking Center. The Match Transactions window opens, as shown in Figure 4-12, with your register displayed in the top and the current downloaded transactions displayed in the bottom.

2. On the Downloaded Transactions tab, click an unmatched item.

3. Click the **Add One To Register** button to add the transaction to your account. A dialog box appears, asking if you want to add directly to the register or enter credit card charges in the form. Click the **Do Not Prompt Me Again** check box if the majority of your transactions are single accounts. Use the form window when entering multiple accounts per charge.

4. Click **OK**. The item is added to your register.

5. Click **Record**. The item is recorded. Repeat for other transactions.

6. Click **Done** when finished.

ADD MULTIPLE TRANSACTIONS AT ONCE

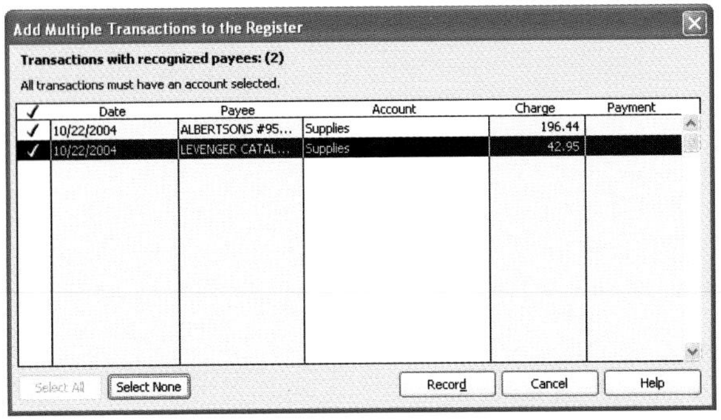

You can use the Add Multiple feature (a new feature in QuickBooks 2005) to add multiple transactions at one time, but you will still need to click the Quick Add button and add vendors that are not currently in your Vendor list. If none of the vendors are in your list, you will have to manually add each one.

1. In the Match Transactions window, click the **Add Multiple** button. The Add Multiple Transactions To The Register window opens.

2. Select the correct account in the Account column for each transaction.

3. Click the **Record** button. The transactions are recorded, and you are returned to the Match Transactions window.

4. Click **Done**.

Figure 4-13: If your beginning balance doesn't match your statement, click the Locate Discrepancies button to view changes made since the last reconciliation.

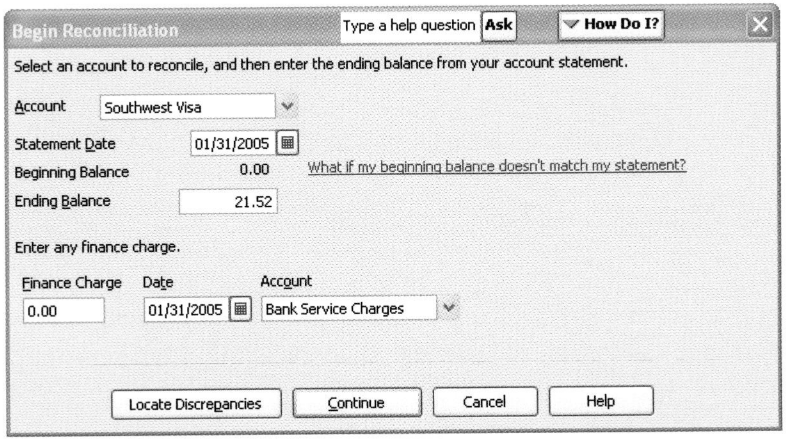

Manage Your Accounts on a Monthly Basis

When you receive your monthly bank or credit card statement, reconciliation is a simple matter of clicking each transaction in QuickBooks to place a check mark next to it. After your reconciliation is complete, you will have the option to write a check for the credit card balance or enter a bill.

Reconcile Credit Card Accounts

To reconcile your credit card accounts:

1. Click the **Banking** menu and click **Reconcile**. The Begin Reconciliation window opens, as shown in Figure 4-13.

2. Click the **Account** down arrow, and click the relevant account. Note that both bank and credit card accounts are listed.

3. Type the ending balance that is listed on your statement, for example, <u>21.52</u>.

4. If this account has finance charges, type them in the Finance Charge field. Enter the date (type the date or click the **calendar** icon, and select the date from a drop-down list).

5. Click the **Account** down arrow located to the right of the Date field, and click the relevant account, for example, **Bank Service Charges**.

6. Click **Continue**. The Reconcile Credit Card window opens, as seen in Figure 4-14.

7. Click individual items to mark them as cleared (a check mark is placed in the left column), or click **Mark All**. In the lower-left area of the screen, you can watch your balances change as you click each item.

8. Click the **Reconcile Now** button when your difference is zero. The Make Payment dialog box appears. The Write A Check For Payment Now option is selected by default.

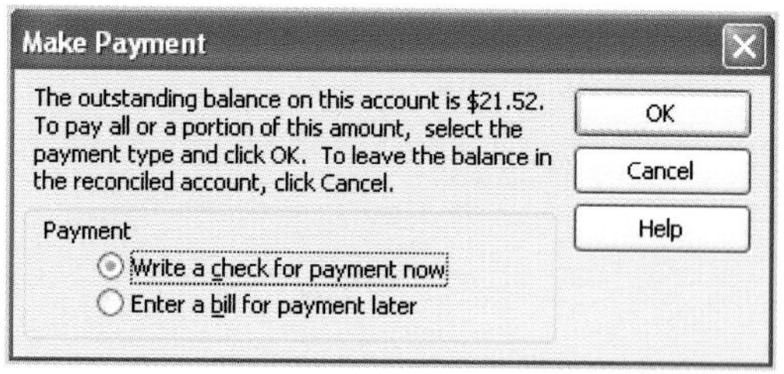

Make Payment

The outstanding balance on this account is $21.52. To pay all or a portion of this amount, select the payment type and click OK. To leave the balance in the reconciled account, click Cancel.

OK
Cancel
Help

Payment
◉ Write a check for payment now
○ Enter a bill for payment later

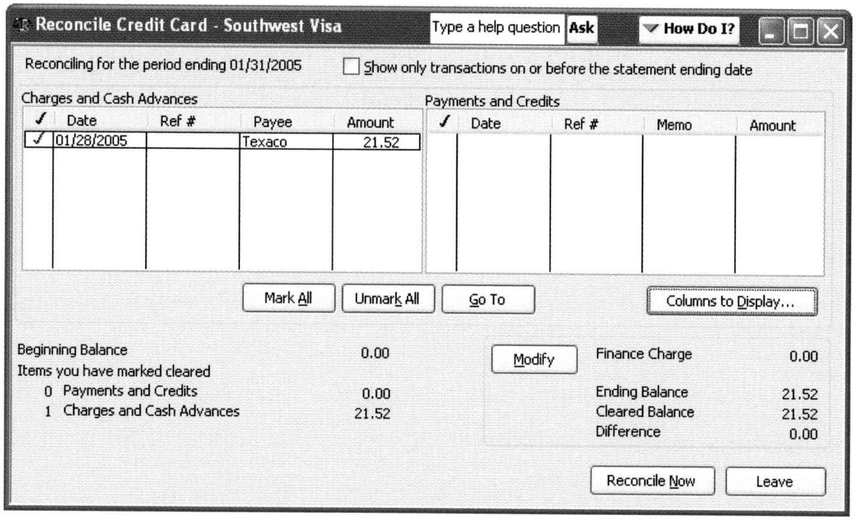

Reconcile Credit Card - Southwest Visa

Type a help question [Ask]   ▼ How Do I?

Reconciling for the period ending 01/31/2005   ☐ Show only transactions on or before the statement ending date

Charges and Cash Advances

✓	Date	Ref #	Payee	Amount
✓	01/28/2005		Texaco	21.52

Payments and Credits

✓	Date	Ref #	Memo	Amount

Mark All   Unmark All   Go To   Columns to Display...

Beginning Balance	0.00	
Items you have marked cleared		
0 Payments and Credits	0.00	
1 Charges and Cash Advances	21.52	

Modify

Finance Charge	0.00
Ending Balance	21.52
Cleared Balance	21.52
Difference	0.00

Reconcile Now   Leave

Figure 4-14: The Reconcile Credit Card window makes it easy to ensure that your credit card entries are accurate and up-to-date.

9. Click **OK**. The Write Checks window opens, and the Select Reconciliation Report dialog box appears. You can choose to view and print reports. Some people like to have them for their records.

10. In the Write Checks window, you may want to edit the amount so as to pay less than the full balance. The first time you write a check to your credit card company, QuickBooks prompts you to add their information to your Vendor list. Edit the check information if needed, and identify it as a check that will be printed or a check sent in the form of an online payment (see the section "Write Checks").

11. Click **Save & Close**.

Reconcile Bank Accounts

Reconciling bank accounts is similar to reconciling credit cards.

1. Click the **Banking** menu and click **Reconcile**. The Begin Reconciliation window opens, as shown in Figure 4-15.

2. If the default account in the Account drop-down list is not the one you want to use, click the down arrow and select the correct account.

3. Click in the **Statement Date** field, and type the date, or click the **calendar** icon and select the date from the drop-down list.

TIP

If you make a mistake entering your dates or amounts in the Begin Reconciliation window, click the **Modify** button in the Reconciliation window to change your entries.

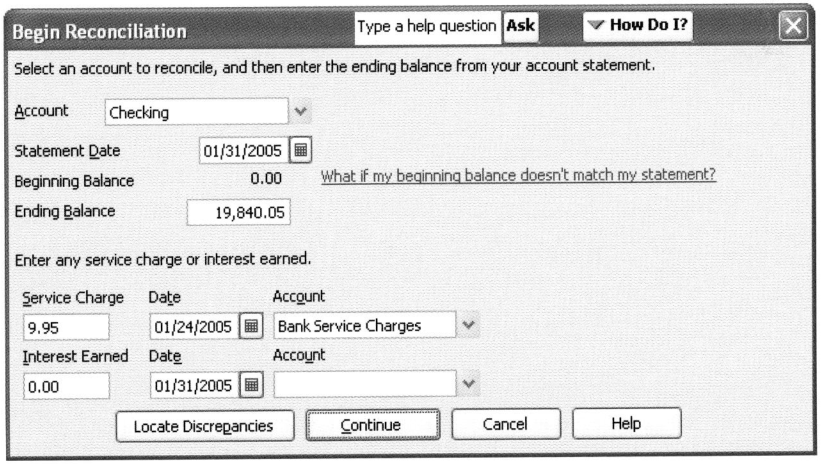

Figure 4-15: Be sure service charges are entered into an expense account and interest accrued is entered into an income account.

Begin Reconciliation	Type a help question	Ask	How Do I?	

Select an account to reconcile, and then enter the ending balance from your account statement.

Account   Checking

Statement Date   01/31/2005

Beginning Balance   0.00   What if my beginning balance doesn't match my statement?

Ending Balance   19,840.05

Enter any service charge or interest earned.

Service Charge   Date   Account
9.95   01/24/2005   Bank Service Charges

Interest Earned   Date   Account
0.00   01/31/2005

Locate Discrepancies   Continue   Cancel   Help

4. Click in the **Ending Balance** field, and type your ending balance as listed in your bank account statement (for example, 19,840.05).

5. Click in the **Service Charge** field, and type the service charge amount, for example, 9.95.

6. Click in the **Date** field, and type the date, or click the **calendar** icon and select the date from the drop-down list.

7. Click the second **Account** down arrow, and click the relevant account, for example, **Bank Service Charges**.

8. If you earn interest on this account, type that amount in the Interest Earned field.

9. Click in the second **Date** field, and type the date, or click the **calendar** icon and select the date from the drop-down list.

10. Click the third **Account** down arrow, and click the relevant account.

11. Click **Continue**. The Reconcile window opens, as seen in Figure 4-16.

12. Click individual items to mark them as cleared. In the lower-left area of the screen, you can watch your balances change as you click each item.

13. Click the **Reconcile Now** button when your difference is zero. The Select Reconciliation Report window opens. Click the type of report you want to see: **Summary**, **Detail**, or **Both**.

14. Click **Display** to see the reports. Click **Print** to create a hard copy of the reconciliation report.

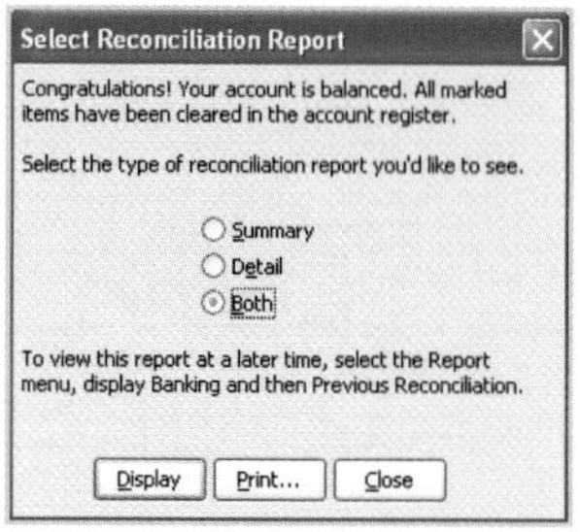

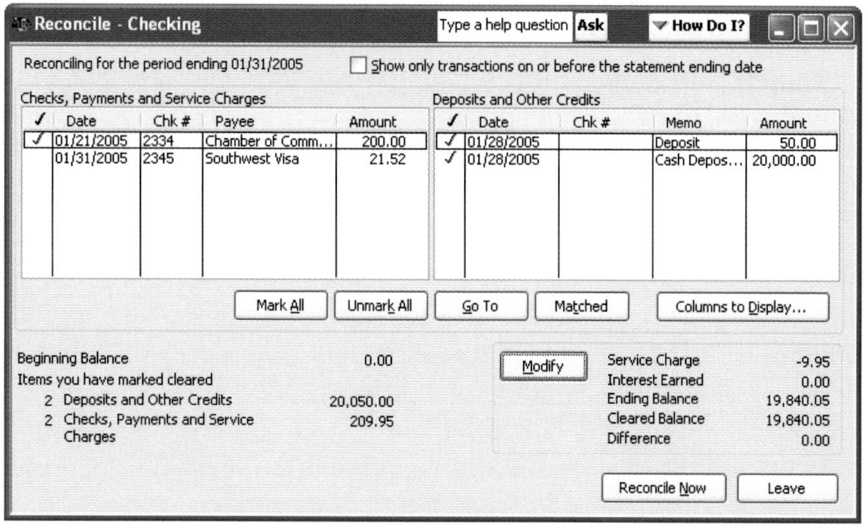

Figure 4-16: Use the Reconcile window to make sure your bank account information is accurate and up-to-date.

How to...

- *Use the Vendor Navigator*

- *Use the Vendor List*

- *Add a Vendor*

- *Merge, Delete, or Make Vendors Inactive*

- *Set Up and Print 1099s*

- *Add Customized Fields to Your Name Lists*

- *Use the Vendor Detail Center*

- *Writing Checks*

- *Enter and Pay Bills*

- *Create Items with Purchase Information*

- *Use Items on a Bill*

- *Memorize Reminder Transactions*

- *Memorize Automatic Transactions*

- *Manage Memorized Transactions*

Chapter 5
Entering and Paying Bills

5

Managing your accounts payable (A/P) and vendors is a large part of staying in business. You have to pay bills, and QuickBooks makes it easy to do. With accurate vendor reports, you may be able to negotiate better discounts or deferred-payment terms. Entering all your expenses is important in knowing how profitable your business is. In addition, if you charge items directly to your clients, you can use QuickBooks to track billable expenses and items so that you don't miss out on any potential chargebacks.

Manage Vendors

Vendors are anyone from whom you purchase items or services. This includes contractors, who are considered 1099 vendors. The IRS requires a Form 1099 be issued at the end of the year to any contractor paid more than a certain amount during the course of the year (currently $600).

Use the Vendor Navigator

The Vendor Navigator is simple to use and includes all of your accounts payable (A/P). Businesses using the cash-based method of accounting will find it easy to write checks directly without first entering the bills. If you wish to use the accrual-based method of accounting, you'll find it easy to enter bills first and then pay them. (See Chapter 2 for more information on accrual- versus cash-based accounting.) To see the Vendor Navigator (as shown in Figure 5-1):

1. Click the **Vendors** menu and click **Vendor Navigator**.

2. Click the **Close** button (the X in the upper-right corner) to close the Vendor Navigator.

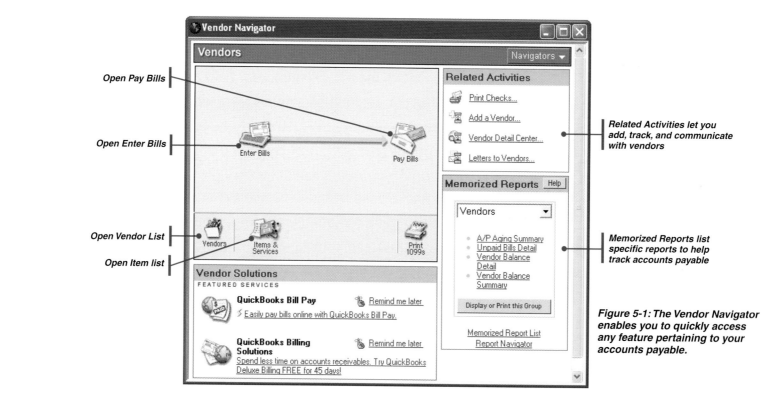

Figure 5-1: The Vendor Navigator enables you to quickly access any feature pertaining to your accounts payable.

NOTE

You can't reorder the Vendor List or the Other list as you can the Customer:Job and Employee lists. The Vendor List and Other list always appear in alphabetical order; however, you can rename vendors so that they appear in a specific place in your list.

Use the Vendor List

The Vendor List is one of the four name lists in QuickBooks, the others being Customer:Job, Employee, and Other. All of the name lists work similarly to the Chart of Accounts (see Chapter 2). Use any of the following methods to open the Vendor List:

Click the **Vend** icon on the icon bar.

–Or–

Click the **Vendors** menu and click **Vendor List**.

–Or–

Click **Vendors** on the Vendor Navigator.

Figure 5-2 shows a Vendor List with three vendors: Chamber of Commerce, Southwest Visa, and Texaco. Each vendor was entered using the Quick Add feature when writing a check (see Chapter 4). Some vendor entries consist only of the name (which is required), whereas other vendor entries include additional information, such as address, phone number, contacts, and so on. The level of detail you require in your reports will dictate how you create your vendor entries.

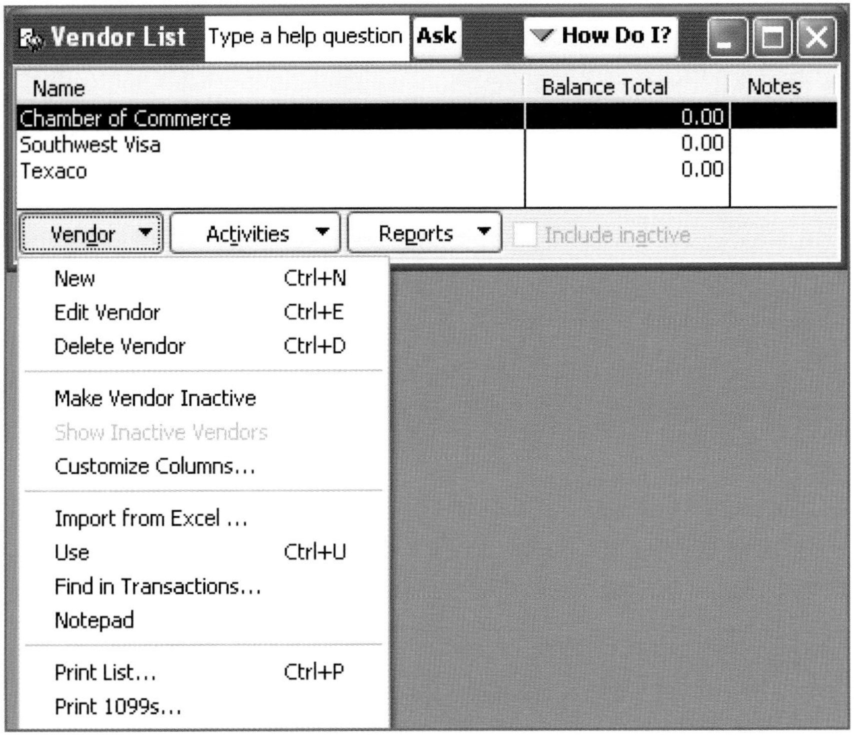

Figure 5-2: From the Vendor List, you can add, edit, and manage your vendors.

NOTE

BG & E is a good example of an easy-to-mistype vendor name. BG&E; B,G & E; BG &E; and B G& E are all completely different to QuickBooks. If the Name Not Found dialog box appears and the vendor is one your company has used before, click **Cancel** to return to the previous window, click the **Name** down arrow, and look up the correct entry.

CAUTION

QuickBooks does not allow duplicate names among lists, so if you have a customer, for example, that is also a vendor, when adding this name to the Vendor List, include a "-v" at the end of the name.

Add a Vendor

QuickBooks offers three ways to add vendors:

- Use the Quick Add feature
- Use the Set Up feature
- Use the Vendor list

Any time you use a name that is not already in QuickBooks' records, the Name Not Found dialog box appears.

- Click **Quick Add** to add just the vendor name to the Vendor List.
- Click **Set Up** to open a New Vendor window. From here you can enter as much or as little information as you want.
- Click **Cancel** to return to the Name field in whatever window you were in previously (for example, Write Checks). This is extremely useful in the event that you mistyped the name.

If the vendor is one your company has used before yet you are prompted to add a new vendor when you type the name, that is a good indication that you made a typo somewhere. Click the **Name** down arrow, and look up the correct entry.

ADD A VENDOR USING QUICK ADD

To add a vendor using Quick Add (from the Write Checks window):

1. Click the **Check** icon on the icon bar.
2. Click in the **Pay To The Order Of** field, and type BG & E.
3. Press the TAB key. The Name Not Found dialog box appears.
4. Click **Quick Add**. The Select Name Type dialog box appears with the Vendor option selected by default.
5. Click **OK**. BG & E is added to your Vendor List, and you are returned to the Write Checks window.
6. Click the **Close** button to close the Write Checks window.
7. Click **No** to confirm that you do not want to record this transaction. The check will not be recorded, but the vendor will be added to the Vendor List.

TIP

The Vendor Name you type should be whatever is easiest for you to remember, such as the company name, phone number, or contact. The name in the Company Name field should be the name you will use to communicate with the vendor.

ADD A VENDOR USING SET UP

To add a vendor using the Set Up feature:

1. Click the **Check** icon on the icon bar.

2. Click in the **Pay To The Order Of** field, and type the vendor name, for example, Cactus Refreshment Services.

3. Press the TAB key. The Name Not Found dialog box appears.

4. Click **Set Up**. The Select Name Type dialog box appears with the Vendor option selected by default.

5. Click **OK**. The New Vendor window opens, as shown in Figure 5-3.

6. Click in the **Company Name** field. Type Refreshment Services. (Cactus Refreshment Services is the name the company does business as (DBA), but Refreshment Services is the legal name of the company, a common practice among companies.)

Figure 5-3: The New Vendor window gives you the ability to store detailed information for a vendor, including an e-mail address or alternate contact information.

New Vendor | Type a help question | **Ask** | ▼ **How Do I?** | ☒

Vendor Name	Cactus Refreshment Services			
Opening Balance		as of 02/08/2004 🔲	How do I determine the opening balance?	OK
				Cancel

Address Info | Additional Info

Company Name	Refreshment Services	Contact	Fred Fishman	Help
Mr./Ms./...	Mr.	Phone	(602) 267-7199	
First Name	Fred	M.I.	FAX	(602) 273-1716	☐ Vendor is inactive
Last Name	Fishman	Alt. Ph.		
Name and Address	Cactus Refreshment Fred Fishman 2328 E. Van Buren Street, Phoenix, AZ 85006	Alt. Contact	Linnea Storm	
		E-mail	sales@cactusrefresh...	
		Print on Check as		
		Refreshment Services		

Address Details

7. Press the TAB key to move to the Mr./Mrs./... field. The entry in the Company Name field automatically populates the Print On Check As field.

8. Type the correct prefix, such as, Mr.

9. Press the TAB key to move to the First Name field, and type the vendor's first name, for example, Fred.

10. Press the TAB key twice to move to the Last Name field, and type the vendor's last name, for example, Fishman.

11. Press the TAB key again. The cursor moves to the Name And Address field, which has been automatically populated with the vendor name and first and last names of your contact. The Contact field has also been updated with the first and last names of your contact.

12. Press the ENTER key and type the vendor's address.

13. Press the ENTER key again, and type the vendor's city, state, and ZIP code.

14. Click in the **Phone** field, and type the vendor's phone number.

TIP

If you use online banking, the account number is a required field. If a vendor doesn't use account numbers, type your name or company name in the Account No. field.

15. Press the **TAB** key to move to the FAX field, and type the vendor's FAX number.
16. Press the **TAB** key twice to move to the Alt. Contact field, and type a name, if necessary.
17. Press the **TAB** key to move to the E-Mail field, and type the vendor's e-mail address, for example, sales@cactusrefreshments.com.
18. Click the **Additional Info** tab to enter more information, as shown in Figure 5-4.
19. Click in the **Account No.** field, and type the account number the vendor uses for you.
20. Press the **TAB** key to move to the Type field. Click the down arrow and click the vendor type, for example, **Supplies**.

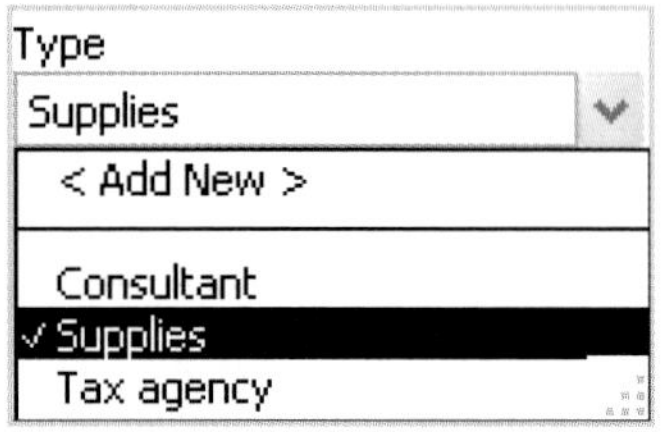

21. Press the **TAB** key to move to the Terms field. Click the down arrow and click the terms type, for example, **Due On Receipt**.
22. When finished, click the **Close** button. The vendor is added to your Vendor List, and you are returned to the Write Checks window.
23. Click the **Close** button to close the Write Checks window.
24. Click **No** to confirm that you do not want to record this transaction. The check will not be recorded, but the vendor will be added to the Vendor List.

Figure 5-4: Use the fields on the Additional Info tab to record further information for a vendor, such as whether this vendor is 1099-eligible.

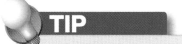

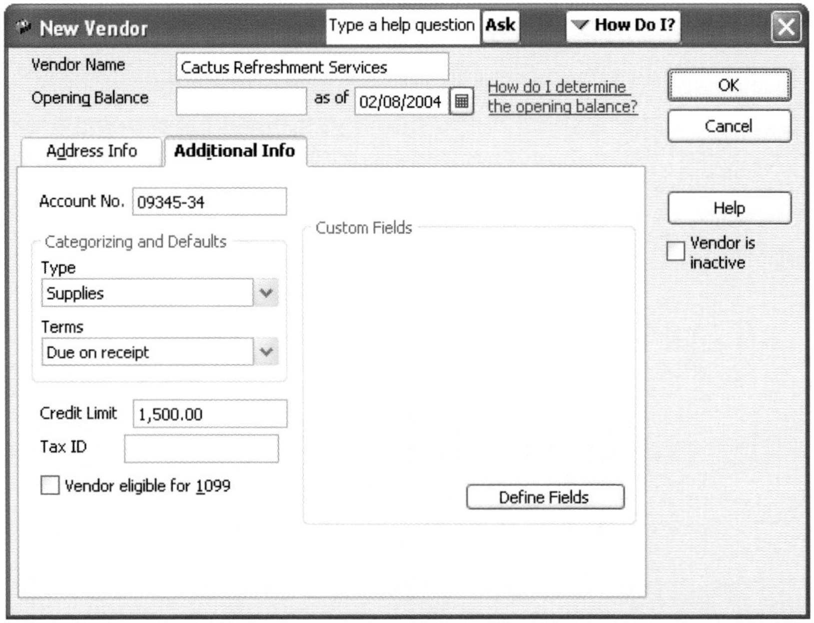

TIP

You can add types and terms on a drop-down list by clicking **Add New**. This will open a dialog box for you to enter the new type or term. This option is common on drop-down lists throughout QuickBooks.

CAUTION

Don't use generic vendors if you want to keep close track of where your money is being spent; however, using generic vendors can come in handy. For example, you can have a generic "Gas Station" vendor or a generic "Texaco" vendor, regardless of location. You can also use "Unknown" if you can't recall a vendor, for example, due to a cash expenditure at an off-brand gas station.

ADD A VENDOR FROM THE VENDOR LIST

The Quick Add and Set Up features are useful when you need to add a new name to any list. You can also directly add vendors to the Vendor List when you establish a new account with a vendor. To add a vendor directly from the Vendor List:

1. Click the **Vendors** menu and click **Vendor List**.

2. From the Vendor List, click the **Vendor** menu button (located at the bottom), and click **New**. The New Vendor window opens.

3. Type your vendor name in the Vendor Name field, for example, Generic Vendor.

4. Click **Next** to continue to enter another vendor. The Next button will appear below the Cancel button on the right side of the New Vendor window when you are entering new vendors from the Vendor List. You can continue to add vendors in this manner.

5. When you are finished adding new vendors, click **OK** and the window will close. The vendors are added to your Vendor List.

EDIT A VENDOR

To edit a vendor:

1. Click the **Vendors** menu and click **Vendor List**. The Vendor List is displayed.

2. Click the vendor whose information you want to edit.

3. Click the **Vendor** menu button (located at the bottom), and click **Edit Vendor**. The Edit Vendor window opens, as shown in Figure 5-5. Make any changes as needed.

4. Click **OK** when you are finished making changes, and the window will close.

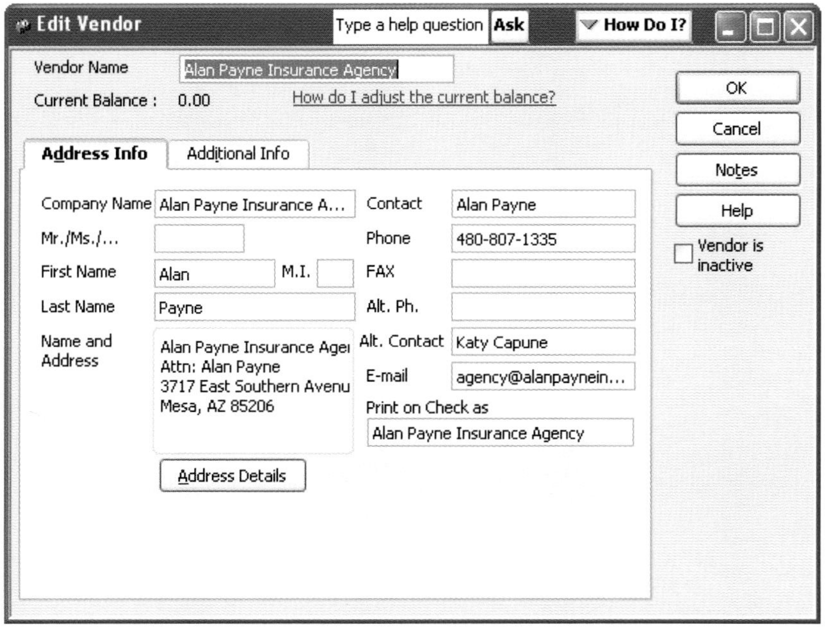

Figure 5-5: Easily change any vendor information by simply clicking in the desired field and editing.

1 2 3 4 5 6 7 8 9 10

TIP

QuickBooks displays reminders each time you open your company file.

NOTE

You can double-click a vendor on the Vendor List to open the Edit Vendor window.

ADD NOTES OR REMINDERS TO A VENDOR

From the Edit Vendor window, you can add notes or reminders regarding a vendor.

1. With the Edit Vendor window open, click the **Notes** button. The Notepad window opens, as shown in Figure 5-6.
2. Click the **Date Stamp** button to automatically enter today's date within the note area.
3. Type your note. Click **OK** if you are finished. If you want to add a reminder, however, click the **New To Do** button. The New To Do window opens.

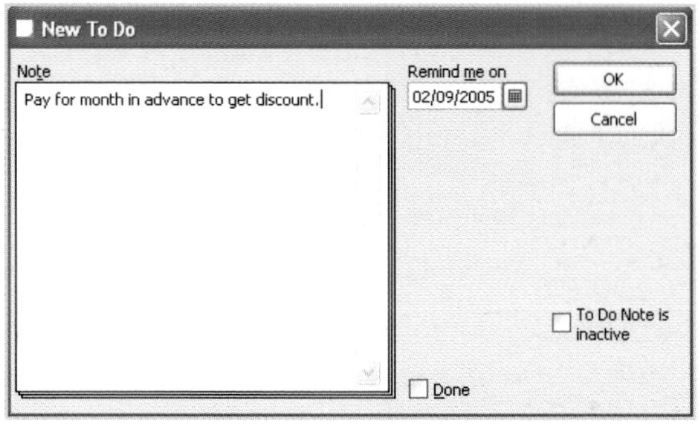

4. Type a reminder in the Note field, for example, Pay for month in advance to get discount.
5. Edit the reminder date. It will be today's date by default.
6. Click **OK** to close the New To Do window.
7. Click **OK** to close the Notepad window. Click **OK** to close the Edit Vendor window. In the Vendor List, notice the blue note icon next to the vendor for whom a reminder exists. You will see a note icon appear in the Notes column next to the vendor.

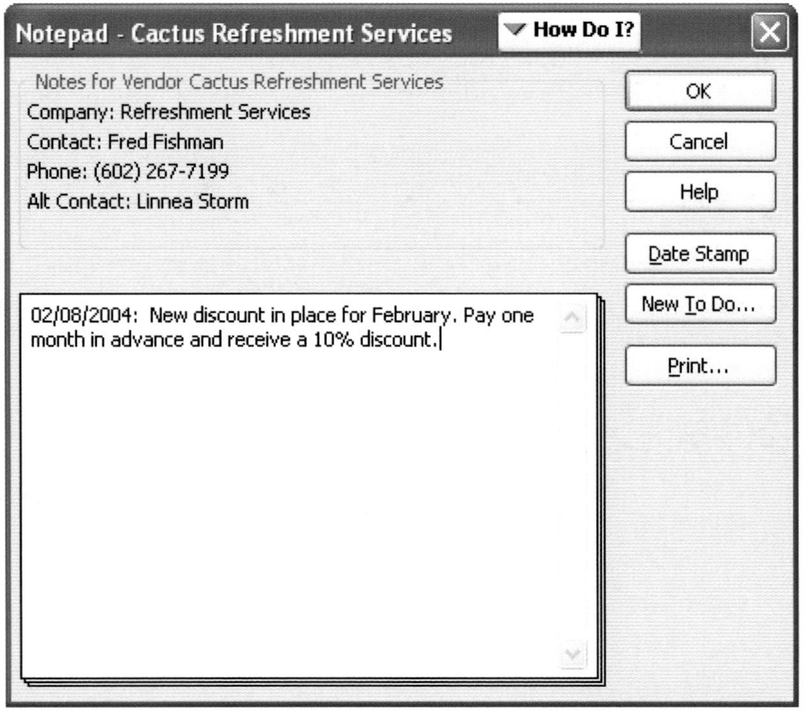

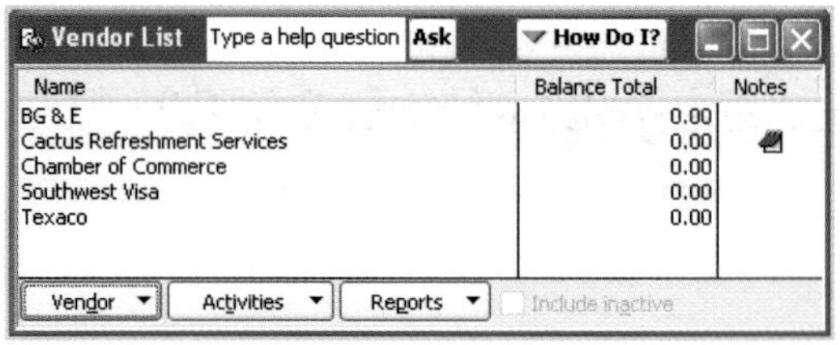

Figure 5-6: You can add notes regarding a vendor beyond what is included in the Vendor List, such as special offers or revised payment terms.

Merge, Delete, or Make Vendors Inactive

When a vendor is listed twice with slightly different names, you can merge the two names so that you don't lose any transactions. If a vendor is entered in QuickBooks but has never been used, you can delete this vendor. If a vendor was once used but isn't any longer, QuickBooks will not allow you to delete this vendor; however, you can make this vendor inactive so that the name no longer appears in your Vendor List. If you start to use the vendor again, you can easily change the status back to active.

MERGE VENDORS

If you change the name of a vendor to one that already exists, QuickBooks asks if you want to merge the information. This is useful if you have entered names incorrectly, such as BG&E and BG & E.

To merge vendors:

1. Click the **Vendors** menu and click **Vendor List**.
2. Click the vendor name you want to merge.
3. From the Vendor List, click the **Vendor** menu button (located at the bottom). Click **Edit Vendor**. The Edit Vendor window opens with the selected vendor name highlighted in blue.
4. Type the name of the vendor with whom you want to merge the first vendor. A dialog box appears asking if you would like to merge these two items.
5. Click **Yes** to complete the merge.

DELETE A VENDOR

You can only delete a vendor if no entries pertaining to it exist.

1. Click the **Vendors** menu and click **Vendor List**. The Vendor List is displayed.
2. Click the vendor name you want to delete.
3. From the Vendor List, click the **Vendor** menu button (located at the bottom). Click **Delete Vendor**. A dialog box appears asking you to confirm this action.
4. Click **Yes** to delete the vendor.

TIP

You can press the **ESC** key to close any window instead of clicking the **Close** button.

Click next to any vendor in the X column to change it from inactive to active.

MAKE A VENDOR INACTIVE

If you've previously used a vendor but no longer plan to, you must mark it inactive since QuickBooks will not allow you to delete this vendor.

1. Click the **Vendors** menu and click **Vendor List**. The Vendor List is displayed.

2. Click the vendor that you want to make inactive.

3. From the Vendor List, click the **Vendor** menu button (located at the bottom). Click **Make Vendor Inactive** (alternatively, you can right-click the vendor name, and click **Make Vendor Inactive**). There is no confirmation dialog box; the vendor immediately becomes inactive and disappears from the Vendor List.

VIEW INACTIVE VENDORS

To view your inactive vendors in your Vendor List:

Click the **Include Inactive** check box, located at the bottom of the Vendor List.

A new column is created to the left of the Name column, designated by an X. That same X is next to any vendor that you have made inactive, as can be seen in the illustration. You can click the X to return the vendor's status to active.

Set Up and Print 1099s

As previously mentioned, contractors are considered 1099 vendors and need to be set up as such in QuickBooks. At the very least, you need to do this to track nonemployee compensation (Box 7 on the 1099 Form). If you're unsure whether you need to track any of the other 1099 categories, check with your accountant. Upon setting up a 1099 vendor, QuickBooks will track the amount you pay to that vendor so that you can print 1099 statements at the end of the year.

SET UP 1099 ACCOUNTS

The IRS tracks different categories under the 1099 Form. Edit your QuickBooks preferences to identify accounts from your Chart of Accounts that should be associated with the categories that pertain to your company.

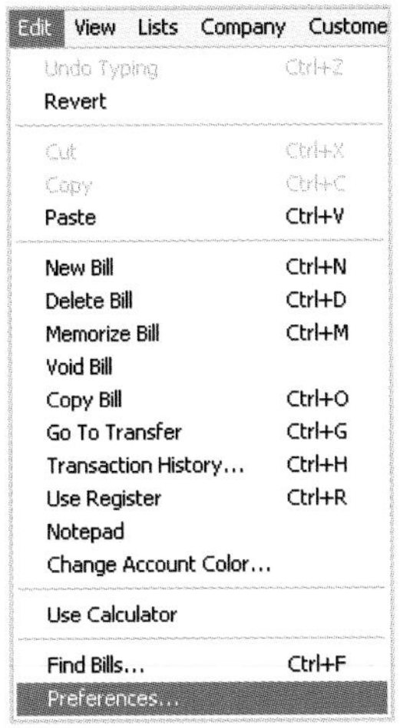

To set up a 1099 account:

1. Click the **Edit** menu and click **Preferences**. The Preferences window opens, as shown in Figure 5-7.

2. Click the **Tax: 1099** button, located on the left, and then click the **Company Preferences** tab.

3. Click the **Yes** option next to Do You File 1099-MISC Forms?

4. Click in the **Account** column next to Box 7: Nonemployee Compensation. Click the down arrow and click **Building Repairs** (under Repairs). QuickBooks will now track expenses in this category paid to 1099 vendors.

5. Click **OK** to close the window and save your preferences.

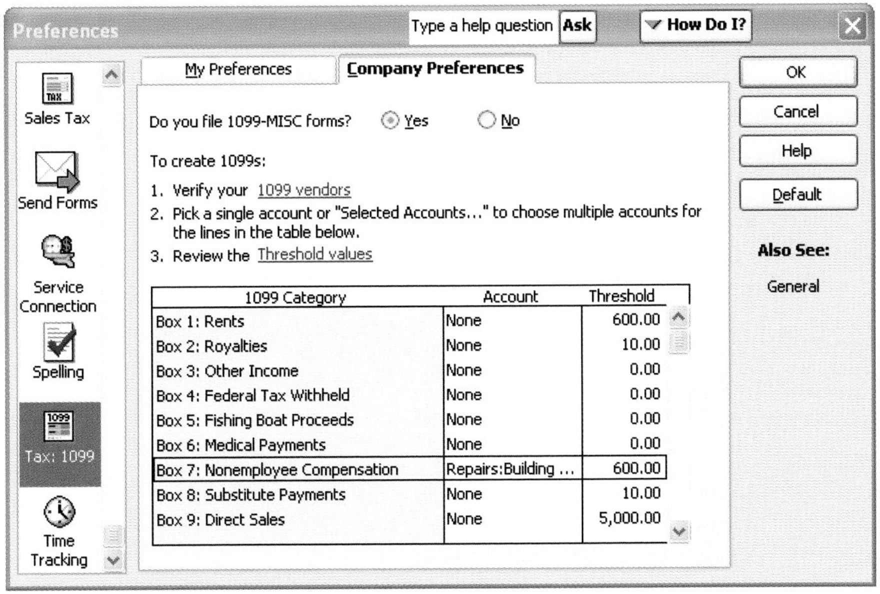

Edit menu:

Edit	View	Lists	Company	Custome
Undo Typing				Ctrl+Z
Revert				
Cut				Ctrl+X
Copy				Ctrl+C
Paste				Ctrl+V
New Bill				Ctrl+N
Delete Bill				Ctrl+D
Memorize Bill				Ctrl+M
Void Bill				
Copy Bill				Ctrl+O
Go To Transfer				Ctrl+G
Transaction History...				Ctrl+H
Use Register				Ctrl+R
Notepad				
Change Account Color...				
Use Calculator				
Find Bills...				Ctrl+F
Preferences...				

Preferences window:

Company Preferences / My Preferences

Do you file 1099-MISC forms? ● Yes ○ No

To create 1099s:
1. Verify your 1099 vendors
2. Pick a single account or "Selected Accounts..." to choose multiple accounts for the lines in the table below.
3. Review the Threshold values

1099 Category	Account	Threshold
Box 1: Rents	None	600.00
Box 2: Royalties	None	10.00
Box 3: Other Income	None	0.00
Box 4: Federal Tax Withheld	None	0.00
Box 5: Fishing Boat Proceeds	None	0.00
Box 6: Medical Payments	None	0.00
Box 7: Nonemployee Compensation	Repairs:Building ...	600.00
Box 8: Substitute Payments	None	10.00
Box 9: Direct Sales	None	5,000.00

Sales Tax, Send Forms, Service Connection, Spelling, Tax: 1099, Time Tracking

OK / Cancel / Help / Default

Also See:
General

Figure 5-7: From the Preferences window, you can customize all facets of QuickBooks.

Reports	Window	Help
Report Navigator		
Memorized Reports	▶	
Process Multiple Reports		
Company & Financial	▶	
Customers & Receivables	▶	
Sales	▶	
Jobs, Time & Mileage	▶	
Vendors & Payables	▶	A/P Aging Summary
Employees & Payroll	▶	A/P Aging Detail
Banking	▶	Vendor Balance Summary
Accountant & Taxes	▶	Vendor Balance Detail
Budgets & Forecasts	▶	Unpaid Bills Detail
List	▶	Accounts Payable Graph
		Transaction List by Vendor
Custom Summary Report		
Custom Transaction Detail Report		1099 Summary
		1099 Detail
QuickReport	Ctrl+Q	
Transaction History		Vendor Phone List
Transaction Journal		Vendor Contact List

SET UP 1099 VENDORS

To set up a 1099 vendor so that QuickBooks can track the amounts paid:

1. Click the **Vendors** menu and click **Vendor List**.

2. From the Vendor List, click the **Vendor** menu button (located at the bottom), and click **New**. The New Vendor window opens.

3. Type your new vendor name, for example, David Gardner, Electrician. Fill in the relevant fields (see the section "Add a Vendor").

4. Click the **Additional Info** tab.

5. Click in the **Tax ID** field. Type the vendor's Tax ID number.

6. Click the **Vendor Eligible For 1099** check box.

7. Click **OK** to close and save this vendor setting.

REVIEW AND PRINT 1099S

Before printing your 1099 forms, you can view 1099-related payments by creating 1099 reports.

1. Click the **Reports** menu, click **Vendors & Payables**, and click **1099 Detail**. A 1099 report is displayed, as shown in Figure 5-8.

2. Click the **Close** button to close the report.

3. Click the **Vendors** menu and click **Vendor List**. From the Vendor List, click the **Vendor** menu button (located at the bottom), and click **Print 1099s/1096**. The Printing 1099-MISC And 1096 Forms window opens. **Last Calendar Year** is selected by default. If you want to use a different range of dates, type them in the **From** and **To** fields (or click the **calendar** icon for each, and select the date).

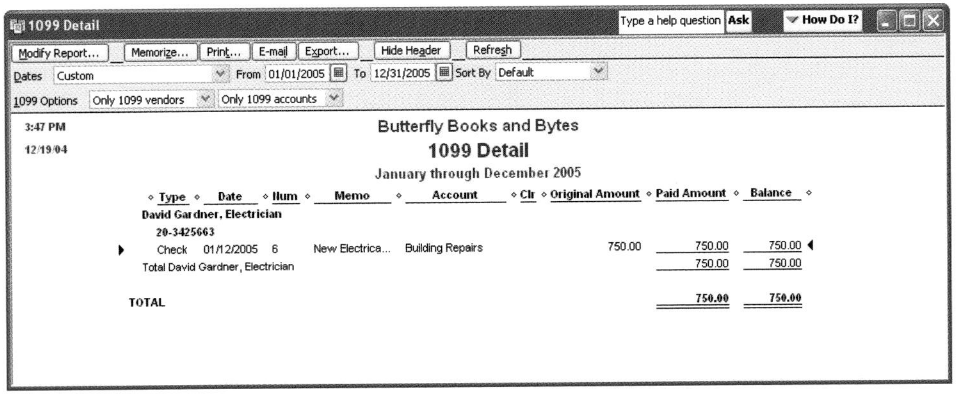

Figure 5-8: 1099 reports are normally run in January to send 1099s to vendors who exceeded the previous year's thresholds.

4. Click **OK**. Provided you have vendors who have been paid the minimum amount (as of this writing, $600.00), a list of 1099-eligible vendors is displayed. If you don't have vendors who have been paid the required amount, a message is displayed notifying you of that and no list is displayed. Figure 5-9 shows a sample list. Note the Valid ID and Valid Address columns. If either of these says NO, you'll need to correct this information in the Edit Vendor window before you print a 1099.

5. Click **Print 1099s**. The Print dialog box appears. Place your 1099 forms in your printer.

6. Click **Print**.

TIP

The 1096 is a summary of all your 1099 vendors who have been paid. Print this after you are finished printing all 1099s.

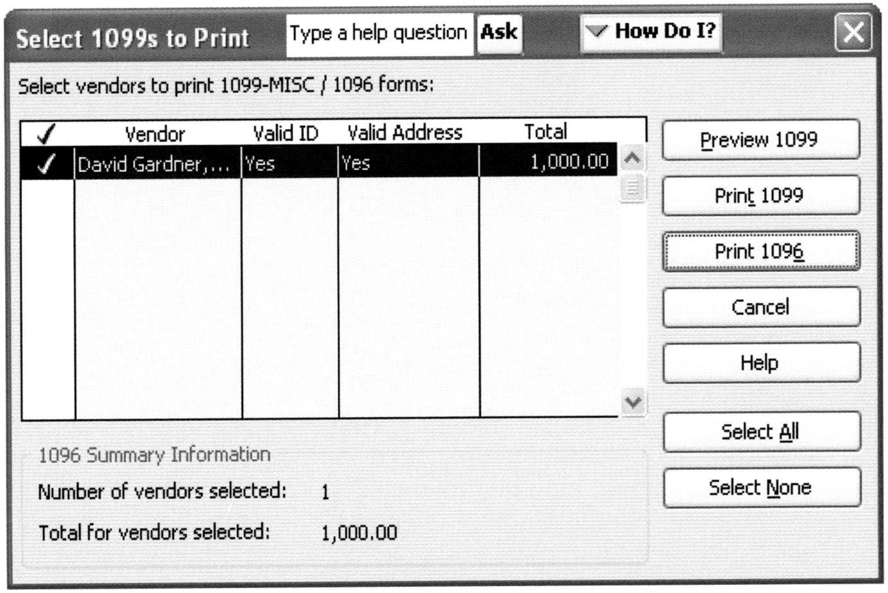

Figure 5-9: View 1099-related reports prior to printing 1099 forms.

Add Customized Fields to Your Name Lists

You may find that you need specific fields that are not included in QuickBooks, for example, a vendor's contractor number or license number. You may also want to track birthdays or special thank-you gifts for employees or customers. Customized fields can be added to all or some of the name lists.

To add customized fields:

1. Click the **Vendors** menu and click **Vendor List**. The Vendor List is displayed.

2. Double-click the vendor name you want to customize. The Edit Vendor window opens.

3. Click the **Additional Info** tab.

4. Click the **Define Fields** button. The Define Fields window opens.

5. In the first Label field, type the name of the custom field you want to create (for example, <u>License Number</u>). The name must be 30 characters or less. Click the **Vendors** and **Employees** check boxes so that this new field is displayed in these name lists.

6. Click **OK**. A dialog box appears, notifying you that custom fields can also be used on your forms. Click **OK**. You are returned to the Edit Vendor window.

7. Click in the field you have just created, and type the relevant information, as shown in Figure 5-10.

8. When finished, click **OK**.

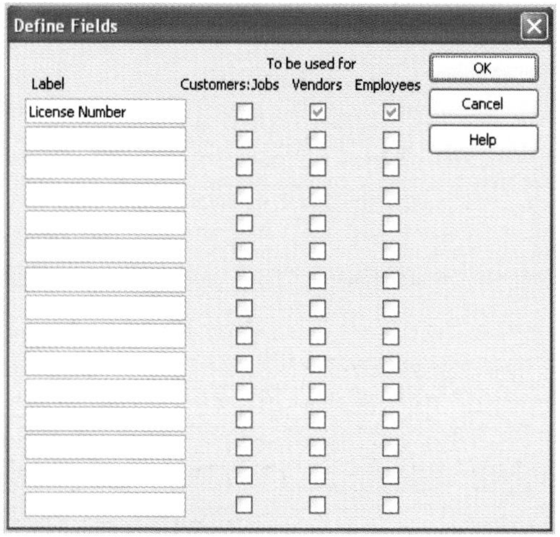

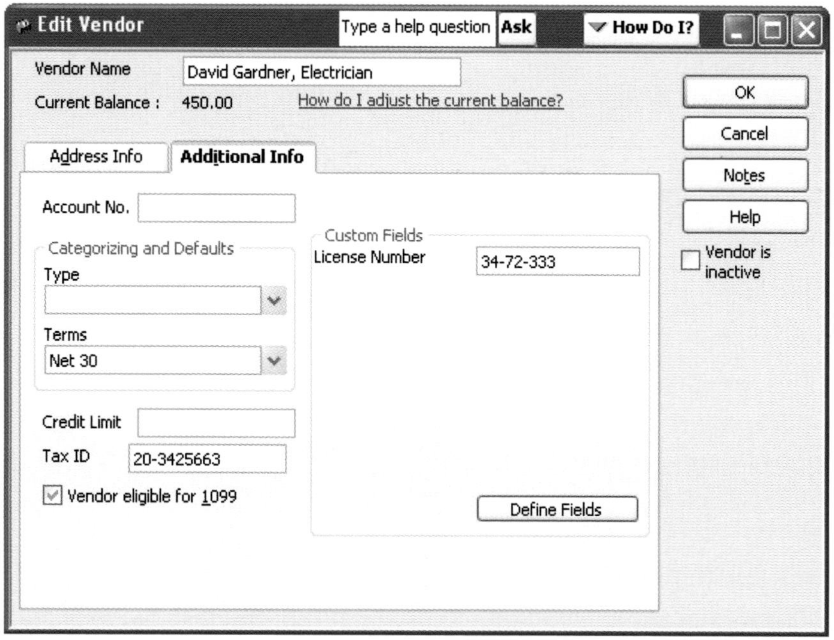

Figure 5-10: Custom fields you create will be added to the Custom Fields area, located on the right side of the window.

Vendor Detail Center

Vendor Detail [Cactus Refreshment Services ▼]   [Centers ▼] [Help]

Contact Information

Edit/More Info

Address:
Cactus Refreshment
Fred Fishman
2328 E. Van Buren Street, Suite ...
Phoenix, AZ 85006

Credit Limit: $1,500.00
Account No.: 09345-34

Contact: Fred Fishman
E-mail: sales@cactusrefreshm...
Phone: (602) 267-7199
FAX: (602) 273-1716

Alt. Contact: Linnea Storm
Alt. Ph.:
Terms: Due on receipt

Decision Tools

To find out about your financial position, click on a link below.

■ Am I borrowing enough money, or too much?

...More Decision Tools

Show: ▼ **Payments Issued**
▼ All   Activities ▼

Transaction	Date	Amount Paid
Check #2	02/09/2005	$54.62
Total		**$54.62**

Show: ▼ **Bills I Haven't Paid**
▼ All   Activities ▼

Transaction	Due Date	Bal. Due
Bill #52642	02/19/2005	$54.62
Total		**$54.62**

Figure 5-11: The Vendor Detail Center provides you with an overview of all vendor-related information.

NOTE

The cash-based method should be used if you are running your business on a cash basis. If you pay your bills using QuickBooks before actually writing the checks, then use the accrual-based method.

Use the Vendor Detail Center

The Vendor Detail Center gives you an overview of your vendor information, including a quick means of seeing pending bills and payments.

To access the Vendor Detail Center:

1. Click the **Vendors** menu and click **Vendor Detail Center**. The Vendor Detail Center is displayed, as shown in Figure 5-11.

2. Click the down arrow at the top of the screen to choose a different vendor.

Pay Bills

With QuickBooks, you can pay your bills in one of two ways, depending on if you use the cash-based method of accounting or the accrual-based method of accounting (see Chapter 2). With the cash-based method, you receive a bill and write a check for it immediately using QuickBooks. With the accrual-based method of accounting, you receive a bill, enter it in QuickBooks, pay the bill, and then write the check for the bill.

Butterfly Books is set up using the accrual-based method because there are multiple employees and the owner wants to have one person enter the bills, but she will be the person who actually writes the checks.

WRITING CHECKS

You can write checks for your business at any time, but set the To Be Printed date or Online Payment date for a period of time before it is due—for example, five to seven business days—to allow for mail delivery and processing. If you handwrite checks, you can still use this process as a reminder to write checks by looking at the Checks To Be Printed list in the Reminders list. (See Chapter 8 for more information.)

To write checks (see Chapter 4 for more information):

1. Click the **Check** icon on the icon bar. The Write Checks window opens. Confirm that you are in the correct account from which to write a check.

2. Press the **TAB** key to move to the Number line. If you are handwriting a check, type the check number. If you are going to print the check or send it online, click the **To Be Printed** or **Online Payment** check boxes.

3. Click in the **Date** line, and type a date that is five to seven days prior to the bill's due date. (Alternatively, you can click the **calendar** icon and select the date from the drop-down calendar.)

4. Click in the **Pay To The Order Of** line, and type the vendor's name.

5. Press the **TAB** key to move to the Amount line, and type the amount to be paid.

6. Click the down arrow under the Account column (in the bottom portion of the screen), and click the relevant account.

7. Click the **Save & Close** button.

Enter and Pay Bills

Although entering bills and then paying them in QuickBooks is a multistep process, it is the best way to accurately track your expenses. In addition to providing a separate date for the date the expense was incurred and the date the expense was paid, QuickBooks warns you if a bill for the same vendor and reference number has already been entered, which will help you avoid duplicate payments.

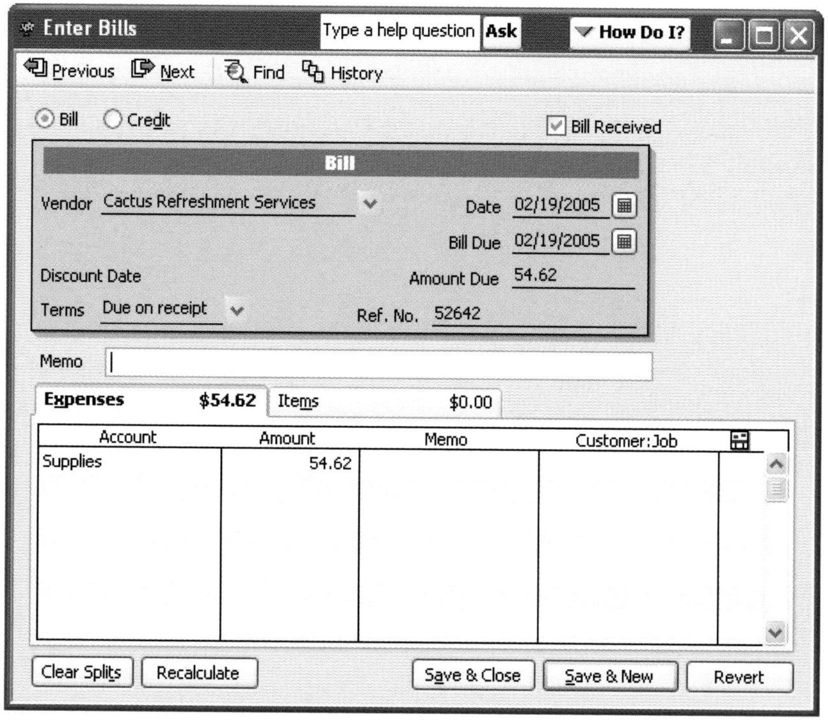

Figure 5-12: From the Enter Bills window, you can enter bills now and pay them later.

ENTER BILLS

To enter bills in QuickBooks:

1. Click the **Vendors** menu and click **Enter Bills**. The Enter Bills window opens, as shown in Figure 5-12.

2. In the purple bill area, click in the **Vendor** line, and type the vendor's name.

3. Press the **TAB** key to move to the Date line. Confirm or type the date you received the bill. (QuickBooks automatically enters today's date by default.)

4. Press the **TAB** key to move to the Bill Due line. QuickBooks automatically calculates the expected due date based on the vendor terms indicated when you added this vendor to your Vendor List. If you need a different date, type it, or click the **calendar** icon and select a date.

5. Press the **TAB** key to move to the Amount Due line, and type the amount.

6. Press the **TAB** key to move to the Terms line, which is automatically filled in for you based on the vendor terms indicated when you added this vendor to your Vendor List. If you change this line, your due date will change accordingly. When you are finished with this bill, QuickBooks asks you if you want to save any changes made to the Terms line.

7. Press the **TAB** key to move to the Reference Number line, and type the invoice number on the billing statement you received (if applicable).

8. Press the **TAB** key twice to move to the Account column, and type the name of the relevant expense account.

9. Click the **Save & Close** button.

TIP

Pay attention to the dates you use when you enter transactions, as those dates will be used to determine when an expense is reflected in your reports. It's better to have a monthly bill of $50 for a recurring expense than to have one month with an expense of $100 and another month with an expense in the same category of $0.

PAY BILLS

To pay bills in QuickBooks:

1. Click the **Vendors** menu and click **Pay Bills**. The Pay Bills window opens, as shown in Figure 5-13.

2. Click the **Show All Bills** option to see a complete list of your pending bills.

3. Click in the column to the left of the Date Due column (designated by a check mark) next to each bill you want to pay. A check mark is displayed next to each bill's due date.

4. In the Payment Method area at the bottom of the window, click the **Payment Method** down arrow, and click **Check**. Click the **To Be Printed** option.

5. Confirm that the date in the Payment Date field allows enough time for the check to arrive by the due date. Change it if necessary.

6. Click the **Pay & Close** button.

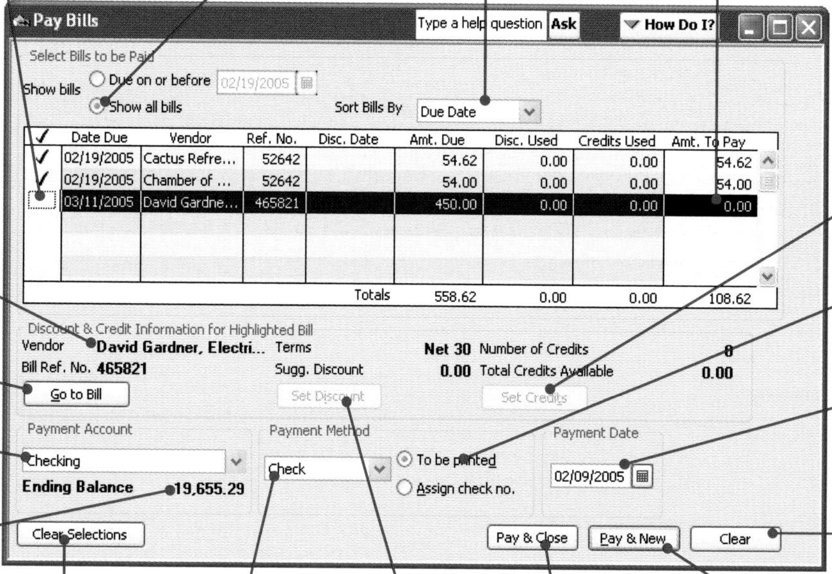

Figure 5-13: The Pay Bills window in QuickBooks presents you with a variety of options when it comes to paying your bills.

Click to insert a check mark next to a bill, indicating it is to be paid

Click to see all bills

Select the order in which bills are sorted

Type the amount of the bill to be paid if different from the default amount

Vendor details for a selected bill

Click to see notes regarding a selected bill

Select the account from which to pay bills

The ending balance of the currently selected bank account changes as bills are selected

Click to apply credits

Choose whether to print your checks or handwrite them (and have QuickBooks assign a check number)

Type the payment date on which checks will be issued

Click to clear all selections and start again

Click to clear bill selections; click again to select all bills

Select a method to pay bills

Click to enter a vendor discount

Click when finished paying bills

Click to pay additional bills using different methods or due dates

Use Cost of Goods Sold Accounts

Cost of Goods Sold accounts are associated with things you purchase for resale, such as books, coffee, and snacks (as is the case with Butterfly Books and Bytes). An important aspect in tracking Cost of Goods Sold accounts is making sure the client gets charged for items purchased specifically on his or her behalf. For example, Butterfly Books and Bytes has ordered and purchased a book at a customer's request (purchase orders and inventory will be discussed in Chapter 7). This item has been received and needs to be entered as a bill and an invoice sent to the customer. In Chapter 3, reimbursements entered directly to accounts was explained. This section will cover creating items associated with Cost of Goods Sold accounts and reimbursements entered using those items.

TIP

You can add a Pay Bills icon to the icon bar for easy access in the future (see Chapter 1).

TIP

Don't pay bills without first confirming their accuracy. Have all bills filed after entry and available for periodic review.

Create Items with Purchase Information

Any charge that will be used on an invoice needs to be set up as an "item" in the Item list that has both income and Cost of Goods (or expense) accounts associated with it. By using items instead of directly using an account, you will be generating transactions that are tied both to the items and to the specific accounts with which they are associated. This helps produce reports on two levels: the account reports provide a high level of information, and the item reports provide a detailed level of information.

To enter items purchased for a specific job:

1. Click the **Item** icon on the icon bar. The Item list is displayed, as shown in Figure 5-14.

Item

Figure 5-14: Items are listed with their associated income accounts but can be set up to be associated with an expense or Cost of Goods Sold account as well.

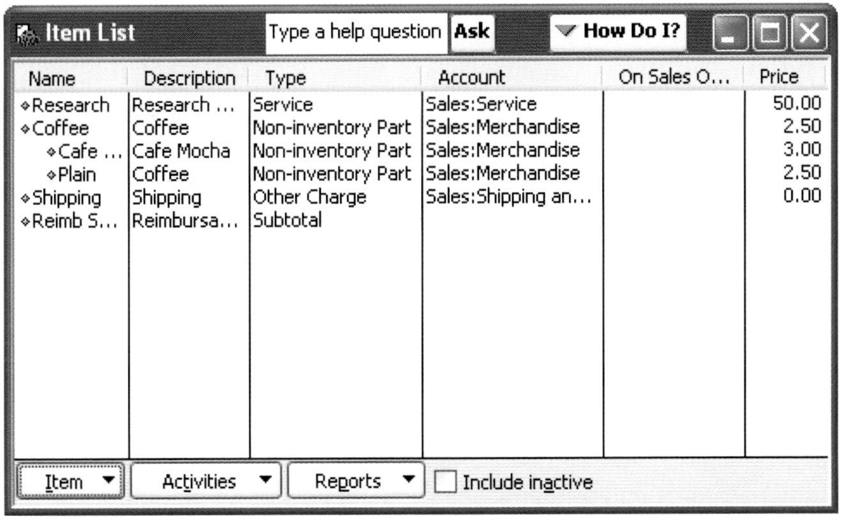

Item List
Type a help question
Ask
How Do I?
Name
Description
Type
Account
On Sales O...
Price
Research | Research ... | Service | Sales:Service | 50.00
Coffee | Coffee | Non-inventory Part | Sales:Merchandise | 2.50
Cafe ... | Cafe Mocha | Non-inventory Part | Sales:Merchandise | 3.00
Plain | Coffee | Non-inventory Part | Sales:Merchandise | 2.50
Shipping | Shipping | Other Charge | Sales:Shipping an... | 0.00
Reimb S... | Reimbursa... | Subtotal
Item
Activities
Reports
Include inactive

TIP

The Cost and Sales Price fields can be edited each time you use an item. If you have a standard cost, type it now. For special-order items, leave both amounts blank as a reminder that they need to be filled in.

CAUTION

QuickBooks requires all item entries to be associated with an account in the Chart of Accounts in order to have accurate accounting and reporting.

2. From the Item list, click the **Item** menu and click **New**. The New Item window opens, as shown in Figure 5-15.
3. Click the **Type** down arrow, and click **Non-Inventory Part**. You can also associate services or other charge items with a Cost of Goods or expense account.
4. Press the **TAB** key to move to the Item Name/Number field. Type a name for the item, for example, Book Order.
5. Click the **This Item Is Purchased For And Sold To A Specific Customer:Job** check box. The New Item window expands to include purchase information as well as sales information.
6. Click in the **Description On Purchase Transactions** field, and type a relevant description, for example, Special Order Books. This information will appear on purchase orders.
7. Press the **TAB** key to move to the Cost field. Whatever you typed in the Description On Purchase Transactions field will appear in the Description On Sales Transactions field (located to the right). This information will appear on sales orders and invoices. You can type a cost or leave it blank if you will be entering a different cost each time.
8. Press the **TAB** key to move to the Expense Account field. Click the down arrow and click an account type. **Purchases** is often selected since it's a Cost of Goods account. Completing the Preferred Vendor field is optional.
9. Click the **Income Account** down arrow, and click a relevant account. Merchandise, for example, is a subaccount of Sales.
10. Click **OK** to save the item and return to the Item list. Click the **Close** button (the X in the upper-right corner) to close the Item list.

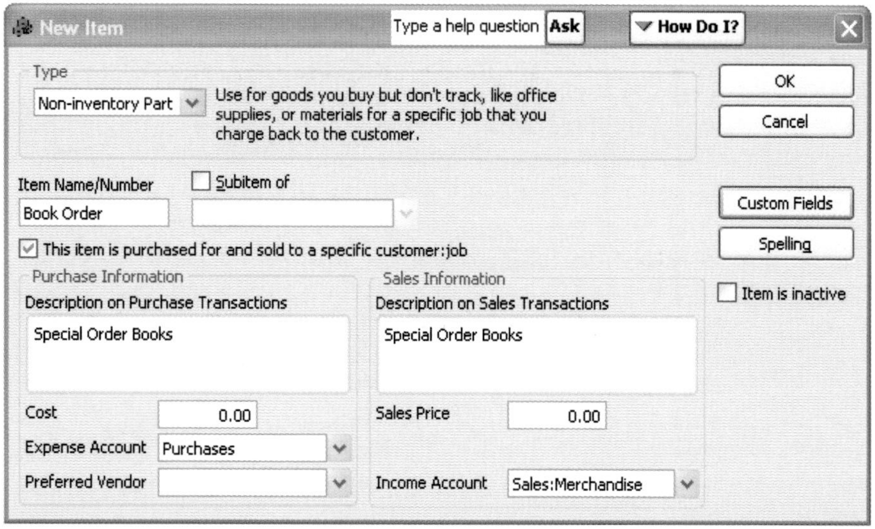

Figure 5-15: Use the New Item window to create an item that is often billed to clients.

TIP

If QuickBooks prompts you to add the vendor name and item name to the relevant lists, do so by clicking **Quick Add** and following the steps in the section "Add a Vendor Using Quick Add."

TIP

If you don't see the item you wish to enter, make sure you are on the Items tab and not on the Expenses tab.

Figure 5-16: Be sure the Items tab is active if you want to enter items in the Enter Bills window.

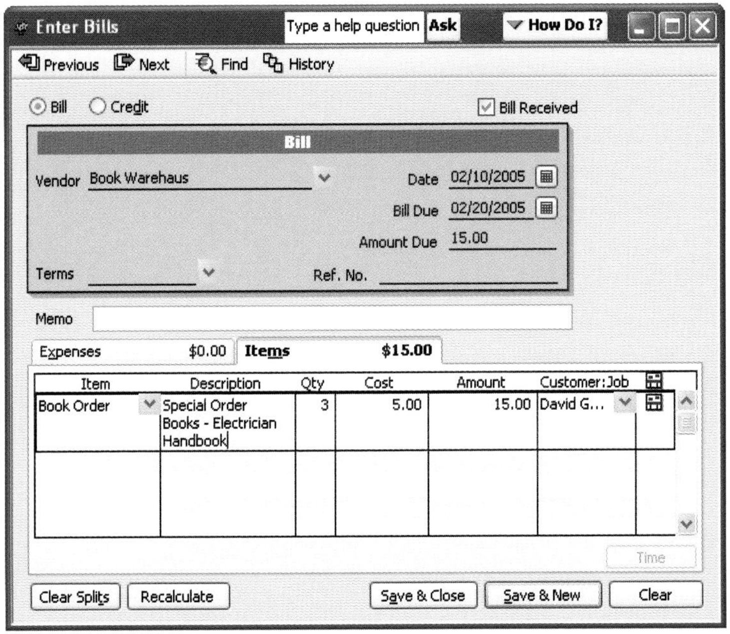

Use Items on a Bill

At the bottom of the Write Checks and Enter Bills windows are two tabs: Expenses and Items. Earlier in this chapter, a bill was entered using the Expenses tab to directly associate the bill with a specific expense. When creating a chargeback for an item, you should use the Items tab to enter the item (which is still associated with an account, as you saw in the previous section). This is especially important for companies that use job costing reports, as it will compare the cost of items to the sale price of items, but only if they are set up as items and then used when entering bills.

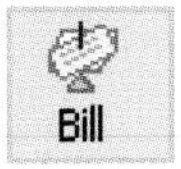

1. Click the **Bill** icon on the icon bar. The Enter Bills window opens (see Figure 5-16).
2. Click in the **Vendor** field, and type the vendor's name, for example, Book Warehaus.
3. Click the **Items** tab, located at the bottom of the Enter Bills window.
4. Click in the **Item** column, and type the item name, for example, Book Order. (Alternately, you can click the down arrow and click the item from the drop-down list if you have already entered it into QuickBooks.)
5. Click in the **Description** column, and type a relevant note.
6. Press the **TAB** key to move to the Quantity column, and type the number of items.
7. Press the **TAB** key to move to the Cost column, and type the amount.
8. Press the **TAB** key twice to move to the Customer:Job column. Type the customer's name. QuickBooks calculates the amount due and populates it in the Amount column and in the Amount Due line in the purple check area. Note the icon in the rightmost column. This is a billing icon that indicates this item is billable to this customer. Click the icon to mark it with an X if you are not going to charge the client for this item.
9. Click the **Save & Close** button when finished. The transaction is entered and the window closes.

Memorize Transactions

Whenever you have a recurring transaction, such as a monthly bill or an invoice, you can have QuickBooks *memorize* it and give you a reminder regarding the transaction, make it available to you when needed, or automatically enter the transaction on a regular basis.

Memorize Reminder Transactions

Each time you enter a bill or write a check, consider whether you will need to perform this task on a recurring basis. If so, memorize this transaction. If it's a fixed amount, such as a rental payment, you can have QuickBooks automatically enter the amount. If it's a variable amount, such as your electric or water bill, you can configure the memorized transaction so that QuickBooks reminds you of the transaction and you can enter the correct amount before recording the transaction.

1. Click the **Bill** icon on the icon bar. The Enter Bills window opens.

2. Enter the bill according to the steps outlined in the previous section "Enter and Pay Bills."

3. Click the **Edit** menu and click **Memorize Bill**. The Memorize Transaction window opens with the vendor's name already in the Name field.

4. Click the **Remind Me** option.

5. Click the **How Often** down arrow, and click the frequency with which you must pay this bill, such as **Monthly**.

6. Click in the **Next Date** field, and type the next date you want to be reminded of this bill. (Alternately, you can click the **calendar** icon and select the date from the drop-down calendar.) Click **OK**. The Memorize Transaction window closes, and QuickBooks memorizes your bill. You are returned to the Enter Bills window.

7. Click the **Save & Close** button in the Enter Bills window.

TIP

This section covers memorizing bills, but you can memorize any type of transaction, such as invoices, transfers, and checks.

Memorize Automatic Transactions

You can have QuickBooks automatically enter checks, bills, or invoices, but make sure the information is accurate.

1. Click the **Check** icon on the icon bar. The Write Checks window opens.
2. Write the check according to the steps outlined in Chapter 4.
3. Click the **Edit** menu and click **Memorize Check**. The Schedule Memorized Transaction window opens.
4. Type a name for this transaction in the Name field, for example, <u>Bank Service Charge</u>.
5. Click the **Automatically Enter** option.
6. Click the **How Often** down arrow, and click **Monthly**.
7. Click in the **Next Date** field, and type a date that is a month away from the bill's current due date. (Alternately, you can click the **calendar** icon, and select the date from the drop-down calendar.)
8. Leave the **Number Remaining** field blank, indicating to QuickBooks that this transaction cycle will never end. (If this were a recurring loan payment, however, you could type the number of payments.) Leave the **Days In Advance To Enter** field at 0 since this is an automatic transaction.
9. Click **OK** when finished.

TIP

When filling in the Days In Advance To Enter field for automatic transactions, consider whether you need to write and mail a check, if it is an online transaction, or if it is automatically deducted from your account.

Manage Memorized Transactions

Every time you memorize a transaction, it is added to the Memorized Transaction list. Review and manage your memorized transactions as often as needed. You can add the Memorized Transaction list to your icon bar if you will be using it on a regular basis (see Chapter 1).

EDIT MEMORIZED TRANSACTIONS

To edit a memorized transaction:

1. Click the **Lists** menu and click **Memorized Transaction List**. The Memorized Transaction list is displayed.
2. Click the memorized transaction you want to edit.

3. Click the **Memorized Transaction** menu button (located at the bottom of the window), and click **Edit Transaction**. The Schedule Memorized Transaction window opens.

4. Click the **Don't Remind Me** option. All other related choices become unavailable.

5. Click **OK**. The changes are saved and the Memorized Transaction list is updated.

GROUP MEMORIZED TRANSACTIONS

You can add groups to your Memorized Transaction list and then add memorized transactions to the groups (see "Move Memorized Transactions").

1. Click the **Lists** menu and click **Memorized Transaction List**. The Memorized Transaction list is displayed.

2. Click the **Memorized Transaction** menu button (located at the bottom of the window), and click **New Group**. The New Memorized Transaction Group window opens.

3. Click in the **Name** field, and type a name for the group, for example, <u>Monthly Bills</u>.

4. Click the **Remind Me** option.

5. Click the **How Often** down arrow, and click **Monthly**.

6. Click in the **Next Date** field, and type the date of the first day in the next month.

7. Click **OK**. The group appears in the Memorized Transaction list; however, at this point the group doesn't contain any transactions. You need to move them to the relevant group.

MOVE MEMORIZED TRANSACTIONS

To move memorized transactions to a group:

1. Click the **Lists** menu and click **Memorized Transaction List**. The Memorized Transaction list is displayed.

2. Move your cursor over the **diamond** icon located to the left of the transaction you want to move. The cursor changes to a four-headed arrow.

3. Drag the transaction to the group of which you want it to be a part, for example, Monthly Bills. A reminder for this transaction will appear every month as part of the Monthly Bills group.

4. Click the **Close** button to close the Memorized Transaction list.

Chapter 6

Selling Products and Services

The QuickBooks customer and accounts receivable (A/R) features include professional invoices and sales receipts, easy tracking of customer accounts, and customer letter templates (see Chapter 8). Items purchased for customers can be added directly to invoices, as can time tracked (see Chapter 9). Estimates created in QuickBooks can be turned into progressive invoices, standard invoices, or sales receipts. You can e-mail, fax, or mail estimates, invoices, and statements to customers, as well as check your business's health with accurate customer, sales, and job-costing reports. Payments can also be received against invoices and deposited. This chapter will cover managing customers, invoicing, receiving payments, and collecting sales tax.

Manage Customers and Jobs

The Customer:Job list tracks information and records regarding your customers—anyone to whom you sell items or services. Jobs are subcategories of customers and can be used for individual projects or departments related to a customer.

Use the Customer Navigator

The Customer Navigator (seen in Figure 6-1) shows options for selling items to a customer and then depositing the money. The first step is to create a sales receipt or an invoice. *Sales receipts* are used when payment is received in full at the time of purchase and goes directly into a deposit.

To open the Customer Navigator:

Click the **Customers** menu. Click **Customer Navigator**.

To close the Customer Navigator:

Click the **Close** button (the X in the upper-right corner).

Opens the Create Estimates window

Opens the Create Invoices window

Opens the Credit Check window

Related Activities help you add, track, and communicate with customers

Opens the Create Sales Orders window (only available in Premier edition)

Opens the Create Sales Receipt window

Opens the Customer: Job List

Opens the Item list

Opens the Customer Manager (if installed on your computer)

Memorized Reports list specific reports to help you track your accounts receivable

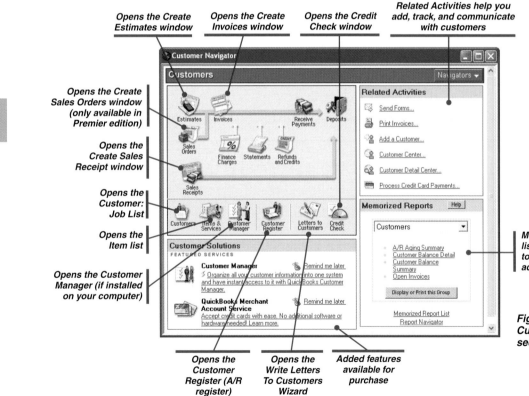

Opens the Customer Register (A/R register)

Opens the Write Letters To Customers Wizard

Added features available for purchase

Figure 6-1: Click any item in the Customer Navigator to see that section of accounts receivable.

The Sales Orders feature is only available in Premier and Enterprise editions of QuickBooks. This feature can be used to track out-of-stock items that customers have requested and are turned into invoices or sales receipts upon receipt of the ordered items.

TIP

The Item list is important to both accounts receivable and accounts payable, as the items are used for job-costing purposes and can be linked to income and expense accounts.

Figure 6-2: From the Customer:Job List, you can add, edit, or otherwise work with your customer information.

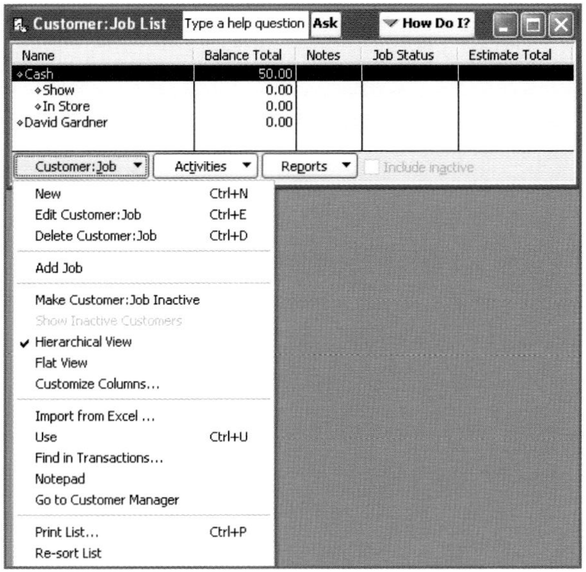

Customer:Job List	Type a help question	Ask	▼ How Do I?	_ □ ☒
Name	**Balance Total**	**Notes**	**Job Status**	**Estimate Total**
◆Cash	50.00			
◆Show	0.00			
◆In Store	0.00			
◆David Gardner	0.00			

Customer:Job ▼	Activities ▼	Reports ▼	☐ Include inactive

New	Ctrl+N
Edit Customer:Job	Ctrl+E
Delete Customer:Job	Ctrl+D
Add Job	
Make Customer:Job Inactive	
Show Inactive Customers	
✓ Hierarchical View	
Flat View	
Customize Columns...	
Import from Excel...	
Use	Ctrl+U
Find in Transactions...	
Notepad	
Go to Customer Manager	
Print List...	Ctrl+P
Re-sort List	

Invoices are used when partial payment or no payment is received at the time of a sale or when services are performed. Invoices can have finance charges or early-payment discounts applied to them, as well as any refunds or credits the customer has outstanding. Statements can be generated to indicate current customer standings. When payments are received, the Receive Payments window is used to apply funds to outstanding invoices. Estimates can also be used to create invoices.

Sales-related information can be quickly accessed in the Customer Navigator through the available links: Customer:Job List, Item list, and Customer Manager (a separate contact-management program that links to QuickBooks).

Clicking the **Customer Register** icon opens a list of transactions, similar to a check register, from which you can select a customer and view all related transactions, sorted in any manner. Clicking the **Letters To Customers** icon opens a wizard that offers a variety of letter templates, including collections (see Chapter 8 for more information).

Clicking the **Credit Check** icon opens a window that allows you to look up a customer's commercial address and verify it (for free) or pull a full credit report (for a fee).

Commonly related activities and reports are listed on the right side of the Customer Navigator. Click each to see the window or report.

Edit Customers in the Customer:Job List

The Customer:Job List is one of the four name lists in QuickBooks, the others being Vendor, Employee, and Others. Adding customers was covered in Chapter 3. Once entered, you can easily edit customers from the Customer:Job List.

The two customers entered using the Quick Add feature for our sample company (Butterfly Books and Bytes) are Cash and David Gardner (see Chapter 3). Cash also has two jobs associated with it, Show and In Store, to indicate where a sale took place. As you continue in your business, this list will expand.

1 2 3 4 5 6 7 8 9 10

TIP

Be consistent in naming your customers. A small business may use the format First Name, Last Name, but a large business that has many employees using QuickBooks should use Last Name, First Name; phone number; or whatever field is easiest to quickly look up.

TIP

Press the **ESC** key instead of clicking the Close button (the X in the upper-right corner) to close any window *without* saving your changes.

EDIT A CUSTOMER IN THE CUSTOMER:JOB LIST

To edit a customer:

1. Click the **Customers** menu. Click **Customer:Job List**.
2. Click the customer you wish to edit, for example, **David Gardner**.
3. Click the **Customer:Job** menu button (located at the bottom of the Customer:Job List).
4. Click **Edit**. The Edit Customer window, as shown in Figure 6-3, opens with the Customer Name field highlighted. Type Gardner, David in this field, replacing the previous entry of "David Gardner."
5. Click **OK** when you are finished making changes.

ADD A NOTE AND A TO DO ITEM TO A CUSTOMER

The Edit Customer window gives you the option of adding notes about a customer. You can use the Notes button, shown in Figure 6-3, to store customer preferences or additional information. You can also create a To Do item regarding a particular customer; for example, you might create a To Do item reminding you to place an order for a customer.

To add a Note item and a To Do item regarding a customer:

1. Click the **Customers** menu. Click **Customer:Job List**.
2. Double-click the customer you want to add a note to, for example, **Gardner, David**.

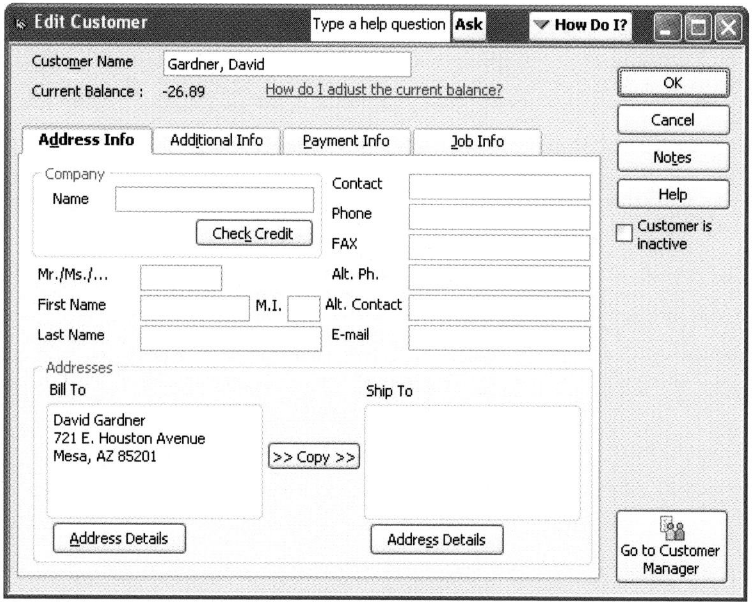

Figure 6-3: The Edit Customer window is similar to the New Customer window, but includes a Notes button and a current balance.

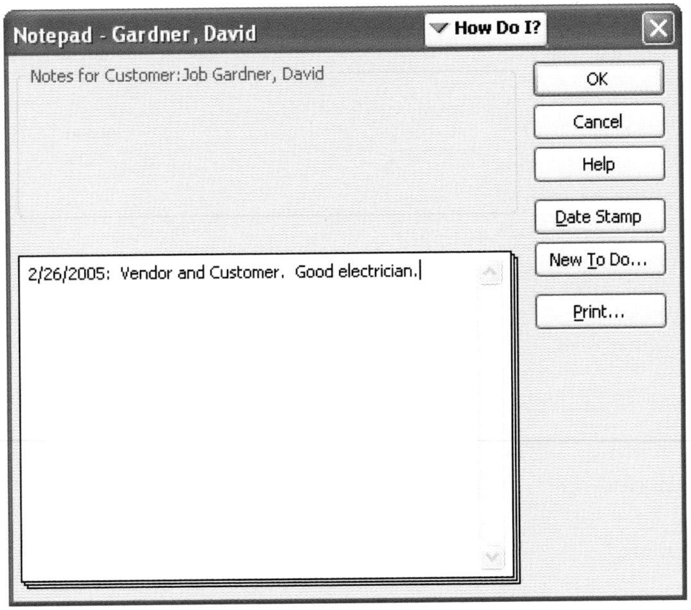

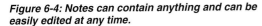
Notepad - Gardner, David

Notes for Customer:Job Gardner, David

OK
Cancel
Help
Date Stamp
New To Do...
Print...

2/26/2005: Vendor and Customer. Good electrician.|

Figure 6-4: Notes can contain anything and can be easily edited at any time.

3. Click the **Notes** button. The Notes window opens, as shown in Figure 6-4.

4. Click the **Date Stamp** button, and QuickBooks automatically enters today's date within the Note area.

5. Type your note, for example, Vendor and Customer. Good electrician.

6. Click the **New To Do** button. A New To Do window opens.

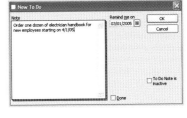

7. Type a reminder.

8. Verify the reminder date.

9. Click **OK** to close the New To Do window.

10. Click **OK** to close the Notes window.

11. Press the **ESC** key on your keyboard to close the Edit Customer window. You will see a note icon displayed in the Notes column next to the customer in the Customer: Job List.

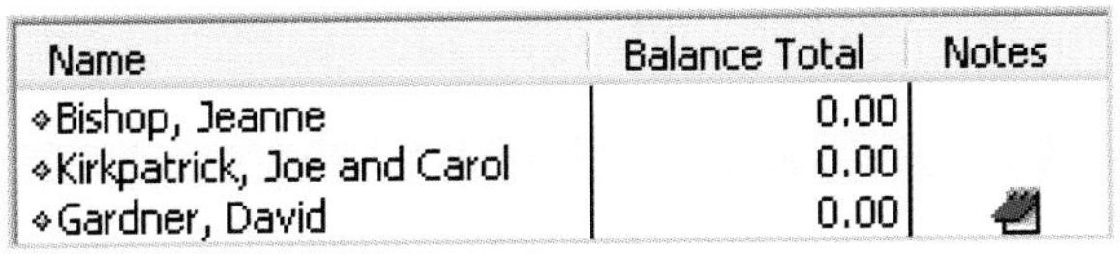

Name	Balance Total	Notes
◆Bishop, Jeanne	0.00	
◆Kirkpatrick, Joe and Carol	0.00	
◆Gardner, David	0.00	📝

CUSTOMER:JOB TABS

The Customer:Job window contains the following four tabs:

1. The **Address Info** tab includes such information as a shipping and mailing address, the ability to add Notes and To Do items, a link to the Customer Manager (if installed on your computer), and a link to a credit-check feature.

2. The **Additional Info** tab includes the following fields:

   - **Customer Type** allows you to create types, thereby classifying your customers in any way that is useful for you.

   - **Customer Terms** allows you to include payment terms. Standard terms, such as due on receipt, net 30, and net 60, are already set up, or you can create custom terms as needed.

   - **Rep** assigns a company representative, who can be either an employee or a subcontractor, to a customer.

TIP

You can double-click any name in a list to open an edit window.

CAUTION

If you collect credit card information for recurring charges, be extra cautious with your user name and password access in QuickBooks.

Preferred Send Method lets you keep track of whether a customer will accept e-mailed invoices or prefers them sent by regular mail.

Sales Tax Info gives the option of identifying a customer as taxable or non-taxable, as well as a place to enter a reseller or nonprofit tax-exempt number.

Price Level can be created to increase or decrease standard item prices, either on an individual basis or a flat percentage increase or decrease for all items.

Custom fields can be created here as well (see Chapter 5 for an example of how this was done for a vendor).

Aliases allow you to create an additional name by which a customer may be recognized.

3. The **Payment Info** tab includes such things as your customer's account number and credit limit, as well as his or her preferred payment method and credit card information.

4. The **Job Info** tab includes such information as job status, start date, projected end date, actual end date, job description, and job type.

NOTE

Sales receipts do not appear in the Customer Detail Center.

Use the Customer Detail Center

One of the options in the Customer Navigator is the Customer Detail Center, shown in Figure 6-5. This feature gives you an overview of your customer's information, including a quick way to see outstanding invoices and payments, which can be a convenient way to look up information quickly when a payment is in dispute.

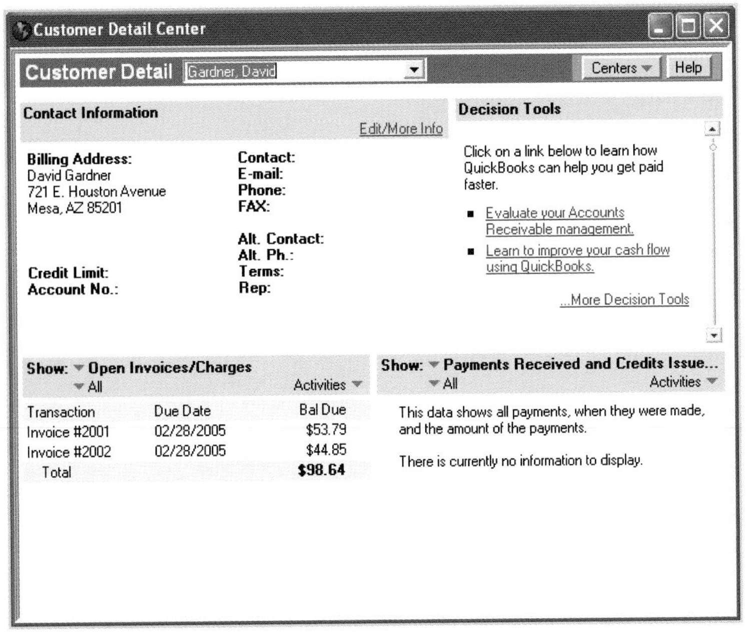

Figure 6-5: This customer has outstanding invoices but has not made any payments.

TIP

If you have multiple business locations in different taxable areas, create a tax item for each taxable area (like a city), and create a matching tax group for each taxable area.

To view the Customer Detail Center:

1. Click the **Customers** menu. Click **Customer Detail Center**. The Customer Detail Center is displayed.

2. Click the **Customer Detail** down arrow (located at the top of the screen) to choose a different customer.

3. Close the Customer Detail Center by clicking the **Close** button.

Track Sales in QuickBooks

Sales are entered using invoices and sales receipts. In order to enter sales, you need to have items to sell. You can use the Quick Add feature to add items as you need them, but it's more accurate to set up items beforehand so that you can be consistent in your data entry. You will also need to set up tax items if you collect taxes. Items and inventory will be covered in more detail in Chapter 7. (See Chapter 3 for information on setting up a non-inventory item.)

Set Up Sales Tax Items

Selling items normally involves collecting taxes. You may need to collect a combination of different taxes that are payable to different tax entities. This section will show you how to set up individual sales tax items and then combine them into sales tax groups, which you will then apply to your invoices and sales receipts.

In our example, Butterfly Books and Bytes must collect a total tax rate of 7.8 percent, the combination of the following three taxes: the city of Mesa (1.5 percent), the state of Arizona (5.6 percent), and Maricopa County (0.7 percent). Research your location to understand what is taxable and to whom the taxes are payable. Make a list and then create the appropriate tax items and groups in the Item list.

NOTE

Some areas may have unusual rules, for example, a state may not charge sales tax for a specific category of items but the county or city does, so a separate sales tax group will need to be set up for that situation.

ACTIVATE SALES TAX IN PREFERENCES

Before you can create a sales tax item, you must activate this feature in QuickBooks.

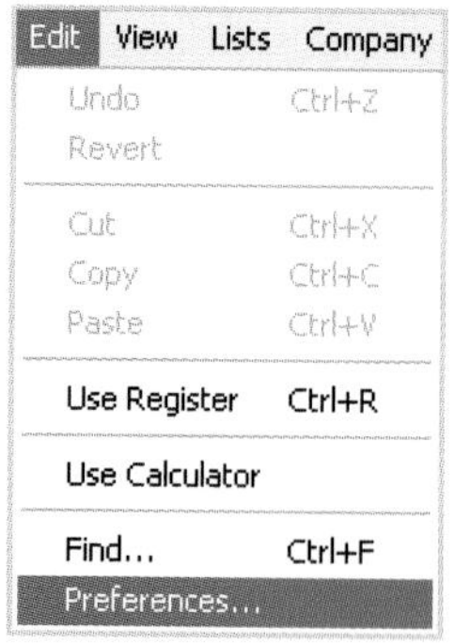

Edit	View	Lists	Company
Undo			Ctrl+Z
Revert			
Cut			Ctrl+X
Copy			Ctrl+C
Paste			Ctrl+V
Use Register			Ctrl+R
Use Calculator			
Find...			Ctrl+F
Preferences...			

1. Click the **Edit** menu and click **Preferences**. The Preferences window opens, as shown in Figure 6-6.

2. Scroll down through the list on the left, and click **Sales Tax**.

3. Click the **Company Preferences** tab.

4. Click **Yes** in the Do You Charge Sales Tax? area. All of the other items on this tab will become available.

5. Click the **Most Common Sales Tax** down arrow. Click **Add New**. The New Item window opens with **Sales Tax Item** selected by default.

6. Press the **TAB** key to move to the Tax Name field. Type the name of the tax, for example, Mesa City Tax.

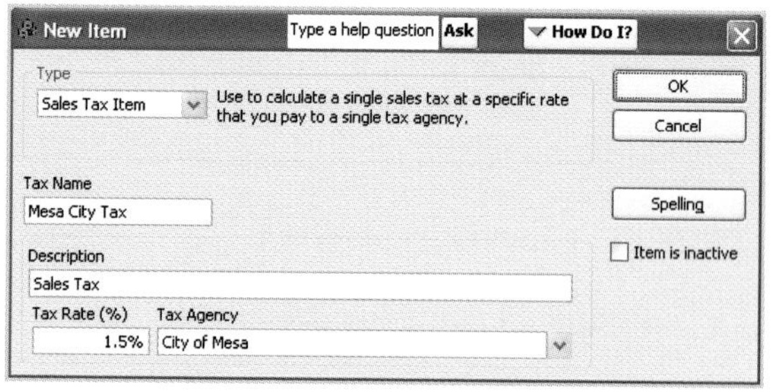

7. Press the **TAB** key to move to the Description field. The words "Sales Tax" are there by default. This wording will appear on invoices and sales receipts. You can change this if you prefer.

8. Press the **TAB** key to move to the Tax Rate field. Type the rate for this *single* tax, for example, 1.5.

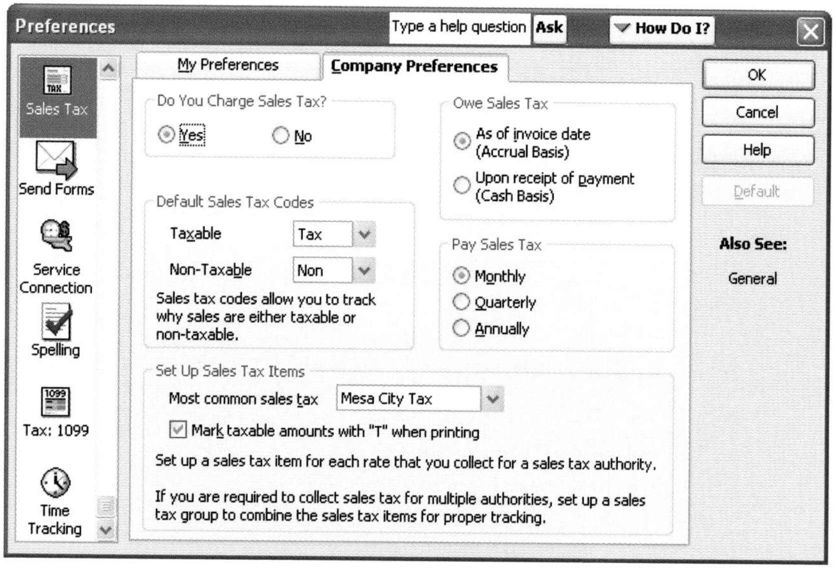

Figure 6-6: You can click different icons in the Preferences window to see more options.

9. Press the **TAB** key to move to the Tax Agency field. Type the agency name, for example, <u>City of Mesa</u>.

10. Press the **TAB** key again. If the Vendor Not Found dialog box appears, click the **Quick Add** button to add this name to your Vendor List.

11. Click **OK** when finished. The New Tax window closes and your item is saved. You are returned to the Preferences window.

12. Click **OK** to save your changes and close the Preferences window. The Updating Sales Tax dialog box appears. Click **Make All Existing Customers Taxable**. Most of your customers will be taxable; you can mark items or customers as non-taxable on an individual basis.

13. Click **OK**. QuickBooks warns you that it needs to close all open windows to make this change.

14. Click **OK**. QuickBooks closes all open windows and makes the change. You can now create additional tax items and tax groups.

CREATE A SALES TAX ITEM

If you have multiple business locations or multiple tax authorities, such as county, city, and state, you will have to collect and pay taxes to multiple agencies. In order to collect multiple taxes (and ensure that you are collecting the correct amounts), you need to enter additional taxes and then group them.

To create an additional sales tax item:

1. Click the **Lists** menu and click **Item List**. The Item list is displayed.

2. Click the **Item** menu button (at the bottom of the screen), and click **New**. The New Item window opens.

3. Click the **Type** down arrow, and click **Sales Tax Item**. Press the **TAB** key to move to the Tax Name field. Type the name of the tax, for example, <u>State of Arizona</u>.

4. Press the **TAB** key to move to the Descrip-tion field. The words "Sales Tax" are there by default. This wording will appear on invoices and sales receipts. You can edit this if you prefer.

NOTE

If your area has only one tax, such as in Maryland, where there are no general local sales taxes, you need only set up a single tax. In many other locations, such as Arizona, you will need to create each single tax and then combine them into a group tax for each area in which you have sales. You then use only the group tax, not the single tax.

TIP

Out-of-state customers are typically not taxable. Some companies create a tax item called Out of State with a zero-percent tax so that they may quickly change the tax item on the invoice instead of individually editing each customer.

TIP

If you have a business such as roofing where you perform work in different locations, you may need to apply the appropriate city tax to each customer. You can mark each customer with the appropriate tax in the Edit Customer window.

5. Press **TAB** to move to the Tax Rate field. Type the rate for this *single* tax, for example, 5.6.

6. Press **TAB** to move to the Tax Agency field. Type the agency name, for example, Arizona Department of Revenue.

7. Press **TAB**. If the Vendor Not Found dialog box appears, click **Quick Add**. You can edit this particular vendor and provide more specific information later if needed.

8. Click the **Next** button. This sales tax item is created and saved, and a New Item window opens. Repeat steps 3-7 to add an additional tax item, for example, Maricopa County tax with a rate of .7 and payable to Maricopa County Department of Revenue.

9. Click **OK** when finished to save your new sales tax items.

CREATE A SALES TAX GROUP

Once you've created the individual tax items for your area, create a tax group to easily apply this group of taxes to each taxable item you sell. This will allow you to show a single tax line on your invoices and sales receipts but track and pay each tax in the tax group individually.

To create a sales tax group:

1. Click the **Lists** menu and click **Item List**. The Item list is displayed.

2. Click the **Item** menu button (located at the bottom of the Item List window), and click **New**. The New Item window opens.

Figure 6-7: A sales tax group is displayed as one tax amount but puts separate amounts into the appropriate accounts of the individual sales tax items of which it is comprised.

Name	Description	Type	Account	On Sales Order	Price
◆Research	Research Services	Service	Sales:Service		50.00
◆Book Order	Special Order Books	Non-inventory Part	Sales:Merchandise		0.00
◆Coffee	Coffee	Non-inventory Part	Sales:Merchandise		2.50
◆Cafe Mocha	Cafe Mocha	Non-inventory Part	Sales:Merchandise		3.00
◆Plain	Coffee	Non-inventory Part	Sales:Merchandise		2.50
◆Maricopa County	Sales Tax	Sales Tax Item	Sales Tax Payable		0.7%
◆Mesa City Tax	Sales Tax	Sales Tax Item	Sales Tax Payable		1.5%
◆State of Arizona	Sales Tax	Sales Tax Item	Sales Tax Payable		5.6%
◆Mesa, Maricopa, State Tax	Sales Tax	Sales Tax Group			7.8%

CHANGING TAX PREFERENCES

Once your tax preferences are set, you may need to mark some items or customers as non-taxable.

MARK ITEMS AS NON-TAXABLE

Once you have activated the Sales Tax feature, tax items will contain a list box where you indicate whether an item should be marked taxable or non-taxable.

To change this setting:

1. Click the **Item** button on the icon bar.
2. Double-click any item, and the Tax Code drop-down list is displayed in the lower-right area.

3. Click the **Tax Code** down arrow, and click **Non-Taxable**.
4. Click **OK**.

MARK CUSTOMERS AS NON-TAXABLE

You may have nonprofit customers or customers with a reseller number that are not required to pay tax. You can modify these customers individually as follows.

1. Click the **Cust** (Customer) button on the icon bar.
2. Double-click an existing customer.
3. Click the **Additional Info** tab. The Tax Code drop-down list is displayed in the lower-left corner in the Sales Tax Information area.
4. Click the **Tax Code** down arrow, and click **Non-Taxable**. The resale number is not required.

3. Click the **Type** down arrow, and click **Sales Tax Group**. Press the **TAB** key to move to the Group Name/Number field. Type the name of the tax group, for example, Mesa, Maricopa, State Tax.

4. Press **TAB** to move to the Description field. The words "Sales Tax" are there by default. This wording will appear on invoices and sales receipts. You can edit this if you prefer.

5. Click in the **Tax Item** column, and a drop-down list will appear, displaying all the tax items you have entered. Click each of the tax items you just created. The total tax will appear at the bottom of the window. Confirm that the total in the Item list is 7.8 percent for the tax group (or whatever the correct total for your tax group is).

6. Click **OK** to save the sales tax group. The New Item window closes, and you are returned to the Item list, where you will see your new tax group included, as shown in Figure 6-7.

Create Invoices

Creating invoices and sales receipts accurately will help you track inventory, know what is selling, and collect your money from your customers.

To create an invoice:

1. Click the **Customers** menu and click **Create Invoices**. The Create Invoices window opens, as seen in Figure 6-8.

2. Click in the **Customer: Job** field, and type your customer's name, for example, Gardner, David. You can also select customers from the drop-down menu, or click the **Quick Add** button to add them if they are a new customer.

3. Press the **TAB** key. A reminder may appear if this customer has outstanding billable time or costs. Click **OK**.

TIP

If a dialog box appears offering a tutorial, as seen here, you can click **Yes** to watch a video. Click **No** if you wish to skip the tutorial at this time. The tutorials are also available in the QuickBooks Learning Center on the Help menu.

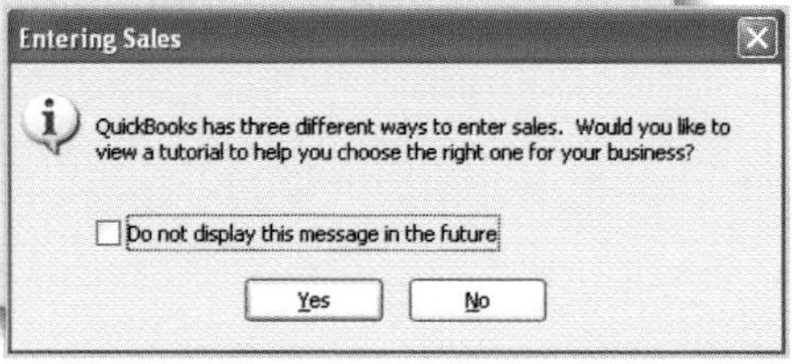

Entering Sales

QuickBooks has three different ways to enter sales. Would you like to view a tutorial to help you choose the right one for your business?

☐ Do not display this message in the future

[Yes] [No]

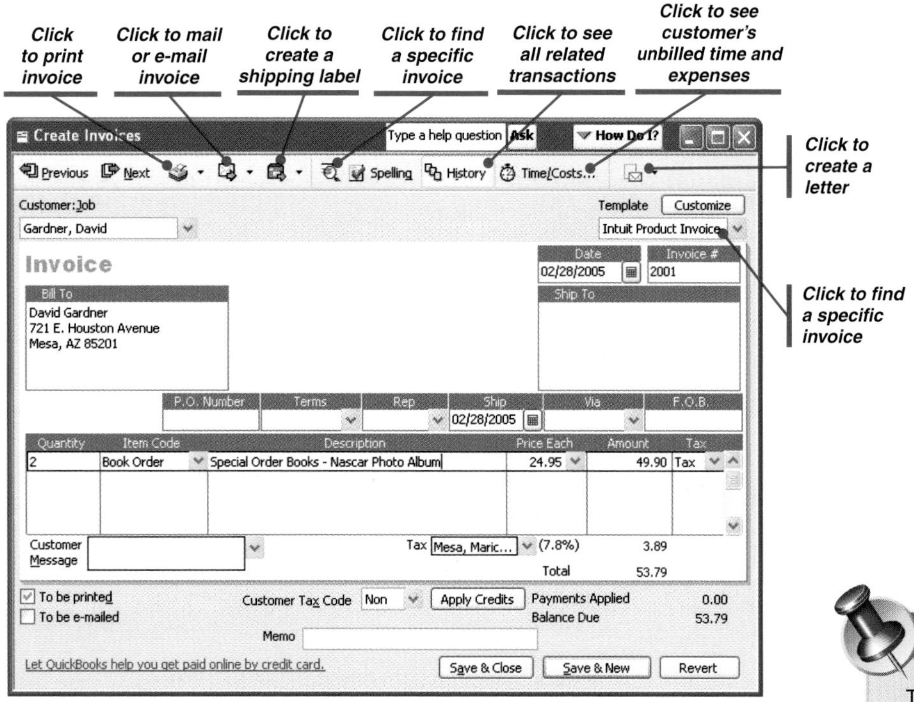

4. Click in the **Date** field to enter the correct date. You can also click the **calendar** icon to choose a date.

5. Press **TAB** to move to the Invoice # field. If this is the first time you've used QuickBooks, your invoice number will be 1. Type <u>2001</u> to start at a higer number. This field will automatically increase by one each time you create a new invoice.

6. Press the **TAB** key to move to the Bill To field. QuickBooks automatically fills in the customer name and any previously provided address information. You may edit this information if you wish.

7. Press the **ENTER** key and type your customer's address, for example, <u>721 E. Houston Avenue</u>.

8. Press **ENTER** and type your customer's city, state, and ZIP code, for example, <u>Mesa, AZ 85201</u>.

9. Press **ENTER** and type your customer's country, if applicable. Press the **TAB** key to move to the Ship To field. This is an optional field, as are PO Number, Terms, Rep, Ship, Via, and F.O.B. If these fields are useful, you may fill them in; however, if they do not apply to your business, you may elect to remove them from your template (see Chapter 8).

10. Click in the **Quantity** field, and type the number of items, for example, <u>2</u>.

Click to print invoice **Click to mail or e-mail invoice** **Click to create a shipping label** **Click to find a specific invoice** **Click to see all related transactions** **Click to see customer's unbilled time and expenses**

Click to create a letter

Click to find a specific invoice

Figure 6-8: Invoices can be customized if you need more or fewer fields than the standard invoice includes.

NOTE

Tax groups allow the customer to see one tax total and you to separately track tax amounts due to each agency.

11. Press the **TAB** key to move to the Item Code field. Type B, and "Book Order" will appear automatically since it is a previously created item.

12. Press **TAB** to move to the Description field. You may see a dialog box regarding tax codes. Click **OK**. Notice that QuickBooks has automatically filled in the Description column (Special Order Books), but this item was set up without a price since each item will be unique.

13. Click at the end of the existing description, and type - Nascar Photo Album.

14. Press the **TAB** key to move to the Price Each column. Type the price for this item, for example, 24.95.

15. Press **TAB** to move to the Amount column. QuickBooks automatically calculates this value for you. A dialog box may appear regarding price levels. Click **OK**.

16. Press **TAB** to move to the Tax column, click the down arrow, and click **Taxable**. (This customer is non-taxable for resale items, but this is a personal item that is not for resale and so can be marked taxable for this area.) The tax appears just above the total amount of the invoice.

17. Confirm that the **To Be Printed** check box is selected (located in the lower-left corner). Click the **Save & Close** button. (If you want to continue entering invoices, click the **Save & New** button.) If you edited the address, as in this example, a dialog box appears, prompting you to confirm the address change. This address will then be corrected in the customer's record and will appear in any future items using this customer.

18. Click **Yes**. The customer's information is updated, and the invoice is saved. You may have a spelling checker open. Click **Close** to cancel the spelling check, or click **Ignore** or **Replace** for each possible error it finds. (You can set your spelling checker preferences by clicking **Edit** and clicking **Preferences**.)

Be sure you accurately enter items and services. If you set up your items correctly and use them correctly on invoices and sales receipts, you will have accurate inventory and sales tracking.

TIP

Once you've viewed a dialog box, if you don't want to continue seeing the same reminder, click the **Do Not Display This Message In The Future** check box.

Edit Invoices

Occasionally you may need to edit an invoice. For example, if you create an invoice based on a customer's phone call and he or she then subsequently changes the order, you will have to correct the original invoice. Click the **Previous** button on the Create Invoice window to return to the invoice (number 2001) you just created.

EDIT A LINE

To edit a line, click in the line anywhere, and make changes as desired. For example, in Invoice 2001:

1. Double-click the word **Nascar** to highlight it. Type <u>NASCAR</u> (all capital letters).
2. Click the **Save & New** button. A dialog box appears, asking if you want to save your changes.
3. Click **Yes**. If the spelling checker appears, click **Close**.

INSERT A LINE

1. Click **NASCAR** to insert a line above this one.
2. Click the **Edit** menu and click **Insert Line**. A new line appears above the currently selected line.
3. Type the quantity for the new line item, for example, <u>2</u>.
4. Press the **TAB** key to move to the Item Code column. Type <u>C</u>, and "Coffee" will appear automatically since it is a previously created item.
5. Press **TAB** to move to the Description column. Notice that Coffee is marked as non-taxable. The tax amount does not change for this invoice as it is only applied to the NASCAR books.
6. Click **Save & New**. A dialog box appears, asking if you want to save your changes.
7. Click **Yes**. If the spelling checker appears, click **Close**.

Edit	View	Lists	Company	Customers
Undo Typing				Ctrl+Z
Revert				
Cut				Ctrl+X
Copy				Ctrl+C
Paste				Ctrl+V
Insert Line				Ctrl+Ins
Delete Line				Ctrl+Del
New Invoice				Ctrl+N
Delete Invoice				Ctrl+D
Memorize Invoice				Ctrl+M
Void Invoice				
Go To Transfer				Ctrl+G
Transaction History...				Ctrl+H
Mark Invoice As Pending				
Use Register				Ctrl+R
Notepad				
Change Account Color...				
Use Calculator				
Find Invoices...				Ctrl+F
Preferences...				

TIP

You can return to a previous invoice and add an item if you have not yet sent it to the customer.

TIP

When your cursor is in the list of items, you have a different list of choices in your Edit menu than when your cursor is in any field in the header (such as the Address field).

DELETE A LINE

To delete a line (still using Invoice 2001 as an example):

1. Click **Coffee** (since this is the line you want to delete).
2. Click the **Edit** menu and click **Delete Line**. The line is immediately deleted; you are not prompted to confirm this action.
3. Click **Save & Close**. A dialog box appears, asking if you want to save your changes.
4. Click **Yes**. If the spelling checker appears, click **Close**.

Charge for Cost of Goods

After purchasing items for a specific customer and marking them as being for that customer, you need to charge the customer for these items on the invoice.

To add a previously purchased item to an invoice:

1. Click the **Customers** menu and click **Create Invoices**. The Create Invoices window opens.
2. Type your customer's name, for example, Gardner, David.
3. Press the TAB key. A reminder may appear if this customer has outstanding billable time or costs.
4. Click **OK**. Confirm the date and customer information. Notice that the invoice number has increased by one from your last invoice entered.
5. Click the **Time/Costs** button located near the top of the invoice. The Choose Billable Time And Costs window opens, as shown in Figure 6-9.
6. Click in the **Use** column to use an item in this list on the current invoice. A check mark will appear in this column.
7. Click **OK**. The Billable Time And Costs window closes. You are returned to the Create Invoices window.

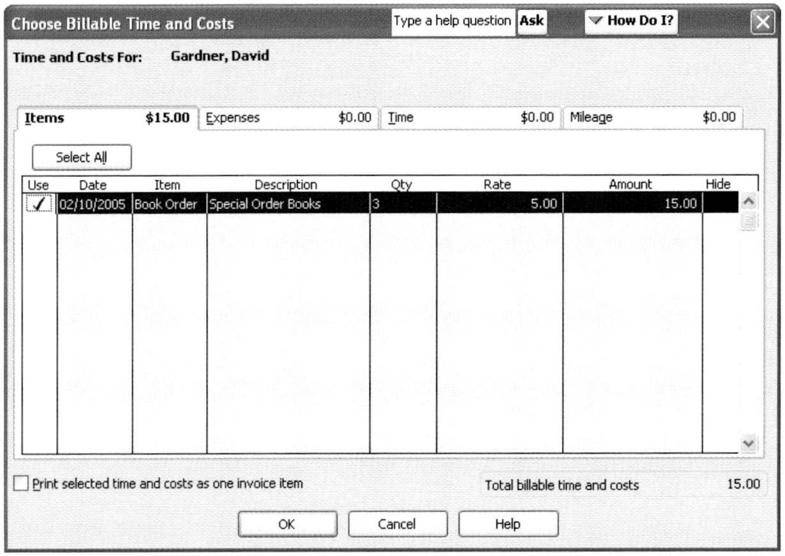

Figure 6-9: Use QuickBooks to track and charge items, expenses, time, or mileage back to your customers.

1 2 3 4 5 6 7 8 9 10

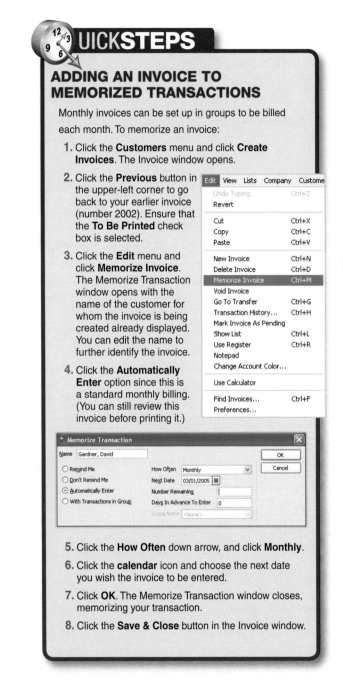

ADDING AN INVOICE TO MEMORIZED TRANSACTIONS

Monthly invoices can be set up in groups to be billed each month. To memorize an invoice:

1. Click the **Customers** menu and click **Create Invoices**. The Invoice window opens.

2. Click the **Previous** button in the upper-left corner to go back to your earlier invoice (number 2002). Ensure that the **To Be Printed** check box is selected.

3. Click the **Edit** menu and click **Memorize Invoice**. The Memorize Transaction window opens with the name of the customer for whom the invoice is being created already displayed. You can edit the name to further identify the invoice.

4. Click the **Automatically Enter** option since this is a standard monthly billing. (You can still review this invoice before printing it.)

5. Click the **How Often** down arrow, and click **Monthly**.

6. Click the **calendar** icon and choose the next date you wish the invoice to be entered.

7. Click **OK**. The Memorize Transaction window closes, memorizing your transaction.

8. Click the **Save & Close** button in the Invoice window.

8. Click in the **Description** field. Click at the end of the existing description, and type - Electrician's Handbook.

9. Press the TAB key to move to the Price Each column. Type the price, for example, 14.95.

10. Press TAB to move to the Amount column. QuickBooks automatically calculates this for you. Since this item is for resale or use in the customer's business, it remains non-taxable. You will need to use your judgment or allow the customer to determine the tax liability for items purchased if he or she has a Tax ID number.

11. Confirm that the **To Be Printed** check box is selected (located in the lower-left corner).

12. Click **Save & Close**. This customer now has two invoices that require payment.

Send Statements to Customers

If you extend credit to customers, chances are you'll need to send them statements. If you run a consulting firm, you may only send statements. Statements are simply a list of charges and payments with dates and descriptions, as well as an aging report at the bottom, listing how long an account has been outstanding.

To create a statement:

1. Click the **Customers** menu and click **Create Statements**. The Create Statements window opens, as shown in Figure 6-10.

2. Confirm the entry in the Statement Date field (by default, it is today's date).

3. Edit the statement's beginning and ending dates by typing them in the Statement Period From and To fields, respectively. Alternatively, you can click the **calendar** icon and select them from the calendar. Use monthly, quarterly, or annual ranges, as you prefer. Statements will show all transactions.

4. Click the **One Customer** option, and a drop-down menu will appear to the right. Click the down arrow and click your customer, for example, **Gardner, David**.

5. Click the **Preview** button. A preview window opens, as shown in Figure 6-11.

6. Click **Print**.

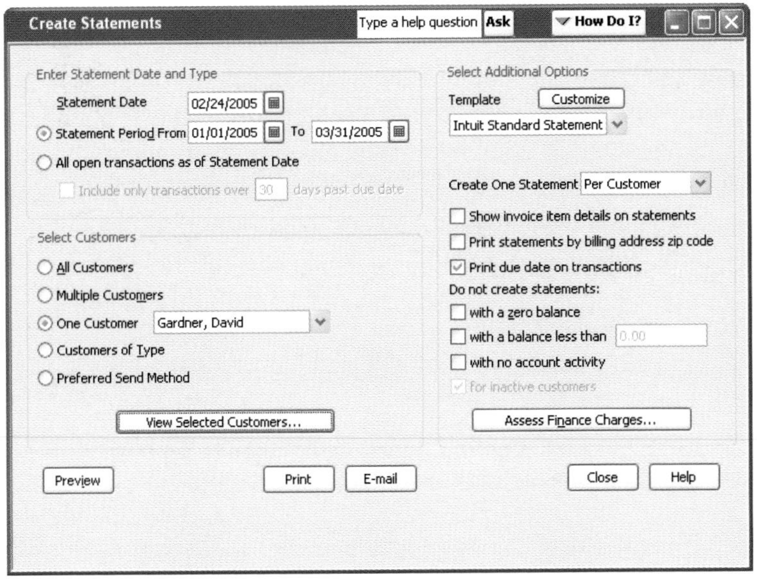

Figure 6-10: You can e-mail, mail, or fax statements, as you can all forms in QuickBooks.

TIP

An estimate can be marked as inactive if it is not accepted and you don't want to delete it.

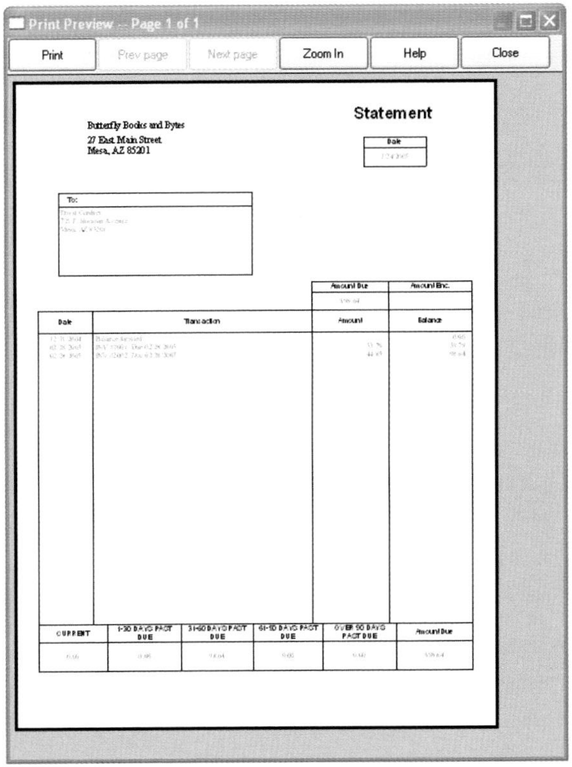

Figure 6-11: Zoom in or out on the invoice by clicking in the statement. Click Close to return to the Create Statements window, where you can edit parameters or e-mail the statement.

NOTE

QuickBooks sorts invoices and sales receipts according to date, not number.

Enter Sales Receipts

Sales receipts are used for any sale paid in full at the time of the transaction, whether paid by cash, check, or credit card. To process sales, you may use a cash register or have a computer set up at your checkout stand. While entering all sales receipts directly into QuickBooks results in more accurate reporting, it may not be practical in terms of employee training and customer volume. Determine if it will work for your business.

To enter sales receipts:

1. Click the **Customers** menu and click **Enter Sales Receipts**. The Enter Sales Receipts window opens, as shown in Figure 6-12.
2. Type your customer's name, for example, Gardner, David. Since he is a previous customer, his name should appear automatically as soon as you type G.

Figure 6-12: You can choose to leave the Enter Sales Receipts window open if you are using a computer as a cash register.

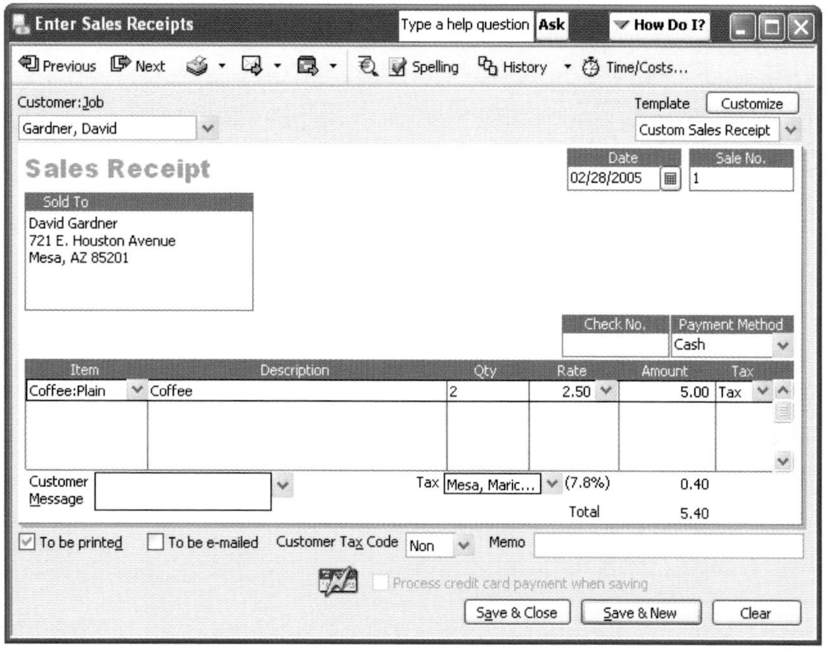

3. Click in the **Date** field to enter the correct date, if necessary. You can also click the **calendar** icon to choose a date from the calendar displayed.
4. Press the **TAB** key to move to the Sale No. field. If this is the first time you've used QuickBooks, your sales receipt number will be 1. This field will automatically increase by one each time you enter a sales receipt.
5. Press **TAB** to move to the Sold To field. QuickBooks automatically enters the name and address. Confirm that the information is accurate.
6. Click in the **Item** field. Type C. Since Coffee is a previously created item, it will appear automatically in a drop-down list, which also contains any sub-items if entered, such as Cafe Mocha or Plain. Click **Plain**.
7. Press the **TAB** key to move to the Description field. QuickBooks automatically enters the price and calculates the total for you.
8. Press **TAB** to move to the Qty (Quantity) field, and type the quantity of items sold, for example, 2.

TIP

If your sales flow is too great to use QuickBooks for each sales receipt, you can use a cash register or other method. Then, at the end of the day, one large sales receipt can be prepared. Make sure you use the correct items and amounts at the end of the day in order to have accurate tracking of items sold and inventory counts. If you use this method, enter your taxes on separate lines as well.

TIP

Whether you use a computer or cash register, if you have a cash drawer, count it out at the end of every shift, and make sure your actual cash matches your cash sales. Errors are easier to find on the day they occur than they are if you wait until the end of the week or month.

9. Click in the **Tax** column, and click **Taxable**. This customer is non-taxable for resale items, but two cups of coffee are not for resale and so can be marked taxable. The tax owed appears just above the total amount due.
10. Upon taking the cash from the customer, click the **Payment Method** down arrow, and click **Cash**.
11. Click the **Print** button near the top of the sales receipt to immediately print a copy for the customer.

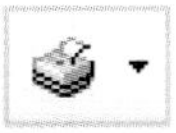

12. Click **Save & New**. The sales receipt is saved and a new, blank one is displayed.

Create Estimates

If you create estimates for your business or do project work that has phases over time, use QuickBooks to generate an estimate and then create invoices based on the estimate as work is completed.

To create an estimate:

1. Click the **Customers** menu and click **Create Estimates**. The Create Estimates window opens, as shown in Figure 6-13.

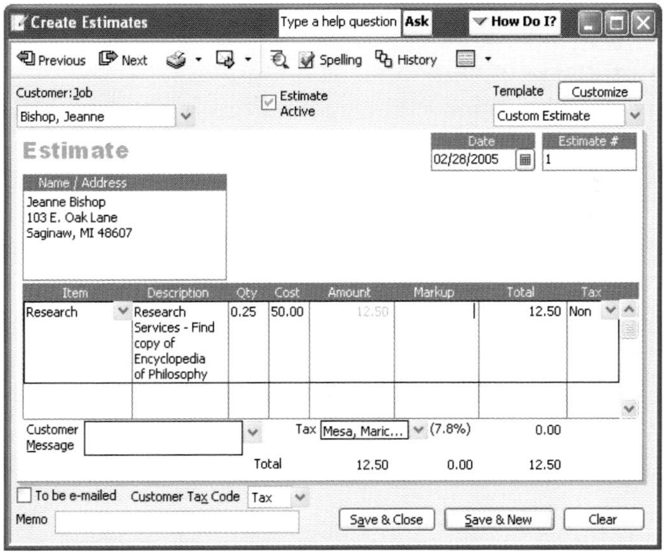

Figure 6-13: The Amount and Markup columns will not be printed or transferred to any invoice created unless you change the templates.

ACCEPTING CREDIT CARDS FROM CUSTOMERS

Credit cards are convenient for clientele and may help boost sales if consumers are your primary market. Unfortunately, accepting credit cards can be inconvenient and expensive and can impede cash flow for you as the merchant.

Accepting credit cards requires that you:

- Have a merchant account set up (you can use PayPal or QuickBooks merchant services)
- Have a credit card machine and perform a manual authorization every time (or use QuickBooks' built-in authorization)
- If using a credit card machine, perform a nightly batch-transfer of all transactions (no money will be disbursed until you do this)
- Receive payments separately from cash and checks
- Track payments separately from cash and checks

When you accept credit card payments, merchant authorization usually involves setting up a deposit directly into your bank account. This "deposit" usually takes place three to five days after the actual transaction. In some cases, this is automatic, but in others (such as PayPal), you will need to initiate the transfer. This "deposit" made by the credit card company may have the transaction fees already removed so that the amount shown on your bank statement will not match the invoice or sales receipt amount unless you have accounted for this charge.

2. Click in the **Customer:Job** drop-down list, and type your customer name. For example, "Bishop, Jeanne."

3. Click in the **Name/Address** field. Type the customer's address.

4. Press the **TAB** key to move to the Date field. Confirm the date.

5. Press **TAB** to move to the Estimate # field. You can leave it as 1, or change it to a larger number if you wish. The number will automatically increase by one each time you create a new estimate.

6. Press **TAB** to move to the Item field. Type <u>Res</u> and Research should appear automatically since this is a previously created item.

7. Press **TAB** to move to the Description field, and all information pertaining to the Research item will populate the other fields automatically based on what you entered when creating this item. Click at the end of the words "Research Services," and type <u>- Find copy of Encyclopedia of Philosophy</u>.

8. Press **TAB** to move to the Quantity column, and type the quantity (which is time in this case), for example, <u>.25</u>.

9. Press **TAB** to move to the Cost field. QuickBooks automatically calculates the total for you.

10. Click the **Print** button if you want to print this estimate.

11. Click the **Save & Close** button. If you changed the address and want to save the changes, click **Yes** when prompted.

This estimate is now active for this customer. You can create an invoice directly from this estimate by clicking the **Invoice** button at the top of the estimate form. This will give you three options by which you can create an invoice from an estimate:

- **Full Amount** directly copies all of the estimate information to the current invoice.
- **Percentage Of Full Amount** gives you the option of entering a flat percentage, which will then be entered along with the item names for all of the items on the estimate.
- **Selected Items And Specific Amounts** opens an additional window in which you will enter specific amounts and/or percentages for each item on the estimate.

> **TIP**
>
> Regardless of which method you use to sell services or products, you will still need to deposit the funds into a bank account.

> **TIP**
>
> For accurate sales reports, always use the Receive Payments window to enter payments in QuickBooks before depositing the money.

Receive Payments

Sales receipts should only be used when payment is received in full at the time of the service being performed or the purchase being made. Invoices are used when some or all of the payment is delayed. When you receive payments against these invoices, you will use the Receive Payments window to enter the information about the payments and apply them to the correct invoices.

Process Cash Payments and Checks

Cash and checks are handled in a similar fashion. The only difference is you need to enter a check number when receiving a payment by check. QuickBooks does provide you with an option to enter a reference number (such as a cash receipt number) when entering cash payments, but this is not required.

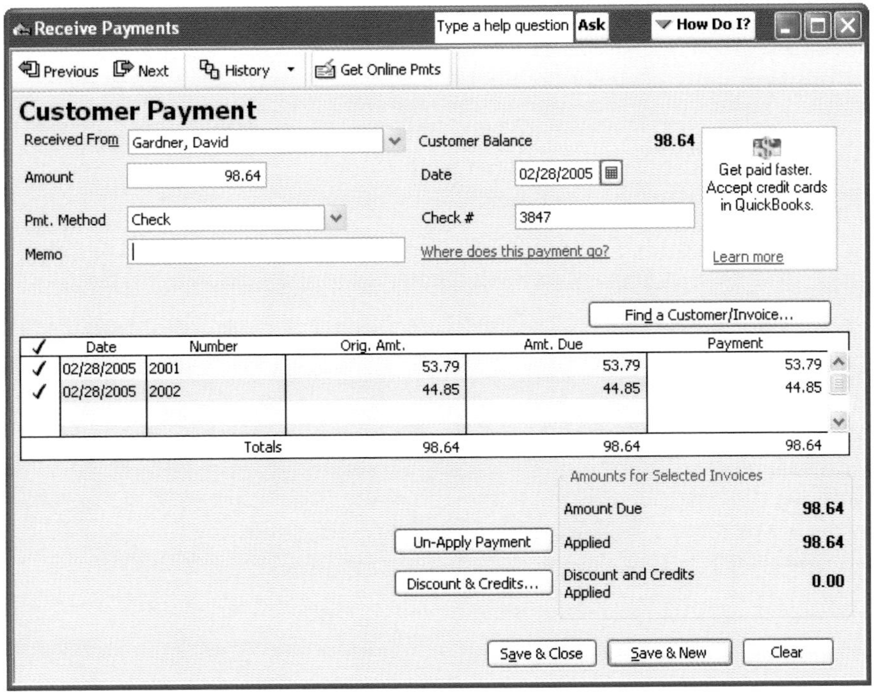

Figure 6-14: Use the Receive Payments window to apply credits and discounts to customers.

To receive payments by check:

1. Click the **Customers** menu and click **Receive Payments**. The Receive Payments window opens, as shown in Figure 6-14.
2. Click in the **Received From** field. Type your customer name, for example, "Gardner, David" (he has two outstanding invoices).
3. Press the **TAB** key to move to the Amount field, and type the amount of the payment you have received, for example, 98.64.
4. Press **TAB** to move to the Date field. QuickBooks automatically marks the outstanding invoices (located in the middle of the window) as paid. Always confirm that the payments are correctly applied.

If you accept checks, be sure you have a policy in place for bad checks. Review the customer's status in the event that you need to halt a shipment, place him or her on COD status, or take other action. Contact the customer immediately to make arrangements for him or her to pay the amount due and any processing fees stated in your policies.

TIP

If you don't have a merchant account and click the Process Visa Payment When Saving check box, a window will open displaying more information on how you can apply and set up a merchant account.

Customer Payment

Received From	Bishop, Jeanne		Customer Balance	12.50
Amount	12.50		Date	02/28/2005
Pmt. Method	Visa		Reference #	4584497
Memo			Where does this payment go?	
Card No.			Exp. Date	/
	□ Process Visa payment when saving			Find a Cust

5. Click in the **Date** field, and type the date you received the payment.

6. Press TAB to move to the Payment Method field. Type the payment method, for example, typing <u>Ch</u> will cause **Check** to be selected.

7. Press TAB to move to the Check # field. Type the check number, for example, <u>3847</u>. Verify that all other information is correct.

8. Click **Save & Close**, and the window closes. If you have received several checks, click the **Save & Next** button to continue entering customer payments.

Process Credit Card Payments

Credit card payments must be processed in a separate deposit since they are not funds you physically have in your hands as you do with cash and checks.

To receive payments by credit card:

1. Click the **Customers** menu and click **Receive Payments**. The Receive Payments window opens.

2. Click in the **Received From** field, and type your customer's name, for example, <u>Bishop, Jeanne</u> (she has one outstanding invoice).

3. Press the TAB key to move to the Amount field, and type the amount of the payment you received, for example, <u>12.5</u>.

4. Press TAB to move to the Date field. QuickBooks automatically marks the outstanding invoice (located in the middle of the window) as paid.

5. Click in the **Date** field, and type the date on which you received the payment.

6. Press the TAB key to move to the Payment Method field. Type the payment method, for example, typing <u>V</u> will cause **Visa** to be selected. This will change the payment portion of the Receive Payment window.

7. Press TAB to move to the Reference # field. If you have run the credit card manually, you can type the approval number, for example, <u>4584497</u>. If you have a merchant account set up with QuickBooks, you need to enter the card number and the expiration date and click the **Process Visa Payment When Saving** check box.

8. Click **Save & Close**. The window closes and the transaction is saved.

TIP

Deposit all monies received in a timely manner. Some businesses do this on a daily basis, but make it no longer than one week to ensure good cash flow, reduce the risk of theft or loss, and prevent customers from wondering about their checks.

Make Deposits

Making a deposit was covered in Chapter 4. The difference this time is that you now have outstanding payments that have been received against invoices but that have not yet been deposited in your bank account.

1. Click the **Banking** menu and click **Make Deposits**. The Payments To Deposit window opens, as shown in Figure 6-15.
2. Click in the column indicated by a check mark next to all check and cash payments (the two payments from David Gardner). These can be combined into one deposit, but credit card payments must be entered in a separate deposit.
3. Click **OK**. The Make Deposits window opens (see Figure 6-16) with the selected payments displayed.
4. Click the **Save & New** button. The current deposit is saved, and you are returned to the Payments To Deposit window. Notice that the outstanding credit card payment is the only deposit remaining in the window.
5. Click the **Select All** button, or click the single payment. Click **OK**. The Make Deposits window opens with the credit card deposit displayed. Depending on how your merchant account is set up, you may have to wait to deposit this amount until you receive a statement or post it a few days in the future so that you don't show money in your bank account that is not really there. Change the date, if desired, and print the deposit.
6. Click **Save & Close**.

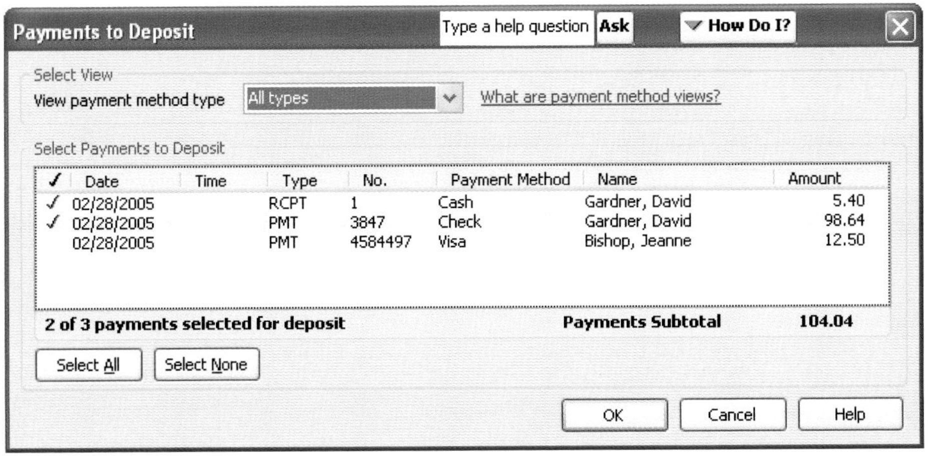

Figure 6-15: Use the View Payment Method Type drop-down list to see just certain types of payments.

Make Deposits — Type a help question | Ask | ▼ How Do I?

🔁 Previous ➡ Next 🖨 Print ▾ 💳 Payments

Deposit To Checking ▾ Date 02/28/2005 📅 Memo Deposit

Click Payments to select customer payments that you have received. List any other amounts to deposit below.

Received From	From Account	Memo	Chk No.	Pmt Meth.	Amount
Gardner, David	Undeposited Funds			Cash	5.40
Gardner, David	Undeposited Funds		3847	Check	98.64

Deposit Subtotal   104.04

To get cash back from this deposit, enter the amount below. Indicate the account where you want this money to go, such as your Petty Cash account.

Cash back goes to   Cash back memo   Cash back amount

Deposit Total   104.04

Save & Close   Save & New   Revert

Figure 6-16: Confirm that the deposit total matches your actual cash and checks in hand.

Create Credit Memos/Refunds Type a help question | Ask | ▼ How Do I?

🔁 Previous ➡ Next 🖨 ▾ 📄 ▾ 🔍 ✔ Spelling 🕮 History ▾ 📧 ▾

Customer:Job   Template | Customize
Gardner, David ▾   Custom Credit Memo ▾

Credit Memo

Customer
David Gardner
721 E. Houston Avenue
Mesa, AZ 85201

Date | Credit No.
02/28/2005 📅 | 2004

P.O. No.

Item	Description	Qty	Rate	Amount	Tax
Book Order	Special Order Books - NASCAR Photo Album	1	24.95	24.95	Tax

Customer Message [ ]   Tax Mesa, Maric... ▾ (7.8%)   1.94

Total   26.89

☑ To be printed ☐ To be e-mailed Customer Tax Code Non ▾ Remaining Credit   26.89

☐ Process credit card credit when saving

Memo [ ]   Save & Close   Save & New   Revert

Figure 6-17: Refer to the original invoice or sales receipt to ensure accurate entries when issuing a credit memo.

Issue Credit Memos

Occasionally, you will have to issue a refund to a customer. QuickBooks accomplishes this through the use of credit memos so that refunds are credited to the correct items and accounts. Credit memos can then be used to create a refund check or to apply a credit toward future purchases.

To issue a credit memo:

1. Click the **Customers** menu and click **Create Credit Memos/ Refunds**. The Create Credit Memos/Refunds window opens, as shown in Figure 6-17.

2. Referring to the invoice or sales receipt you are generating the credit memo against, enter the corresponding information for your customer and the item(s) being returned. Be sure to confirm the tax settings and quantities, as well as price.

3. Click the **Print** button if you want to print a copy of the credit memo for the customer.

4. Click **Save & Close**. If the spelling checker appears, click **Close**. The Available Credit dialog box appears with **Retain As An Available Credit** selected by default.

5. Click **OK**, and the credit memo process will be complete.

To apply this credit memo to future purchases, in the Receive Payments window, click the **Credits** button after you have entered the customer name.

TIP

Even though QuickBooks provides a place for cash back on your deposit, a more accurate business practice is to deposit all items received and take cash out separately.

Chapter 7
Managing Inventory Items

Inventory can include raw materials, works in progress, and finished goods. Some companies may just buy and sell specific items, while others combine or assemble items. Smaller service companies may not need to track inventory if they purchase items specifically for customers and do not keep any items on hand. This chapter will review the inventory-tracking feature QuickBooks provides that allows you to order, receive, build, and sell inventory items while tracking all information along the way. The chapter will also examine purchase orders and shipping.

> **NOTE**
>
> Creating non-inventory items and service items was covered in Chapter 3, and tax items were covered in Chapter 6.

Create and Purchase Inventory Items

The buying and selling of non-inventory items is best carried out by accurately entering them as expenses and charging them back to customers (see Chapter 6). However, if you handle a number of items on a regular basis and keep them in stock, inventory items can be tracked as well. An *inventory assembly* (available only in Premier or Enterprise editions) is a compilation of inventory items. If you don't want to use assemblies (or don't have the correct edition), item groups can serve the same function.

Activate Inventory in Preferences

Before you can use the inventory feature in QuickBooks, you must first activate it from within the Preferences settings.

1. Click the **Edit** menu and click **Preferences**. The Preferences window opens, as shown in Figure 7-1.
2. Scroll down the left side, and click **Purchases And Vendors**. Click the **Company Preferences** tab.
3. Click the **Inventory And Purchase Orders Are Active** check box.
4. Click **OK** to save your preferences and close the window. Click **OK** if you receive a warning that QuickBooks needs to close all open windows. You now have the ability to use inventory and purchase orders in QuickBooks.

Figure 7-1: Inventory warnings can be turned off, but this is not recommended.

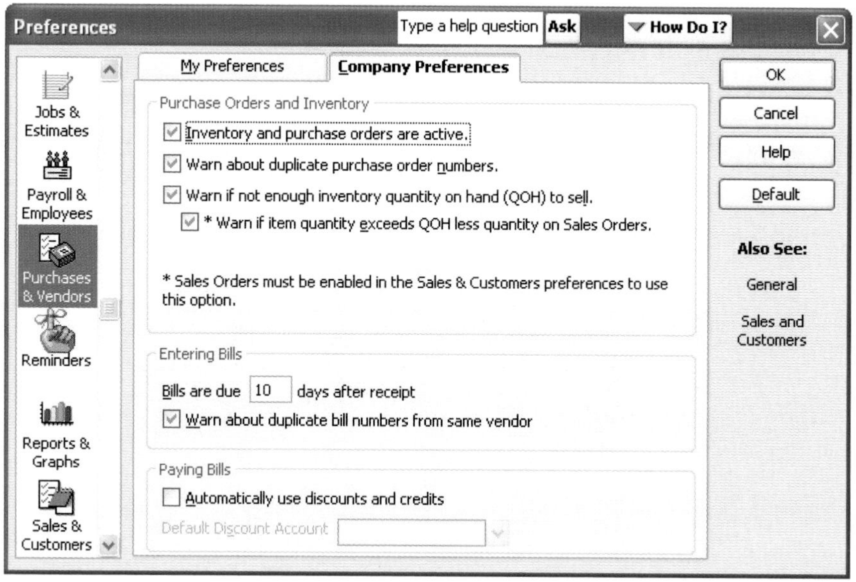

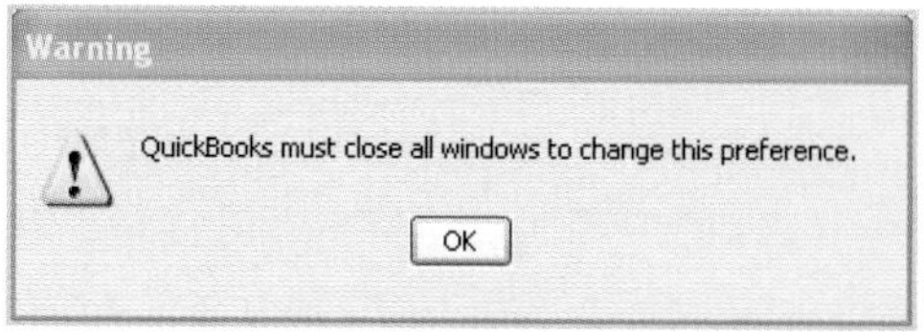

NOTE

Once inventory is activated, Inventory Part and Inventory Assembly will be available on your Item Type list.

Create Inventory Items

The Inventory Part item is used for inventory you buy, track, and sell.

1. Click the **Lists** menu and click **Item List**. The Item list is displayed.

2. Click the **Item** menu and click **New**. The New Item window opens, as shown in Figure 7-2.

3. Click the **Type** down arrow, and click **Inventory Part**.

4. Press the **TAB** key to move to the Item Name/Number field. Type the item name, for example, Coffee Mugs.

5. Click in the **Description On Purchase Transactions** field. Type a description, for example, Decorative Coffee Mugs.

6. Press **TAB** to move to the Cost field. The text in the Description On Purchase Transactions field is copied in the Description On Sales Transaction field. Type the cost of the item (that is, the price the item cost you), for example, 2.50.

7. Click in the **Sales Price** field. Type the price of the item (that is, what the customer must pay), for example, 7.50.

Type

| Inventory Part |
| Service |
| √ Inventory Part |
| Inventory Asse... |
| Non-inventory Part |
| Other Charge |
| Subtotal |
| Group |
| Discount |
| Payment |
| Sales Tax Item |
| Sales Tax Group |

Figure 7-2: You can enter multiple items by clicking the Next button instead of the OK button.

New Item

Type a help question | Ask | How Do I?

Type
Inventory Part — Use for goods you purchase, track as inventory, and resell.

OK
Cancel
Next
Custom Fields
Spelling

Item Name/Number ☐ Subitem of
Coffee Mugs

Purchase Information — Sales Information

☐ Item is inactive

Description on Purchase Transactions — Description on Sales Transactions
Decorative Coffee Mugs — Decorative Coffee Mugs

Cost	2.50	Sales Price	7.50
COGS Account	Cost of Goods Sold	Ta**x** Code	Tax
Preferred Vendor		Income Account	Sales:Merchandise

Inventory Information

| Asset Account | Reorder Point | On Hand | Total Value | As of |
| Inventory Asset | 10 | 144 | 360.00 | 01/01/2005 |

8. Click the **Income Account** down arrow, and click **Merchandise** (a subaccount of Sales).

9. Click the **COGS Account** down arrow, and click **Cost Of Goods Sold**.

10. Click the **Tax Code** down arrow, and click **Tax** (provided the item is a taxable item).

11. Click the **Asset Account** down arrow, and click **Inventory Asset**.

12. Click the **Preferred Vendor** down arrow, and click the vendor you normally purchase from (this field is optional.)

13. Click in the **Reorder Point** field. This is the point at which QuickBooks will remind you to reorder when your inventory reaches this amount (this field is optional). Type a number, for example, 10.

TABLE 7-1: COMPARISON OF ASSEMBLY ITEMS TO GROUPS

GROUP ITEM	INVENTORY ASSEMBLY ITEM
Includes any combination of item types.	Includes only inventory part items and other inventory assembly items.
Option to list individual items or just the group item.	Lists only the assembly item name, not the individual items.
No preset reports, but more detailed custom reports can be created.	Included in standard preset inventory reports.
Inventory quantity on hand is adjusted for each item at the time of sale.	Inventory quantity on hand is adjusted for each item when the inventory assembly item is identified as having been built.
Sales tax is calculated individually for each item in the group item.	Sales tax is calculated as it is listed for the single assembly item even if each item's tax code differs.
Group items cannot be included in other group items or in inventory assembly items.	Assembly items can be used within other assembly items and group items.
Group item price is calculated from the items in the group (which can include discounts or additional-charge items).	Assembly item price is set to anything you specify.
Group item can include any combination of taxable and non-taxable items.	Single assembly item must be designated as a single tax type.
Easy to keep detailed track of your inventory; and customers receive clear, easy-to-read invoices.	Gives you information such as the date that items were assembled, quantity, cost, and component lists; customers receive a single-line item invoice.
If you show each item in your group, you can quickly enter a lot of line-item detail. Just type the group name, and all the details will appear for the customer.	Shows assembled items as separate from individual inventory items. If you have things packaged together, you won't mistake a part (as in a group) as individually available since the component parts will have already been deducted from the quantity on hand.
You can sell items as part of a group or on an individual basis. Best for package deals.	You can set reminders to create new assembly items as you sell them.

14. Press the **TAB** key to move to the On Hand field. Type 144 as a sample beginning inventory quantity.

15. Press **TAB** to move to the Total Value field. QuickBooks automatically computes this amount for you based on the amount in the Cost field. Adjust it if it is not accurate due to a discount or some other reason. Confirm the date on which the inventory was obtained in the As Of field. Type your start date in this feld if the inventory was purchased before then.

16. Click **OK** to save your selections and close the window. The inventory item is created and will appear in the Item list, along with the inventory balance.

Once you have created an inventory item, you will be able to use it on purchase orders, invoices, estimates, sales orders, credit memos, and sales receipts.

A second inventory item, Gift Baskets, has been entered in the sample file. They cost $2.50, the sale price is $4.95, the reorder point is 10, and the on-hand quantity is 50. You may add this item to QuickBooks for practice purposes if you wish.

Create and Build Inventory Assembly Items

To package items together, you can use an inventory assembly or an item group. Table 7-1 provides a comparison of the two methods. There are two parts to creating an assembly: creating the item and then building it.

CREATE AN INVENTORY ASSEMBLY ITEM

An inventory assembly item (only available in QuickBooks Premier or Enterprise editions) can only include inventory items that have been created. Once incorporated into the assembly, the number of those inventory items used in the component will be decreased accordingly. You can set any price you like for the assembly regardless of the costs of the components used for the assembly.

TIP

Creating inventory parts using actual part numbers, such as ISBN numbers, can make for great tracking, but then you need to know the number to look up or enter anything. Choose what works best for your company.

To create an inventory assembly item:

1. Click the **Lists** menu and click **Item List**. The Item list is displayed.
2. Click the **Item** menu and click **New**. The New Item window opens, as shown in Figure 7-3.
3. Click the **Type** down arrow, and click **Inventory Assembly**. This assembly will contain two coffee mugs with certificates for one free order of coffee placed in a basket and covered with cellophane and tied with a ribbon. The coffee mugs and baskets are inventory items; the cellophane and ribbon are supply items.
4. Press the **TAB** key to move to the Item Name/Number field. Type the item name, for example, Coffee Gift Pack.
5. Click in the **Description** field. What you type in this field will be displayed on your invoices. Type a description, for example, Coffee Gift Pack.
6. Press **TAB** to move to the Sales Price field. Type the price for the customer, for example, 19.95.
7. Click the **Income Account** down arrow, and click **Merchandise** (a subaccount of Sales).
8. Click the **COGS Account** down arrow, and click **Cost Of Goods Sold**.
9. Click the **Tax Code** down arrow, and click **Tax** (provided the item is a taxable item).
10. Click the **Asset Account** down arrow, and click **Inventory Asset**.
11. Click in the **Item** field in the Components Needed area. Type C and "Coffee Mugs" will appear automatically since this is a previously created item.
12. Press the **TAB** key to move to the Qty (Quantity) field. QuickBooks fills in the Description field from the item (you cannot edit this information in this field). Type a quantity for this assembly, for example, 2.

Figure 7-3: Different fields are available for different item types.

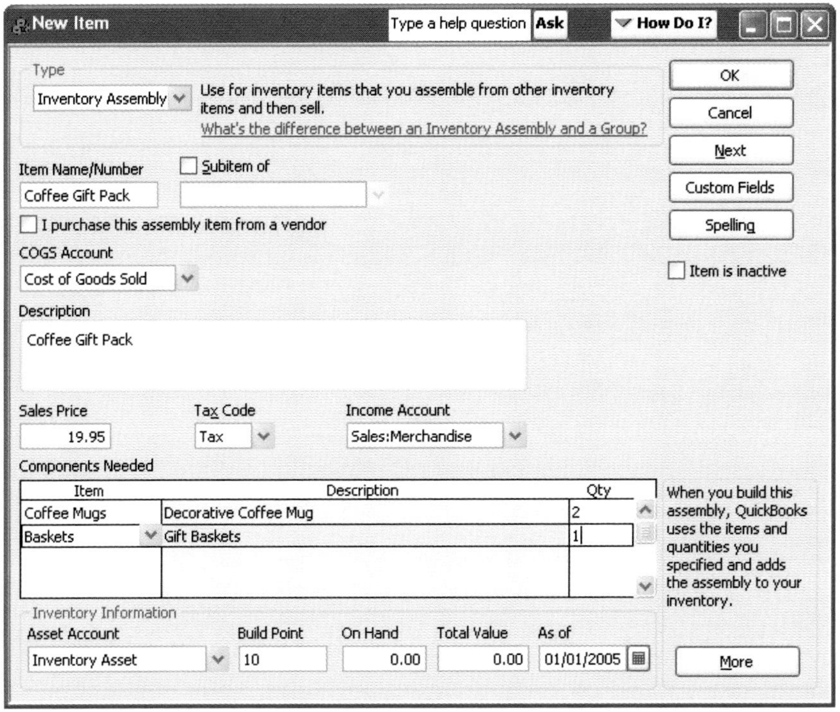

CAUTION

If you enter a quantity on hand for inventory assembly items in the New Item window, QuickBooks will assume those assemblies have already been created from other items and will not use existing inventory items, but it will add those as an inventory adjustment. Therefore, make sure you don't enter your items twice.

NOTE

If you need to track a detailed history of assemblies, labor, or other items involved in manufacturing items, you may need to track the process in some other manner, as QuickBooks will only track the combined costs of the inventory assembly items.

13. Press **TAB** to move to a new line in the Item field. Type Baskets (if you entered this item as previously suggested).
14. Press **TAB** to move to the Qty (Quantity) field. Type a quantity for this assembly, for example, 1.
15. Click in the **Build Point** field. This is the point at which QuickBooks will remind you to reorder when your inventory reaches this amount (this field is optional). Type a number, for example, 10.
16. Click **OK** to save the inventory assembly item and close the window.

You will now see the Item list with your two new inventory items and the new inventory assembly item displayed, as shown in Figure 7-4.

BUILD AN INVENTORY ASSEMBLY ITEM

Now that you have created an inventory assembly item, you need to use the Build Assemblies window to build it. This "adds" assembly item units and "deducts" inventory items. You will see this change in the Quantity column of the Items list, as well as on inventory reports.

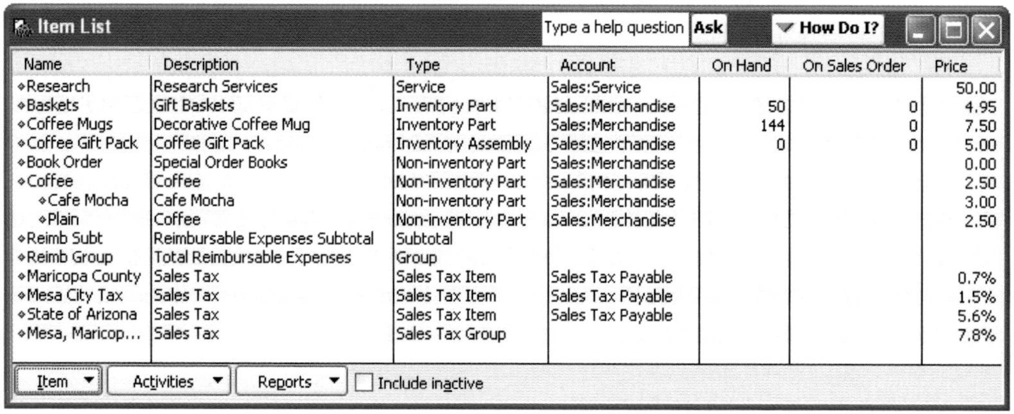

Name	Description	Type	Account	On Hand	On Sales Order	Price
Research	Research Services	Service	Sales:Service			50.00
Baskets	Gift Baskets	Inventory Part	Sales:Merchandise	50	0	4.95
Coffee Mugs	Decorative Coffee Mug	Inventory Part	Sales:Merchandise	144	0	7.50
Coffee Gift Pack	Coffee Gift Pack	Inventory Assembly	Sales:Merchandise	0	0	5.00
Book Order	Special Order Books	Non-inventory Part	Sales:Merchandise			0.00
Coffee	Coffee	Non-inventory Part	Sales:Merchandise			2.50
Cafe Mocha	Cafe Mocha	Non-inventory Part	Sales:Merchandise			3.00
Plain	Coffee	Non-inventory Part	Sales:Merchandise			2.50
Reimb Subt	Reimbursable Expenses Subtotal	Subtotal				
Reimb Group	Total Reimbursable Expenses	Group				
Maricopa County	Sales Tax	Sales Tax Item	Sales Tax Payable			0.7%
Mesa City Tax	Sales Tax	Sales Tax Item	Sales Tax Payable			1.5%
State of Arizona	Sales Tax	Sales Tax Item	Sales Tax Payable			5.6%
Mesa, Maricop...	Sales Tax	Sales Tax Group				7.8%

Figure 7-4: Inventory items and inventory assemblies show you the current on-hand and on-order amounts.

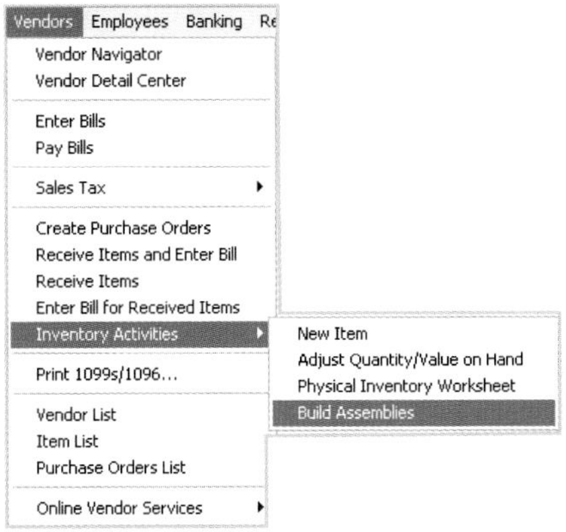

1. Click the **Vendors** menu, click **Inventory Activities**, and click **Build Assemblies**. The Build Assemblies window opens, as shown in Figure 7-5.

2. Click the **Assembly Item** down arrow, and click **Coffee Gift Pack**.

3. Click in the **Quantity To Build** field (located below the Components Needed To Build area), and type the number of items you have actually created, for example, 20.

4. Press the **TAB** key to move to the Date field, and type the date on which the items were created.

5. Press **TAB** twice to move to the Memo field, and type any pertinent information, for example, Jenny created 5 each of blue, red, yellow and green cellophane-wrapped gift packs.

6. Click the **Build & Close** button.

Your Item list will now show an increase in the assembly items on hand (20) and a decrease in the baskets (30) and coffee mugs (104). Cellophane, coffee coupons, and labor are not accounted for in this procedure since they are considered supplies.

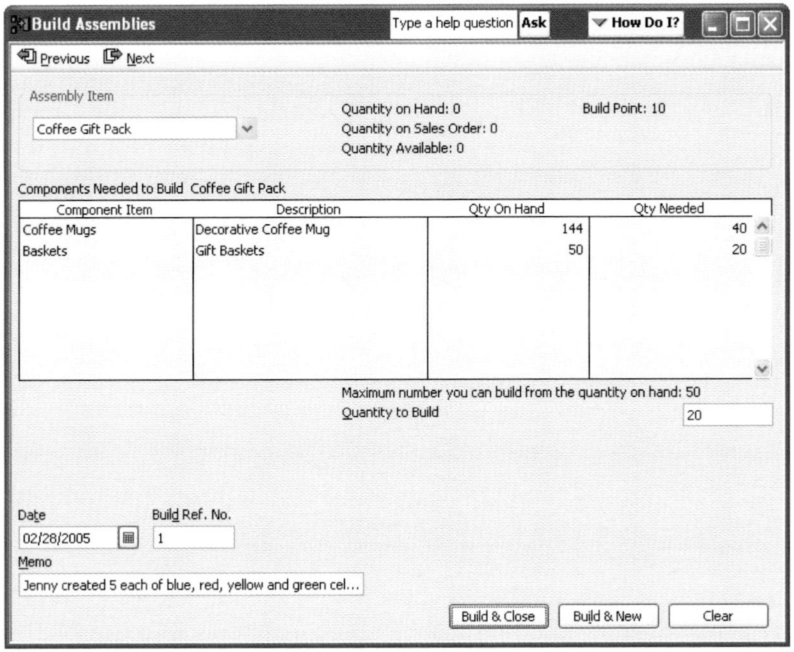

Figure 7-5: You can disassemble these inventory assemblies by reopening this window and reducing the quantity or deleting the transaction altogether if the gift packs are not selling.

Create Inventory Groups

Another method whereby you can create a product that consists of multiple items, especially if those items are not all inventory items, is to create a group. This section will show you how to create the same gift basket that was created as an inventory assembly item in the previous section. (Assembly items and groups work interchangeably.)

1. Click the **Lists** menu and click **Item List**. The Item list is displayed.

2. Click the **Item** menu and click **New**. The New Item window opens, as shown in Figure 7-6.

3. Click the **Type** down arrow, and click **Group**.

4. Press the **TAB** key to move to the Group Name/Number field. Type a group name, for example, Coffee Gift Pack 2 (the "2" is needed because you can't use the same name as another item).

Figure 7-6: You don't see sales price, income account, cost of goods sold account, tax code, and asset account information as you do on other items because each of these fields will be pulled from the items used in the group.

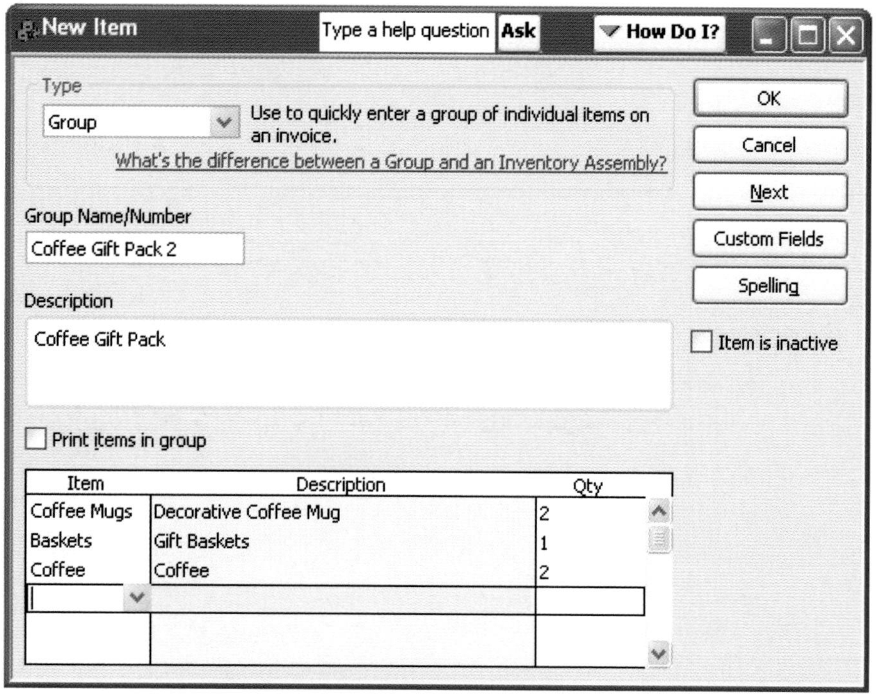

5. Click in the **Description** field. What you type in this field will be displayed on your invoices. Type a description, for example, Coffee Gift Pack.

6. Click in the **Item** field (located at the bottom of the window). Type C and "Coffee Mugs" will appear automatically since this is a previously created item.

7. Press the **TAB** key to move to the Qty (Quantity) field. Type a quantity for this group, for example, 2.

8. Press **TAB** to move to a new line in the Item field. Type Baskets (if you entered this item previously as suggested).

9. Press **TAB** to move to the Qty (Quantity) field. Type a quantity for this group, for example 1.

10. Press **TAB** to move to a new line in the Item field. Type Coffee (if you previously entered this item).

11. Press **TAB** to move to the Qty (Quantity) field. Type a quantity for this group, for example, 2.

12. Click **OK** to save the group and close the window.

You will now see the Item list with your new group item. The biggest difficulty with this method is that the total price comes completely from the items being added up when entered in an invoice.

Notice in Figure 7-6 that you have the choice to show the group components in any form. In some cases, you may wish to break out the group, while in others, you may prefer that the group appear as a single line item on an invoice or sales receipt.

You can return to a group and add more items as needed, and if the item has not yet been entered into QuickBooks, you can add it on the fly. Consider adding employee labor time (as a service item) and a discount item or other charge item to bring the total customer price of the group to your desired price level.

Use Purchase Orders

Purchase orders are a written request by your business for goods or services, containing product descriptions, quantities, terms, shipping instructions, prices, and approvals. Even if you don't specifically track inventory, using purchase orders helps ensure that the supplies you order are received and paid for without paying for items you didn't order. The larger your company, the more important it is to have purchase-order procedures in place. If you're the only employee in your business, you will likely remember what you ordered and when, but when one person is responsible for ordering items, another receives them, and a third pays for them, purchase orders will help make sure everyone is on the same page.

To create a purchase order:

1. Click the **Vendors** menu and click **Create Purchase Orders**. The Create Purchase Orders window opens, as shown in Figure 7-7.
2. Click the **Vendor** down arrow, and click the name of the vendor from whom you wish to purchase an item, for example, Book Warehaus.
3. Click in the **Vendor** area, located below the Vendor drop-down list. QuickBooks will automatically fill in any existing information. Confirm the name and address, or type it in the field if it is not complete. Confirm the Ship To address as well.
4. Click in the **Item** field. Type Book Order. This is a custom order, not an inventory order, so additional information will need to be added.
5. Press the **TAB** key to move to the Description field. Select the text "Special Order Books," press the **DELETE** key, and type the following information, which you will need to order the product:
   - SQL The Complete Reference, Second Edition
   - Author(s): James Groff, Paul Weinberg
   - ISBN: 0072225599
6. Press **TAB** to move to the Quantity field. Type the quantity you are ordering, for example, 3.
7. Press **TAB** to move to the Rate field. Type your cost per item, for example, 4.05.
8. Press **TAB** to move to the Customer field. If you are ordering these items for a specific customer, type his or her name here, for example, Kobinski, John.
9. Press **TAB** to move to the Amount field. The Customer:Job Not Found dialog box appears since John Kobinski is not in the Customer list. Click **Quick Add** to just add his name to the Customer:Job list. QuickBooks automatically calculates the figure in the Amount field. If you change the amount, QuickBooks will divide the amount by the quantity and will change the rate accordingly.

TIP

Check to see if your vendor supports drop ship, which allows you to send a product directly to your customer from your supplier. This is especially useful for Internet-based companies.

Figure 7-7: Forms look similar throughout QuickBooks. The same items are used on purchase orders as are used on all other forms.

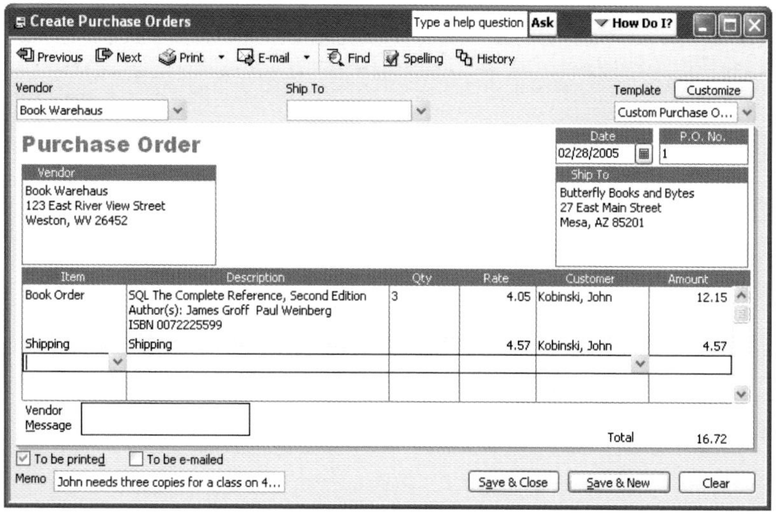

NOTE

Purchase orders for inventory are handled the same as custom orders, although they do not need to have the customer listed. Items will be added to inventory when they are received.

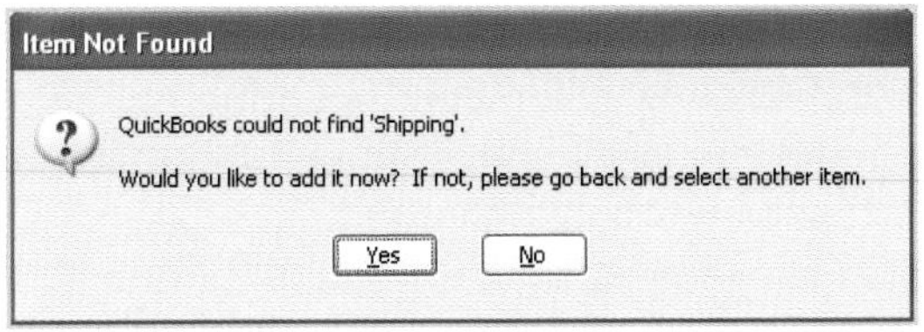

Item Not Found

? QuickBooks could not find 'Shipping'.

Would you like to add it now? If not, please go back and select another item.

[Yes]   [No]

Figure 7-8: When you use the Quick Add feature to add an item, such as shipping, that you suddenly realize you need, you can always edit it later.

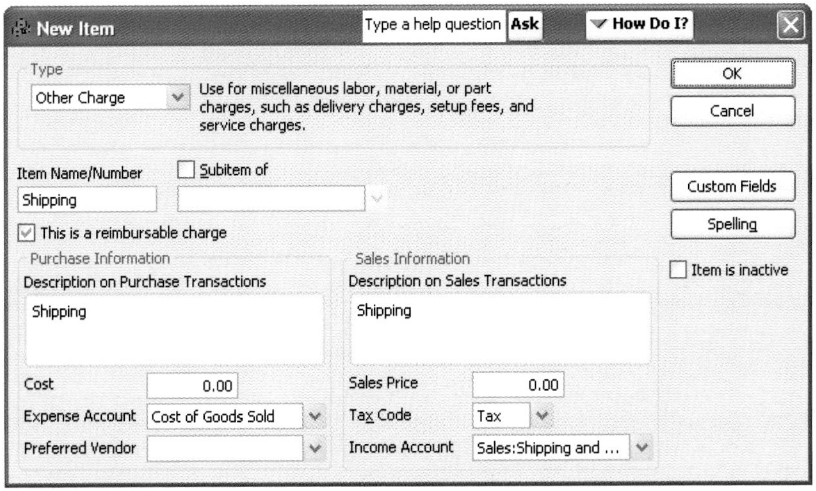

New Item

Type a help question | Ask   ▼ How Do I?   [X]

Type
Other Charge   Use for miscellaneous labor, material, or part charges, such as delivery charges, setup fees, and service charges.

[OK]
[Cancel]

Item Name/Number   ☐ Subitem of
Shipping

[Custom Fields]
[Spelling]

☑ This is a reimbursable charge

☐ Item is inactive

Purchase Information
Description on Purchase Transactions
Shipping

Sales Information
Description on Sales Transactions
Shipping

Cost   0.00
Expense Account   Cost of Goods Sold ▼
Preferred Vendor

Sales Price   0.00
Tax Code   Tax ▼
Income Account   Sales:Shipping and ... ▼

10. Press **TAB** to move to a new line in the Item field, and type <u>Shipping</u> to add the shipping costs to send this product to your customer.

11. Press **TAB** to move to the Description field. The Item Not Found dialog box appears since an item called "Shipping" is not in the Item list. Click **Yes** to add this item to your Item list. The New Item window opens.

12. In the New Item window, click the **Type** down arrow, and click **Other Charge**.

13. Press **TAB** to move to the Item Name/Number field. QuickBooks automatically inserts the Shipping item.

14. Click the **This Is A Reimbursable Charge** check box. This will cause the Purchase Information area to appear in the Item window, as seen in Figure 7-8.

15. Click in the **Description On Purchase Transactions** field. Type the item name as you wish it to appear on your purchase order, for example, <u>Shipping</u>.

16. Press **TAB** to move to the Cost field. If you have a standard cost, type it here. You can always edit the Description and Amount fields each time you use this item.

17. Click the **Income Account** down arrow, and click **Shipping And Handling** (a subaccount of Sales). All other fields in this window are optional.

18. Click **OK** to save this item and return to the Create Purchase Orders window.

19. Press the **TAB** key twice to move to the Rate field. Type the cost of shipping, for example, <u>4.57</u>.

20. Press **TAB** to move to the Customer field. Type the customer name. In this case, since John Kobinski has now been added to the Customer list, typing <u>Ko</u> will cause "Kobiniski, John" to automatically appear.

21. Click in the **Vendor Message** field. Type a relevant message, for example, <u>Please rush this order.</u>

22. Press **TAB** to move to the Memo field. Type a relevant note to remind you what the purchase order is for, for example, <u>John needs three copies for a class on 4/1/05.</u>

23. Click the **Save & Close** button. If the spelling checker appears, use it to check your spelling, or click **Close**. If the Name Information Change dialog box appears, click **Yes** to accept the address change.

NOTE

If you receive items and bills separately, you can click the Receive Items and the Enter Bills For Received Items commands to open windows similar to the Enter Bills window. They function in similar ways.

Figure 7-9: From the Enter Bills window, you can use the Select PO button (located near the bottom) to review pending purchase orders.

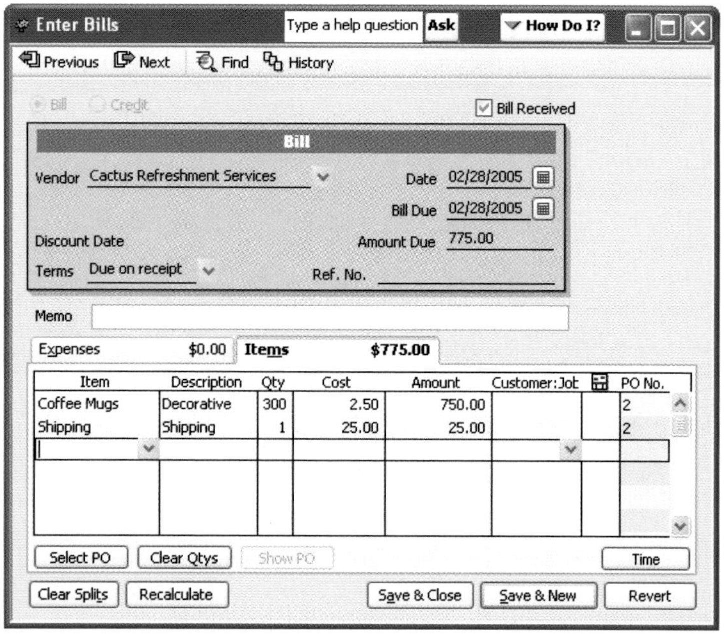

Receive Items

When deliveries arrive from vendors, you need to receive the items in QuickBooks, either as inventory items or regular items. The purchase orders will then be marked as received, inventory will be added (if applicable), and a bill will be generated for payment. The receipt of special orders is handled just as the receipt of inventory is; however, the items are not marked as inventory, so consider creating the invoice to send to your customer at the time you place the order (use the Sales Order feature in the Premium edition) or upon receiving the special-order item.

RECEIVE ITEMS AND ENTER BILLS

If you've received items along with an invoice from your vendor, use the Receive Items And Enter Bill feature. If you've only received a packing slip and not a bill, use the Receive Items feature.

1. Click the **Vendors** menu and click **Receive Items And Enter Bill**. The Enter Bills window opens, as shown in Figure 7-9.
2. Click the **Vendor** down arrow, and click the vendor name from whom you have received a shipment, for example, Cactus Refreshment Services.
3. Press the **TAB** key to move to the Date field. A dialog box will appear, informing you that you have open, or pending, purchase orders and asking you if you wish to receive against them.

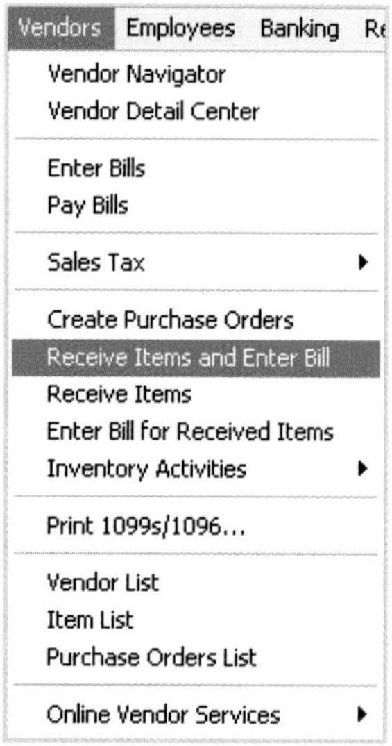

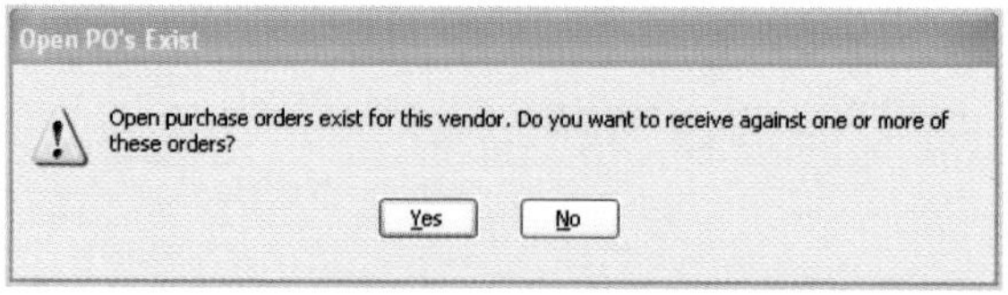

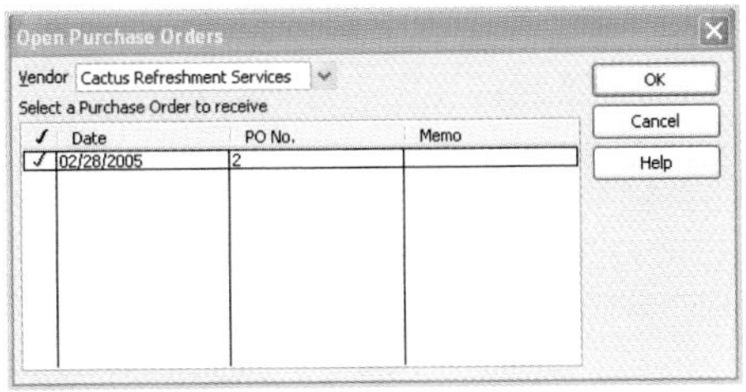

4. Click **Yes**. The Open Purchase Order window opens, listing all outstanding purchase orders for this vendor. Click the purchase order that matches the items received.

5. Click **OK**. You are returned to the Enter Bills window. The items from the purchase order are entered into the Item list at the bottom of the window. If this were a partial shipment, you could adjust the quantity received.

6. Click the **Save & Close** button.

The inventory items have now been added to inventory, and a bill has been entered for payment.

Ship Items

Once you've ordered and received items for your customers, your next actions depend on your type of business. In a retail store, customers normally walk in and collect their items. In other companies, you may need to ship or deliver items. In such cases, you need to make sure you have the correct items and that they are sent to the correct location.

Packing slips typically include all the product information and quantities but not the price information. Thus, it is simply a modified invoice or sales receipt form. QuickBooks includes a default packing slip, or you can create your own by customizing your forms (see Chapter 8). Use the Print menu on an invoice to print a packing slip based on the invoice. Printing a packing slip from a sales receipt requires customizing a form and printing the sales receipt twice, once with the prices, once without.

USE PACKING SLIPS

1. Click the **Edit** menu. Click **Preferences**. The Preferences window opens, as shown in Figure 7-10.

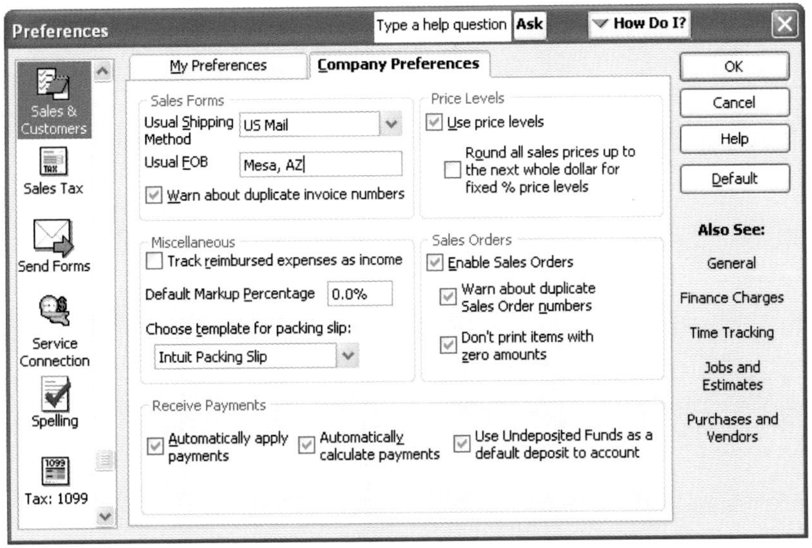

Figure 7-10: You can also select your default shipping method and freight origin when creating packing slips.

TIP

Use discount items to track specific discounts, such as coupons or referrals. For one-time negotiated discounts, enter the same item onto the invoice or sales receipt, and enter a negative amount so that the discount is credited back to the same account as the initial purchase.

Figure 7-11: Double-click any reminder to see the actual item to which it refers.

Due Date	🗲	Description	Amount
		To Do Notes	
		Bills to Pay	-1,531.39
		Overdue Invoices	3.24
		Checks to Print	-77.62
		Invoices/Credit Memos to Print	114.39
02/28/2005		2001 - Gardner, David	53.79
02/28/2005		2002 - Gardner, David	44.85
02/28/2005		2003 - Bishop, Jeanne	12.50
02/28/2005		2004 - Gardner, David	-26.89
02/28/2005		2005 - Harris, Kelvin	30.14
		Sales Receipts to Print	5.40
		Sales Orders to Print	30.14
		Purchase Orders to Print	-827.08
		Memorized Transactions Due	0.00
		Assembly Items to Build	
		Alerts	
		Deposit payroll taxes	
		Reconcile your accounts	
		Make depreciation entries	

Reminders — Type a help question — Ask — How Do I?

[Custom View] [Collapse All] [Expand All]

Print Packing Slip — Type a help question — Ask — How Do I?

Settings | Fonts

Printer name: hp officejet 7100 series on Ne03: — [Options...]

Printer type: Page-oriented (Single sheets)

Note: To install additional printers or to change port assignments, use the Windows Control Panel.

Print on:
○ Intuit Preprinted forms.
● Blank paper.
○ Letterhead.

Note: The form Template provides additional print settings such as Logo selection. Templates are accessed by selecting Templates from the List menu.

☐ Do not print lines around each field.

Number of copies: 1

[Print] [Cancel] [Help] [Preview] [Align]

2. Scroll down the left side, and click **Sales And Customers**. Click the **Company Preferences** tab.

3. Click the **Choose Template For Packing Slips** down arrow, and click **Intuit Packing Slip**. You can choose any invoice template, including those you customize.

4. Click **OK**.

CREATE PACKING SLIPS

If you marked all your invoices to be printed, they will be listed in your Reminders list. From here, you can review and choose the invoices for which you need to print packing slips. These packing slips can also be used as pick-up slips in a warehouse.

To open your Reminders list:

1. Click the **Company** menu and click **Reminders**. The Reminders list is displayed, as shown in Figure 7-11.

2. Double-click **Invoices/Credit Memos To Print** (since this is the specific reminder with which you want to work) to expand the list under it.

3. Double click **Invoice #2005 - Harris, Kelvin**. This invoice is displayed.

4. Click the **Print** down arrow, and click **Print Packing Slip**. A dialog box may appear regarding shipping labels, which are also available on the Print menu.

Preview
Print...
Print Batch...
Print Packing Slip
Print Shipping Label...
Print Envelope...
Order Forms & Envelopes...

5. Click **OK**. The Print Packing Slip dialog box appears, as shown in Figure 7-12.

6. Click the **Print** button.

Figure 7-12: Click the Preview button (on the right) if you want to see the layout of your packing slip and check it for accuracy before printing.

Use the Shipping Manager

QuickBooks can be integrated with FedEx and UPS so that you can create shipping labels directly from your invoice within QuickBooks by automatically filling in the shipping label with information from the invoice.

SEND A PACKAGE VIA UPS

1. Click the **Invoice** button on the icon bar. The Create Invoice window opens. Click the **Previous** button to return to an invoice requiring shipment, such as Invoice #2005.

2. Click the **Ship** down arrow, and click **Ship UPS Package**. The Shipping Manager For UPS window opens, displaying a form with your customer information already filled in, as shown in Figure 7-13.

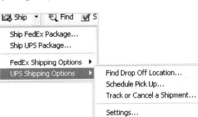

3. Click the **Service** down arrow, and click your shipping method (for example, **Ground**, **Next Day**, **2nd Day**, and so on).

4. In the Package area, click in the **Weight** field. Type the package weight in pounds, for example, 2.

5. In the Package area, click in the **Declared Value** field. Type the package value in dollars, for example, 30.

6. Click the **Rate Quote** button (located near the lower-right area of the window). A rate quote is displayed.

7. Click the **Close** button. You are returned to the Shipping Manager For UPS window. If you are satisfied with the rate quote, click **Ship Now**. A label is sent to your printer. The Shipping Manager closes, and you are returned to the Create Invoices window.

8. Click **Save & Close**.

Figure 7-13: Package information is the only area required (it is not copied from the invoice). Size, Delivery Confirmation, and COD are all optional sections.

TIP

In the Shipping Manager, you can click the **Settings** button (located at the bottom of the screen), and elect to have labels display on your screen without printing, or you can print a test label.

SEND A PACKAGE VIA FEDEX

1. Click the **Invoice** button on the icon bar. The Create Invoice window opens. Click the **Previous** button to return to an invoice requiring shipment, such as Invoice #2005.

2. Click the **Ship** down arrow, and click **Ship FedEx Package**. The Quick-Books Shipping Manager Shipping Form window opens, displaying a FedEx form with your customer information already filled in, as shown in Figure 7-14.

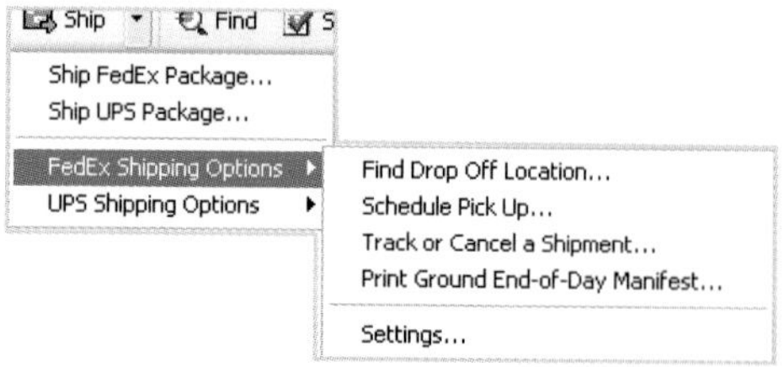

3. In the Step 1 area (at the top of the screen), click your shipping method (for example, **FedEx Express**, **FedEx Ground**, or **COD service**).

4. In the Packaging area (on the right side of the screen), click in the **Weight** field, and type the package weight in pounds.

5. In the Special Handling And Shipment Options area, click in the **Declared Value** field, and type the package value in dollars.

6. Click the **Rate Quote** button (located near the lower-right area of the window). A rate quote is displayed.

7. Click the **Close** button. You are returned to the QuickBooks Shipping Manager Shipping Form window. If you are satisfied with the rate quote, click **Ship Now**. A label is sent to your printer. The Shipping Manager closes, and you are returned to the Create Invoices window.

8. Click **Save & Close**.

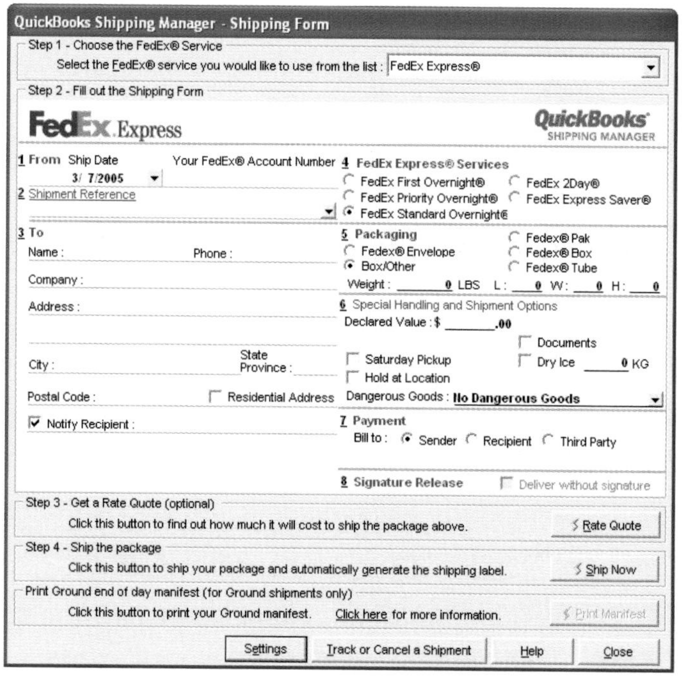

Figure 7-14: Package information is the only area required (it is not copied over from the invoice). Size, Delivery Confirmation, and COD are all optional sections.

TIP

You can group your items in a variety of ways. Consider grouping them by location to facilitate inventory checks.

Monitor and Maintain Inventory Items

QuickBooks provides options for you to take physical inventory and adjust for errors, theft, breakages, or other inaccuracies in your inventory. If you have slow-moving or large items, you can do an inventory on an infrequent basis. If you have small, expensive items, you may want to closely monitor storage and do random or frequent inventories.

Take Inventory

To take inventory, you need a list of your inventory items. You should do a monthly inventory if possible—at the very least take your inventory once a year.

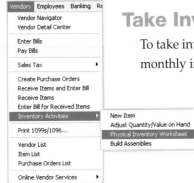

1. Click the **Vendors** menu. Click **Inventory Activities** and click **Physical Inventory Worksheet**. A Physical Inventory Worksheet report appears, as shown in Figure 7-15.

2. Click **Print**. The Print dialog box appears. Click **Print** again.

3. Click the **Close** button (the X in the upper-right corner) to close the report window. If QuickBooks prompts you to memorize this report, click **No**.

You can now use this inventory worksheet to physically check your inventory against what you have listed in QuickBooks. When you have completed your physical inventory, you can adjust it in QuickBooks if necessary.

Figure 7-15: In the Physical Inventory Worksheet report, inventory items and inventory assemblies are grouped separately.

Manually Adjust Inventory

1. Click the **Vendors** menu. Click **Inventory Activities** and click **Adjust Quantity/Value On Hand**. The Adjust Quantity/Value On Hand window opens, as shown in Figure 7-16.

2. Click in the **New Quantity** field. Type the actual count of mugs, for example, <u>402</u>.

3. Click the **Adjustment Account** down arrow, and click **Supplies**. In this case, these mugs were taken for office use. If they had been broken or lost, however, you would perhaps want to create an expense account to reflect that.

4. Click **Save & Close**.

Your inventory has now been updated and the appropriate expense account charged. If you need to use multiple expense accounts, click the **Save & New** button, and add multiple inventory adjustments, each with its own account.

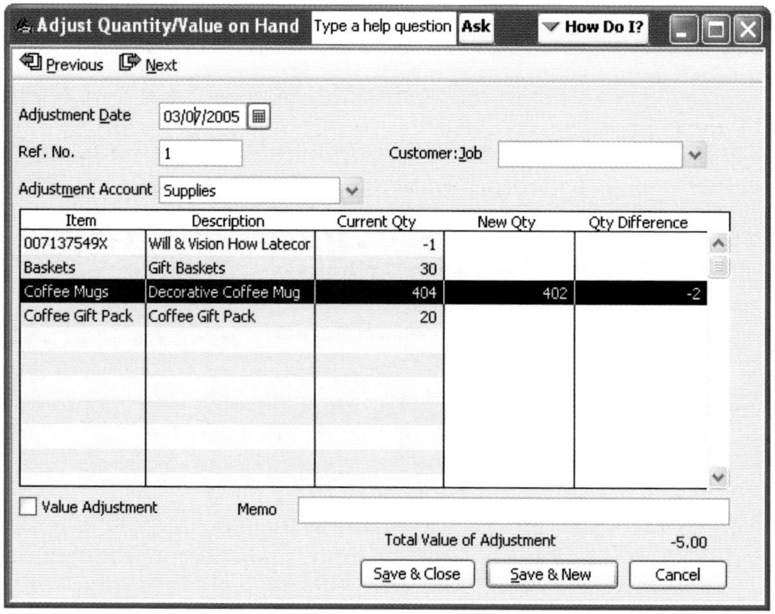

*Figure 7-16: Use the Customer:
Job field (not available in the Basic
edition) to correct errors involving
any incorrect entries of items so
that they can be charged correctly
for job-costing reports.*

How to...

- *Automate Your Backup*

- *Restore Your Data*

- *Verify Your Data*

- *Work with an Accountant's Copy*

- *Storing Your Backups*

- *Network Your QuickBooks File*

- *Customize Company Preferences*

- *Customize My Preferences*

- *Use the Find Feature*

- *View Reminders*

- *Write Collection Letters to Customers*

- *Create Mailing Labels*

- *Customize Forms*

Chapter 8

Customizing and Maintaining QuickBooks

QuickBooks can be customized to meet your specific needs and adjusted to fit your interaction with it. For example, the Preferences section has a long list of company and personal preferences, and you can customize your icon bar (see Chapter 1). Commonly used preferences will be covered in this chapter, as well as other changes, such as customizing forms, maintaining your data, and communicating with your customers. Each QuickBooks company file can be customized to meet your needs and preferences. Experiment with the various settings to determine what works best for you. Any change you make can be easily changed it back if it doesn't suit your needs.

Maintain and Access Your Data

The most important thing in accounting is to maintain your data. Remember that all of your QuickBooks data is stored in a single file with a .qbw file extension. When you back it up, it is compressed into another single file with a .qbb file extension. Backing up your data is covered in Chapter 1. If you need to restore your data, you need to uncompress your .qbb file back into a .qbw file.

Automate Your Backup

Chapter 1 covered manual backups. If you want to back up your data every day or every time you use your file, you can schedule automatic backups. QuickBooks provides you with two options for automated backups:

- Set automatic backups that take place when you close the company file (every time or at set intervals).

- Schedule automatic backups at specific times. You can be away, but the computer must be on.

SET AUTOMATIC BACKUPS

1. Click the **File** menu and click **Back Up**. The QuickBooks Backup window opens, as shown in Figure 8-1.

2. Click the **Schedule Backup** tab.

3. Click the **Automatically Back Up When Closing The Data File Every** check box.

4. Click in the **Times** field, and type how often you wish the backup to occur, for example, 1 (every time you close the file). If you typed 2, for example, QuickBooks would back up the file every other time it was closed.

5. Click **OK**.

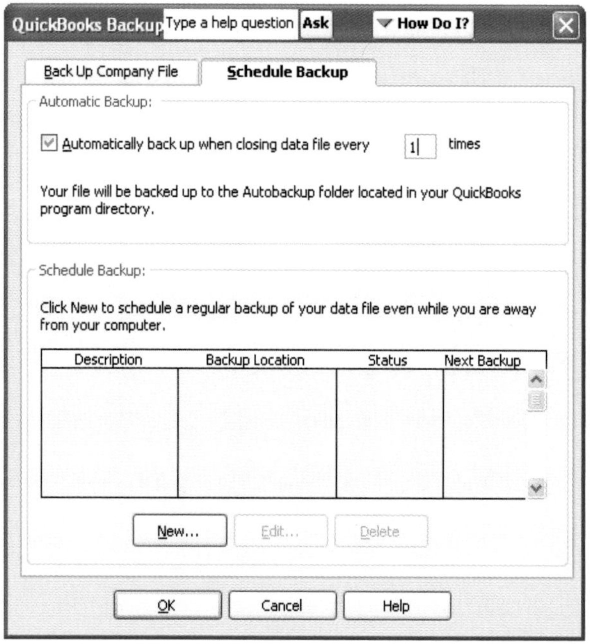

SCHEDULE REGULAR BACKUPS

1. Click the **File** menu. Click **Back Up**. The QuickBooks Backup window opens.

2. Click the **New** button, located near the bottom of the window. The Schedule Backup window opens, as shown in Figure 8-2.

Figure 8-1: When scheduling an automatic backup, the number in the Times field dictates how frequently the file is backed up upon being closed.

TIP

Automatic backups store all the previous versions of your company file. If you want to automatically limit the number stored, in the Schedule Backup window, click the **Number Of Backups To Keep** check box, and type how many backup versions QuickBooks should save before writing over an earlier version.

Figure 8-2: Back up your company file to a thumb drive or other removable drive for the most security.

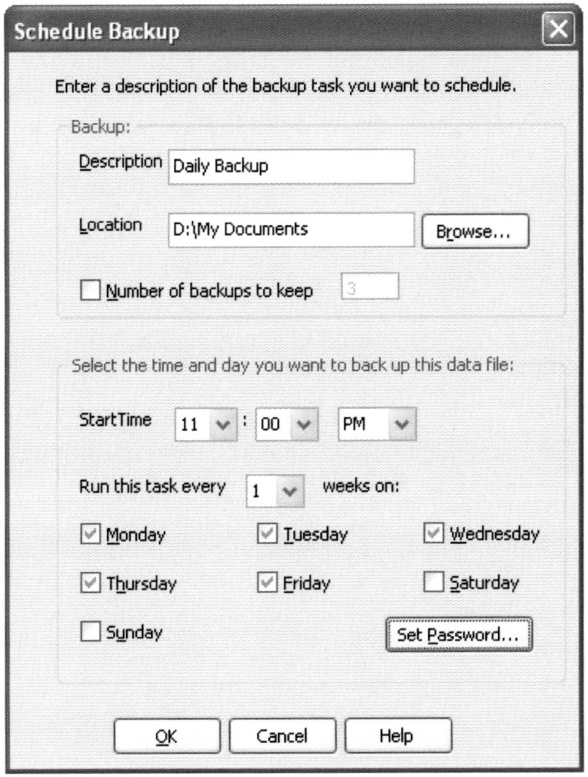

3. Click in the **Description** field, and type a description for your backup, for example, Daily Backup.
4. Click the **Browse** button. A Folder list dialog box appears. Select a destination for your backup.
5. Click **My Documents**. Click **OK** to close the Folder list and return to the Schedule Backup window.
6. Click the days on which you want your backup to run, for example, **Monday**, **Tuesday**, **Wednesday**, **Thursday**, and **Friday**.
7. In the Start Time area, click the **hour** down arrow, and click the hour you wish the backup to occur, for example, **11**.
8. In the Start Time area, click the **minute** down arrow, and click the minute you wish the backup to occur, for example, **00**.
9. In the Start Time area, click the **AM/PM** down arrow, and click the desired time of day, such as **PM**.
10. Click the **Set Password** button. The Enter Windows Password dialog box appears. If you are required to enter a password when Windows starts up (this is different from your QuickBooks password), type it here. Unattended backups cannot take place unless you provide your Windows user name and password.

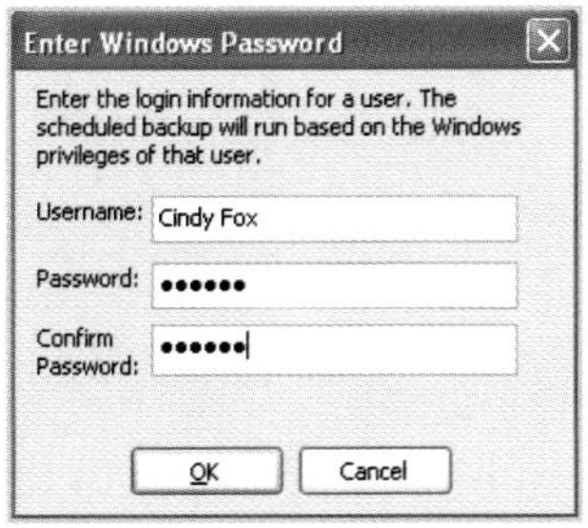

11. Click **OK** to close the Enter Windows Password window.
12. Click **OK** to close the Schedule Backup window.
13. Click **OK** to close the QuickBooks Backup window.

Restore Your Data

You will need to restore your data if, for example, you have a hard disk crash, a stolen computer, or a possible corrupt company file. After remedying whatever situation caused you to lose your data, you will need to reinstall QuickBooks and then restore your data.

1. Click the **File** menu and click **Restore**. The Restore Company Backup window opens, as shown in Figure 8-3. Leave the default settings in place, as they should be accurate for your purposes.

2. In the Get Company Backup From area, if the current location and file name are not correct, click the **Browse** button. The Restore From dialog box appears.

3. In the Restore Company Backup To area, if the current location and file name are not correct, click the **Browse** button. The Restore To dialog box appears.

4. Click the **Restore** button when you have confirmed the locations of your files.

Figure 8-3: The .qbb (backup) file name and location are shown at the top. The .qbw file name (the one you normally use) and location are shown at the bottom.

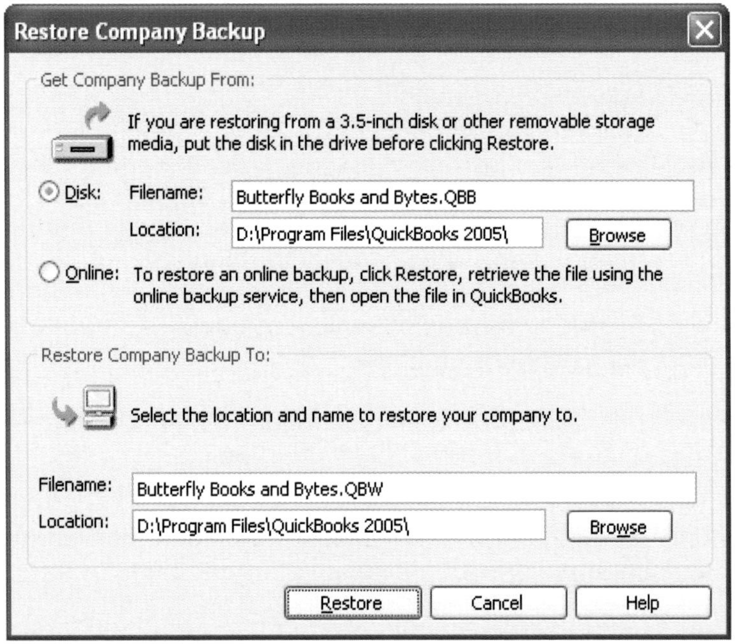

5. If you are choosing to replace an existing file, a Backup dialog box will appear, prompting you to confirm this action. (If you are unsure, click **No** to return to the Restore Company Backup window, and choose another name for your restore file.)

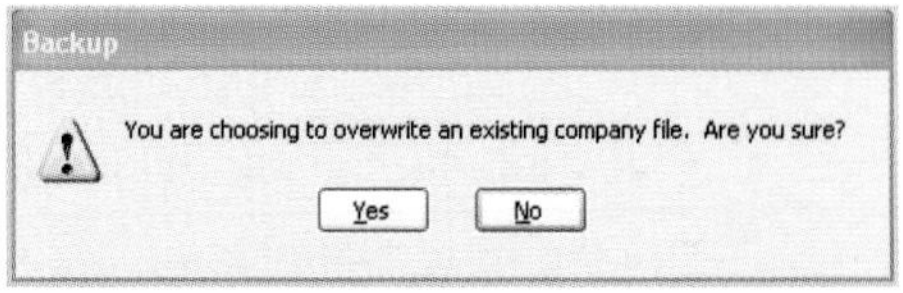

6. Click **Yes**. A Delete Entire File dialog box appears, asking you again to confirm this action.

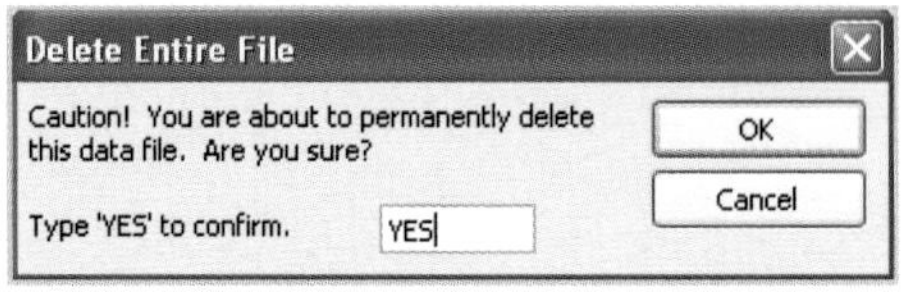

7. If you are sure you want to proceed with the deletion, type YES in the confirmation box. Click **OK**. The restore operation begins and the QuickBooks Login dialog box appears.

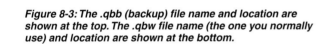

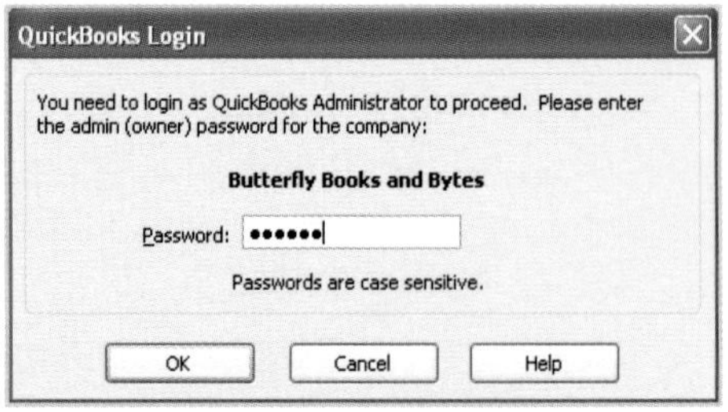

CAUTION

Don't overwrite a newer copy of your data with an older backup. Always rename your current working file before restoring another file in case of any problems.

Verify Data

Before verifying your data, QuickBooks will need to close all open windows.

Do you want to continue?

OK   Cancel

8. Type your password, if required, and click **OK**. The restore operation continues, and a final dialog box appears when the restoration is complete.

9. Click **OK**.

QuickBooks Information

Your data has been restored successfully.

OK

Verify Your Data

If you have any concerns about your data being corrupted, such as strange entries or links not working correctly, you can check it by verifying your data.

1. Click the **File** menu, click **Utilities**, and click **Verify Data**. A Verify Data dialog box may appear, notifying you that you need to close all open windows before proceeding.

2. Click **OK**. If all is well, the following dialog box will appear.

QuickBooks Information

QuickBooks detected no problems with your data.

OK

If you see a dialog box stating that your data is corrupted, you will be directed to use the Rebuild Data feature (you can also access this by clicking the **File** menu and clicking **Utilities**). If the Rebuild Data feature fails, you should contact Intuit for support.

Work with an Accountant's Copy

In addition to creating a backup for emergencies, you may need to give a copy of your data to your accountant. You can accomplish this in one of two ways:

- **Create a normal backup** to give to your accountant for review; however, this file cannot be merged back into your company file.

  –Or–

- **Create an accountant's copy of your data**, which can be returned and reintegrated into your QuickBooks company file.

STORING YOUR BACKUPS

It's convenient and easy to store all your financial data in one file, but when (not if) a computer crashes, computer programs can be restored, but data cannot unless you have a backup.

A *backup* is a compressed copy of your data. You may store your data on a floppy disk, CD-ROM, DVD, or online. Keep this backup file offsite in case of flood, fire, or theft.

STORE YOUR BACKUP ONLINE

Online storage of your backup is easy when you have a high-speed connection, and is automatically stored offsite.

STORE YOUR BACKUP ON A FLOPPY DISK

Floppies are convenient and reusable; however, some newer computers do not include floppy drives. As your file grows, you may need multiple floppies, which prevents unattended backups and makes a backup failure more likely.

STORE YOUR BACKUP ON TAPE

Tape is great for backing up large amounts of data. If you have a tape drive for your entire computer system, make sure your QuickBooks file is included. Again, make sure the tape is stored offsite. If you ever need to retrieve that data, you will need to have the same type of tape drive and software to access the drive.

Continued...

TIP

The audit trail preference can be useful for tracking employee entries, but it can cause the QuickBooks data file to dramatically increase in size.

Whichever method you choose, you will want to save the file in the proper location in order to transfer it to your accountant. You can e-mail your file to your accountant or physically deliver it to him or her on your accountant's preferred media, such as floppy, CD, or flash drive.

While you have an accountant's copy in existence, you *can* use your QuickBooks file to:

- Create, edit, and delete transactions
- Add and edit list items

While you have an accountant's copy in existence, you *cannot* use your QuickBooks file to:

- Delete, move, or rename a list entry
- Create subaccounts

Table 8-1 lists the actions that your accountant can and cannot perform on the copy of your QuickBooks file you give to him or her.

TABLE 8-1: CHANGES ACCOUNTANT CAN AND CANNOT MAKE

ACCOUNTANT CAN:	ACCOUNTANT CANNOT:
View lists, transactions, and reports; add new items to the Chart of Accounts, Item list, and To Do Notes list; edit account and tax information for existing items	Delete, reorganize, or make list entries inactive, including memorized reports
Enter and memorize general journal transactions, adjust inventory value and quantities	Enter, edit, delete, or memorize any transaction other than general journal and inventory adjustment entries
Create and print new reports, including 1099, 941, 940, and W-2 forms	Export any changes made to 1099, 941, 940, or W-2 forms or employee YTD payroll setup transactions to your copy

CLOSING YOUR BOOKS

Unlike many accounting programs, QuickBooks allows you to make changes to your accounting files at any time. Although this is convenient, it can be a problem if information is changed after it has already been filed with the IRS or other agencies.

To prevent changes before a certain date:

1. Click the **Edit** menu and click **Preferences**. The Preferences window opens, as shown in Figure 8-4.

2. Scroll up the list to the left, and click **Accounting**.

3. In the Closing Date area, click in the **Date Through Which Books Are Closed** field, and type the end date of your fiscal year.

4. Click the **Set Password** button. The Set Closing Date Password dialog box appears.

5. Type a password you will remember, and click **OK**.

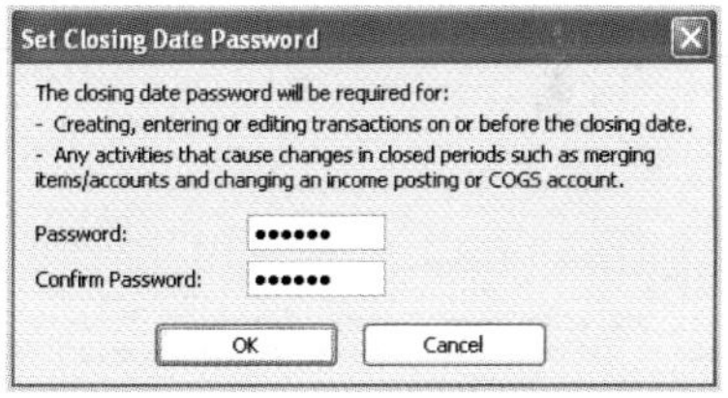

Changes made before this closing date will require the use of the password, which will help ensure that no accidental changes are made.

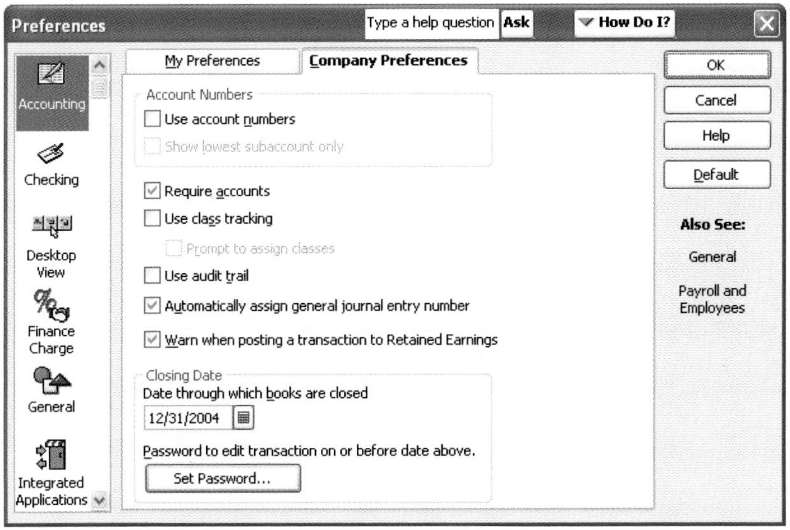

Figure 8-4: Only the Admin user of QuickBooks can change or modify company preferences.

CAUTION

Certain QuickBooks features require you to be in single-user mode. A dialog box will notify you when this is necessary. You can easily switch to single-user mode, complete your task, and switch back to multiuser mode. Others will need to exit the file, however, before you do this.

Network Your QuickBooks File

If you have purchased a multiuser pack, more than one person can use QuickBooks at one time (the Basic edition does not support this feature). This allows the owner, a bookkeeper, and a person at the checkout counter to all enter transactions at the same time.

To allow multiple users to access the file at one time:

1. Connect your computers together using a network (use a contractor if you are not comfortable doing this).

2. Determine on which computer the data file will reside. This computer must be on at all times when others need to access the file. It should be the most stable computer and not need to be rebooted. Preferably, this is a computer that no one uses for daily work.

3. Install the QuickBooks program (the same version) on all computers that need access.

4. Open QuickBooks on the computer on which the file is installed.

5. Set up multiple users (see Chapter 2).

6. Ensure that your file is set to open in multiuser mode by clicking the **File** menu and clicking **Switch To Multi-User Mode**.

Others can now access the file as well.

CAUTION

Shut down QuickBooks at the end of each day to avoid data corruption that can be caused by losing power overnight.

TIP

Reboot your computers on a daily basis to keep your computer from freezing up.

Edit Your QuickBooks Preferences

Preference settings are available in QuickBooks, for the entire company file (Company Preferences) or for the current user (My Preferences). Some preferences require that you close all open windows before making changes, so finish any transactions in progress before changing your preferences.

TABLE 8-2: COMPANY PREFERENCES

PREFERENCE	COMPANY PREFERENCES
Accounting	Account numbers, classes, audit trail, general journal entries, retained earnings, closing date, and password
Checking	Voucher account names, check updating when printed, check field order, duplicate check number warning, autofill payee information, account associations for creating paychecks and paying liabilities, and payee aliasing for online banking
Finance Charge	Annual interest rate, maximum charge, grace period, finance charge account, calculations on finance charges, date, and printing
General	Time and year format; turn off name update (not recommended)
Integrated Applications	Control access to your QuickBooks file from other programs (such as the Intuit Customer Manager)
Jobs and Estimates	Edit estimate titles, warn about duplicate numbers, hide zero amounts, and activate estimates and progress invoicing
Payroll and Employee	Activate payroll and set preferences for printing pay stubs and vouchers, workers' comp, and employee list (see Chapter 9)
Purchases and Vendors	Activate inventory and purchase orders, warn about quantity on hand, and set default for bill-pay dates (see Chapter 7 for information on inventory)
Reminders	Set lists or summaries for each section and reminder dates (see the QuickSteps "Viewing Reminders" in this chapter for more information)
Reports and Graphs	Set accrual or cash basis for reports and set account names, aging report options, and cash flow accounts (see Chapter 10)
Sales and Customers	Set sales form, price levels, sales orders, reimbursed expenses, default markup, and receive payment settings (see Chapter 6 and in this chapter)
Sales Tax	Set sales tax, codes, and payments (see Chapter 6 for information on charging sales tax and Chapter 9 for information on paying sales tax)
Send Forms	Customize default text for e-mailing forms
Service Connection	Allow automatic login to business services and downloading of messages
Tax:1099	Set thresholds for 1099 creation and relate to accounts (see Chapter 5 for more information)
Time Tracking	Turn on time tracking and set day of week (see Chapter 9 for more information)

Customize Company Preferences

Company preferences affect the entire company file and should only be changed by the business owner or accountant after careful consideration.

1. Click the **Edit** menu and click **Preferences**.

2. Scroll down the left side to find the icon for the section you wish to change. Click the icon for that section.

3. Make your selections. When finished, either:

   ● Click **OK** to save and close.

   –Or–

   ● Click **Cancel** if you have made an error.

Table 8-2 lists the specific company preferences in QuickBooks that you can change. Keep in mind that a change to your company preferences affects all QuickBooks users.

TABLE 8-3: MY PREFERENCES

PREFERENCE	MY PREFERENCES
Accounting	Autofill memos for general journal entry
Checking	Account associations for writing checks, paying bills, paying sales tax, making deposits, and online banking
Desktop View	View single or multiple windows; have the Navigator show on startup; and change desktop settings, color scheme, and links to operating system monitor and sound settings
General	Field movement, beeping, decimal point placement, warnings for editing or deleting a transaction, messages, recall transactions, show tool tips, and use today's date (default) versus the last used date
Reminders	Show reminders when opening a company file
Reports and Graphs	Refresh report settings, prompting for report option modification each time you run a report, and graphing options for slower computers
Service Connection	Option to save files and whether to close your browser when using Web Connect
Spelling	Turn spelling checker on or off and control what it does or does not check

Figure 8-5: When conducting a search from the Find window, click the Reset button to clear all entries and start a new search.

Customize My Preferences

Personal preferences are unique to each user in QuickBooks.

1. Click the **Edit** menu and click **Preferences**.

2. Scroll down the left side to see the section you wish to change. Click the icon for that section.

3. Make your selections. When finished, either:

   ● Click **OK** to save and close.

   –Or–

   ● Click **Cancel** if you have made an error.

Table 8-3 lists the specific user preferences in QuickBooks that you can change. Changes made here only affect the currently logged-in user.

Use the Find Feature

The Find feature in QuickBooks can be used to quickly find a transaction. It has a Simple and an Advanced tab. Try both methods of searching and use whichever one you find works better for you.

THE SIMPLE TAB

1. Click the **Edit** menu and click **Find**. The Find window opens, as shown in Figure 8-5.

2. Click the **Simple** tab (if it is not already active).

3. Click the **Transaction Type** down arrow, and click the type of transaction you are searching for, for example, **Invoice**.

4. Click the **Customer:Job** down arrow, and click your customer's name.

5. Click **Find**.

The Find window will display a list of invoices for the customer you selected. If you get a large list, you can add more restrictions, such as date range, invoice, or amount. If you want to see all transaction types at the same time, you'll need to use the Advanced tab. The Simple tab can only be used to search for one type of transaction at a time.

1. Click the **Edit** menu and click **Find**. The Find window opens.

2. Click the **Advanced** tab, as shown in Figure 8-6. For each filter you click in the list, the options to the right of the Filter list will change accordingly.

3. Click the **Transaction Type** down arrow, and click **Invoice**.

4. Click **Name** in the Filter list.

5. Click the **Name** down arrow, and click your customer's name.

6. Click **Find**.

The Find window displays all transactions and line items associated with the customer you selected.

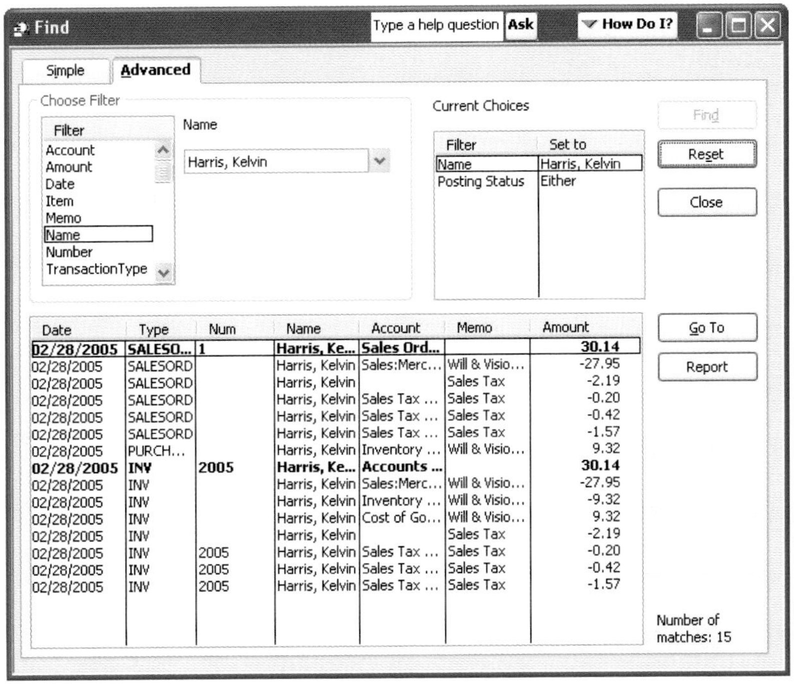

TIP

Double-click any transaction in the Find window to open that transaction for reviewing, editing, or printing.

TIP

Click the **Report** button to generate a report based on the items retrieved using the Find feature.

Figure 8-6: The Advanced tab has a list of filters showing all the searchable fields in QuickBooks.

View Reminders

You can view the Reminders list at any time, but it's convenient when reminders appear each time you open QuickBooks, especially if you do not use QuickBooks every day.

VIEW REMINDERS AT ANY TIME

To view your Reminders list:

Click the **Company** menu and click **Reminders**.

Double-click any bold section header to expand the section and see section items. Double-click any section item to open that item to review, print, or update it.

CUSTOMIZE REMINDERS

To customize the Reminders list:

1. Click the **Edit** menu and click **Preferences**.

2. Click the **Reminders** icon in the scroll bar on the left.

3. Click the **Personal** tab and click **Show Reminders When Opening A Company**.

4. Click the **Company** tab. For each item on the list, choose one of the following:

   • **Show Summary** lists the section header with items hidden.

   • **Show List** lists each item in the section.

   • **Don't Remind Me** does not show any item or header in the section.

5. For items with dates, type the number of days for each reminder in the relevant field.

6. Click **OK** to save your change and close the Preferences window.

To Do items are listed as a section of the Reminders list, or you can view them individually by clicking the **Company** menu and clicking **To Do List**.

> **TIP**
>
> All letters can be customized to meet your company's specific needs.

> **TIP**
>
> To send marketing and other letters, click **Prepare Customer Letters** instead of Prepare Collection Letters.

Communicate with Customers

When communicating with your customers in writing, you can print (and send by regular mail), e-mail, or fax forms and letters. When sending forms (such as invoices) by e-mail, you can customize the default e-mail text aimed at customers in the Preferences section.

Write Collection Letters to Customers

Collection efforts can be unpleasant, but they need to be done. To make it easier, QuickBooks provides you with collection reports (see Chapter 10), statements (see Chapter 6), and form letters you can use when writing collection letters to your customers.

To write a collection letter:

1. Click the **Customers** menu, click **Customer Letters With Envelopes**, and click **Prepare Collection Letters**. The Letters And Envelopes Wizard starts, as shown in Figure 8-7.
2. Leave the default options selected in the first two sections (**Both** and **Customer**). In the third section, click **1 Day Or More**.
3. Click **Next**. A list of customers and the amounts due is displayed, as shown in Figure 8-8. They are all selected by default.

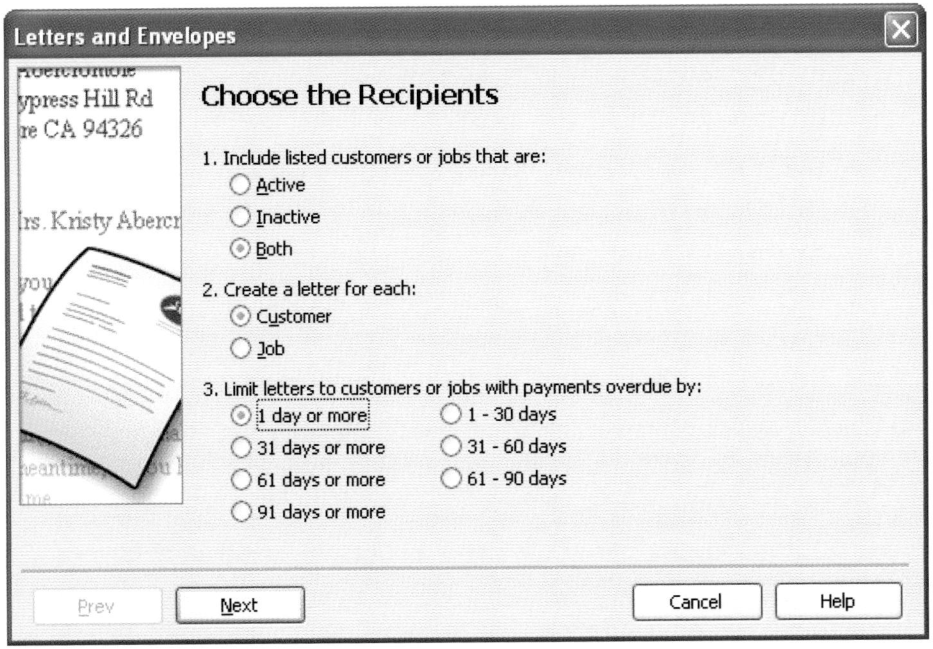
Letters and Envelopes
Choose the Recipients
1. Include listed customers or jobs that are:
Active
Inactive
Both
2. Create a letter for each:
Customer
Job
3. Limit letters to customers or jobs with payments overdue by:
1 day or more
1 - 30 days
31 days or more
31 - 60 days
61 days or more
61 - 90 days
91 days or more
Prev
Next
Cancel
Help

Figure 8-7: The Letters And Envelopes Wizard can help make your collection efforts easier by providing form letters that you customize.

CAUTION

The letter-writing feature in QuickBooks requires you to have Microsoft Word 2000 or later.

4. Click **Next**. Click the type of letter you want to send.

5. Click **Next**. Type your name and title in the fields provided.

7. Click **Next**. QuickBooks creates the letters and opens Word. If any information is missing, QuickBooks will notify you. Click **OK** if this occurs.

8. Your letter is displayed with any missing information indicated, as shown in Figure 8-9. You can edit the letter directly in Word.

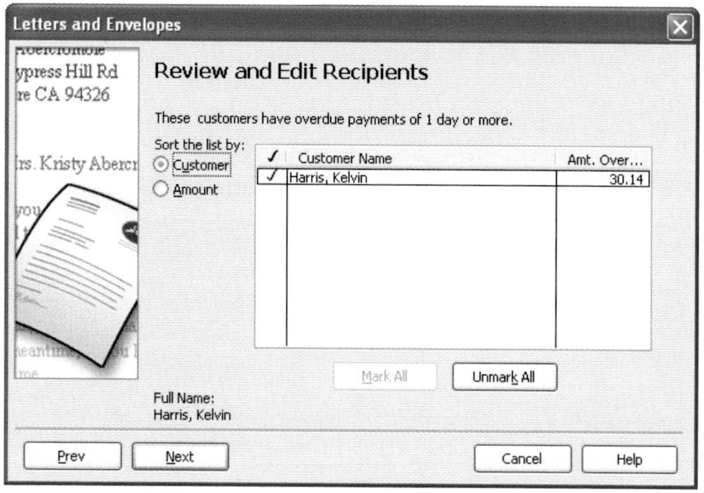

Letters and Envelopes

ypress Hill Rd
re CA 94326

Review and Edit Recipients

These customers have overdue payments of 1 day or more.

Sort the list by:
- ⦿ Customer
- ○ Amount

✓	Customer Name	Amt. Over...
✓	Harris, Kelvin	30.14

Mark All   Unmark All

Full Name:
Harris, Kelvin

Prev   Next   Cancel   Help

Figure 8-8: Click the check mark in the left column to deselect a customer.

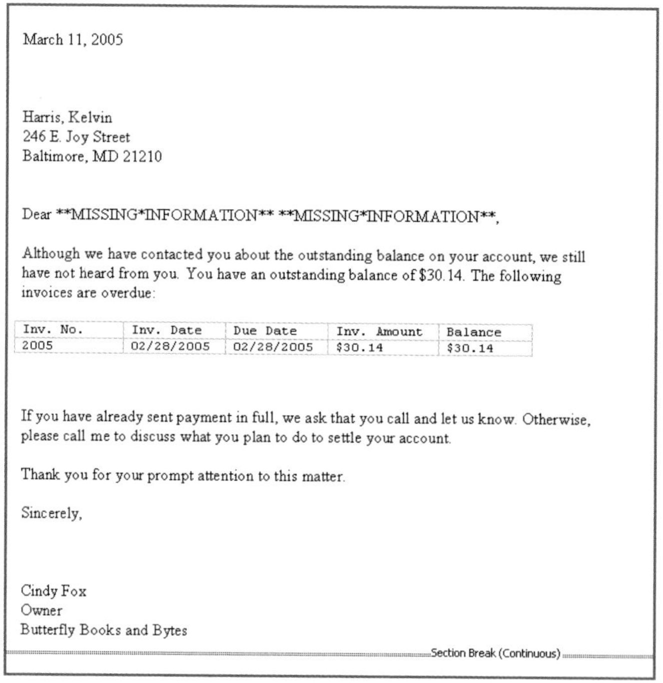

Figure 8-9: Provide the missing information (in this case, first name and last name) in the customer information area, or edit your template so that it is more generic.

March 11, 2005

Harris, Kelvin
246 E. Joy Street
Baltimore, MD 21210

Dear **MISSING*INFORMATION** **MISSING*INFORMATION**,

Although we have contacted you about the outstanding balance on your account, we still have not heard from you. You have an outstanding balance of $30.14. The following invoices are overdue:

Inv. No.	Inv. Date	Due Date	Inv. Amount	Balance
2005	02/28/2005	02/28/2005	$30.14	$30.14

If you have already sent payment in full, we ask that you call and let us know. Otherwise, please call me to discuss what you plan to do to settle your account.

Thank you for your prompt attention to this matter.

Sincerely,

Cindy Fox
Owner
Butterfly Books and Bytes

Section Break (Continuous)

9. In Word, click the **File** menu and click **Print**.

10. In Word, click the **Close** button (the X in the upper-right corner). Save the document when Word prompts you, if desired.

11. Return to the QuickBooks window. A list of options when printing letters or envelopes is displayed.

12. Click **Next**. The Envelope Confirmation window opens. Review the information shown and click the **Delivery Point Barcode** check box if you so desire. Large mailings may receive a discount from the Post Office if they include a barcode, and they also ensure accuracy of mail delivery.

13. Click **OK**. Word opens again so you can print your envelope, as seen in Figure 8-10.

14. Click **OK**. Your envelope is printed and you are returned to QuickBooks. If your envelope did not print correctly, click the **Prev** button on the wizard to try again.

15. Click **Finish**.

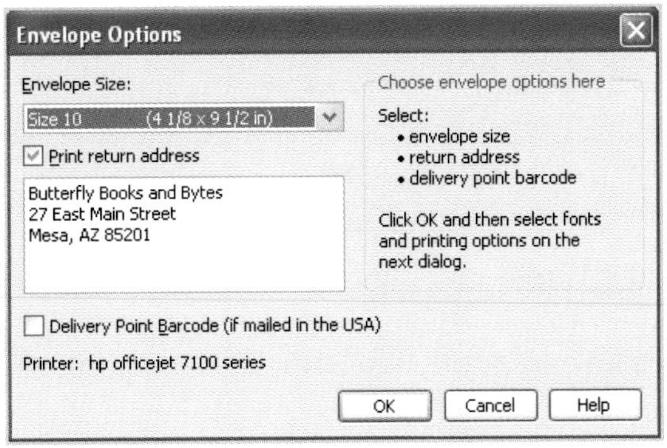

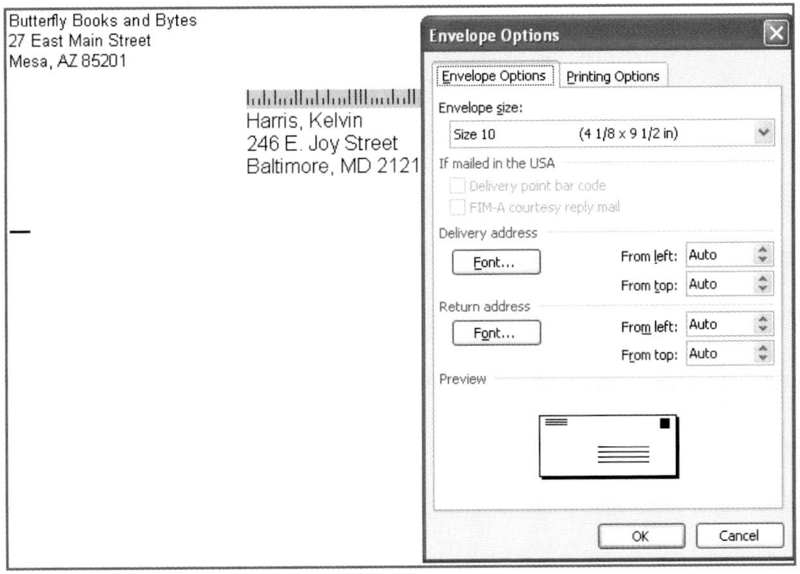

Figure 8-10: Load your envelopes before clicking OK.

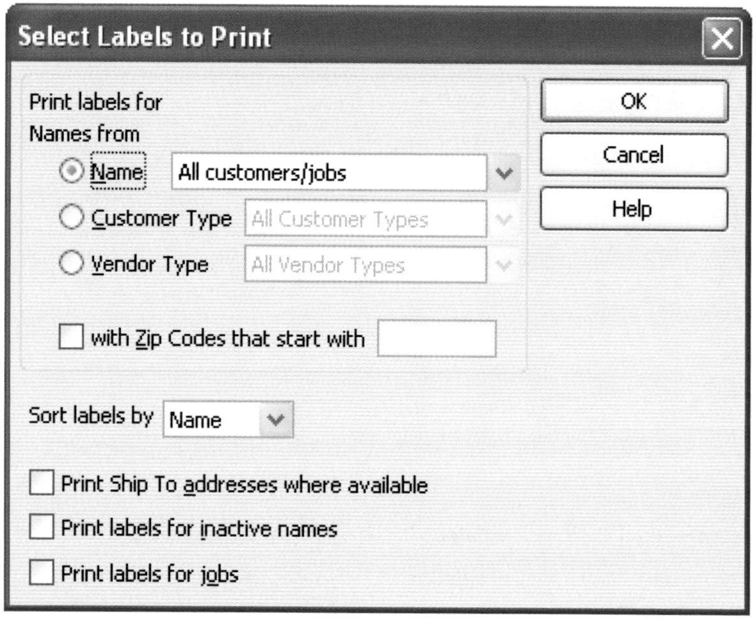

Figure 8-11: You can print and sort labels according to type or ZIP code.

Figure 8-12: Print your labels on plain paper first to make sure they will correctly line up.

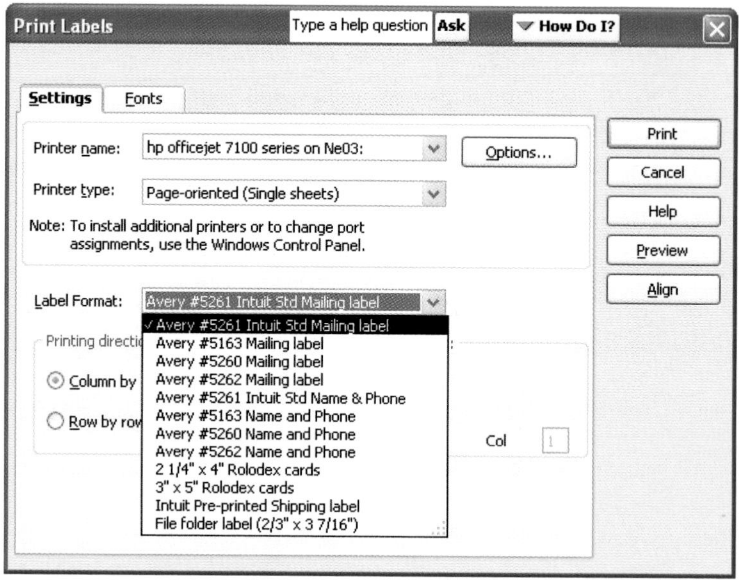

Create Mailing Labels

If you don't have Word or want to send a flyer or other item requiring a label instead of writing a letter, you can easily create mailing labels in QuickBooks.

1. Click the **File** menu, click **Print Forms**, and click **Labels**. The Select Labels To Print window opens, as shown in Figure 8-11. Select the relevant options for printing and/or sorting your labels.

2. Click **OK**. The Print Labels dialog box appears, as shown in Figure 8-12.

3. Click the **Label Format** down arrow, and click your label type, for example, **Avery #5261 Intuit Std. Mailing Label**.

4. Click **Print**. Your mailing labels are printed.

Customize Forms

All of the sales forms in QuickBooks can be customized to meet your needs. This section will demonstrate how to create a new custom invoice, but the procedure is the same for all of the following forms:

- Invoice
- Credit Memo
- Sales Receipt
- Purchase Order
- Statement
- Estimate
- Sales Order

CREATE A NEW INVOICE TEMPLATE

1. Click the **Lists** menu and click **Templates**. The Templates list is displayed.

2. Click the **Templates** menu button (located near the bottom), and click **New**. The Select Template Type dialog box appears.

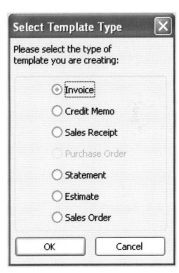

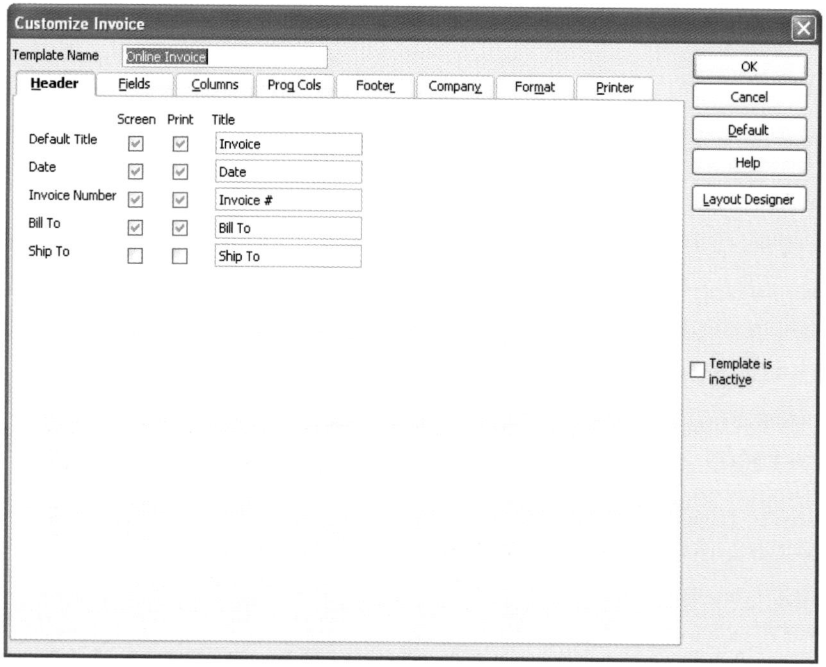

Figure 8-13: *If you're not sure what a particular option does, change it and then view your changes in the Layout Designer.*

3. Click **Invoice** and click **OK**. The Customize Invoice window opens, as shown in Figure 8-13.

4. Click in the **Template Name** field, and type the name of your new invoice, for example, Online Invoice.

5. Click each tab to review your customizing options, and make any changes you desire. See Table 8-5 for a description of each tab's contents.

6. Click **OK**. The new Online Invoice form is now in the Templates list.

TABLE 8-5: OPTIONS WHEN CUSTOMIZING A FORM

TAB	DESCRIPTION
Header	Fields that will print on the top of every page of the form (for example, an invoice)
Fields	Fields that normally print directly below the header on every page of the form
Columns	The main part of the invoice where items, a description, and amount are listed
Prog Cols	Progressive columns can be included to give more information on related estimates when creating a progressive invoice
Footer	Fields that will print on the bottom of each page of the form; includes a text box that you can use to include warranty or return information on every invoice
Company	Options for printing a company logo, name, address, phone number, fax number, e-mail address, and web address; this information is pulled from entries on the Company menu (click **Company** and click **Company Information**)
Format	Options for changing the font of certain sections, printing page numbers, trailing zeros, and adding a status stamp (such as paid, pending, and so on)
Printer	Option to use the default printer or to specify a specific printer for this form (useful for multipart forms printing on a dot-matrix printer)

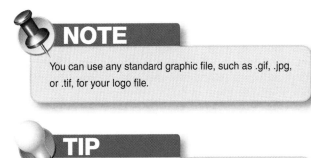

Figure 8-14: In addition to standard company information, you can include your web site address, e-mail address, and company logo in your invoices.

ADD COMPANY INFORMATION AND A LOGO TO AN INVOICE

When adding your company information and logo to an invoice, be sure you have entered it correctly first by clicking the **Company** menu, clicking **Company Information**, and verifying the entries.

1. Click the **Lists** menu and click **Templates**. The Templates list is displayed.

2. Click the form to which you want to add the company information and logo, for example, **Online Invoice**. Click the **Templates** down arrow, and click **Edit Template**. The Customize Invoice window opens, as shown in Figure 8-14.

3. Click the **Company** tab. Click the **Print Web Site Address** check box.

4. Click **Use Logo**. A Select Image dialog box appears. Navigate to the location of your company logo, and click that image.

5. Click **Open**. A dialog box appears, informing you that the image will be copied to a directory in QuickBooks.

6. Click **OK**. You are returned to the Customize Invoice window.

7. Click **OK**. Your changes to the invoice form are saved. If you receive an error message regarding the overlapping of fields, click **Skip**.

![NOTE]
You can use any standard graphic file, such as .gif, .jpg, or .tif, for your logo file.

![TIP]
A square image will work best for your logo, but you can resize the image in the Layout Designer.

To move or resize objects on your form, use the Layout Designer. This feature is especially useful when using window envelopes for invoices. You can arrange the layout, print the document, and fold and stuff it into a test envelope, thus saving you time addressing envelopes.

To use the Layout Designer:

1. Click the **Lists** menu and click **Templates**. The Templates list is displayed.

2. Double-click the form you want to customize using the Layout Designer, for example, **Online Invoice**. The Customize Invoice window opens.

3. Click the **Layout Designer** button. The Layout Designer opens, as shown in Figure 8-15.

4. You now have the following options:

   - Click any item and drag it to a new location.

   - Click any item and press the **DELETE** key to remove it from the layout view (some items cannot be removed).

   - Right-click anywhere in the layout view to see a menu of commands, for example, Undo. You can also add fields, images, or text boxes anywhere you like.

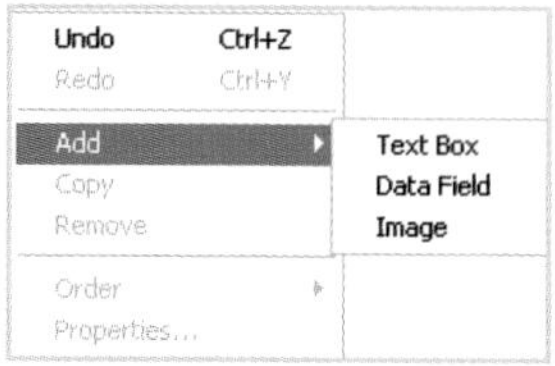

5. When you are finished editing, click **OK** to save your changes (or click **Cancel** if you wish to discard your changes). Your changes are saved and you will exit the Layout Designer. (If you click Cancel, a dialog box appears, prompting you to confirm that you want to discard your changes, and you will then exit the Layout Designer.)

6. Click **OK** to save your changes and exit the Customize Invoices window.

You can create as many customized forms as you like, but it is best to have one form of each type for ease of readability, and only create extra forms if needed for specific customers or purposes.

Figure 8-15: The green shaded areas represent standard window envelope placement. Print and fold a form to confirm it fits your envelopes.

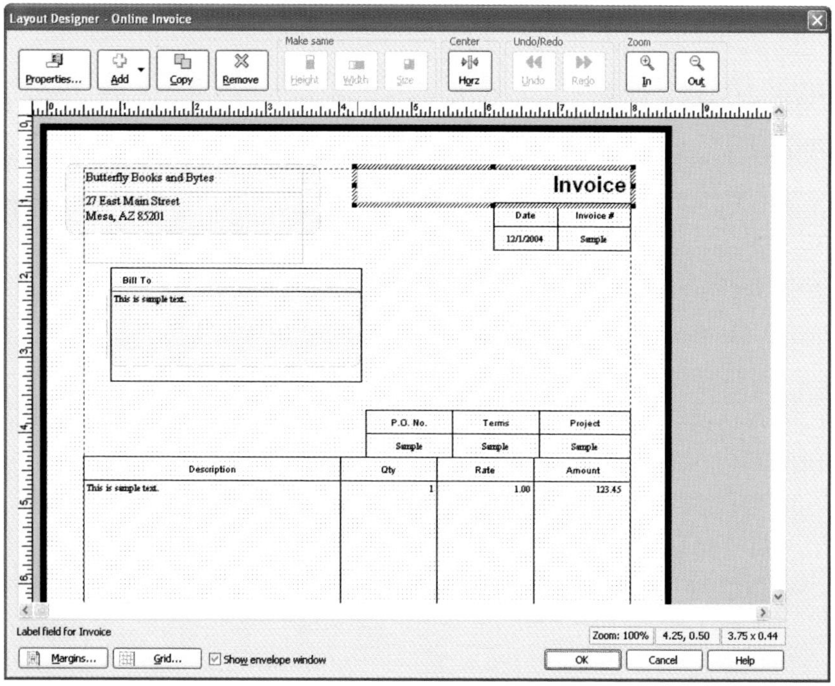

How to...

- *Activate Payroll in Preferences*
- *Set Up Payroll*
- *Choosing a Payroll Service*
- *Set Up Company Information*
- *Enter Default Payroll Settings*
- *Enter and Review Employee Information*
- *Create Paychecks*
- *Print Paychecks*
- *Edit or Void Paychecks*
- *Turn on Time Tracking*
- *Entering a Single Activity*
- *Enter Weekly Timesheets*
- *Review and Pay Payroll Taxes*
- *Review and Pay Sales Taxes*

Chapter 9
Paying Employees and Taxes and Tracking Time

Employees help a business grow, but having employees requires a whole new area of tracking. Companies need to track employee information, hours, and payroll items. In addition to tracking your employee hours for payroll purposes, you can use time tracking to track billable hours to charge back to customers. This chapter will cover both uses of time tracking. Payroll can be set up manually or automated through Intuit's payroll system. Both methods will be addressed in this chapter. You also need to pay payroll taxes and sales taxes, which will also be addressed in this chapter.

9

CAUTION

An Employer Identification Number (EIN) is required to run payroll. This number is assigned by the IRS upon request. Visit www.irs.gov to obtain the necessary paperwork.

NOTE

QuickBooks defaults will be correct for most companies, but if you need to change your printing preferences, workers' compensation preferences, or employee defaults, those options are all available in the Preferences window.

Set Up Payroll Options

The Employee list is similar to the other lists in QuickBooks, but employee forms have unique fields to help you track employee information. Before you can use any payroll feature, however, you need to make sure payroll is enabled in your QuickBooks file, choose which payroll method you will use (see the "Choosing a Payroll Service" QuickSteps), and then set up employees in QuickBooks.

Activate Payroll in Preferences

The first step in setting up payroll is to make sure it is enabled in Preferences. Once you've done this, you'll need to choose a payroll service, set up your company and employees, enter any year-to-date information (if you have been running payroll another way), and then check your payroll data.

To activate payroll:

1. Click the **Edit** menu and click **Preferences**. The Preferences window opens.

2. Click the **Payroll & Employees** icon on the left, and click the **Company Preferences** tab. The Payroll & Employees Company Preferences are displayed, as shown in Figure 9-1.

3. Click the **Full Payroll** option to activate payroll and have additional features available on this tab.

4. Click **OK** to close the Preferences window.

You can come back to this window at any time if you need to change your preferences.

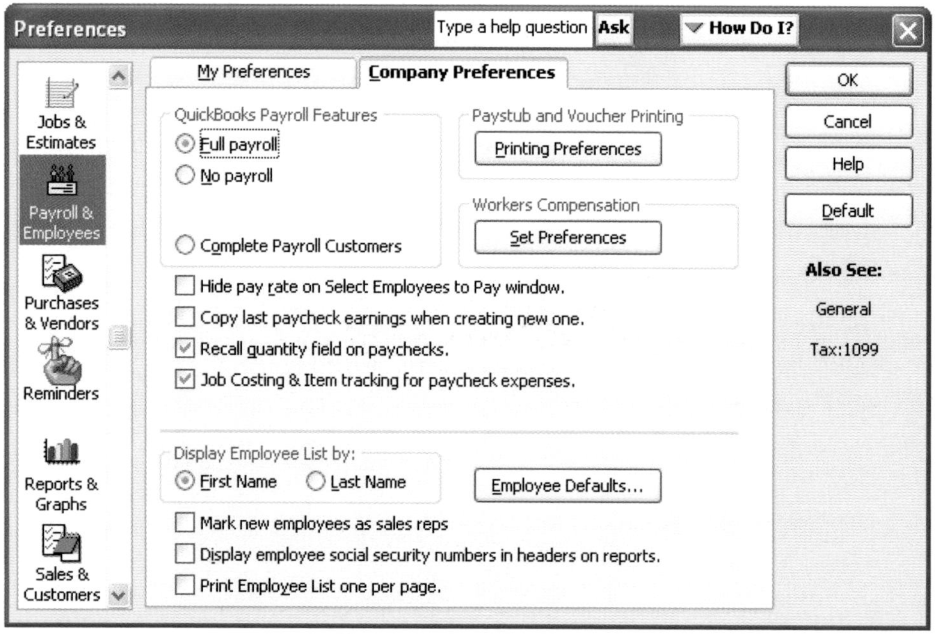

Figure 9-1: There are no personal preferences settings available in Payroll & Employees.

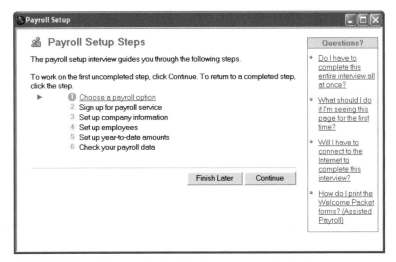

Figure 9-2: You will return to this list after each step. A check mark indicates that a step is complete.

QuickBooks Payroll Service Signup

As soon as you go online to complete your signup, your QuickBooks Payroll subscription will begin. You will also be given the opportunity to sign up for Direct Deposit.

Click Sign Up Now to go online and continue the QuickBooks Payroll signup.

Federal Employer Identification Number (EIN)	20-1234567

Company Legal Name	BUTTERFLY CONSULTING LLC
Legal Address	27 EAST MAIN STREET
City	MESA
State	AZ
Zip Code	85201

Sign Up Now

Cancel   Back   Continue

Set Up Payroll

QuickBooks provides a Payroll Setup Wizard that steps you through your initial setup. You can exit the payroll setup at any time and return later to complete the setup if needed.

To set up your payroll:

1. Click the **Employees** menu, click **Payroll Services**, and click **Set Up Payroll**. If you don't see this choice on your menu, be sure you have the payroll feature activated in your Preferences (see "Activate Payroll in Preferences"). The Payroll Setup window opens, as shown in Figure 9-2.

2. Click the **Continue** button to see a listing of the payroll options. See the "Choosing a Payroll Service" QuickSteps for more information on what you should choose.

3. Make your selection and click the **Continue** button. You are returned to the step overview.

4. Click the **Continue** button again, and enter your EIN in the Payroll Service Signup window (see Figure 9-3) if it has not already been entered into QuickBooks.

5. Click the **Sign Up Now** button. QuickBooks will go online to activate your subscription. If you don't have your EIN, credit card information, or Internet access, click **Back** to return to the steps overview. (This step is optional.)

Figure 9-3: You may cancel the payroll setup at this point if you don't yet have an EIN and activate your subscription later.

CAUTION

You will need to go online to activate your payroll, which will require a credit card payment and your federal Employer Identification Number (EIN). You can still set up payroll and then activate your system later if you don't have these items at this time.

QUICKSTEPS

CHOOSING A PAYROLL SERVICE

QuickBooks offers five levels of payroll services. Table 9-1 compares the features of the different Payroll Services, while Table 9-2 shows estimated costs for comparison.

- **Manual Payroll** requires that you manually calculate and enter the tax rates for your employees. Your accountant can give you the correct amounts to enter for withholding. There are no charges and no guarantees of accuracy.

- **Standard Payroll** allows you to fully control the payroll process, but includes tax tables that are updated on a regular basis to automatically calculate withdrawal amounts.

- **Enhanced Payroll** includes all the Standard Payroll features, as well as information for state tax forms. This level is recommended for companies with 1 to 250 employees.

- **Assisted Payroll** includes more features than Enhanced Payroll, such as making federal and state payroll tax payments from your payroll bank account; filing all required federal and state payroll tax forms; preparing, printing, and mailing employee W-2 forms; and filing your company's W-3 forms with the IRS.

- **Complete Payroll** is an Intuit service that is fully outsourced; you do not need to enter your payroll information into QuickBooks. You can call in your information, and the service processes, prints, and delivers your paychecks to you. They will also prepare and file payroll tax forms, make payroll tax deposits on your behalf, and provide reports. You can download information from the Internet for QuickBooks reporting.

To learn more about any service or find pricing information:

   Click the **Employees** menu, click **Payroll Services**, and click **Learn About Payroll Options**.

Although you can choose to receive updates on a CD-ROM and subscribe via phone, Internet access is required to use direct deposit, to download payroll updates, or to use Assisted Payroll. Complete Payroll does not require any QuickBooks interaction.

TABLE 9-1: COMPARISON OF PAYROLL SERVICES FEATURES

PAYROLL FEATURES	STANDARD	ENHANCED	ASSISTED	COMPLETE
Full QuickBooks integration	✔	✔	✔	
QuickBooks payroll reports (Complete Payroll provides data-import option with 40 additional reports online)	✔	✔	✔	✔
QuickBooks payroll calculations	✔	✔	✔	
Print paychecks and pay stubs from QuickBooks (Complete Payroll can also print for you for an additional fee)	✔	✔	✔	✔
Integrated direct deposit ability (for additional fee)	✔	✔	✔	✔
Calculate net-to-gross paycheck amounts		✔	✔	✔
Track workers' compensation		✔		✔
QuickBooks Employee Organizer (or "HR Assistant") provides employee management tools (for additional fee)	✔	✔	✔	✔
QuickBooks federal and state payroll tax table updates	✔	✔	✔	
Generate and print latest federal forms, such as 940, 940EZ, 941, W-2, W-3, 1099-MISC, and 1096	✔	✔	Service	Service
Generate and print latest state forms		✔	Service	Service
Federal and state electronic payroll tax deposit and filing completed for you with "No Penalties" guarantee			✔	✔
Local payroll tax deposit and filing completed for you				✔
Enter payroll information online or by phone (additional fee for phone use).				✔
Preparation and filing of state new hire reports and calculation and preparation of third-party checks (such as garnishments)				✔

TABLE 9-2: COMPARISON OF AVERAGE COSTS OF PAYROLL SERVICES FOR BIWEEKLY PAYROLL SERVICES

STANDARD PAYROLL	ENHANCED PAYROLL	ASSISTED PAYROLL	COMPLETE PAYROLL
$17/month ($199 billed annually); flat fee (unlimited number of employees)	$25/month ($299 billed annually); flat fee (unlimited number of employees)	$79/month for up to 10 employees; $106/month for 20 employees	$84/month for up to 5 employees; $112/month for 10 employees; $184/month for 20 employees

TIP

You may be assigned EINs from state and local tax agencies in addition to your federal EIN. Keep a folder of communications and information from each agency with which you are dealing.

Set Up Company Information

Your company setup includes your state information—such as your state agency identification numbers; withholding percentages; and payroll items, such as salary, hourly, benefits, and garnishes; federal and state agency payment vendors; and your default setting for new employees.

SET UP STATE PAYROLL ITEMS

1. After you have completed the online activation or returned to the steps overview, click **Continue**. The Company Setup Tasks window opens, showing the list of items to complete, including payroll taxes, payroll items, liability vendors, and default payroll settings.

2. Click the **Continue** button to complete the first task (set up payroll taxes). A list of states is displayed, from which you can choose your state-level payroll.

3. Click every state for which you collect or pay a payroll tax, and click the **Continue** button. A list of rates is displayed for your review.

4. Click the **Continue** button to enter your state information, including company identification numbers, as seen in Figure 9-4 using Arizona as an example.

5. Click the **Continue** button. If you chose multiple states, you will be prompted to enter the pertinent information for each one. Enter the information and click the **Continue** button. When you have entered all the state information, you are returned to the Company Setup Tasks list.

Arizona Payroll Taxes

Tax Payment Information

Arizona State Withholding Number	`99999999` *99999999* Located on Forms A1-WP, A1-QRT (see State Withholding Number). AZ Department of Revenue, (800) 843-7196 or (602) 255-2060.
Arizona Dept. of Economic Security Account Number	`9999999-9` *9999999 9 or 9999999-9* Located on Form UC-018 (see ARIZONA ACCOUNT NUMBER). Arizona Department of Economic Security, (602) 248-9396.

Rates and Limits

	Company Rate	Employee Rate	Taxable Wage Limit
AZ – Withholding	none	table	none
AZ – Unemployment Company *	Jan-Mar `2.1` % Apr-Jun `2.1` % Jul-Sep `2.1` % Oct-Dec `2.1` %	none	$7,000
AZ – Job Training Tax	`0.1%` ▾	none	$7,000

* Enter percentages without the preceding two decimal places. Examples: enter 3.1% as 3.1, not .031. Enter .25% as .25, not .0025.

[Cancel]   [Back]   [Continue]

Company Payroll States

Select all states for which your company collects or pays payroll taxes.

☐ Alabama	☐ Indiana	☐ Nebraska	☐ Rhode Island
☐ Alaska	☐ Iowa	☐ Nevada	☐ South Carolina
☑ Arizona	☐ Kansas	☐ New Hampshire	☐ South Dakota
☐ Arkansas	☐ Kentucky	☐ New Jersey	☐ Tennessee
☐ California	☐ Louisiana	☐ New Mexico	☐ Texas
☐ Colorado	☐ Maine	☐ New York	☐ Utah
☐ Connecticut	☐ Maryland	☐ North Carolina	☐ Vermont
☐ Delaware	☐ Massachusetts	☐ North Dakota	☐ Virginia
☐ Florida	☐ Michigan	☐ Ohio	☐ Washington
☐ Georgia	☐ Minnesota	☐ Oklahoma	☐ Washington DC
☐ Hawaii	☐ Mississippi	☐ Oregon	☐ West Virginia
☐ Idaho	☐ Missouri	☐ Pennsylvania	☐ Wisconsin
☐ Illinois	☐ Montana	☐ Puerto Rico	☐ Wyoming

[Cancel]   [Back]   [Continue]

Figure 9-4: Your state will look different and may have no tax requirements. Check with local agencies.

9

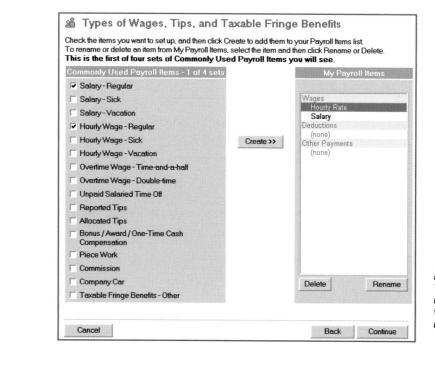

TIP

If you mistakenly add an item to your list that you don't want, click the item to select it, and click the **Delete** button at the bottom. You can also click an item to select it, and click the **Rename** button to rename it.

SET UP PAYROLL ITEMS

Payroll items can be set up as part of the payroll setup. They are also accessible on the Lists menu on the Payroll Item list. A wizard will step you through the process of adding additional payroll items if you need to make changes later.

1. Click the **Continue** button to move to the next task (enter payroll items). A window opens, as seen in Figure 9-5.

2. Click the check box next to each item you want to add. Click the **Create** button in the middle of the window to add them to the My Payroll Items list on the right side.

3. Click the **Continue** button to go through each of the four screens:

   - Types of Wages, Tips, and Taxable Fringe Benefits
   - Insurance Benefits
   - Retirement Benefits
   - Other Payments and Deductions

4. When you are finished adding items, you are returned to the Company Setup Tasks list.

5. Click the **Continue** button to move to the next step and add the tax agencies to which you make payments as vendors. The Tax Payment Information window opens.

6. Review the tax payment information, correct if necessary, and then click the **Continue** button. If you chose additional items, you will see a list of those items with the vendors and account numbers displayed.

7. Click the **Continue** button until you return to the Company Setup Tasks list.

Figure 9-5: Salary – Regular and Hourly Wage – Regular are the most commonly used items. If your company offers sick, vacation, and overtime pay, select the relevant items.

If you have a weekly or monthly salary amount, type the amount in the Hourly/Annual Rate field followed by the asterisk (*), indicating multiplication, and then the number of periods in a year, such as <u>2450 * 12</u> or <u>700 * 52</u>. QuickBooks automatically calculates the amount.

Enter Default Payroll Settings

Default settings are for those payroll items that most people in your company have in common, such as hourly wage, health insurance, vacation, and sick time. If you have multiple employees, establishing default payroll settings will allow you to easily add new employees with your standard, preferred settings, as well as edit those items that are different for each employee added.

1. Click the **Continue** button to move to the final company task (enter default payroll settings). The Default Payroll Settings For New Employees window opens.

2. Click the **Continue** button if you do *not* want to set up default settings. You are returned to the Company Setup Tasks list. (This step is optional.) Otherwise, click the **Edit** button. The Employee Defaults window opens, as shown in Figure 9-6.

3. Click the **Pay Period** down arrow, and click your company's pay period (**Daily**, **Weekly**, **Bi-Weekly**, **Semi-Monthly**, **Quarterly**, **Annually**).

4. Click in the **Item Name** column under the Earnings area, and a down arrow will appear. Click this down arrow to see the income choices you have available. Click the most commonly used income type, for example, **Salary**.

5. Press the **TAB** key to move to the Hourly/Annual Rate column. Type the appropriate rate for the income type you chose. Continue to add items in this area (if necessary) until complete.

6. Click the **Use Time Data To Create Paychecks** check box if you will be using the timesheet or single-time entry in QuickBooks.

7. If you have common additions or deductions, click in the **Item Name** column under the Additions, Deductions And Company Contributions area, and click a common item.

8. Press the **TAB** key to move to the Amount column, and type the amount (per pay period). Continue to add items in this area until complete.

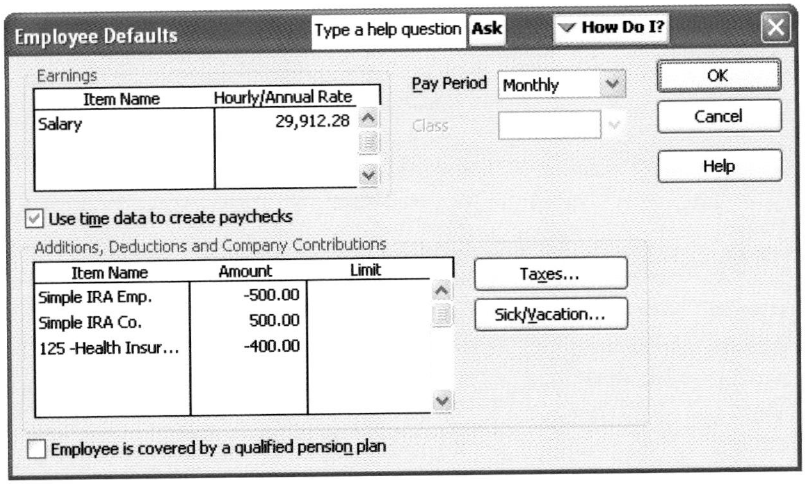

Figure 9-6: Use the Employee Defaults window to set up the most commonly used employee settings.

TIP

You do not have to use the default settings. They are there to help you; any item can be changed for each new employee.

Taxes Defaults

Federal | **State** | Other

State Worked
State AZ ☑ SUI (Company Paid)

State Subject to Withholding
State AZ

OK
Cancel
Help

NOTE

Click **Reset Hours Each New Year**? in the Sick or Vacation sections if your company policy dictates that unused time is lost at the end of the year.

ENTER DEFAULT TAX SETTINGS

1. From the Employee Defaults window, click the **Taxes** button. The Taxes Default window opens so that you can enter federal, state, and local tax settings.

Taxes Defaults

Federal | State | Other

Filing Status Single

Subject to
☑ Medicare
☑ Social Security
☐ Advance Earned Income Credit
☑ Federal Unemployment Tax (Company Paid)

OK
Cancel
Help

2. Click the **Filing Status** down arrow, and click the most common filing status (**Single**, **Married**, **Married Using Single**, or **Don't Withhold**).

3. In the Subject To area, click the check boxes for items related to your company's employees.

4. Click the **State** tab and choose the state your company's employees typically work in and the state they typically live in (pay taxes in).

5. Click the **SUI** check box if you need to pay state unemployment insurance.

6. Click the **Other** tab if you need to enter custom taxes not covered by the Federal and State tabs.

7. Click **OK** to close this window and return to the Employee Defaults window. Answer any questions that may appear.

ENTER SICK AND VACATION DEFAULTS

1. From the Employee Defaults window, click the **Sick/Vacation** button. The Sick & Vacation Defaults window opens.

Sick & Vacation Defaults

Sick
Accrual period
Every paycheck
Hours accrued per paycheck   5:00
Maximum number of hours   120:00
☐ Reset hours each new year?

Vacation
Accrual period
Every paycheck
Hours accrued per paycheck   10:00
Maximum number of hours   240:00
☐ Reset hours each new year?

OK
Cancel
Help

2. In the Sick area, click the **Accrual Period** down arrow, and click the relevant period for sick-time accrual (**Beginning Of Year**, **Every Paycheck**, or **Every Hour On Paycheck**).

3. Press the TAB key to move to the Hours Accrued Per Paycheck field, and type the number of hours.

TIP

The Employee List button in the Employee Setup window displays the Employee list. You can also click the **Employees** menu and then click **Employee List** to access it at any time.

4. Press the **TAB** key to move to the Maximum Number Of Hours field, and type the number of hours.

5. Press the **TAB** key to move to the Hours Accrued Per Paycheck field in the Vacation area, and type the number of hours.

6. Press the **TAB** key to move to the Maximum Number Of Hours field, and type the number of hours.

7. Click **OK** to close the window and return to the Employee Defaults window.

8. Click **OK** to close the window and return to the Default Payroll Settings window.

9. Click the **Continue** button to return to the Company Setup Tasks list.

10. Click the **Done** button to return to the Payroll Setup Steps window.

Enter and Review Employee Information

In order to pay employees, you must first set them up in QuickBooks. Use the Payroll Setup window to initially set up employees, and then use the Employee list to manage your employees. The Employee Navigator gives you an overview and links to employee tasks and information.

SET UP EMPLOYEES

To set up employees from the Payroll Setup Steps window:

1. Click the **Continue** button on the Payroll Setup Steps window. The Employee Setup window opens.

2. Click the **Add Employee** button. The New Employee window opens, as seen in Figure 9-7.

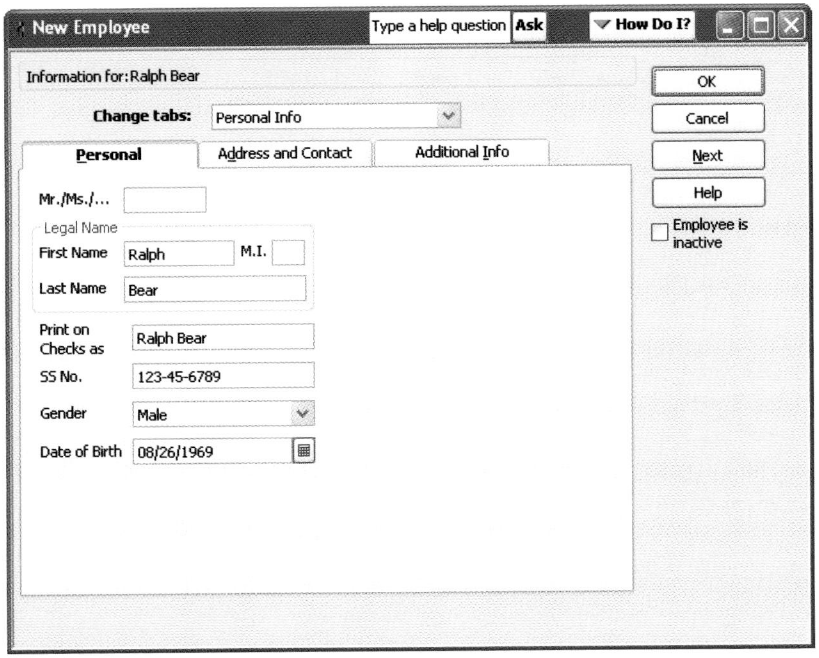

Figure 9-7: The Change Tabs drop-down list presents different choices from the visible tabs.

3. Click in the **First Name** field, and type the employee's first name.

4. Press the TAB key to move to the Last Name field, and type the employee's last name.

5. Press the TAB key. QuickBooks automatically fills in the Print On Checks As field with the employee's name. Confirm that the name is correct.

6. Press the TAB key to move to the SS No. field, and type the employee's social security number. Fill in the Gender and Date Of Birth fields if desired.

7. Click the **Address And Contact** tab, and enter the relevant information. (This step is optional.)

8. Click the **Additional Info** tab, and enter the relevant information. (This step is optional.)

9. Click the **Change Tabs** down arrow, and click **Payroll And Compensation Info**. A new tab is displayed, as shown in Figure 9-8.

10. Review and change any information that does not pertain to this employee.

11. Click the **Change Tabs** down arrow, and click **Employment Info**. A new tab is displayed that includes hire date, release date, and employee type.

12. Review and change any information that does not pertain to this employee.

13. Click **OK** when you are finished adding employees. You are returned to the Payroll Setup window.

14. Click the **Continue** button to return to the Employee Setup window.

15. Click the **Continue** button to return to the Payroll Setup Steps window.

Figure 9-8: Default payroll information is entered for each new employee.

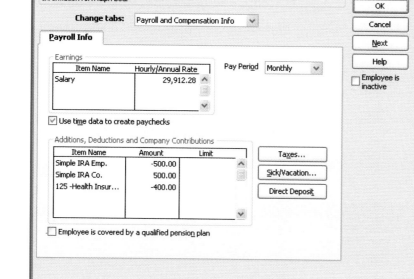

CAUTION

Read the choices carefully to determine your need. If you are starting a new company, are at the beginning of the year, or have not yet paid any employees, you do not need to use this section.

TIP

This information only needs to be done once in a QuickBooks file and not at all if you don't meet the criteria. Consult your tax professional for additional assistance in this area.

YEAR-TO-DATE INFORMATION

If your company has employees that have been paid through some prior payroll method, you will need to adjust the current balance of liabilities.

1. Click the **Continue** button in the Payroll Setup Steps window. The Enter Year To Date Payroll Amounts In QuickBooks window opens.
2. Click **Cancel**.
3. Click **Finish** to close the Set Up YTD Amounts window and return to the Payroll Setup window.
4. Click the **Continue** button to return to the Payroll Setup Steps window.
5. Click **Done** to close the Payroll Setup Steps window.

Be sure to review and check your data when you run payroll for the first time. After a few payroll periods, you will be more comfortable with the mechanism of running payroll and more confident of your payroll settings.

EMPLOYEE NAVIGATOR

The Employee Navigator gives you an overview of employee and payroll options, and allows you to click any icon for quick access to a related section.

To view the Employee Navigator:

Click the **Employees** menu and click **Employee Navigator**. The Employee Navigator window opens, as shown in Figure 9-9.

From here you can perform all employee-related reports, activities, forms, and timesheets. Click the **Close** button (the red X in the upper-right corner) when finished.

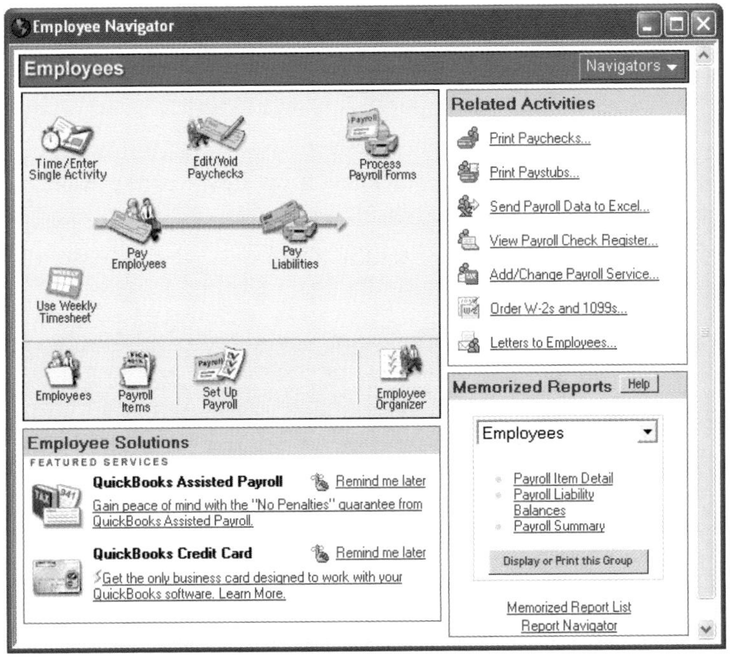

Figure 9-9: Access time, employee, and payroll functions from the Employee Navigator or from the Employees menu.

Run and Maintain Payroll

Payroll can be established on a weekly, biweekly, monthly, or annual basis. It's important to be consistent and choose a frequency that works for your company. You must use the Create Paycheck feature and not the Write Checks feature in order to have accurate withholdings, although you can use the same checking account.

Create Paychecks

To create paychecks:

1. Click the **Employees** menu and click **Pay Employees**. The Select Employees To Pay window opens, as shown in Figure 9-10. If you get an error message, return to the Payroll Setup window, and make sure your payroll selection is activated (see "Activate Payroll in Preferences").

2. Click the **Bank Account** down arrow, and click the bank account against which you are writing payroll checks. If you only have one bank account, you can use it for regular checks and payroll checks, but just make sure to always create paychecks using this window.

3. Click the **To Be Printed** option in the Paycheck Options area if you will be using your printer or online banking service to create checks. You can choose to handwrite or directly deposit funds and enter the check number if desired.

4. Click in the **Check Date** field, and choose the date the check will be printed.

5. Click in the **Pay Period Ends** window, and type the final date of the pay period for which you are paying.

6. Click the employee names you will be entering paychecks for, if not already selected.

> **CAUTION**
>
> You may see a dialog box regarding year-to-date amounts. Confirm that you do not need to enter them, or return to the Setup YTD Amounts window before creating paychecks. Do *not* create paychecks before entering YTD amounts if they need to be entered.

> **NOTE**
>
> In the Select Employees To Pay window, you will *not* see vendors (subcontractors), employees identified as owners, inactive employees, or employees with a release date earlier than the current pay date.

Figure 9-10: Future paychecks will include the data in the Last Pay Period End column and the option to create paychecks based on hours from the last paycheck.

Preview Paycheck

Ralph Bear

Pay Period 01/01/2005 - 01/31/2005

☐ Use Direct Deposit

Earnings

Item Name	Rate	Hours	Customer:Job	Service Item
Salary	2,492.69			

Total Hours: 0:00

Sick Available 5:00
Vacation Avail. 10:00
Sick Accrued 5:00
Vac. Accrued 10:00

☐ Do not accrue sick/vac

Other Payroll Items

Item Name	Rate	Quantity
Simple IRA Emp.	-500.00	
Simple IRA Co.	500.00	
125 -Health Insurance (pre-t...	-400.00	

Company Summary (adjusted)

Item Name	Amount	YTD
Simple IRA Co.	500.00	500.00
Social Security Company	154.55	154.55
Medicare Company	36.14	36.14
Federal Unemployment	19.95	19.95
AZ - Unemployment Company	16.95	16.95

Employee Summary (adjusted)

Item Name	Amount	YTD
Salary	2,492.69	2,492.69
Simple IRA Emp.	-500.00	-500.00
125 -Health Insurance (pre-t...	-400.00	-400.00
Federal Withholding	-335.00	-335.00
Social Security Employee	-154.55	-154.55
Medicare Employee	-36.14	-36.14
AZ - Withholding	-167.00	-167.00

Check Amount: 900.00

Create   Cancel   Help

☐ Enter net/Calculate gross
What's this?

Figure 9-11: Review and edit any amounts needed with the exception of YTD amounts.

Select Paychecks to Print

Bank Account Payroll Checking   First Check Number 144

Select Paychecks to print, then click OK.
There is 1 Paycheck to print for $900.00.

✓	Date	Employee	Amount
✓	02/01/2005	Ralph Bear	900.00

OK
Cancel
Help
Select All
Select None
Preferences

Show: ⦿ Both   ○ Paychecks   ○ Direct Deposit

Figure 9-12: Confirm that the check number matches the next number on your check stock.

7. Click the **Create** button. The Preview Paycheck window opens, as shown in Figure 9-11. Amounts will be automatically entered for you if a payroll service has been activated. Otherwise, you will need to manually enter the amounts.

8. Click the **Create** button. The paycheck is created and ready for printing, and you are returned to the Select Employees To Pay window. You may now print paychecks or close this window.

Print Paychecks

Once you have created paychecks, you need to print them. The process of creating them calculates taxes, tracking both the employee balances and what you owe the tax agencies.

To print paychecks:

1. Click the **Employees** menu and click **Pay Employees**. The Select Employees To Pay window opens.

2. Click the **Print Paychecks** button. The Select Paychecks To Print window opens, as shown in Figure 9-12, listing current paychecks waiting to be printed. If you don't have any checks listed, make sure you followed the steps in the "Create Paychecks" section.

3. Click all the employees for whom you wish to print checks, and confirm that the bank account and check number are correct.

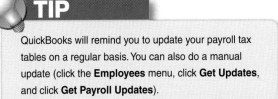

TIP

QuickBooks will remind you to update your payroll tax tables on a regular basis. You can also do a manual update (click the **Employees** menu, click **Get Updates**, and click **Get Payroll Updates**).

Print Checks

Type a help question **Ask**   ▼ **How Do I?**   ☒

You have 1 check to print for $900.00

| **Settings** | Fonts | Partial Page |

Printer name: hp officejet 7100 series on Ne03: ▼   Options...

Printer type: Page-oriented (Single sheets) ▼

Note: To install additional printers or to change port
assignments, use the Windows Control Panel.

Check Style

○ Standard   ◉ Voucher   ○ Wallet

Number of copies: 1

☐ Print company name and address.

☐ Use logo

Print

Cancel

Help

Logo

Figure 9-13: If your company name, address, and logo are not already printed on the check, click the Print Company Name And Address and Use Logo check boxes.

4. Click **OK**. The Print Checks window opens, as shown in Figure 9-13.

5. Load your checks correctly in the printer, and verify that the correct printer is selected in the Printer Name field.

6. In the Check Style area, click the option that corresponds to the type of check you have. Most paychecks are printed on voucher-style checks, which have a check on the top and the deduction information on the bottom of an 8.5" x 11" sheet.

7. Click **Print**. The check is sent to your printer, and you are asked to confirm that it printed correctly.

8. Click **OK** if it printed correctly; the dialog box closes and the paycheck is updated with the check number. If it did not print correctly, type the check number that did not print correctly so that it will be marked to be printed again.

Did check(s) print OK?   ☒

Remember to sign your checks!
If check 144 printed correctly, click OK
to continue. Otherwise, type the number of the check
which printed incorrectly and then click OK.

First incorrectly printed check: |

OK   Help

9. Close the Select Employees To Pay window.

Once paychecks are created, you can also print them by clicking the **File** menu, clicking **Print Forms**, and clicking **Paychecks**.

Edit or Void Paychecks

With QuickBooks, you can edit, void, review, or reprint a paycheck. If an employee has lost a paycheck or you need to make changes after creating it but before printing, you can make those changes, but don't change a check that is unaccounted for.

To edit or void a paycheck:

1. Click the **Employees** menu and click **Edit/Void Paychecks**. The Edit/Void Paychecks window opens.

2. Click in the beginning and ending date fields, and choose the date range during which the paycheck you are looking for was written.

CAUTION

Make sure your year-end closing date is set so that you do not accidentally edit payroll checks on which you have already paid company taxes. See Chapter 8 for more information on closing dates.

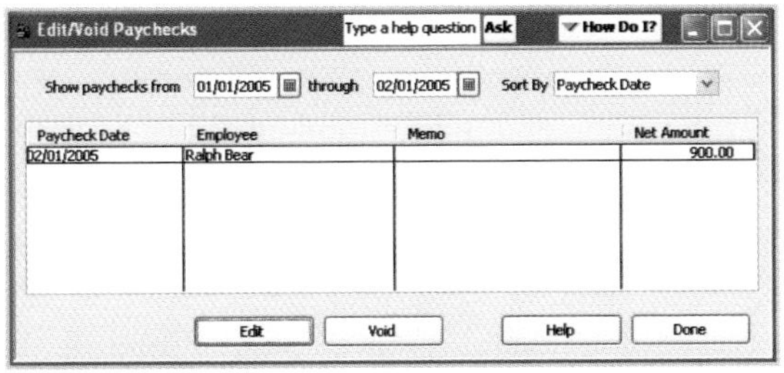

3. Click the check you wish to void or edit. If you need to void the check, click the **Void** button. Click the **Edit** button to view the check for reviewing, editing, or printing, as shown in Figure 9-14.

4. At this point, you can:

   - Click the **Print** button to print the check now

   - Click the **To Be Printed** check box if you want to print the check later

   - Click the **Paycheck Detail** button to open the Review Paycheck window, as shown in Figure 9-15

5. After making any changes necessary, click **OK** to return to the Paycheck window.

6. Click **Save & Close** to save your changes and close the window.

7. Confirm that you wish to save your changes if asked.

8. Click the **Done** button to close the Edit/Void Paychecks window.

At any time you can click the **Revert** button to discard your changes and start again.

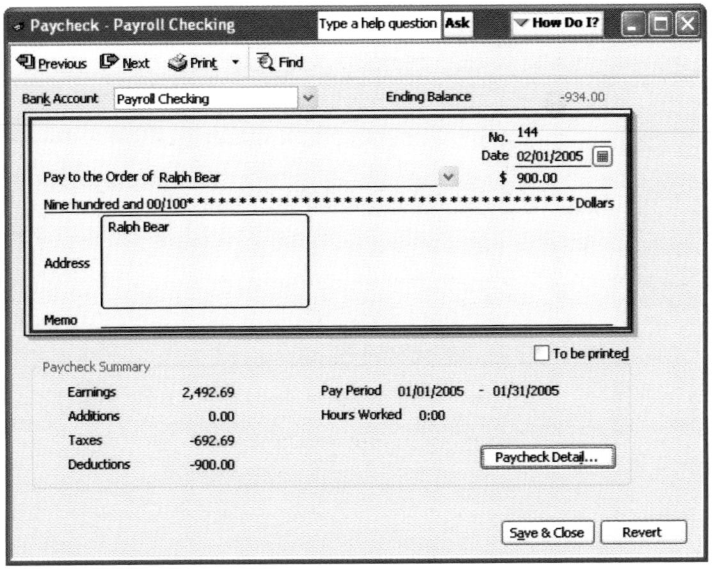

Figure 9-14: A paycheck looks different from an average check and has additional details available.

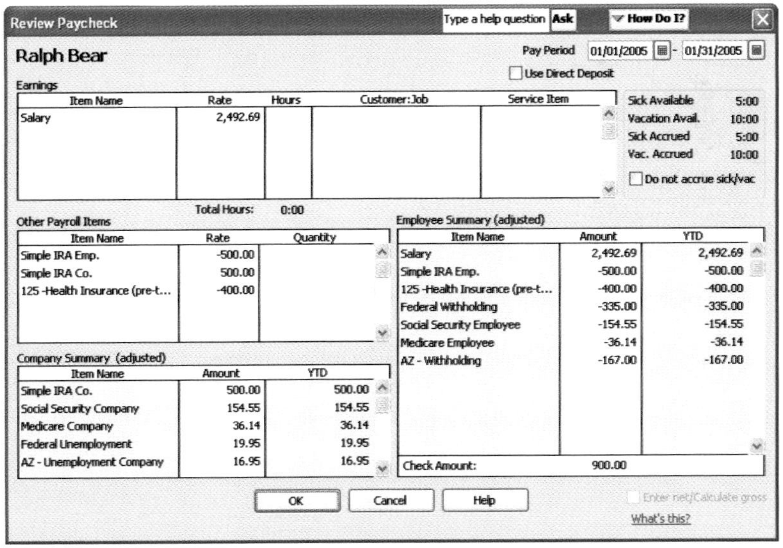

Figure 9-15: From the Review Paycheck window, you can edit any item entered incorrectly and then reprint the check.

TIP

There is a separate time program included with QuickBooks (all versions but Basic), but importing information can get confusing and cumbersome. Use this program if you need to specifically track a lot of small periods of time by many people. Otherwise, manually enter data.

Track Time

The ability to track time is not available in QuickBooks Basic, but is available in all other versions. It is used to enter employee hours for payroll, billable hours for customer billing, or both. Time can be tracked within QuickBooks as a single entry for each activity or as a weekly timesheet.

Turn on Time Tracking

Before you can use the time-tracking feature, you need to activate it in Preferences.

1. Click the **Edit** menu and click **Preferences**.

2. Click the **Time Tracking** icon on the left, and click the **Company Preferences** tab, as seen in Figure 9-16.

3. In the Do You Track Time? area, click **Yes**.

4. Click the **First Day Of Work Week** down arrow, and choose the day you will use as your first day of the week for payroll. This will be used for entering time on a weekly basis.

5. Click **OK**. Your preferences are saved and the window closes.

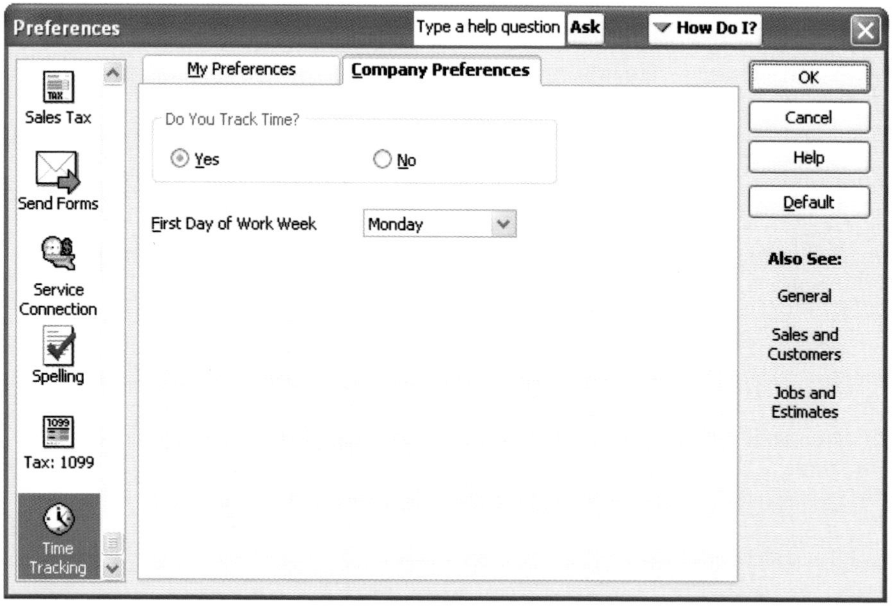

Figure 9-16: There are no personal preferences settings available in Time Tracking.

QUICKSTEPS

ENTERING A SINGLE ACTIVITY

Enter a single activity for individual entries or to time an event. Use the weekly timesheets (see "Enter Weekly Timesheets") to enter hours for the week.

1. Click the **Employees** (or **Customers**) menu, click **Time Tracking**, and click **Time/Enter Single Activity**. The Time/Enter Single Activity window opens.

2. Confirm or correct the date. Today's date is displayed by default, which you *must* use to use the timer.

3. Press the **TAB** key to move to the Name field, and type the name of the employee or subcontractor whose time you are tracking.

4. Press the **TAB** key to move to the Customer:Job field, and type the name of the customer for whom you are tracking time.

5. Press the **TAB** key to move to the Service Item field, and type the service item.

6. Press the **TAB** key to move to the Time field in the Duration area. Type the time such as 1:15. To time an activity, click the **Start** button. The timer will start from the time you have entered until you click **Stop**, click **Pause**, or close the window.

7. Click the **Billable** check box if you need to charge this time back to the customer.

8. Click the **Payroll Item** down arrow, and choose a relevant payroll item if the activity is for an employee.

9. Press the **TAB** key to move to the Notes section, and type any notes pertaining to this time activity.

10. Click **Save & Close**.

Enter Weekly Timesheets

Entering single activities is useful for occasional use or for keeping detailed notes, but weekly timesheets are more streamlined for many entries. Use weekly timesheets to enter payroll-related timesheets and/or billable time that will be charged to customers.

To enter weekly timesheets:

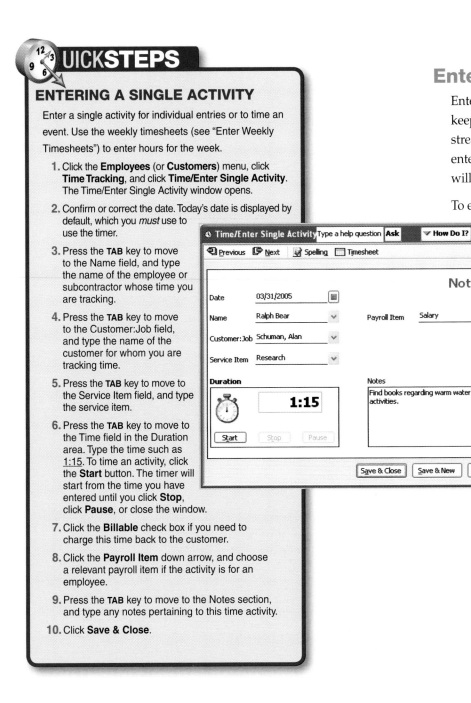

1. Click the **Employees** (or **Customers**) menu, click **Time Tracking**, and click **Use Weekly Timesheet**. The Weekly Timesheet window opens, as shown in Figure 9-17.

2. Confirm or correct the date. Use the **Previous** and **Next** buttons at the top of the timesheet to move to earlier or later dates, respectively.

3. Click in the **Name** field, and type the name of the employee or subcontractor whose time you are tracking.

4. Press the **TAB** key to move to the Customer:Job field, and type the name of the customer for whom you are tracking time.

NOTE

Activities will appear on both single-activity and weekly timesheets, so it doesn't really matter which way you enter them; use whichever method is more convenient for you.

NOTE

When you enter a payroll item in the timesheet, all other columns become optional (except Time).

TIP

If you don't wish to bill a line item to a customer, click the billable icon in the far right column so that it has a red X through it, as in the second line of Figure 9-17.

5. Press the **TAB** key to move to the Service Item field, and type the service item for which you are tracking time.

6. Click the **Payroll** down arrow, and choose the relevant payroll item if this time activity is for an employee.

7. Press the **TAB** key to move to the Notes field, and type any notes pertaining to this time activity. You can control how the text wraps by clicking the **Wrap Text In Notes** field check box, located at the bottom.

8. Press the **TAB** key to move to the relevant Day field. Type the time in either hours and minutes, such as 2:15, or in hours and fractions of an hour, such as 2.25.

9. Click **Save & Close** (or click **Save & New** to continue adding time activities).

Using weekly timesheets is the best way to enter payroll time data. When you next create a paycheck, QuickBooks will ask if you wish to use the time data available.

Figure 9-17: Make sure you are on the correct date before you start entering activities, or you will lose your information when you move to the correct date.

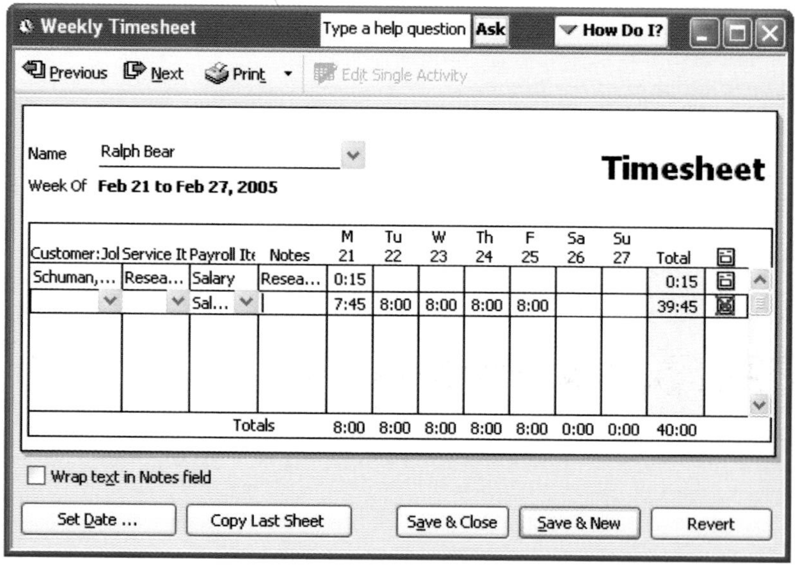

Paying Taxes

Once you have tax items set up, QuickBooks tracks your taxes and gives you an easy way to pay everyone, including Uncle Sam, your local state agencies, your employees, and, of course, yourself. Your responsibilities as an employer include paying all withholdings on your scheduled basis, and QuickBooks makes this easy.

Review and Pay Payroll Taxes

Most companies need to pay payroll taxes at least quarterly, although some companies pay them monthly. Verify with your local tax agencies the frequency with which you need to pay any taxes. Before paying taxes, you can run a payroll report to review your payments, withholdings, and amounts due to tax agencies.

RUN A PAYROLL REPORT

To run a payroll report:

1. Click the **Reports** menu, click **Employees And Payroll**, and click **Payroll Summary**. A report is displayed similar to that pictured in Figure 9-18.

2. Click the **Close** button when finished reviewing this report.

See Chapter 10 for information on customizing and memorizing reports.

> **TIP**
>
> Both federal and state (if using QuickBooks Enhanced Payroll service) payroll forms are available for you to process, print, and mail. Click the **Employees** menu and click **Process Payroll Forms**.

Figure 9-18: Add the Payroll Summary report to your icon bar for easy access and review.

	Modify Report...	Memorize...	Print...	E-mail	Export...	Hide Header	Refresh	

Dates: This Calendar Quarter From 01/01/2005 To 03/31/2005 Columns Employee

2:47 PM
01/04/05

Butterfly Books and Bytes
Payroll Summary
January through March 2005

	Ralph Bear			TOTAL		
	Hours	Rate	Jan - Mar 05	Hours	Rate	Jan - Mar 05
Employee Wages, Taxes and Adjustments						
Gross Pay						
Salary			2,492.69			2,492.69
Total Gross Pay			2,492.69			2,492.69
Deductions from Gross Pay						
125 -Health Insurance (pre-tax)			-400.00			-400.00
Simple IRA Emp.			-500.00			-500.00
Total Deductions from Gross Pay			-900.00			-900.00
Adjusted Gross Pay			1,592.69			1,592.69
Taxes Withheld						
Federal Withholding			-335.00			-335.00
Medicare Employee			-36.14			-36.14
Social Security Employee			-154.55			-154.55
AZ - Withholding			-167.00			-167.00
Total Taxes Withheld			-692.69			-692.69
Net Pay			900.00			900.00
Employer Taxes and Contributions						
Federal Unemployment			19.95			19.95
Medicare Company			36.14			36.14
Social Security Company			154.55			154.55
AZ - Unemployment Company			16.95			16.95
Simple IRA Co.			500.00			500.00
Total Employer Taxes and Contributions			727.59			727.59

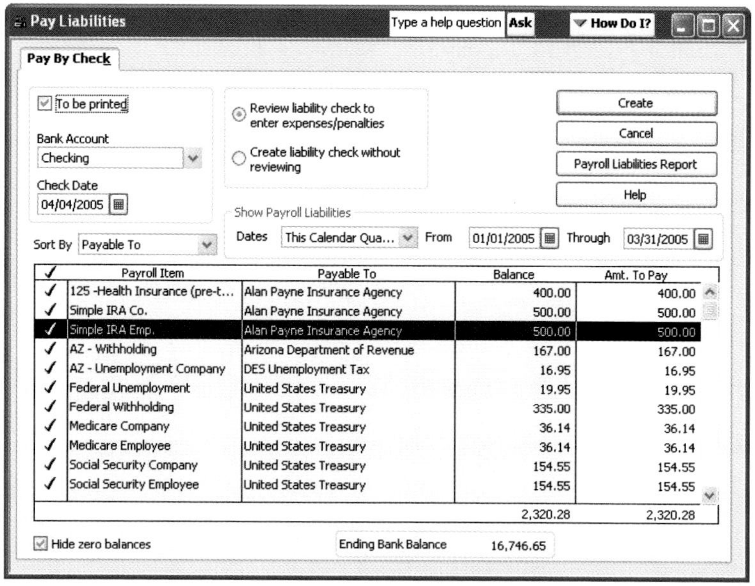

Figure 9-19: You can choose to pay all or part of any liabilities.

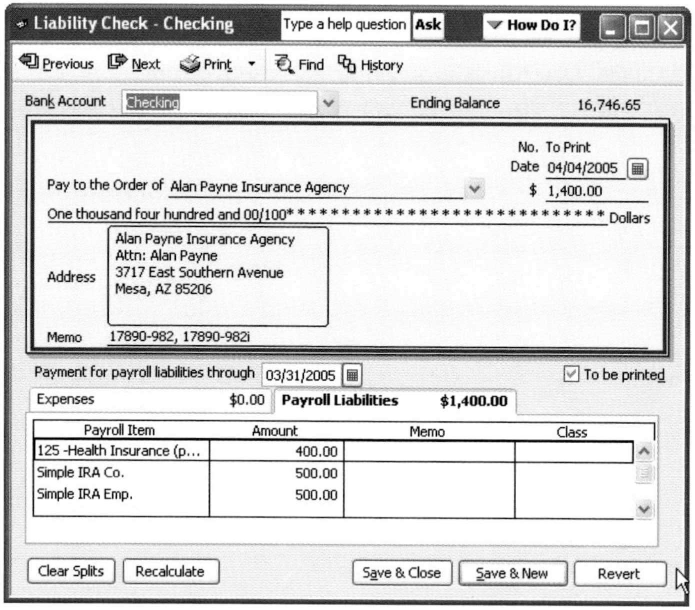

Figure 9-20: The Liability Check window looks similar to the Write Checks window, but is tied to liability tracking. Don't write checks from the Write Checks window to pay liabilities.

PAY LIABILITIES

You can generate checks to pay taxes and other liabilities (such as insurance, garnishments, and so on.)

To pay liabilities:

1. Click the **Employees** menu, click **Process Payroll Liabilities**, and click **Pay Payroll Liabilities**.

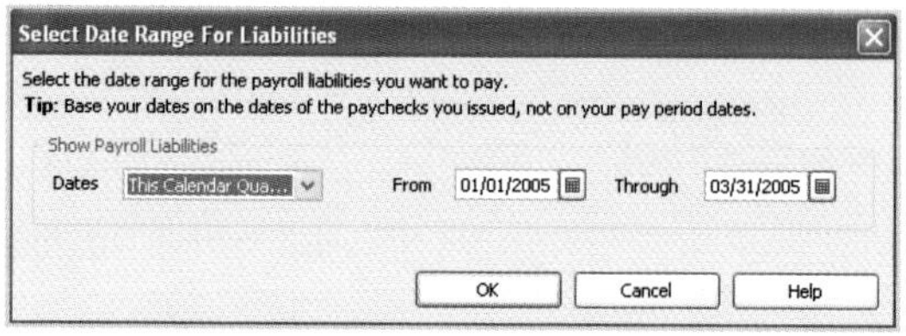

2. Select the date range for your payment, and click **OK**. The Pay Liabilities window opens, as shown in Figure 9-19.

3. Click the items you wish to pay to place a check mark in the leftmost column.

4. Click the **Create** button. The Pay Liabilities window closes, and the Liability Check window opens, as shown in Figure 9-20. If you chose more than one liability, click the **Next** button to review all checks. You can print the checks now or later (if you are going to print them later, click the **To Be Printed** check box).

5. Click the **Close** button (the red X in the upper-right corner) to close the Liability Check window.

Review and Pay Sales Taxes

If you charge sales tax, you need to pay the related tax agencies on a regular basis. See Chapter 6 for information on setting up sales tax items in QuickBooks. A monthly basis is the most common time frame, but check your local requirements.

To pay sales tax:

1. Click the **Vendors** menu, click **Sales Tax**, and click **Pay Sales Tax**. The Pay Sales Tax window opens, as shown in Figure 9-21.

2. Click the **Pay From Account** down arrow, and click the relevant bank account.

3. Press the TAB key to move to the Check Date field. Type the date to be printed on the check.

4. Press the TAB key to move to the Show Sales Tax Due Through field. Type the closing date of the sales tax for which you are paying.

5. Click the sales tax items you wish to pay to place a check mark in the leftmost column.

6. Click the **To Be Printed** check box, or type a check number in the Starting Check No. field if you are printing them.

7. Click **OK**. The window closes, and checks have now been generated for the appropriate vendors. Be sure to print the checks or send them online.

Be sure to keep on top of your tax payments. QuickBooks makes it easy to create checks for the correct amounts as long as all of your entries are being made correctly.

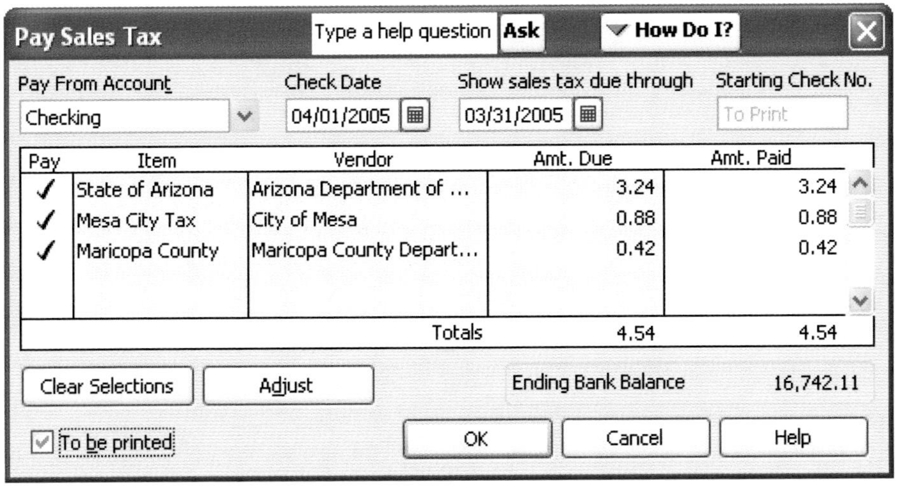

Pay	Item	Vendor	Amt. Due	Amt. Paid
✓	State of Arizona	Arizona Department of …	3.24	3.24
✓	Mesa City Tax	City of Mesa	0.88	0.88
✓	Maricopa County	Maricopa County Depart…	0.42	0.42
		Totals	4.54	4.54

Pay Sales Tax · Type a help question · Ask · How Do I?

Pay From Account: Checking · Check Date: 04/01/2005 · Show sales tax due through: 03/31/2005 · Starting Check No.: To Print

Clear Selections · Adjust · Ending Bank Balance · 16,742.11

☑ To be printed · OK · Cancel · Help

Figure 9-21: Returns and credits against your liabilities will be listed here as well.

How to...

- *Use the Report Navigator*
- *Use the Report Menu*
- *Set Report Preferences*
- *Use the Button Bar*
- *Customize Reports*
- *Memorize Reports*
- *Use Memorized Reports*
- *Organize Memorized Reports*
- *Printing to a File*
- *Print Reports*
- *E-Mailing Reports in PDF Format*
- *Export Reports*

Chapter 10

Creating Reports

One of the most powerful features of QuickBooks is flexible, immediate reporting. Create a report almost as fast as you think about it from a wide assortment of preset reports, or customize any report to meet your company's needs. Then memorize it for easy report generation on a regular basis. In addition to standard reports, graphs are available for certain views, and all reports can be exported to Microsoft Excel, where they can be manipulated and have additional graphs generated. Reports can also be e-mailed in PDF format. Budgeting and forecasting are additional features that help you step back and see where your business has been and where it is going. This chapter will discuss all these features and what you can do with them.

1 2 3 4 5 6 7 8 9 10

CAUTION

Reports are only as accurate as the data from which they are created. Enter all of your information on a daily basis and make a commitment to accuracy.

TIP

Click the **More** link at the end of each report description on the Report Navigator for more detailed information.

Create Company and Financial Reports

A paperless office is a wonderful thing. With QuickBooks, a click of the button changes a daily report to monthly or sorts clients from alphabetical order into their various spending levels. You can get immediate answers to questions without having printed a thing or waiting for accounting or data personnel.

Use the Report Navigator

If you are unfamiliar with accounting terminology or are looking for a report whose name you do not know, use the Report Navigator to preview sample reports and create reports using your own data.

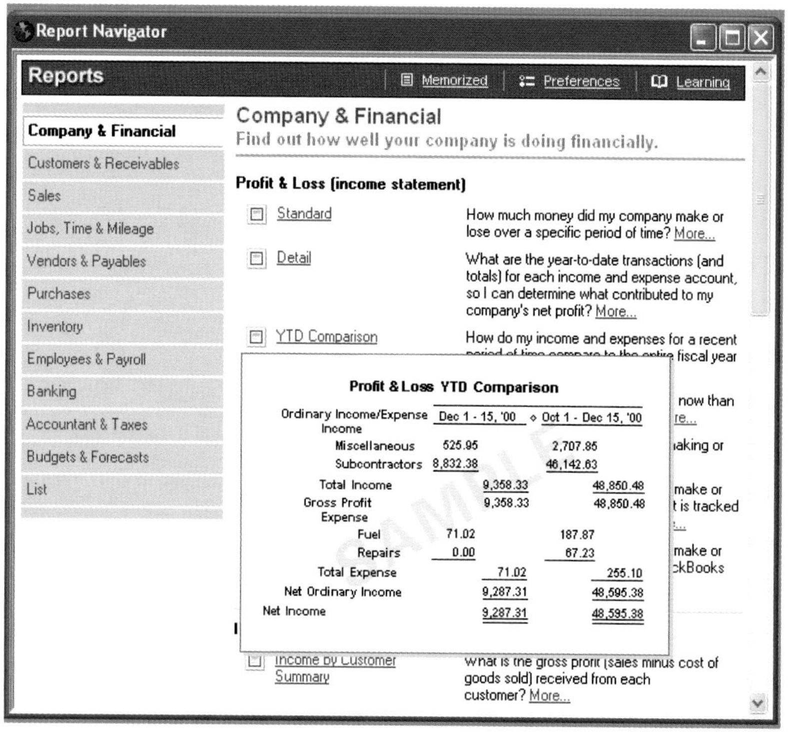

To view the Report Navigator:

1. Click the **Report** menu and click **Report Navigator**. The Report Navigator window opens, as shown in Figure 10-1.
2. Click a topic in the list on the left to see a detailed list of the reports available and a description of each, for example, click **Company & Financial**.
3. Click the name of the report you want to create, for example, click **Standard** (under Profit & Loss). The report is displayed with default settings, as shown in Figure 10-2.
4. Click the **Close** button (the red X in the upper-right corner) to close the report.

Figure 10-1: Move your mouse pointer over any of the small icons to see a sample report.

TIP

Customize your report and then click the **View** menu and click **Add Report To Icon Bar** for quick access.

REPORT GROUPS

Reports are grouped into the following categories:

- **Company & Financial** includes traditional business reports, such as profit and loss, income and expense statement, balance sheet, and cash flow. Profit and loss and balance sheet reports include graphs as well.

- **Customers & Receivables** includes accounts receivable aging reports on overdue customers, customer balances, phone number and contact, and price lists reports.

- **Sales** includes reports broken down by customer, item, rep, and open sales orders.

- **Jobs, Time & Mileage** includes job profitability reports, job estimate versus actual reports, time reports, and mileage reports.

- **Vendors & Payables** includes accounts payable aging reports on overdue bills, vendor balances, phone number and contact lists, 1099s, and sales tax reports.

- **Purchases** includes reports broken down by vendor, item, or purchase order.

- **Inventory** includes valuation and stock status reports, including pending builds (see Chapter 7 for more information on inventory).

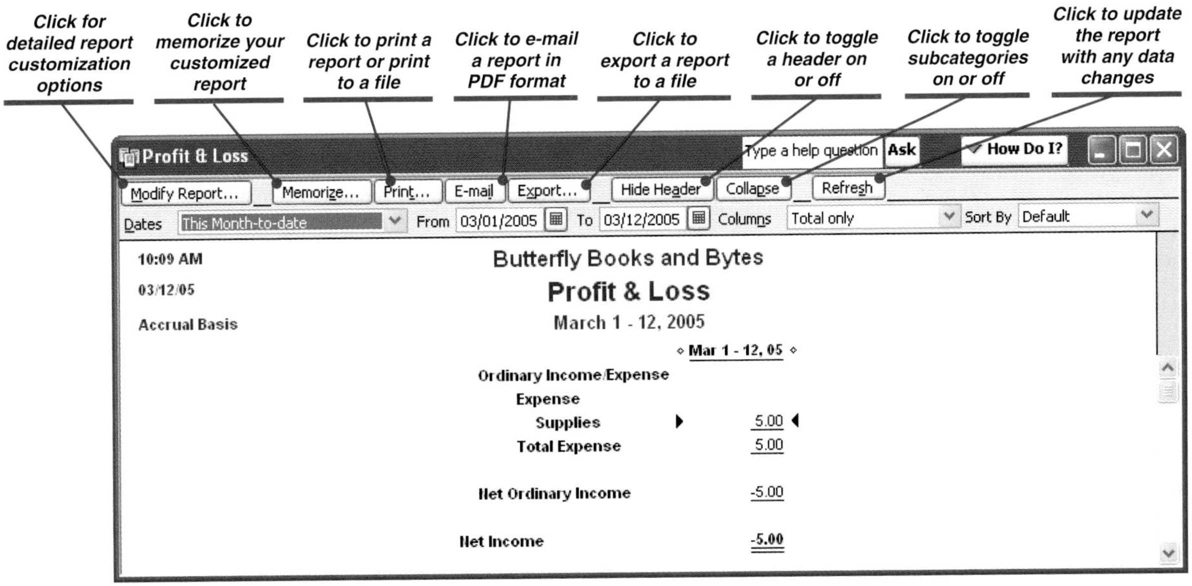

Figure 10-2: You can customize reports by using the buttons and drop-down menus at the top of each report window.

TIP

You can print any list while viewing the List window by clicking the **File** menu and clicking **Print List**. Try this method, as well as the report method, to see which you prefer.

- **Employees & Payroll** includes reports on payroll items, transactions, liabilities, employee earnings, employee withholdings, contact lists, and paid time off.

- **Banking** includes deposit reports; check reports, including missing checks; and reconciliation reports, including discrepancies.

- **Accountant & Taxes** includes reports on account activities, such as trial balances, general ledger, audit trail, journal, account listings, fixed-asset listing, and income tax preparation information.

- **Budgets & Forecasts** includes budget overview reports, budgeted costs versus actual costs reports, budget profit and loss forecast overviews, and forecasted income versus actual income.

- **List** includes phone number and contact lists for all name groups, and lists of accounts, items, payroll items, fixed assets, terms, To Do notes, and memorized transactions.

Reports	Window	Help	
Report Navigator			
Memorized Reports		▶	
Process Multiple Reports			
Company & Financial	▶		Profit & Loss Standard
Customers & Receivables	▶		Profit & Loss Detail
Sales	▶		Profit & Loss YTD Comparison
Jobs, Time & Mileage	▶		Profit & Loss Prev Year Comparison
Vendors & Payables	▶		Profit & Loss by Job
Purchases	▶		Profit & Loss by Class
Inventory	▶		Profit & Loss Unclassified
Employees & Payroll	▶		Income by Customer Summary
Banking	▶		Income by Customer Detail
Accountant & Taxes	▶		Expenses by Vendor Summary
Budgets & Forecasts	▶		Expenses by Vendor Detail
List	▶		Income & Expense Graph
Custom Summary Report			Balance Sheet Standard
Custom Transaction Detail Report			Balance Sheet Detail
			Balance Sheet Summary
QuickReport		Ctrl+Q	Balance Sheet Prev Year Comparison
Transaction History			Net Worth Graph
Transaction Journal			
			Statement of Cash Flows
			Cash Flow Forecast

Use the Report Menu

Create reports and graphs from the Report menu on a regular basis. QuickBooks Pro and Basic versions have fewer reports than seen here, but the groupings are similar. The best way to learn what each report does is to run it.

1. Click the **Report** menu and click the grouping you wish to use, for example, **Company & Financial**, as shown in Figure 10-3.

2. Click the report name you want to run, such as **Balance Sheet Standard**. The report window opens, as shown in Figure 10-4.

3. Review the report and click the **Close** button (the X in the upper-right corner) when finished.

Figure 10-3: Use the graphs available in a group for a pictorial representation of your data.

```
Butterfly Books and Bytes
        Balance Sheet
       As of March 12, 2005
                           ◇ Mar 12, 05 ◇
ASSETS
   Current Assets
      Checking/Savings
         Checking              ▶ 19,836.83 ◀
         Payroll Checking           -34.00
         Total Checking/Savings   19,802.83

      Accounts Receivable
         Accounts Receivable         3.25
         Total Accounts Receivable   3.25

      Other Current Assets
         Inventory Asset          1,120.68
         Total Other Current Assets  1,120.68

      Total Current Assets        20,926.76

   TOTAL ASSETS                    20,926.76

LIABILITIES & EQUITY
   Liabilities
      Current Liabilities
         Accounts Payable
            Accounts Payable      1,531.39
            Total Accounts Payable  1,531.39

         Other Current Liabilities
            Sales Tax Payable        4.54
            Total Other Current Liabilities  4.54

         Total Current Liabilities   1,535.93

      Long Term Liabilities
         Startup Loan - Personal  30,000.00
         Total Long Term Liabilities  30,000.00

      Total Liabilities           31,535.93

   Equity
      Opening Bal Equity         -9,615.00
      Net Income                   -994.17
      Total Equity              -10,609.17

   TOTAL LIABILITIES & EQUITY      20,926.76
```

Figure 10-4: When you move from a different accounting system to QuickBooks, running a balance sheet for the same date in both systems is a good way to ensure that your new system is correctly set up.

COMMON REPORTS

Common reports in QuickBooks include the following:

- **Profit and Loss Statement** (located under Company & Financial) lists all income and expenses, and then calculates the difference, showing your profit (or loss). View year-to-date (YTD) comparisons or previous year comparisons to see trends in your business. This report is also known as an income statement.

- **Balance Sheet** (located under Company & Financial) shows a snapshot of your business on a specific date. The current value of assets, liabilities, and equity (the difference between assets and liabilities) is shown. Equity is also considered to be the net worth of the business.

- **Employee, Vendor, or Customer Contact List** lists the names, addresses, and phone numbers, as well as specific related fields, of whichever group you choose. Each contact list is located under the related grouping.

- **Payroll Report** (located under Employees & Payroll) lists the wages and taxes paid on paychecks, which is useful to have on hand when filing forms at the end of each tax period.

- **Sales Reports by Item, Customer, or Rep** (available under Sales) allows you to see where sales are the strongest. A sales graph shows you a pictorial representation, with both a pie and bar chart that you can customize according to item, customer, or rep.

- **Budget Reports** (located under Budget & Forecasts) reflect where you stand in relation to your budget, thus allowing you to evaluate your business's success against your plan and consider alternatives, such as adjusting income and expenses or altering your budget.

TIP

Zoom in by double-clicking any number in a report to see either a subreport of the transactions that make up an amount or the transaction itself. Keep double-clicking subsequent reports that open to zoom into the transaction in greater detail.

TIP

Right-click any item in a graph to see the dollar amount of the corresponding section.

GRAPHING INFORMATION

In addition to printed reports, you can create graphs to see a pictorial representation of your data. As with reports, you can double-click any (graphical) total to open a subgraph or subreport summarizing how that total was calculated. You can then double-click items in that subreport to zoom into the actual transactions.

To create a graph-based report:

1. Click the **Reports** menu and click the grouping you wish to use, for example, **Company & Financial**.

2. Click **Income & Expense Graph**. The graph is displayed, as shown in Figure 10-5.

3. Review the graph and click the **Close** button (the X in the upper-right corner) when finished.

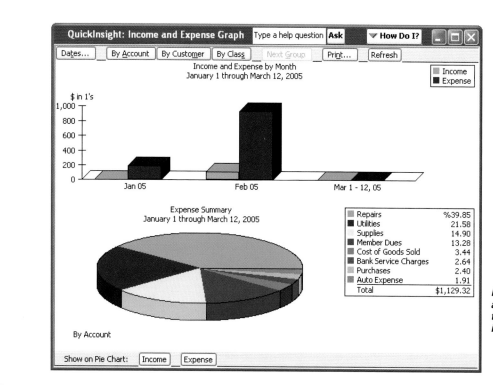

Navigate and Modify Reports

Standard reports in QuickBooks are based on default settings that most people use; however, your business may require different settings. You can modify any report at any time to get the information you need. Memorize reports for recurring use, and add a report to the icon bar for frequent use.

Figure 10-5: Click the Income button at the bottom of the graph to change the pie chart display from expense to income accounts.

Set Report Preferences

QuickBooks contains a number of preferences that you can set to affect all reports. Reports & Graphs (used as an example here) have both My Preferences and Company preferences.

To set report preferences:

1. Click the **Edit** menu and click **Preferences**. The Preferences window opens, as shown in Figure 10-6.

2. Scroll through the list on the left, and click **Reports & Graphs**.

3. Click the **My Preferences** tab. Select from among the following settings:

   - **Prompt Me To Modify Report Options Before Opening A Report** opens the Modify Report window each time a report is run. This is useful if you always customize a report; otherwise, this feature may slow you down. Try it if you are unsure. You can always turn it off again.

   - **Refresh Automatically** will rerun the report when any change is made in QuickBooks that affects the report. If you are on a network or have a large, slow data file, you may choose to be prompted to refresh or simply not refresh while you're looking at a report. Each report window has a Refresh button you can click at any time.

   - **Graphs** can be drawn in two dimensions (2-D) or in patterns instead of in full color (see Figure 10-5 for an example of a full-color graph). Patterns are useful if you're printing reports on a black-and-white printer instead of a color printer. You can change this feature when printing, and then change it back when you are finished.

Figure 10-6: You can modify reports according to personal preferences, as well as company preferences.

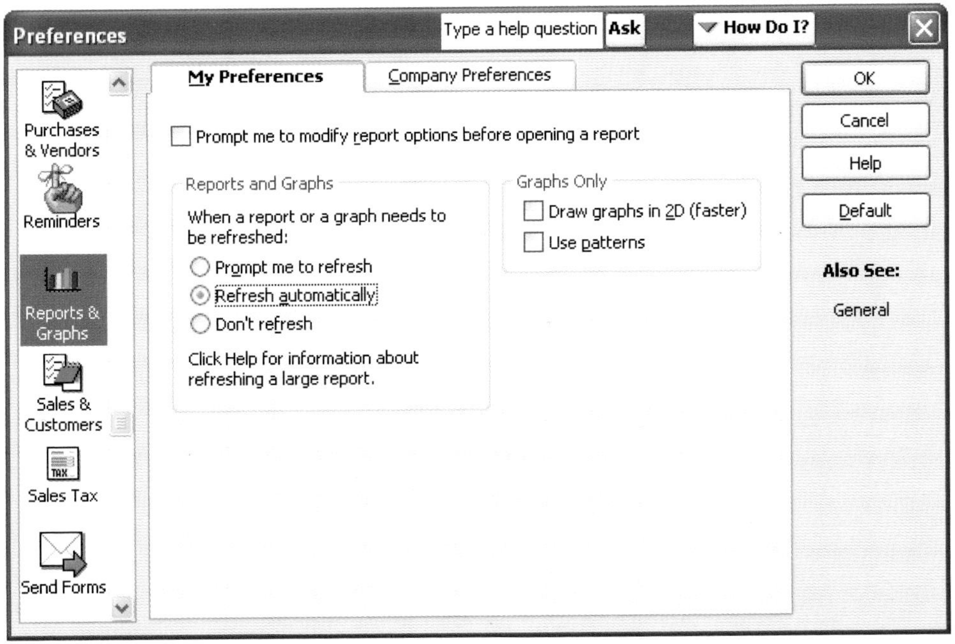

CAUTION

In a multiuser setting, only the Admin user can change company preferences.

4. Click the **Company Preferences** tab. You'll see the choices presented in Figure 10-7. Select from the following:

   - **Summary Reports Basis** affects summary reports only. Accrual shows sales as income when you enter a sale and bills as expenses when you enter a bill, regardless of whether invoices or bills have been paid. Cash shows sales as income when you receive payments and bills as expenses when you pay them. This preference doesn't affect individual transaction-based reports or 1099 reports, which are always on a cash basis. You can change sales tax liability reports in the Sales Tax section of Preferences.
   - **Aging Reports** sets the date to calculate the number of overdue days on aging reports. Each invoice has a transaction date and a due date. The due date may be 30 days later if the customer is net 30. You can age from either the date the transaction occurred or the due date.
   - **In the Reports - Show Accounts For Area, Name Only** is the most common setting and makes the report easy to read. Use the description (or both) if you prefer. The description used will be the one you entered when you set up the account in the Chart of Accounts.
   - The **Classify Cash** button allows you to change where accounts appear in any given section of a report. Only change this on the advice of an accountant.

5. Click **Cancel** to close the window without making any changes.
6. Click the **Format** button. The Report Format Preferences window opens, as shown in Figure 10-8. Any changes you make here will affect all reports. The choices are the same for all reports (see "Customize Reports" later in this chapter for more information).
7. Click **Cancel** to close the window without saving your changes, or click **OK** if you have made changes you wish to save. You are returned to the Preferences window.
8. Click **OK** to save your preferences and close the window.

Figure 10-7: Changing the defaults here changes the settings of all reports, with the exception of memorized custom reports.

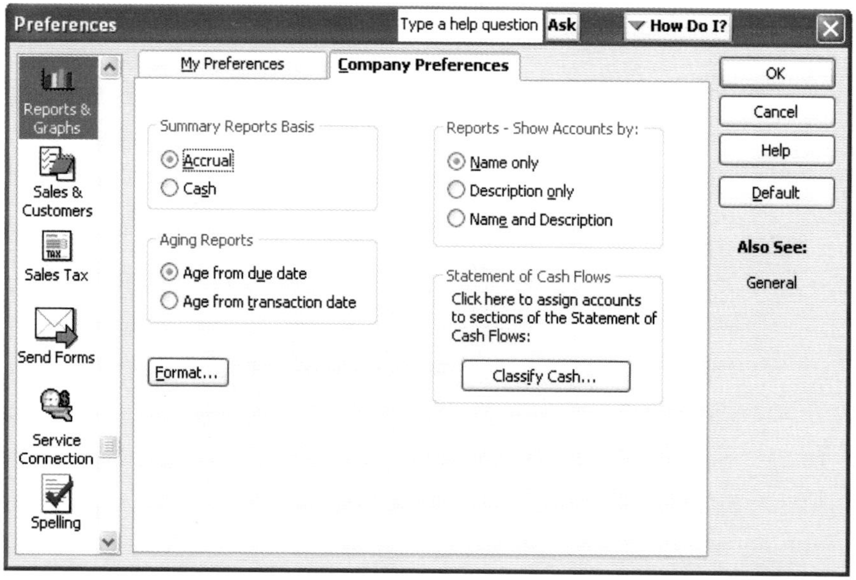

Use the Button Bar

At the top of every report in QuickBooks is a button bar. To view and experiment with report settings using the Profit & Loss report as an example:

Click the **Reports** menu, click **Company & Financial**, and click **Profit & Loss Standard**. The Profit & Loss Standard report is displayed, as shown in Figure 10-8.

CHANGE THE DATE RANGE

In the bottom row of the button bar, the Dates down arrow includes commonly used preset date ranges, such as Today, This Week, This Month, This Quarter, This Year, Year to Date, Last Week, Last Month, and so on.

To change the date range:

Click the **Dates** down arrow, and select the date range you wish.

–Or–

1. Click in the **From Date** field, and select a date.

2. Click in the **To Date** field, and select a date.

3. Click anywhere in the report to refresh the report and use the new dates.

TIP

The Dates down arrow is helpful, but you can customize the date range to any settings you wish.

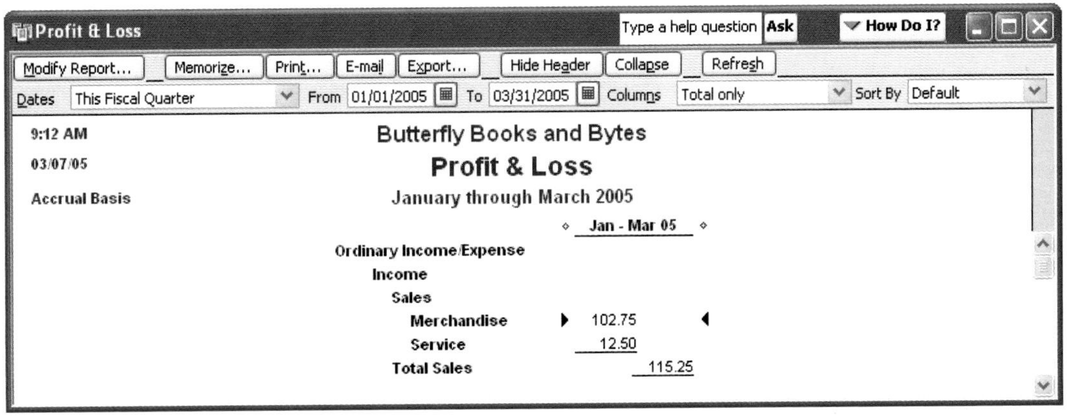

Profit & Loss											Type a help question	Ask	▾ How Do I?			

Modify Report... Memorize... Print... E-mail Export... Hide Header Collapse Refresh

Dates This Fiscal Quarter ▾ From 01/01/2005 ▦ To 03/31/2005 ▦ Columns Total only ▾ Sort By Default ▾

9:12 AM
03/07/05
Accrual Basis

Butterfly Books and Bytes
Profit & Loss
January through March 2005

◇ __Jan - Mar 05__ ◇

Ordinary Income/Expense
Income
Sales
Merchandise ▸ 102.75 ◂
Service 12.50
Total Sales 115.25

Figure 10-8: Categories with down arrows change the report immediately. If you set custom dates, click the report to have the date range take effect.

REPORT COLUMNS

Most reports open with only totals displayed unless they are a comparative report (comparing a current period to another period), but you can use the Columns field to see sublevels of data in your date range. You can view your data broken down into periods, such as day, week, month, quarter, and so on; or by different topics, such as Customer:Job, Rep, Payee, Terms, and so on. Each report will have different choices.

SORT BY FIELD

The Sort By field allows you to sort by different items.

Click the **Sort By** down arrow, and click a field.

Summary reports typically can only be sorted by account or amount. Detailed reports can be sorted by any of the fields

RESIZE COLUMNS

Small diamonds separate each column in a report. By dragging these diamonds, you can shrink the columns to fit on your page or expand them to show all data.

To resize an account column:

Move your mouse pointer over the diamond to the right of the account column name, and drag to the desired size.

To resize all data columns at once:

1. Move your mouse pointer over the diamond to the right of a column name, and drag to the desired size. When you release the mouse button, a dialog box appears asking if you want to make all the columns the same size.

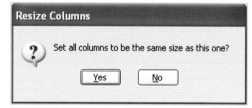

2. Click **Yes** if you wish to make all columns the same size, or click **No** to just resize a single column.

> **CAUTION**
>
> Clicking the **Revert** button will return the report to its default date range.

Customize Reports

In addition to the quick changes you can make using the button bar, there are a large number of changes you can make to each report. Each change you make to an individual report will affect only that report and will be lost if you close the report without memorizing it. To make global changes to all reports, see the "Set Report Preferences" section earlier in this chapter.

To customize any report:

1. Click the **Modify Report** button. The Modify Report window opens, as seen in Figure 10-9.
2. Click the tab that corresponds to the area you want to modify, and make your changes. If you want the Modify Report window to open every time you run a report, choose that option under Preferences (see "Set Report Preferences").

Figure 10-9: The ability to modify a report according to date, columns, or sort order is available in the Modify Report window, as well as on the button bar.

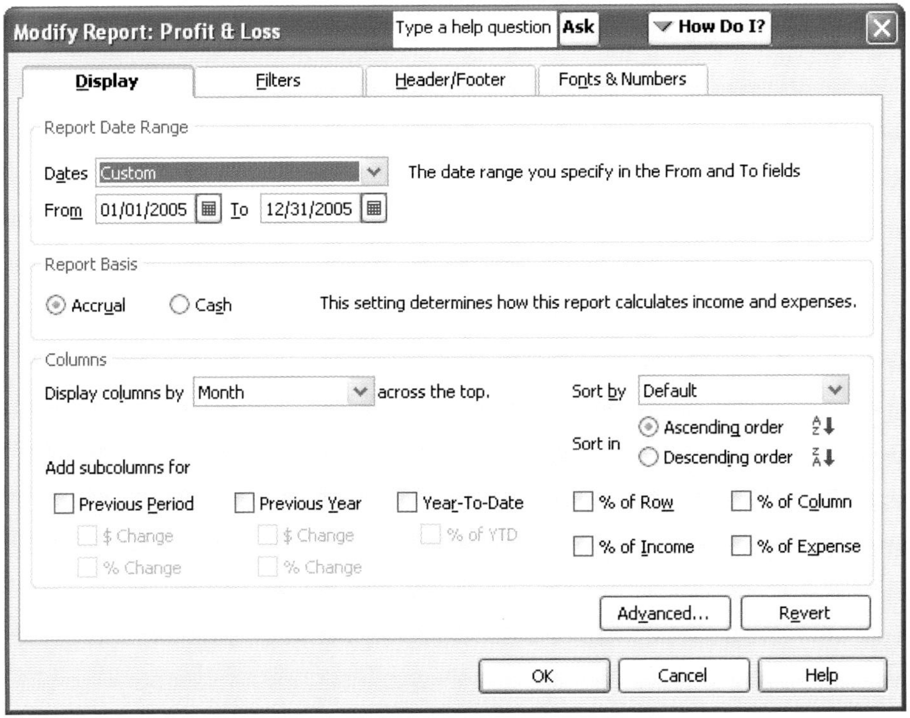

EDIT THE DISPLAY

The best way to learn how any option affects your report is to run a report, and then change one item at a time to see the corresponding result.

1. With any report open, click the **Modify Report** button. The Modify Report window opens with the Display tab active.
2. Choose any of the following options:
   - Click the **Dates** down arrow to choose preselect-ed dates, or type specific dates in the From and To fields.
   - Click the **Accrual** or **Cash** option to indicate which basis you would like the report to display.
   - Click the **Display Columns By** and **Sort By** down arrows to choose preselected options. You can also choose to sort by ascending (0-9, A-Z) or descending (Z-A, 9-0) order.
   - Click the desired additional columns in the Add Subcolumns For area to display comparison or percentage information.

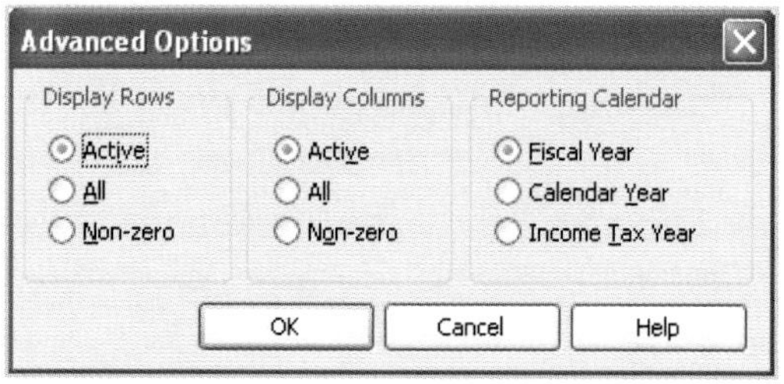

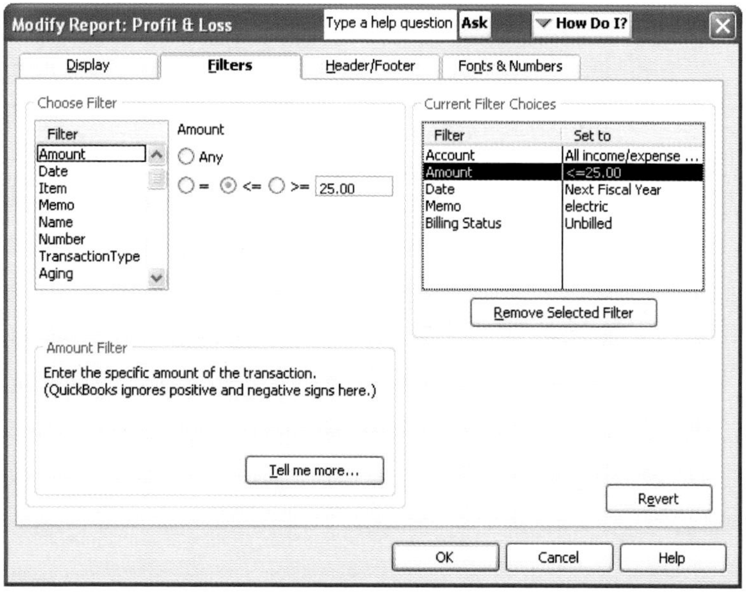

3. Click the **Advanced** button to see additional choices:

- In the Display Rows area, **Active** is selected by default. Click **All** to see inactive accounts in addition to active accounts, or click **Non-Zero** to hide accounts with no activity for the selected period.

- In the Display Columns area, **Active** is selected by default. Click **All** to see inactive accounts in addition to active accounts, or click **Non-Zero** to hide accounts with no activity for the selected period.

- In the Reporting Calendar area, **Fiscal Year** is selected by default. Click **Calendar Year** to use the range of January 1–December 31, or click **Income Tax Year** if it is different from your fiscal and calendar years.

4. Click **OK** when finished to close the Advanced Options window.

5. Click **OK** when finished to close the Modify Report window.

FILTER REPORT CONTENT

The Filters tab on the Modify Report window is a powerful feature. It allows you to control what data is shown by limiting (filtering) the data used to generate the report. There are approximately 50 filters: all the fields in QuickBooks, including accounts, names, dates, statuses, vendor type, customer type, and custom fields.

1. With any report open, click the **Modify Report** button. The Modify Report window opens.

2. Click the **Filters** tab, as seen in Figure 10-10.

3. In the Choose Filter area (on the left), scroll through the list and click a filter. Each filter will have a variety of choices, including one or more of the following:

- A drop-down list of choices to further refine the filter (when using the Account or Names filters)

- Equal To, Less Than, or Greater Than options (for example, in Figure 10-10, with the amount filter selected, amount options appear to the right)

TIP

Click **Transaction Type** filter to see *only* one or more types of transactions, such as invoices, checks, deposits, payments, and so on.

Figure 10-10: Experiment with various filters to create custom memorized reports.

10

TIP

You can use custom fields from name lists to create specific reports by filtering for that customized field. Scroll all the way down in the filter list to find your customized fields.

TIP

Change the default report settings in the Preferences section. Click the **Edit** menu, click **Preferences**, and then click **Reports & Graphs**.

- Date range fields (when using the Date filter)
- Text fields (when using the Memo or Number filters)
- Status options (when using the Billing Status and Cleared filters)

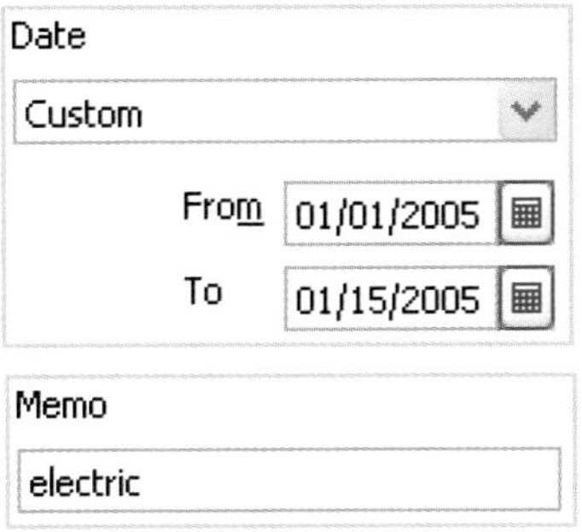

Date
Custom
From
01/01/2005
To
01/15/2005
Memo
electric

4. To deselect a filter, click the relevant name in the Current Filter Choices area (located on the right side of the window), and click the **Remove Selected Filter** button.
5. Click **OK** when finished to save your changes and close the Modify Report window.

MODIFY REPORT HEADERS AND FOOTERS

Headers and footers appear either at the top or bottom of a page, respectively. You can include headers and footers on all pages or have a header on just the first page and/or a footer on all pages thereafter.

1. With any report open, click the **Modify Report** button. The Modify Report window opens.
2. Click the **Header/Footer** tab, as seen in Figure 10-11.
3. Change any section you want by clicking in the relevant field and typing the new text, or by choosing an item from the related drop-down list. To prevent any section of the header or footer from printing, click the relevant check box to deselect it.
4. Click **OK** when finished to save your changes and close the Modify Report window.

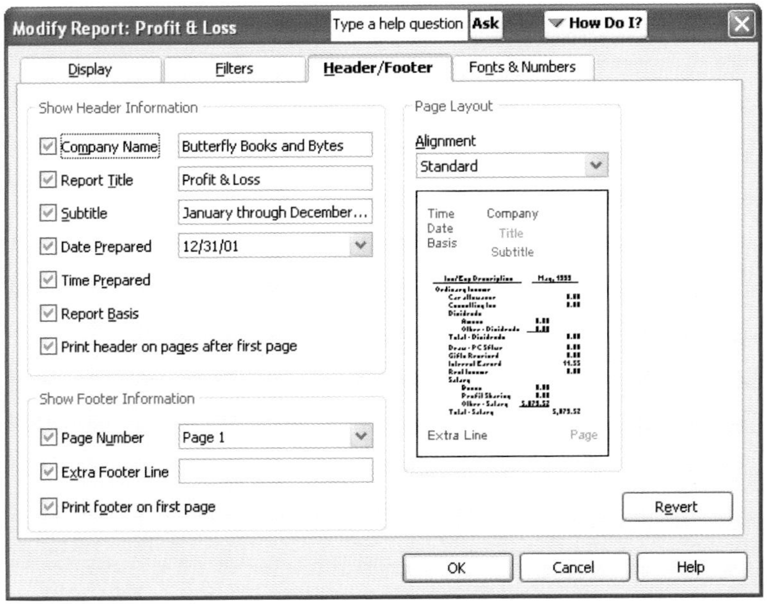

Modify Report: Profit & Loss
Type a help question
Ask
How Do I?
Display
Filters
Header/Footer
Fonts & Numbers
Show Header Information
Company Name
Butterfly Books and Bytes
Report Title
Profit & Loss
Subtitle
January through December...
Date Prepared
12/31/01
Time Prepared
Report Basis
Print header on pages after first page
Show Footer Information
Page Number
Page 1
Extra Footer Line
Print footer on first page
Page Layout
Alignment
Standard
Time
Date
Basis
Company
Title
Subtitle
Extra Line
Page
Revert
OK
Cancel
Help

Figure 10-11: Use the small sample report to guide you in placing each section of the header and footer.

MODIFY FONTS AND NUMBERS

Fonts and numbers can be set so that your reports reflect your company's preferences.

1. With any report open, click the **Modify Report** button. The Modify Report window opens.

2. Click the **Fonts & Numbers** tab, as seen in Figure 10-12.

3. In the Change Font For list, located on the left, click the report element for which you would like to change fonts, and an example will appear to the right, showing the font color, size, and type currently in place for that report element.

4. Click the **Change Font** button. A dialog box appears, from which you can change the following properties:

   - **Font** is the "look" of the text and numbers on the report. Click each type to see a preview of what it will look like in the lower-right area of the dialog box.

   - **Font Style** displays text in bold, italics, or regular typeface.

   - **Size** is measured in points. 72 points is equal to one inch. The most common sizes for reports are 8, 10, and 12.

   - **Effects** include strikeout (~~example~~) and underline (example).

   - **Color** can be used to emphasize or customize reports.

5. Click **OK** to apply your choices to the element you selected and close the dialog box.

6. Customize how numbers are displayed by selecting from among the following options on the right side of the Fonts & Numbers tab:

   - In the **Show Negative Numbers** area, you can choose to display negative numbers normally, in parentheses, or with a trailing minus. Click the **In Bright Red** check box if you prefer.

   - In the **Show All Numbers** area, you can choose to show all numbers divided by 1000 (for large numbers), suppress zero amounts, and only display whole dollar amounts.

7. Click **OK** when finished to save your changes and close the Modify Report window.

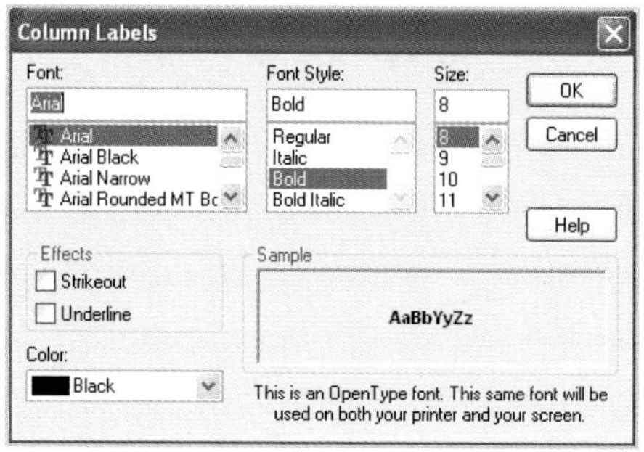

Figure 10-12: Make changes to fonts and numbers, and then click OK to see the result.

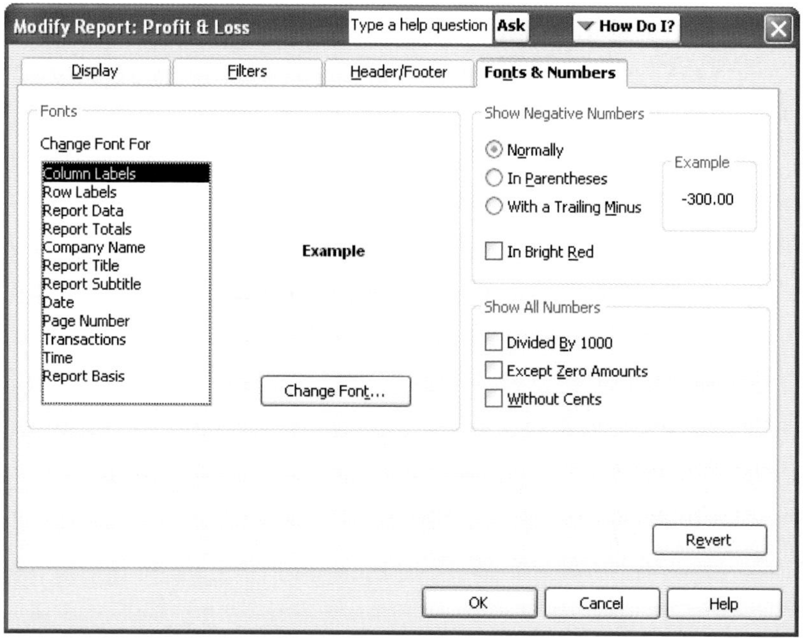

TIP

Click the **Save In Memorized Group** check box if you want to add the report to an existing group or to a custom group you have added.

Memorize Reports

When you memorize reports, you are memorizing the settings, not the data. To memorize a report:

1. Click the **Edit** menu and click **Memorize**. The Memorize Report dialog box appears with the current name of the report highlighted.

2. Edit the report name or type a new name.

3. Click **OK** to memorize the report.

Memorize Report

Name: Profit & Loss

☐ Save in Memorized Report Group: Accountant

OK   Cancel

Use Memorized Reports

When you memorize a report, it is added to your Reports menu, either directly under the Memorized Reports submenu or under the custom grouping you chose. You can have many reports open at the same time, either by opening each individually or by running a group of reports at once.

RUN A SINGLE MEMORIZED REPORT

To run a single memorized report:

Click the **Reports** menu, click **Memorized Reports**, and click the report you want to run, as shown in Figure 10-13. The report is displayed.

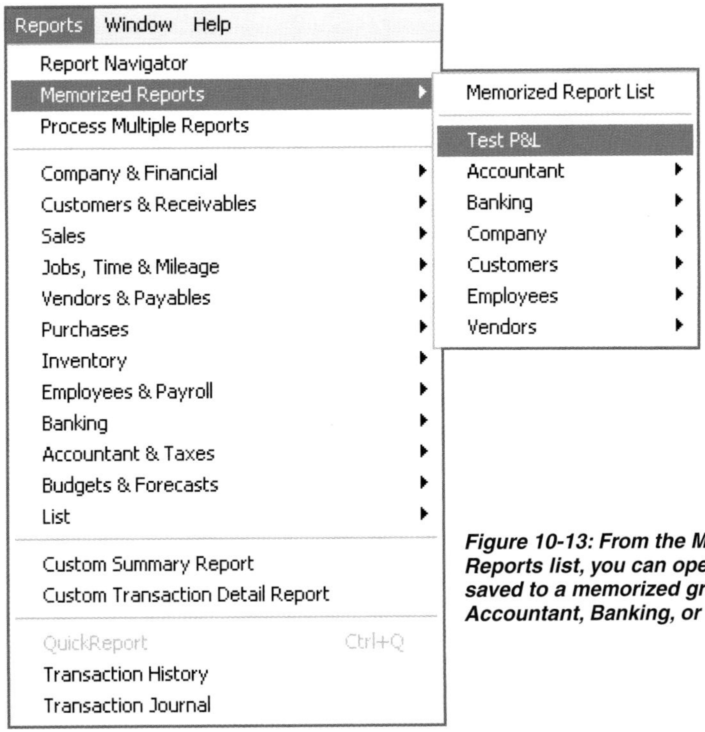

Reports Window Help

Report Navigator
Memorized Reports   ▶   Memorized Report List
Process Multiple Reports

Company & Financial   ▶   Test P&L
Customers & Receivables   ▶   Accountant   ▶
Sales   ▶   Banking   ▶
Jobs, Time & Mileage   ▶   Company   ▶
Vendors & Payables   ▶   Customers   ▶
Purchases   ▶   Employees   ▶
Inventory   ▶   Vendors   ▶
Employees & Payroll   ▶
Banking   ▶
Accountant & Taxes   ▶
Budgets & Forecasts   ▶
List   ▶

Custom Summary Report
Custom Transaction Detail Report

QuickReport   Ctrl+Q
Transaction History
Transaction Journal

Figure 10-13: From the Memorized Reports list, you can open a report saved to a memorized group, such as Accountant, Banking, or Company.

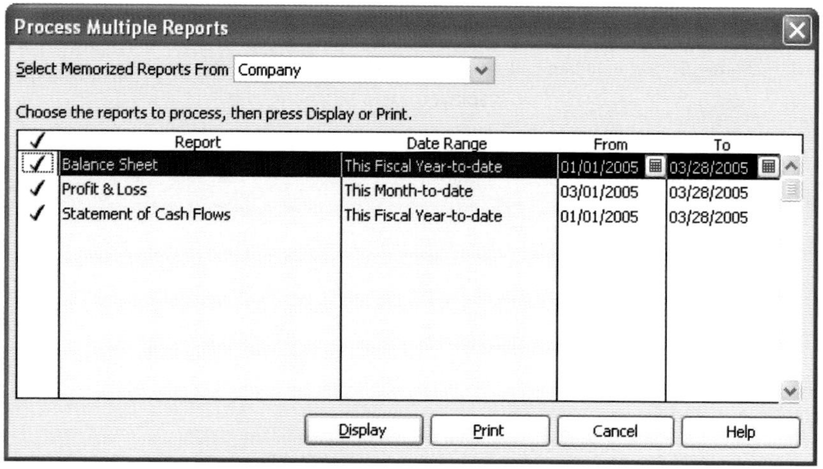

Figure 10-14: All reports in a selected group are run by default.

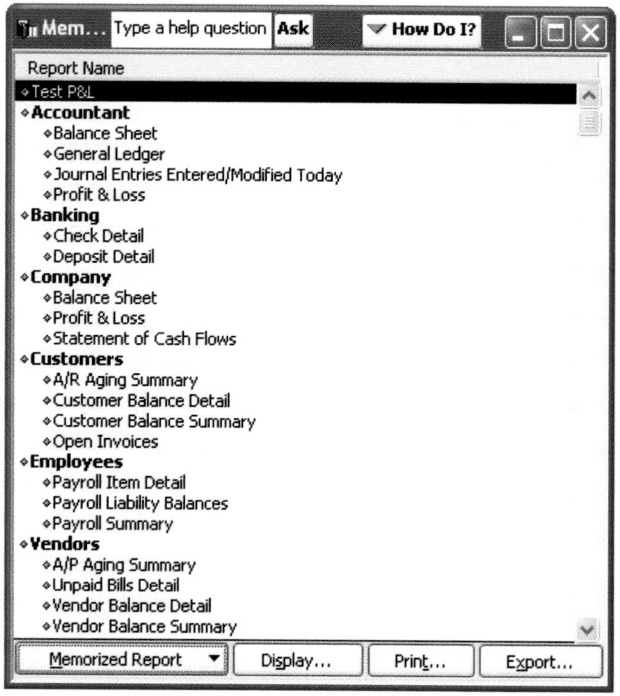

Figure 10-15: Move reports to groups by dragging the diamonds up, down, left, or right.

RUN A GROUP OF MEMORIZED REPORTS

To run multiple reports:

1. Click the **Reports** menu and click **Process Multiple Reports**. The Process Multiple Reports window opens, as shown in Figure 10-14.

2. Click the **Select Memorized Reports From** down arrow, and click the group, for example, **Company**. The report area, in the lower half of the screen, displays all the reports in that memorized group.

3. Click the **Display** button. The reports are run and the Process Multiple Reports window closes.

4. Review the reports. When finished, you can close the window or print the reports.

Organize Memorized Reports

If you customize and memorize reports often, over time, those reports may be difficult to find in a single list. Luckily, you can organize your memorized reports according to topics that make sense for your business.

GROUP REPORTS

Custom groups can be added to the Reports menu, and reports can be moved to different groups using the Memorized Reports list, which is similar to other lists found throughout QuickBooks.

To create a new group:

1. Click the **Reports** menu, click **Memorized Reports**, and click **Memorized Reports List**. The Memorized Reports list is displayed, as shown in Figure 10-15.

2. Click the **Memorized Report** menu button (located at the bottom of the screen), and click **New Group**. The New Memorized Report Group dialog box appears.

New Memorized Report Group

Name: Weekly Reports

OK   Cancel

3. Type the name of your new group, such as, <u>Weekly Reports</u>.

4. Click **OK**. The group is added to your Memorized Reports list.

5. Click the **Close** button (the X in the upper-right corner) to close the list.

Refer to Chapter 3 for more information on moving items in a list.

EDIT MEMORIZED REPORT NAMES

To edit the names of your reports:

1. Click the **Reports** menu, click **Memorized Reports**, and click **Memorized Reports List**. The Memorized Reports list is displayed.

Edit Memorized Report

Name: Profit & Loss

☑ Save in Memorized Report Group: Company

OK   Cancel

2. Right-click the report you want to edit, and click **Edit Memorized Report**. The Edit Memorized Report dialog box appears.

3. Type a new name for the report. Click the **Save In Memorized Report Group** check box, click the down arrow, and choose the new group that you want this report to be a part of, if desired.

4. Click **OK** to save the new name and/or group.

TIP

QuickBooks comes with standard memorized reports, but you can change these. When you close a standard memorized report, QuickBooks will ask if you wish to replace the existing report with the modified one.

PRINTING TO A FILE

In addition to exporting and printing reports, you can print directly to a file, which is useful for transferring information to another program.

1. Click the **Print** button on any report window. The Print Reports dialog box appears. (Figure 10-16 shows this window with settings for printing to a printer).

2. In the Print To area, click the **File** option.

3. Click the down arrow located to the right of the File option, and select the preferred file type:

   - **ASCII Text File** keeps the layout intact but removes all formatting and saves the file with a .txt file extension.

   - **Comma Delimited File** saves just the data in the report, with each column of information separated by commas and saved with a .csv file extension.

   - **Tab Delimited File** saves just the data in the report, with each column of information separated by tabs and saved with a .txt file extension.

4. Click the **Print** button. The Create Disk File dialog box appears. Type a file name and choose a location to save the file.

Print, E-Mail, and Export Reports

Viewing reports on your computer screen is a fast, easy way to see how your business is doing. However, most businesses need to distribute reports as well, and some may also need to export information into another program. You can do all of that using QuickBooks. At the top of the report window on the button bar are the Print, E-Mail, and Export buttons (next to the Modify Report and Memorize Report buttons). Click any of these to open the related dialog boxes.

| Modify Report... | Memorize... | Print... | E-mail | Export... | Hide Header | Collapse | Refresh |

Figure 10-16: Click Print if you have a short report and don't need to worry about formatting.

Print Reports

Type a help question | **Ask** | ▼ **How Do I?**

Settings   Margins

Print to:
- ⦿ Printer: hp officejet 7100 series on Ne03: [Options...]
- ◯ File: ASCII text file

Note: To install additional printers or to change port assignments, use the Windows Control Panel.

Orientation:
- ⦿ Portrait
- ◯ Landscape

Page Range:
- ⦿ All
- ◯ Pages:
  - From: 1 To: 9999

Page Breaks:
- ☑ Smart page breaks (widow/orphan control)
- ☐ Page break after each major grouping

Number of copies: 1

- ☐ Fit report to 1 page(s) wide
- ☐ Print in color (color printers only)

[Print] [Cancel] [Help] [Preview]

TIP

To fit more columns on a report, click **Landscape** in the Print Reports window. This will print your report horizontally. You can also use legal-sized (8.5" x 14") paper.

Figure 10-17: Click anywhere in the report preview to zoom in. Click again to zoom out.

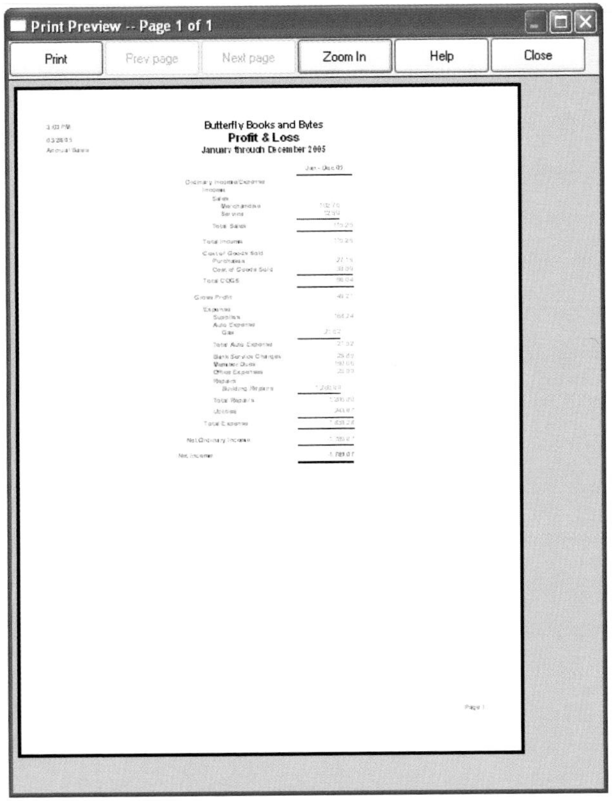

Print Reports

Printing a report is the most common way of distributing information. To print a report:

1. Click the **Print** button on any report window. The Print Reports dialog box appears, as in Figure 10-16.
2. In the Print To area, click the **Printer** option and choose from among the following options:
   - Click the **Printer** down arrow to select an alternate printer if the default printer is not the one you want to use.
   - Click the **Options** button if you want to change settings specific to your printer. A separate dialog box appears. Click **OK** when finished to close that dialog box.
   - In the Orientation area, click the **Landscape** option to change the page orientation to horizontal. Portrait (vertical orientation) is the default selection.
   - In the Page Range area, click the **Pages** option and type the page numbers you want to print if you don't want to print all pages in a report.
   - In the Page Breaks area, click the **Smart Page Breaks** and **Page Break After Each Major Grouping** check boxes if you have a long report and want to make it easier to read by providing "natural" breaks. (This may make the report print on more pages.)
   - Click the **Fit Report To** check box, and type the number of pages wide in the field, for example, 1.
3. When finished, click the **Preview** button to see how the report will look when printed, as shown in Figure 10-17.
4. If the preview is acceptable, click **Print**. The report is sent to the printer, and the preview window closes. If the report is not acceptable, click **Close** and make further adjustments as needed.

E-MAILING REPORTS IN PDF FORMAT

E-mailing reports is convenient, but be aware that there are no guarantees of confidentiality or that the correct person will receive the e-mail. Preview a report before you send it to be sure it will be readable to the person who receives it.

To e-mail reports:

1. Click the **E-Mail** button on any report window. The Edit E-Mail Information window opens, as shown in Figure 10-18.

2. In the To field, type the e-mail address of the person to whom you are sending the report.

3. In the Cc field, type any other e-mail addresses to whom you would like to send the report.

4. Edit the default e-mail text to add any pertinent information, such as the purpose of the attached report or any information that is needed to understand the report's significance.

5. Click the **Send Now** button.

Invoices and other forms give you the option to send them later, but reports are always sent immediately.

Export Reports

QuickBooks has a number of links to the Microsoft Office suite of products, including the letter writing wizard covered in Chapter 8, which sends information to Word. Report information can be sent directly to Microsoft Excel, a spreadsheet application. Although QuickBooks has a variety of report customization options available, for raw data manipulation, exporting reports to Microsoft Excel allows you to create detailed budgets, create projection estimates, create "What If?" scenarios, perform more detailed analysis, and import to or compare to other programs' data.

BASIC EXPORTING

To export a report:

1. Click the **Export** button on any report window. The Export Reports window opens, with the **A New Excel Workbook** option selected by default, as shown in Figure 10-19.

Figure 10-18: Send a report to yourself before sending it to others to see how it appears.

Edit E-mail Information

Edit the e-mail information as necessary, and then send your form.

To	owner@azcts.com
Cc	
From	info@butterflybooks.org
Subject	Report from Butterfly Books and Bytes

E-mail Text

Please review the attached report. Feel free to contact us if you have any questions.

Thank you.

Edit Default Text
Check Spelling

[Your Report will be attached to the message as a PDF file]

Send Now   Cancel   Help

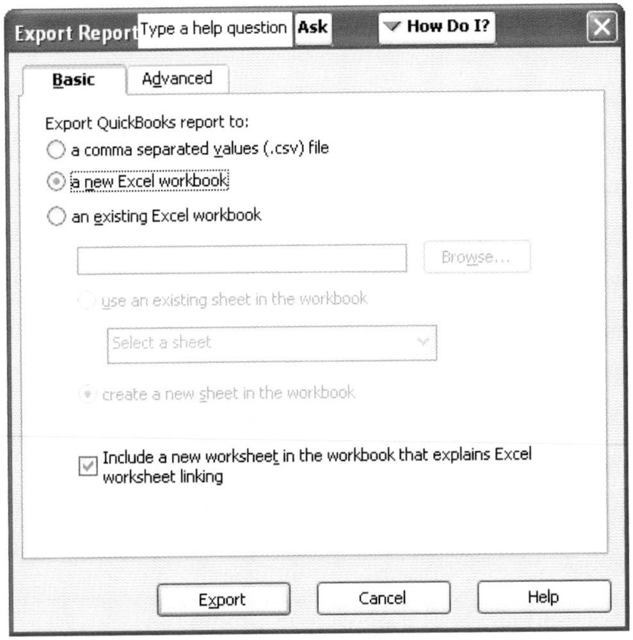

Figure 10-19: You must have Microsoft Excel installed to export information to Excel files.

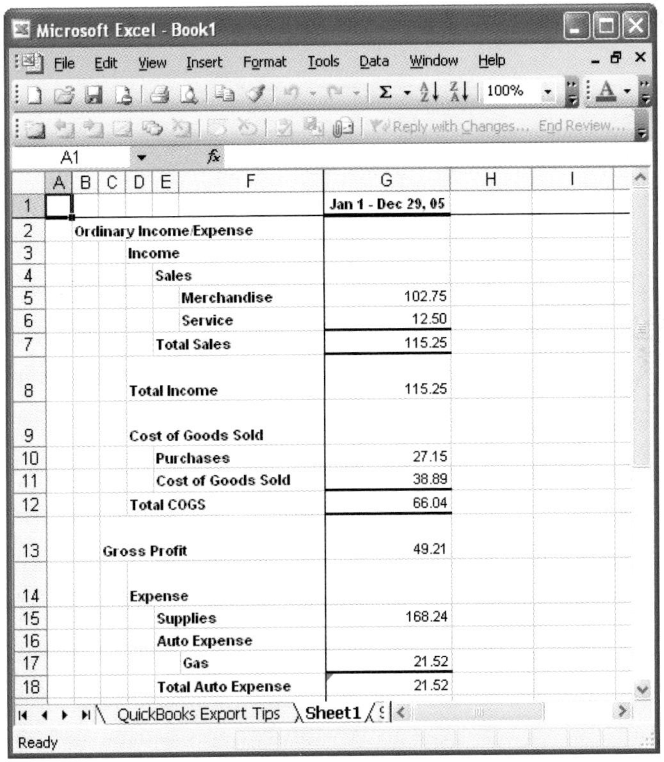

Figure 10-20: Data exported to Excel is a copy of the current report information and can be manipulated as desired without affecting the original QuickBooks data.

2. Click the **Export** button to transfer the report to a new Excel file. QuickBooks will open Excel and create a new page, as seen in Figure 10-20. Choose from among the following options in the Export Reports window:

- Click **A Comma Separated Values (.csv) File** to create a file for import into any other data program, such as a Microsoft Access database.

- Click **An Existing Excel Workbook** to add this report as a new page in any current Excel file. This is a good way to collect monthly information in a file.

- You can also choose to include a page in Excel that will explain the export process by clicking the check box at the bottom of the window.

3. From Excel, you can choose to print, view, or save the file. Click the **Close** button (the X in the upper-right corner) to close Excel.

You can also export customer data and other items from QuickBooks by clicking the **File** menu and then clicking **Export**.

ADVANCED FEATURES

You can also customize the appearance and content of your exported file.

1. Click the **Export** button on any report window. The Export Reports window opens. Click the **Advanced** tab to see the options shown in Figure 10-21.

2. Choose from among the following:

   - Click the formatting options to choose whether to include formatting information in Excel or use Excel's default font (the first area).

   - Click the Excel options to set the initial Excel preferences for this report page (the middle area).

   - Click the printing options to set how the page will print in Excel (the bottom area).

3. From Excel, you can choose to print, view, or save the file. Click the **Close** button (the X in the upper-right corner) to close Excel.

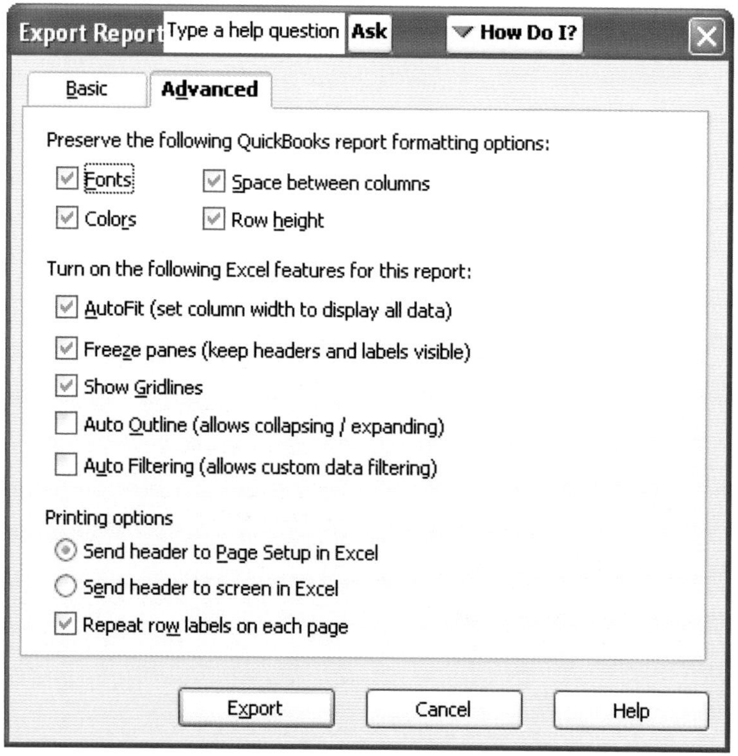

Export Report | Type a help question | **Ask** | ▼ **How Do I?** | ✕

| Basic | **Advanced** |

Preserve the following QuickBooks report formatting options:

☑ Fonts   ☑ Space between columns
☑ Colors   ☑ Row height

Turn on the following Excel features for this report:

☑ AutoFit (set column width to display all data)

☑ Freeze panes (keep headers and labels visible)

☑ Show Gridlines

☐ Auto Outline (allows collapsing / expanding)

☐ Auto Filtering (allows custom data filtering)

Printing options

⊙ Send header to Page Setup in Excel

○ Send header to screen in Excel

☑ Repeat row labels on each page

[Export]   [Cancel]   [Help]

Figure 10-21: To just export the report data, clear the top four formatting check boxes.

Note: Italicized page numbers indicate definitions of terms.

Numbers

1099s
preferences for, 169
printing from Vendor Navigator, 96
setting up and printing, 104–107

Symbols

– keyboard shortcut, using previous day's date, 23
+ keyboard shortcut, using for next day's date, 23

A

account numbers, including in online banking, 100
Account Listing report, example of, 66
account lists, printing, 65–66
Accountant & Taxes reports, description of, 206
accountant's copies, working with, 165–166
accounting files, closing, 167
Accounting preferences
for Company preferences, 169
for My preferences, 170
accounting flow, learning from Navigators, 12
accounting–related tasks, examples of, 15
accounts. See also bank accounts; user accounts
for 1099s, 104–105
asset accounts, 44
balance sheet accounts, 55–56
bank accounts, 43–44
changing to subaccounts, 60
Cost of Goods Sold accounts, 58
creating, 62
deleting, 63
editing, 64
equity accounts, 45
making inactive, 64
moving and sorting, 59–61
moving within lists, 60
renaming and merging, 65
setting up for credit cards, 87–88
transferring funds between, 87
types of, 42–43, 55
Accounts list in Banking Navigator, description of, 74
accounts, types of. See also bank accounts; Chart of Accounts; user accounts
accrual–based accounting
versus cash–based accounting, 35, 109
setting preferences for, 35
activities, entering for Time Tracking, 197
Activities menu button, description of, 59
Add Multiple feature, using with online business credit cards, 91
Adjust Quantity/Value on Hand window, displaying, 160
Administrator's Name password, storing, 33

Advanced tab in Find feature, options on, 171
aging reports, setting preferences for, 210
ALT key, identifying keyboard shortcuts with, 21
ALT+F4 keyboard shortcut, exiting QuickBooks with, 21
annual tasks, examples of, 15
A/P (accounts payable), relationship to Vendor Navigator, 96
assemblies. See inventory assembly items
asset accounts
creating, 44
examples of, 56
Assisted Payroll service, description of, 184
audit trails, tracking employee entries with, 166
automatic backups
effect of, 163
setting, 162

B

backups, 7
automating, 162–163
scheduling regularly, 162–163
storing, 166–167
balance sheet accounts
components of, 55–56
definition of, 42
Balance Sheet reports
description of, 207
example of, 55
balances, tracking with Customer:Job lists, 67–69
bank account registers, viewing and editing, 86
bank accounts. See also accounts; online banking
creating, 43–44, 75
enabling for use with online banking, 77
reconciling, 91, 93–94
transferring funds between, 87
Banking Navigator
accessing, 74
features of, 73–74
Banking reports, description of, 206
Banking Solutions, definition of, 74
Banking menu, keyboard shortcut for, 22
banks, choosing, 75–76
Begin Reconciliation window, displaying, 91, 93
beginning balances, matching with statements, 91
Billable Time/Costs dialog box, displaying, 129
bills
entering, 111
entering when receiving items, 154–155
paying, 112
receiving separately from items, 154
setting preferences for, 35
using items on, 115
books, closing, 167
Budget reports, description of, 207
Budgets & Forecasts reports, description of, 206

Build Assemblies window, displaying, 149
business credit cards, managing, 87, 90–91
business type, selecting, 32
Butterfly Books and Bytes sample company
setting up sales taxes for, 125–129
significance of, 27
using accrual–based accounting with, 109
button bar, using, 211–212

C

cash payments, processing, 139–140
cash–based accounting
versus accrual–based accounting, 35, 109
setting preferences for, 35
CD–ROMs, storing backups on, 167
changes, preventing, 167
charges
for Cost of Goods, 133–134
versus credits, 88
on invoices as items, 113–114
Chart of Accounts, 21. See also accounts; bank accounts; user accounts
viewing registers through, 86
abbreviation for, 8
categories within, 42–43
contents of, 10, 54
description of, 51
opening, 54–55
selecting window for, 11
check registers, example of, 86
Checking preferences, setting for Company preferences, 169
checks
editing, voiding, and deleting, 81
ordering, 78–79
printing, 81
processing, 139–140
protecting, 111
writing, 79–81, 110
classes, setting preferences for, 35
Close button, location of, 6
closing date, definition of, 48
closing QuickBooks 2005, 22
collection letters, writing, 173–175
columns
customizing in lists, 61
fitting on reports, 221
resizing, 212
Columns tab in forms, description of, 178
companies, starting, 28
Company & Financial reports, description of, 205
company information
adding to invoices, 179
setting up for payroll, 185–186
Company preferences
description of, 169

Company tab in forms, description of, 178
company files
closing, 22
completing General section of, 28–36
completing Income & Expenses section of, 36–38
definition of, 4
gathering information and choosing start dates for, 27
identifying, 5
opening, 5–7, 12
recording location of, 32
updating to work with QuickBooks 2005, 7
Company Information tab in General section, options on, 31–33
Company menu
keyboard shortcut for, 22
lists in, 50
company work flow
arranging icons for, 16
determining, 15
Complete Payroll service, description of, 184
contact information for companies, entering, 31
Cost of Goods Sold accounts
charges for, 133–134
description of, 58
using, 113–115
cost of goods, definition of, 38
Create Credit Memos/Refunds window, displaying, 142
Create Invoices window, displaying, 130
Create Purchase Orders window, displaying, 152
Create Statements window, displaying, 135
Create Invoice forms, opening, 21
credit card accounts
reconciling, 91–93
setting up, 87–88
credit card payments, processing, 140
credit cards
accepting from customers, 138
definition of, 42
entering transactions for, 88–89
managing for businesses, 87
Credit Check icon, features of, 121
credit memos, issuing, 142
credits
versus charges, 88
entering for vendors, 111
.csv (comma–separated value) files, importing and exporting, 223
CTRL+A keyboard shortcut, opening Chart of Accounts lists with, 9, 21
CTRL+D keyboard shortcut,
deleting items with, 21
deleting transactions with, 21

CTRL+E keyboard shortcut, editing list items with, 21
CTRL+F keyboard shortcut, opening Find windows with, 21
CTRL+I keyboard shortcut, opening Create Invoice forms with, 21
CTRL+J keyboard shortcut, opening Customer:Job lists with, 21
CTRL+M keyboard shortcut, memorizing transactions with, 21
CTRL+N keyboard shortcut, opening Enter New Item windows with, 21
CTRL+P keyboard shortcut, opening Print windows with, 21
CTRL+Q keyboard shortcut, viewing QuickReports with, 21
CTRL+T keyboard shortcut, opening Memorized Transactions lists with, 21
CTRL+W keyboard shortcut, opening Write Checks forms with, 21
CTRL+DEL keyboard shortcut, deleting lines with, 21
CTRL+INS keyboard shortcut, inserting new lines with, 21
Customer Contact List reports, description of, 207
Customer Detail Center, using, 124–125
Customer lists
    contents of, 51
    opening, 14
Customer Navigator
    components of, 120
    opening and closing, 120
Customer Register icon, features of, 121
Customer Message list, description of, 51
customer names, selecting, 68
Customer:Job lists
    adding customers to, 68
    adding jobs to, 69
    definition of, 120
    description of, 51
    features of, 121
    opening, 21
Customer:Job window, tabs in, 123–124
customers
    accepting credit cards from, 138
    adding notes and To Do items to, 122–123
    designating as vendors, 69
    determining, 41
    editing in Customer:Job lists, 121–124
    marking as non-taxable, 129
    naming, 70
    naming consistently, 122
    sending statements to, 134–135
Customers & Receivables reports, description of, 205
Customers menu, keyboard shortcut for, 22
Customize Invoice window, displaying, 178, 179

D

daily/weekly tasks, examples of, 15
data
    restoring, 164–165
    verifying, 165
data entry, keyboard shortcuts for, 21
data files, opening and restoring, 4
date range, changing in button bar, 211
date fields, keyboard shortcuts for, 23
dates. See also start dates
    adjusting when writing checks, 81
    confirming for entries, 23
    entering for transactions, 112
Days in Advance To Enter field, filling in, 117
default payroll settings, entering, 187–189
default setting, explanation of, 4
Define Fields window, displaying, 108
deleting
    accounts and subaccounts, 63
    checks, 81
    deposits, 83
    vendors, 103
deposit slips, printing, 85
deposit summaries, creating, 85
deposits
    editing and deleting, 83
    making, 82–83, 141
Desktop View preferences, description of, 170
desktop, customizing with View menu, 13–14
dialog boxes, opening company files with, 12
Did check(s) print OK? dialog box, appearance of, 194
discount items, using, 155
drop ship, definition of, 152
DVDs, storing backups on, 167

E

EasyStep Interview
    beginning, 28–29
    completing Income Details section of, 39
    Income Details section of, 39–40
    leaving, 37
    navigating, 30
    Opening Balances section of, 41–45
    returning to, 30
    What's Next section of, 45–46
Edit Customer window, displaying, 122
Edit E-mail Information screen, displaying, 222
Edit Vendor window, displaying, 101, 108
edit windows, opening in lists, 124
Edit Item window, displaying, 72
Edit menu, keyboard shortcut for, 22
Edit/Void Paychecks window, displaying, 195
EIN (Employer Identification Number)
    assignment of, 185
    entering, 31
    requirement for payroll, 182

e-mailing invoices, 132
Employee Defaults window, displaying, 187
Employee lists
    description of, 51
    displaying, 189
Employee Navigator, using, 191
Employee reports, description of, 207
Employees & Payroll reports, description of, 206
employees, setting up, 189–190
Enhanced Payroll service, description of, 184
Enter Bills feature in Vendor Navigator, accessing, 96
Enter Bills window, displaying, 111, 115, 154
Enter Credit Card Charges icon, adding to icon bar, 89
Enter Sales Receipts window, displaying, 136
Enter New Item windows, opening, 21
Entering Sales dialog box, displaying, 130
entries, confirming dates for, 23
Envelope Options window, displaying, 175
equity accounts
    creating, 45
    examples of, 56
estimates, creating, 137–138
Excel, exporting reports to, 223
exiting QuickBooks 2005, 22
expense accounts
    creating, 38
    entering service charges in, 93
    description of, 57
expenses versus fixed assets, 56
Export Report window, displaying, 223–224
exporting reports, 222–224

F

F1 keyboard shortcut, opening Help windows with, 21
F2 keyboard shortcut, showing QuickBooks product information with, 21
federal payroll forms, accessing, 199
FedEx, sending packages by means of, 158
fields
    customizing for name lists, 108
    navigating with keyboard shortcuts, 21
Fields tab in forms, description of, 178
File menu, keyboard shortcut for, 22
Filename For New Company window, opening, 32
files
    finding, 13
    opening in multi-user environments, 26
    printing to, 220
    using, 26
Finance Charge preferences, description of, 169
Find feature, using, 170, 171
Find windows, opening, 21
fixed asset items, description of, 151
Fixed Asset list, description of, 51

fixed assets versus expenses, 56
flash drives, storing backups on, 167
floppy disks, storing backups on, 166
flowcharts in Banking Navigator, example of, 74
fonts, modifying in reports, 216
Footer tab in forms, description of, 178
footers, modifying in reports, 215
Format tab in forms, description of, 178
forms
    customizing, 177–180
    examples of, 10
    moving and resizing objects on, 180
    navigating with keyboard shortcut, 21
    ordering, 78–79
    for payroll, 199
fringe benefit payroll items, setting up, 186
funds, transferring between accounts, 87

G

General preferences
    for Company preferences, 169
    for My preferences, 170
General section of company files
    Company Information tab in, 31–33
    completing, 28–29
    Preferences tab in, 34–36
    Start Date tab in, 36
    Welcome tab in, 29–30
graphs, creating, 208
group items, description of, 151
groups
    adding to memorized transactions, 118
    versus assembly items, 146
    creating for sales taxes, 128–129
    using with items, 159
    using with reports, 218–219

H

H keyboard shortcut, using for date of last day of month, 23
Header tab in forms, description of, 178
headers
    modifying in reports, 215
    toggling in reports, 205
Help menu
    keyboard shortcut for, 22
    using, 20
Help questions, asking, 19
Help windows, opening, 21
Hourly/Annual Rate column, accessing for payroll, 187
How Do I? drop-down menu, using, 20

I

icon bar
    adding Enter Credit Card Charges icon to, 89
    location of, 6
    description of, 8

editing, 15
features of, 10
planning, 15
toggling on and off, 13
icon buttons, adding separators between, 18
icons
adding to icon bars, 15, 18
arranging for company flow, 16
customizing, 17
deleting, 16
editing, 17
rearranging order of, 17
inactive vendors, viewing, 104
inactive accounts, reviewing, 64
income accounts
creating, 36–37
description of, 57
Income Details section of EasyStep Interview,
editing, 39–40
Income & Expenses section of company files
creating expense accounts from, 36–37
creating income accounts from, 36–37
Income and Expense Accounts, definition of, 42
income tax forms, selecting, 31
Integrated applications preferences, description
of, 169
inventory
activating in Preferences, 144
adjusting manually, 160
definition of, 143
taking, 159
using purchase orders with, 153
inventory assembly items
building, 148–149
creating, 146–148
description of, 151
disassembling, 149
versus groups, 146
tracking detailed history of, 148
inventory groups, creating, 150–151
inventory items, creating, 145–146
Inventory Part items, using, 145–146
inventory parts
creating, 147
description of, 151
Inventory reports, description of, 205
Inventory topic of Income Details section,
completing, 40
invoice templates, creating, 177–178
invoice types, setting preferences for, 34
invoices
adding company information and logos to, 179
adding previously purchased items to, 133–134
adding to memorized transactions, 134
creating, 129–131
definition of, 39, 121

editing, 132
e-mailing, 132
including items on, 113–114
zooming in and out of, 135
Item lists
capacity of, 53
importance of, 121
opening, 14
tracking services, inventory, and taxes with, 70
Item List window, displaying, 113, 128, 148
item names, adding to lists, 115
Item Not Found dialog box, appearance of, 153
Item Types list, description of, 52
items. See also non-inventory items
adding to invoices, 133–134
creating with purchase information, 113–114
deleting, 21
entering for inventory, 145
grouping, 159
marking as non-taxable, 129
matching with statements, 92
packaging for inventory, 146–148
receiving, 154–155
receiving separately from bills, 154
shipping, 155–156
using on bills, 115
Items & Services feature in Vendor Navigator,
accessing, 96
Items topic of Income Details section, completing,
40

J
jobs
adding to Customer:Jobs lists, 69
definition of, 67
tracking with Customer:Job lists, 67–69
Jobs and Estimates preferences, description of, 169
Jobs, Time & Mileage reports, description of, 205

K
K keyboard shortcut, using for date of last day of
week, 23
keyboard shortcuts. See also Shortcut list
accessing menus with, 21
for data entry, 21
for date fields, 23
for lists, 21
using, 21

L
labels
creating and printing, 176
displaying in Shipping Manager, 158
Landscape Larry sample company file, opening, 5–6
Layout Designer, using, 180
Learning Center, components of, 6
Letters and Envelopes window, displaying, 173–174
Letters To Customers icon, features of, 121

liabilities, paying, 200
liability accounts
creating, 43–44
examples of, 56
lines
editing and inserting in invoices, 132–133
inserting and deleting, 21–22
lines of credit, adding, 43
List reports, description of, 206
list items, editing, 21
List Name button, description of, 58
lists
adding item names to, 115
adding vendor names to, 115
capacity of, 53
customizing columns in, 61
examples of, 10
keyboard shortcuts for, 21
moving accounts within, 60
opening edit windows in, 124
printing, 206
restoring default order of, 61
sorting, 60
types of, 53
Lists menu
contents of, 50–51
keyboard shortcut for, 22
lists of accounts, printing, 65–66
logos, adding to invoices, 179

M
M keyboard shortcut, using for date of first day of
month, 23
mailing labels
creating and printing, 176
displaying in Shipping Manager, 158
main lists, description of, 53
Make Deposits window
confirming deposit totals in, 142
options in, 82–83
Make Payment window, displaying, 92
Manual Payroll service, description of, 184
Match Transactions window, opening, 90
memorized reports
creating, 217
editing, 219
organizing, 218–219
using, 217–219
Memorized Reports list in Banking Navigator,
description of, 74
memorized transactions
adding invoices to, 134
editing, 117–118
grouping, 118
moving, 118

Memorized Transactions lists
description of, 51
opening, 21
capacity of, 53
memorizing reports, 205
menu bar
location of, 6
description of, 8
features of, 9
menus, accessing with keyboard shortcuts, 21–22
merging vendors, 103
Modify Report window, displaying, 213–216
monthly/quarterly tasks, examples of, 15
multi-user environments
enabling, 168
opening files in, 26
setting up, 46–48
My preferences, descriptions of, 170

N
name lists
adding customized fields to, 108
description of, 53
managing information with, 67–69
using with deposits, 83
Name Not Found dialog box, appearance of, 98
Navigators. See also windows
accessing, 6
Employee Navigator, 191
learning accounting flow from, 12
Vendor Navigator, 96
New Account window, displaying for credit cards,
87
New Employee window, displaying, 189–190
New Item window, displaying, 70–71, 114, 145,
147, 150, 153
New Vendor window, displaying, 99–100
New Customer form, displaying, 68
non-inventory items. See also items
description of, 151
examples of, 40
entering, 72
nonprofit organizations, "customers" of, 41
non-taxable items, marking, 129
notes
adding to customers, 122–123
adding to vendors, 102
numbers, modifying in reports, 216

O
online banking. See also accounts; bank accounts
activating, 76–77
enabling bank accounts for, 77
including account numbers in, 100
Online Banking Center, features of, 84

online business credit card transactions, receiving and entering, 90–91
online storage of backups, using, 166
online transactions, sending and receiving, 84
Open Window List
  location of, 6
  toggling on and off, 13
  using, 11
Opening Balances section of EasyStep Interview, completing, 41–45
other charge items, description of, 151
Other Names list, description of, 51
Out of State tax items, creating, 128

P

packages, sending via UPS and FedEx, 157–158
packing slips
  creating, 156
  printing, 156
  using, 155–156
passwords
  entering, 33
  for online banking accounts, 78
Pay Bills feature in Vendor Navigator, accessing, 96
Pay Bills window, displaying, 112
Pay Liabilities window, displaying, 200
Pay Sales Tax window, displaying, 201
paychecks
  creating, 192–193
  editing and voiding, 194–195
  printing, 193–194
payment items, description of, 151
payment methods, adding with Quick Add button, 83
Payment Method list, description of, 51
payments
  receiving, 39, 139–142
  setting preferences for, 35
Payments to Deposit window, displaying, 141
payroll
  activating in Preferences, 182–183
  entering salary amounts for, 187
  entering YTD (year–to–date) amounts for, 192
  setting up, 183
Payroll and Employee preferences, description of, 169
payroll costs, examples of, 184
payroll forms, accessing, 199
payroll items, setting up for states, 185–186
payroll reports
  description of, 207
  running, 199
payroll services, choosing and comparing, 184
payroll settings, entering defaults for, 187–189
Payroll Setup window, displaying, 183

payroll taxes
  example of, 185
  reviewing and paying, 199–200
Payroll Item list, description of, 51
PDF format, e–mailing reports in, 222
Physical Inventory Worksheet, example of, 159
preferences
  for reports, 209–210
  for shipping methods, 155
Preferences window
  activating inventory in, 144
  activating payroll in, 182–183
  activating sales tax in, 126–127
  customizing for companies, 169
  displaying, 105
Preferences tab in General section, options on, 34–36
Prepare Customer Letters feature, using, 173
Preview Paycheck window, displaying, 193
Price Levels dialog box, displaying, 131
Price Level lists
  capacity of, 53
  description of, 51
Print Checks window, displaying, 194
Print Deposit Slips window, displaying, 85
Print Labels window, displaying, 176
Print Packing Slip window, displaying, 156
Print Preview window, displaying, 221
Print Reports window, displaying, 220
Print windows, opening, 21
Printer tab in forms, description of, 178
printing
  1099s, 96, 104–107
  checks, 81
  deposit slips, 85
  to files, 220
  invoices, 132
  lists, 206
  lists of accounts, 65–66
  mailing labels, 176
  packing slips, 156
  paychecks, 193–194
  reconciliation reports, 94
  reports, 205, 221
Process Multiple Reports window, displaying, 218
product–based company, example of, 5–6
Profit & Loss statements, 211
  description of, 207
  example of, 57, 205
Prog Cols tab in forms, description of, 178
progress invoicing, setting preferences for, 34
purchase information, creating items with, 113–114
purchase orders, using, 151–153
Purchases and Vendors preferences, description of, 169
Purchases reports, description of, 205

Q

.qbw files
  explanation of, 5
  opening, 12
quarterly tasks, examples of, 15
Quick Add feature
  adding payment methods with, 83
  adding vendors with, 98
QuickBooks bank accounts. See bank accounts
QuickBooks Information dialog box, appearance of, 165
QuickBooks 2005
  accomplishing tasks in, 8
  closing, 11, 22
  customizing, 12–18
  exiting, 21, 22
  finding help within, 19–21
  migrating to, 26
  opening with Start menu, 4
  registering, 8
QuickBooks family, editions in, 2–3
QuickBooks product information, showing, 21
QuickBooks window, overview of, 8–12
QuickFacts
  Accepting Credit Cards from Customers, 138
  Choosing a Bank, 75
  Gathering Data for a New Company File, 28
  Naming Customers, 70
  Receiving Payments, 39
  Storing Your Backups, 166
  Understanding Item Types, 151
  Understanding Cost of Goods Sold, 58
  Using Accrual–vs. Cash–Based Accounting, 36
QuickReports, viewing, 21
QuickStatements, features of, 80
QuickSteps
  Adding an Invoice to Memorized Transactions, 134
  Changing Tax Preferences, 129
  Choosing a Payroll Service, 184
  Creating Liability Accounts, 44
  Editing an Account, 64
  E–mailing Reports in PDF Format, 222
  Entering a Single Activity, 197
  Opening Other Company Files (.qbw), 12
  Printing to a File, 220
  Registering QuickBooks, 8
  Sending and Receiving Online Transactions, 84
  Transferring Funds between Accounts, 87
  Updating Older Company Files to Work with QuickBooks 2005, 7
  Writing Checks, 110

R

R keyboard shortcut, using for date of last day of year, 23
Receive Payments window, displaying, 139
Reconcile Credit Card window, displaying, 92
reconciliation reports, printing, 94
reconciling
  bank accounts, 91, 93–94
  credit card accounts, 91–93
registering QuickBooks 2005, 8
registers
  for bank accounts, 86
  examples of, 10
Related Activities list in Banking Navigator, description of, 74
reminder transactions, memorizing, 116
reminders, adding to vendors, 102
Reminders lists
  description of, 50
  opening for packing slips, 156
  setting preferences for, 35
  viewing and customizing, 172
Reminders preferences
  for Company preferences, 169
  for My preferences, 170
report columns, changing in button bar, 212
report content, filtering, 214–215
report groups, examples of, 205–206
report headers and footers, modifying, 215
Report menu, using, 206
Report Navigator, using, 204–206
report preferences, setting, 209–210
report settings, changing defaults for, 215
reports
  customizing, 205, 213
  editing display of, 213–214
  e–mailing in PDF format, 222
  exporting, 222–224
  exporting to files, 205
  fitting columns on, 221
  generating from Find feature, 171
  graphing, 208
  memorizing, 21, 205, 217–219
  modifying, 213
  modifying fonts and numbers in, 216
  moving to groups, 218
  for payroll, 199
  Physical Inventory Worksheet, 159
  printing, 205, 221
  printing reconciliation reports, 94
  sampling, 204
  types of, 207
  updating, 205
  zooming into, 207

Reports and Graphs preferences
   for Company preferences, 169
   for My preferences, 170
Reports menu, 59
   contents of, 52
   keyboard shortcut for, 22
   printing lists of accounts from, 65–66
Research service item, setting up, 70–71
Resize Columns dialog box, displaying, 212
Restore Company Backup window, displaying, 164
restoring data, 4, 164–165
Review Paycheck window, displaying, 195
Rock Castle sample company file, opening, 5–6

S

salary amounts, entering for payroll, 187
Sales and Customers preferences, description of, 169
Sales Order feature, availability of, 121
sales receipts, entering, 136–137
sales reports
   description of, 205, 207
   ensuring accuracy of, 139
Sales Tax Codes dialog box, displaying, 131
sales taxes, reviewing and paying, 201
sales tax groups
   creating, 128–129
   description of, 151
sales tax items
   activating in Preferences, 126–127
   description of, 151
   setting up, 127–128
Sales Tax preferences, description of, 169
sales orders, setting preferences for, 34
sales receipts, definition of, 39
Sales Rep list, description of, 51
Sales Tax Code list, description of, 51
Schedule Backup window, displaying, 163
Schedule Memorized Transaction window, displaying, 117
Select Employees To Pay window, displaying, 192
Select Labels to Print window, displaying, 176
Select Name Type window, displaying, 98
Select Paychecks to Print window, displaying, 193
Select Reconciliation Report window, displaying, 94
Select Template Type dialog box, displaying, 177
Send Forms preferences, description of, 169
service charges, entering in expense accounts, 93
Service Connection preferences
   for Company preferences, 169
   for My preferences, 170
service items
   description of, 151
   entering, 70–71

service–based company, example of, 5–6
Set Up feature, adding vendors with, 99–100
SHIFT+TAB keyboard shortcut, navigating forms with, 21
Ship Via list, description of, 51
shipping items, 155–156
Shipping Manager, using, 157–158
Shortcut list, turning on and off, 14. See also keyboard shortcuts
Sick & Vacation Defaults window, displaying, 188
Simple tab in Find feature, options on, 170
single–user mode, switching to, 167
Sort By field, changing, 212
sorting lists, 60
spelling check, using with invoices, 131
Spelling preferences, description of, 170
SSN (social security number), entering, 31
Standard Payroll service, description of, 184
Start Date tab in General section, options on, 36
start dates, choosing, 26–27. See also dates
Start menu, opening QuickBooks with, 4
state payroll forms, accessing, 199
state payroll items, setting up, 185
statements
matching beginning balances with, 91
   matching items with, 92
   sending to customers, 134–135
subaccounts
   changing accounts to, 60
   creating, 63
   creating under expense accounts, 38
   deleting, 63
sublists
   capacity of, 53
   description of, 53
submenus, displaying, 9
subtotal items, description of, 151
Switch To Multi–User mode, using, 26

T

T keyboard shortcut, using for today's date, 23
TAB keyboard shortcut, navigating forms with, 21
tapes, storing backups on, 166
tasks, examples of, 15
tax groups, features of, 130
tax preferences, changing, 129
tax settings, entering defaults for, 188
Tax:1099 preferences, description of, 169
taxes
   paying, 199–201
   setting up, 127
Taxes Defaults window, displaying, 188
templates, creating for invoices, 177–178
Templates window, displaying, 177
Templates list, description of, 51
terms and types, adding for vendors, 100

Terms list, description of, 51
Time Tracking feature
   setting preferences for, 34, 169
   turning on, 196–198
timesheets, entering, 197–198
title bar, location of, 6
To Do items, adding to customers, 122–123
To Do List, contents of, 50
toggle item, definition of, 13
toolbar. See icon bar
tracking time. See Time Tracking feature
transactions
   deleting and memorizing, 21
   entering dates for, 112
   entering for credit cards, 88–89
   memorizing, 116–118
   opening, 171
   receiving and entering for online business credit
      cards, 90–91
transferring funds between accounts, 87
tutorial videos, accessing, 6
Type list, description of, 51
types and terms, adding for vendors, 100

U

Updating Sales Tax window, displaying, 127
UPS, sending packages by means of, 157
user accounts, setting up, 47–48. See also accounts; bank accounts
User List window, displaying user accounts in, 48, 52

V

Vehicle list, description of, 51
Vendor Detail Center, using, 109
Vendor lists
   adding vendors from, 101
   description of, 51
   using, 97
vendor names
   adding to lists, 115
   entering, 106
Vendor Navigator, using, 96
Vendor Profiles list, contents of, 51
Vendor reports, description of, 207
vendor information, entering, 42
Vendor menu, contents of, 52
vendors
   adding, 98–102
   adding notes or reminders to, 102
   adding types and terms for, 100
   definition of, 95
   deleting, 103
   designating customers as, 69
   editing, 101
   entering credits for, 111
   making inactive, 104

   merging, 103
   setting up for 1099s, 106
Vendors & Payables reports, description of, 205
Vendors menu, keyboard shortcut for, 22
Verify Data dialog box, appearance of, 165
version, definition of, 2
View menu
   customizing desktop with, 13–14
   keyboard shortcut for, 22
voiding paychecks, 194–195

W

W keyboard shortcut, using for first day of week, 23
wage payroll items, setting up, 186
weekly timesheets, entering, 197–198
weekly tasks, examples of, 15
Welcome tab in General section, options on, 29–30
What's Next section of EasyStep Interview, completing, 45–46
Window menu, using, 14
windows. See also Navigators
   displaying and resizing, 14
   switching between, 11
Windows menu, keyboard shortcut for, 22
Write Checks feature, benefits of, 80
Write Checks forms, opening, 21

Y

Y keyboard shortcut, using for first day of year, 23
YTD (year–to–date) amounts, entering for payroll, 192

International Contact Information

AUSTRALIA
McGraw-Hill Book Company Australia Pty. Ltd.
  TEL +61-2-9900-1800
  FAX +61-2-9878-8881
  http://www.mcgraw-hill.com.au
  books-it_sydney@mcgraw-hill.com

CANADA
McGraw-Hill Ryerson Ltd.
  TEL +905-430-5000
  FAX +905-430-5020
  http://www.mcgraw-hill.ca

GREECE, MIDDLE EAST, & AFRICA
  (Excluding South Africa)
McGraw-Hill Hellas
  TEL +30-210-6560-990
  TEL +30-210-6560-993
  TEL +30-210-6560-994
  FAX +30-210-6545-525

MEXICO (Also serving Latin America)
McGraw-Hill Interamericana Editores S.A. de C.V.
  TEL +525-1500-5108
  FAX +525-117-1589
  http://www.mcgraw-hill.com.mx
  carlos_ruiz@mcgraw-hill.com

SINGAPORE (Serving Asia)
McGraw-Hill Book Company
  TEL +65-6863-1580
  FAX +65-6862-3354
  http://www.mcgraw-hill.com.sg
  mghasia@mcgraw-hill.com

SOUTH AFRICA
McGraw-Hill South Africa
  TEL +27-11-622-7512
  FAX +27-11-622-9045
  robyn_swanepoel@mcgraw-hill.com

SPAIN
McGraw-Hill/Interamericana de España, S.A.U.
  TEL +34-91-180-3000
  FAX +34-91-372-8513
  http://www.mcgraw-hill.es
  professional@mcgraw-hill.es

UNITED KINGDOM, NORTHERN,
EASTERN, & CENTRAL EUROPE
McGraw-Hill Education Europe
  TEL +44-1-628-502500
  FAX +44-1-628-770224
  http://www.mcgraw-hill.co.uk
  emea_queries@mcgraw-hill.com

ALL OTHER INQUIRIES Contact:
McGraw-Hill/Osborne
  TEL +1-510-420-7700
  FAX +1-510-420-7703
  http://www.osborne.com
  omg_international@mcgraw-hill.com